John Jortin

Sermons on Different Subjects

Volume II.

John Jortin

Sermons on Different Subjects
Volume II.

ISBN/EAN: 9783337160685

Printed in Europe, USA, Canada, Australia, Japan

Cover: Foto ©Lupo / pixelio.de

More available books at **www.hansebooks.com**

SERMONS

ON

DIFFERENT SUBJECTS,

BY THE LATE REVEREND

JOHN JORTIN, D. D.

Archdeacon of LONDON, Rector of St. DUNSTAN in the East, and Vicar of KENSINGTON.

THE THIRD EDITION.

VOLUME II.

DUBLIN:

Printed for Meſſrs. WHITESTONE, SLEATER, WILLIAMS, WILSON, HALLHEAD, FLIN, JENKIN, BEATTY, WHITE, BURTON, and PARKER.

M DCC LXXVIII.

CONTENTS.

SERMON I.

The Sower.

MATTH. xiii. 8.

But other fell into good ground, and brought forth fruit, some an hundred fold, some sixty fold, some thirty fold.

p. 1

SERMON II.

The Rich Man and Lazarus.

LUKE xvi. 31.

If they hear not Moses and the Prophets, neither will they be persuaded, though one rose from the dead. p. 14

SERMON III.

The intermediate State between Death and the Resurrection.

MATTH. xxii. 32.

God is not the God of the dead, but of the living. p. 26

SERMON IV.

The Nature of bad Habits.

JEREMIAH xiii. 23.

Can the Æthiopian change his skin, or the leopard his spots? then may ye also do good, that are accustomed to do evil.

P. 39

SERMON V.

Uprightness.

PROV. x. 9.

He that walketh uprightly, walketh surely; but he that perverteth his ways shall be known. P. 51

SERMON VI.

The Difference of Duties.

MATT. xxii. 35.

Then one of them—asked him a question—saying, Master, which is the great commandment in the Law? p. 64

CONTENTS.

SERMON VII.

The Penitent Thief.

LUKE xxiii. 42, 43.

And he said unto Jesus; Lord, remember me, when thou comest into thy kingdom. And Jesus said unto him, Verily I say unto thee, to-day shalt thou be with me in Paradise.
p. 76

SERMON VIII.

Anger.

COLOSS. iii. 8.

But now you also put off all these; anger, wrath, malice.
p. 89

SERMON IX.

Honour.

1 SAM. ii. 30.

For them that honour me, I will honour.   p. 102

SERMON X.

Secret Things.

DEUTER. xxix. 29.

The secret things belong unto the Lord our God, but those things which are revealed belong unto us, and to our children for ever, that we may do all the works of this law. p. 115

SERMON XI.

Blasphemy against the Holy Ghost.

MATTH. xii. 31.

All manner of sin and blasphemy shall be forgiven unto men: but the blasphemy against the holy Ghost shall not be forgiven unto men. p. 127

SERMON XII.

The Love of the World.

1 JOHN ii. 15.

Love not the world, neither the things that are in the world. p. 140

SERMON XIII.

Mortality.

PSALM ciii. 15, 16.

As for man, his days are as grass; as a flower of the field, so he flourisheth; for the wind passeth over it, and it is gone, and the place thereof shall know it no more.

p. 153

SERMON XIV.

Meekness.

MATTH. v. 5.

Blessed are the meek. p. 165

SERMON XV.

Religious Retirement.

MATTH. xiv. 23.

And when he had sent away the multitudes, he went up into a mountain apart to pray. p. 178

SERMON XVI.

Future State of the Good.

MATTH. xiii. 43.

Then shall the righteous shine forth as the sun in the kingdom of their father. p. 192

SERMON XVII.

Charity.

1 COR. xiii. 13.

And now abideth faith, hope, charity, these three; but the greatest of these is charity. p. 204

SERMON XVIII.

Living peaceably.

ROM. xii. 18.

If it be possible, as much as lieth in you, live peaceably with all men. p. 218

CONTENTS.

SERMON XIX.

Afflictions.

PSALM cxix. 71.

It is good for me that I have been afflicted. p. 231

SERMON XX.

Envy.

1 COR. xiii. 4.

Charity envieth not.—— p. 243

SERMON XXI.

The Conversion of Cornelius.

ACTS x. 22.

And they said, Cornelius the centurion, a just man, and one that feareth God, and of good report among all the nation of the Jews, was warned from God by an holy Angel to send for thee into his house, and to hear words of thee. p. 256

CONTENTS.

SERMON XXII.

The Security of the Wicked without Foundation.

LUKE xii. 20.

But God said unto him, Thou fool, this night thy soul shall be demanded of thee. p. 269

SERMON XXIII.

Agur's Request.

PROV. xxx. 7.

Two things have I required of thee; deny me them not before I die. Remove far from me vanity and lies; give me neither poverty nor riches, feed me with food convenient for me: lest I be full, and deny thee, and say, Who is the Lord? or lest I be poor and steal, and take the name of my God in vain. p. 282

SERMON XXIV.

Humility.

1 PETER v. 5.

— Be clothed with humility. p. 295

SERMON XXV.

Resignation.

MATTH. xxvi. 39.

O my Father, if it be possible, let this cup pass from me: nevertheless, not as I will, but as thou wilt.   p. 308

SERMON XXVI.

Future Judgment.

ROM. ii. 6.

Who will render to every man according to his deeds.
p. 321

SERMON XXVII.

Keep thy Foot.

ECCLES. v. 1.

Keep thy foot when thou goest into the house of God, and be more ready to hear than to give the sacrifice of fools; for they consider not that they do evil.   P. 334

SERMON XXVIII.

Faith.

ACTS xvii. 11.

These were more noble than those in Thessalonica, in that they received the word with all readiness of mind, and searched the Scriptures daily, whether those things were so. P. 347

SERMON XXIX.

Life and Immortality.

2 TIM. i. 10.

—Who hath brought life and immortality to light through the Gospel. p. 360

SERMON XXX.

The Gifts of the Spirit.

ACTS i. 8.

But ye shall receive power, after that the holy Ghost is come upon you. P. 373

SERMON XXXI.

Unlawfulness of Persecution.

LUKE xiv. 23.

And the Lord said unto the servant; Go out into the highways and hedges, and compel them to come in, that my house may be filled. p. 385

SERMON XXXII.

The Sign of Jonas.

MATTH. xii. 39.

An evil and adulterous generation seeketh after a Sign, and there shall no Sign be given to it, but the Sign of the prophet Jonas. p. 399

SERMON XXXIII.

The Thorn in the Flesh.

2 COR. xii. 7.

Lest I should be exalted above measure through the abundance of the revelations, there was given to me a thorn in the flesh, the messenger of Satan to buffet me. p. 412

SERMON XXXIV.

Evil-speaking.

TITUS iii. 2.

To speak evil of no man.   p. 425

SERMON XXXV.

Self-love.

2 TIM. iii. 2.

Men shall be lovers of their own selves.   p. 437

SERMON I.

MATTH. xiii. 8.

But other fell into good ground, and brought forth fruit, some an hundred fold, some sixty fold, some thirty fold.

THE parable of the sower was designed by our Saviour to represent the different effects which his doctrine then had upon different persons, and which religion and the word of God hath and will have in all times and places.

But, before we consider the several persons described in the parable, it is well worthy of our observation to consider how the distinct operations of divine assistance, and of human liberty, may fairly and naturally be inferred from it.

Revealed religion is here represented as good seed sown in the ground by the Husbandman. God, or our Saviour Jesus Christ, is the Husbandman. Revealed religion is the gift of God: of ourselves we could never have discovered it. It is a restoration of natural religion to an ignorant and a wicked world, which had in a manner lost all due apprehensions, all just and practical notions of God, of duty, of future rewards and punishments: it is also an improvement of natural religion, containing new dissuasives from wickedness, and new motives to amendment and righteousness.

In one sense, all that we have is derived from God, who gave us our souls and our bodies, our natural qualities and affections; most justly therefore in this sense may we ascribe to our great Author all that we are, and all that belongs to us, except our sins. But amongst other good gifts he imparted to us self-motion, power, activity, and liberty; and He, who made us without ourselves, cannot save us without ourselves, without our own concurrence and co-operation, and the free exertion of our natural powers. All this is implied plainly enough in the parable of the sower. Human art and human industry cannot make the seeds which are sown, or the ground into which they are cast; these are created of God: but the soil must be prepared and cultivated by human labour, or else no fruit will grow in it. So as to the spiritual harvest, religion is the gift of God, and the human understanding is the gift of God: but the application of the heart and mind to the word and to the will of God is free and voluntary.

In this parable our Saviour hath described four sorts of hearers of the word.

The first sort are thus described: Some seeds fell by the way-side, and they were trodden down, and the fowls came and devoured them up. That is, says our Lord, when any one heareth the word of the kingdom, and understandeth it not, that is to say, regardeth it not, then cometh the Wicked One, the Devil, and catcheth away that which was sown in his heart, lest he should believe, and be saved: this is he which received the seed by the way-side.

When any one heareth the word, and understandeth it not. Our Saviour cannot here intend to signify, that his word ever becomes unprofitable to any persons, either through the natural weakness of their understanding, which renders them unable to discern his mind; or through the darkness or obscurity of the word preached; since then the blame would fall, not upon the hearers, whose ignorance would be unavoidable and invincible but upon the Preacher, who delivered it so darkly, or who offered it to men incapable of receiving it. But the word which we translate, *to understand*, means

in

in this, and in some other places, to consider a thing, and lay it to heart, with an intention to make a right use of it.

The Devil is here said to snatch the word away from such persons, lest they should profit by it. The entrance of evil into the world is ascribed to the Devil, as to the first cause of it, and he is called the *Evil One*, by way of eminence, as being the first rebel against God and goodness. When it is said, that the Devil enters into the heart of a sinner, it is an Hebrew way of speaking, which is not to be taken too rigorously, and pressed too far; for the Devil is said to do whatsoever is executed and performed by the unruly lusts of men, which are accounted as his instruments. The Gospel accommodates itself in style and phrase to the Jewish conceptions and forms of speech; but then it takes care to ascribe no such power and prevalence to the Devil as shall lay the tempted person under a necessity of sinning; and it always supposes that the inducements and the assistances to well-doing are far stronger than the incentives and instigations to evil, if a man will act like a rational creature, and use his best endeavours, and exert his own powers: so that whether it be an evil spirit, or whether it be only an evil disposition in the man himself, which prompts him to iniquity, it is all one, since he ought to repel and reject such assaults and temptations, and sins entirely by his own choice and fault.

When a man heareth the word, and regardeth it not, then cometh the Evil one and taketh it away. The meaning seems to be no more than this; He who hath no consideration, no sober and serious and settled respect for religion, when his duty is propounded to him, gives no attention to it; it makes no impression upon him; his own vicious habits, and the bad example, and the contagious society of wicked persons, who are the children of the wicked One, are more prevalent than the word of God, and soon blot out the faint and floating remembrance

remembrance of it; the man goes on in his thoughtless iniquity, and steddily pursues his evil courses. This is he who received seed by the way-side.

Seed falling upon the hard highway cannot possibly take root, and bring forth fruit. It lies exposed and unguarded, the sun burns it, the frost kills it, the wind disperses it, the rain washes it away, the foot of the passenger and of the beast tramples and crushes it, the birds of the air pick it up and eat it. Sad image and melancholy representation of the worst sort of sinners! These are the persons, who, as our Saviour says, have eyes, and see not, ears, and hear not, and whose hearts are hardened like a rock; these are they to whom he would not explain his parables, because they were unworthy of it, and because instruction would have been thrown away upon them; these are they, who, when John the Baptist made his appearance with austere severity, said he was mad; and when Christ conversed, and taught with mild condescension, said he was a drunkard, a glutton, and a keeper of bad company. They disliked the doctrines, and therefore they were resolved to find fault with the teachers. Such are those who have entered betimes, and continued long in the service of the Devil, who are slaves to vices and to bad habits, who have extinguished all reason, reflection, and natural conscience, and whom no ordinary methods can reclaim. The word is preached to them; and they trample it under foot, treat it with the utmost scorn and contempt, and revile and ridicule those who offer them good advice. They lie out of the reach of persuasion and instruction, and nothing less than some grievous calamity can awaken them. But from their deplorable condition others may take due warning, lest, by departing from their duty, and neglecting a timely reformation, they should, through the deceitfulness of sin arrive to such a hardened state: and this seems to be the only use for which these incorrigible offenders serve in this world:

world: they stand forth, not as marks and friendly lights to guide and direct the passenger, but as examples to be shunned, and signals of danger and death to those who shall approach them.

The next sort of hearers, as they are less wicked, so they are more frequent, and are set forth to us in the parable under the image of stony ground. Some seed fell upon stony places, where they had not much earth, and forthwith they sprang up; but because they had no deepness of earth, when the sun was up, they were scorched; and because they had not root they withered away. Now he that received the seed into stony places, the same is he that heareth the word, and anon with joy receiveth it, and for a time believeth. Yet he hath not root in himself, but dureth for a while; for when tribulation or persecution ariseth because of the word, by and by he is offended.

These are persons who have conscience, reason, and reflection; who can discern the amiable and the profitable nature of religion, and the folly and danger of vice; who can sometimes give attention to the word of God, approve it as right and fit, speak and think honourably of it, and of those who practise it, and even entertain purposes of acting suitably to it: but they have no steddiness, resolution, and perseverance, and so are not proof against trials and temptations. They are such as are elegantly described in the prophet Ezechiel: Son of man, says God to the prophet, the children of thy people came unto thee, and they sit before thee as my people, and they hear thy words, but they will not do them: for with their mouth they shew much love, but their heart goeth after their covetousness. And (a) lo, thou art unto them as a very lovely song of one that hath a
pleasant

(i) Hard are the ways of truth, and rough to walk,
Smooth on the tongue discours'd, pleasing to th' ear,
And tuneable as silvan pipe or song. Milton, Par. Reg. I. 478.

pleasant voice, and can play well on an instrument; for they hear thy words, but they do them not. Moral precepts and religious arguments appear fair and lovely in idea, but are found grievous in practice and execution; and the paths of righteousness, which make a fine landskip in description, are rough, steep, and tedious to ascend. Such is the effect of religion upon those who have some taste and natural discernment, but no steddy love of goodness. They are such as our Saviour represents in another place under the image of the man who built his house upon the sand, and the rain and the wind beat upon it, and the storm blew it down, and the flood swept it away. They are like the young man who came to Christ offering to do any thing that should be required of him; but when Christ would have favoured and honoured him so far as even to take him for a companion and disciple if he would relinquish his possessions, he went away sorrowful. Our Saviour and his Apostles had many such half-disciples and imperfect converts, sincere perhaps at the first, but weak and unsteddy; and he had such wavering persons in view, when he spake this parable of the sower. When the Gospel was first preached, many embraced it, and continued in it for a time, whilst the course of things ran tolerably smooth: but when persecution was to be endured, they departed and fell away. In the morning, whilst the refreshing dew was upon the earth, the divine seed suffered no detriment, though lodged in stony ground; but when the heat increased, and the burning sun shone upon it, it withered and died.

We live not now in times of such kind of distress, and so are not put to the same trial: but if we were in the very same condition, we may be morally certain that a great apostasy would ensue, and that many nominal Christians would forsake their religion. To judge whether a man would be faithful under great trials, it is to be considered, whether he be found faithful under smaller experiments of his integrity and resolution. There are, from without, two everlasting temptations in all times and places, namely, loss and gain, and by the behaviour of a person under trials of these kinds, a tolerable judgment may be formed of his disposition. If he will part with nothing, and endure no inconvenience to do that which he knows to be right, or if he will not scruple to obtain worldly advantages by sordid, fraudulent, violent, and iniquitous methods, he can be no true disciple of Christ.

The third sort of hearers mentioned in the parable, who are by far the most numerous, are those gay, luxurious, dissipated, or worldly-minded persons, who are set forth to us under the image of ground over-run with weeds and thorns.

Some seed fell among thorns, and the thorns sprang up and choaked them. He that received seed among the thorns is he that heareth the word; and the cares of this world, and the deceitfulness of riches, and the pleasures of this life, and the lusts of other things, entering in, choak the word, and he becometh unfruitful.

To this class of people religion is presented and propounded, and they assent to it, and receive it, and call themselves Christians; but many things arise between them and their duty, many avocations and impediments, which prevent the word of God from having a due effect upon their hearts, and they are here enumerated.

Such are, in the first place, the cares of this life, which, when they are admitted and nourished and encouraged, seize upon the whole man, and so fill the head, and so occupy the hours, that the attention is entirely fixed on worldly affairs, and no leisure is allowed for concerns of the spiritual kind; and as no person can bear the toil and fatigue of being always contriving, projecting, labouring, and plodding, and some amusement must intervene, the times for recreation are with

such

such persons the times when other Christians are attending the public worship of God, or meditating on things sacred and serious at home. And thus religious considerations are totally banished, and not permitted to have even the smallest intervals; and then the man may be pronounced to be dead to God and to Christ, and alive only to the world.

The deceitfulness of riches is here represented as having the same bad effect. When the love of wealth is predominant and engrosses the affections, it produces an eagerness to acquire it, a proud trust and confidence in it, a settled resolution to preserve and increase it by any methods, and in defiance of honesty and humanity, and an esteem or contempt of other persons, according as they are rich or poor; and then Mammon alone is worshipped, and the love of God is expelled from the heart.

The pleasures of life are another source of evil, another cause why the word of God can produce no good effect upon the minds and manners of men; indeed they are the most common, the most deceitful, the most prevalent and the most pernicious, of all temptations. They are those pleasures of life, which are called the works of the flesh, as intemperance, and debauchery of every kind, which depress and sink the soul in sensuality, and entirely alienate it from God and goodness; they are also those pleasures which though they are not directly and essentially vicious, yet are inlets and incentives to vice, such as the conveniences of life, and the objects agreeable to the senses, when they are too studiously sought after and collected, and too much indulged, a circle of perpetual amusements, and an immoderate pursuit of vain diversions. These are bad instructors, which teach men to banish serious thoughts, to neglect their duty to God and to their neighbour, and even their own calling, and their private concerns, and their temporal welfare, to live in perpetual dissipation, to connect themselves with loose and profligate persons,

and

and to run into expences which they cannot afford; and hence arife temptations to a fad variety of follies and vices, the portion of thofe who are lovers of pleafure more than lovers of God. To this our Saviour adds, the lufting after other things, namely, defires of magnificence and fplendor, of flattery and popular applaufe, of power and pre-eminence, and in a word immoderate affections for any thing that is temporal and tranfitory.

From this melancholy fcene prefented to us in the review of perfons deaf to the voice of Reafon and to the calls of the Gofpel, feeking their own deftruction, and walking in thoughtlefs unconcern, till darknefs overwhelms them, let us turn our confideration to the laft fort of hearers mentioned with applaufe by our Saviour, and defcribed under the fimilitude of good ground. Other feed fell into good ground, and brought forth fruit, fome an hundred fold, fome fixty fold, fome thirty fold. He that received feed into the good ground, is he that heareth the word, and underftandeth it, and receiveth it into a good and honeft heart, which alfo beareth fruit with patience, and bringeth forth, fome an hundred fold, fome thirty, fome fixty.

In this parable there is a beautiful gradation, from the bad to the good (*b*). The feed which fell on the highway comes not up at all; the feed upon ftony ground comes

---

(*b*) An old Commentator (Theophylact) expounding this parable fays, See how a fmall number there is of good men, and how few are faved, fince only a fourth part of the feed was preferved. His remark is not juft, but is foreign from the purpofe, as may eafily be fhewed. In this parable of the Sower, there are three claffes of bad men, and one of good: In the parable of the talents, there are two good fervants, and one bad; and in the parable of the virgins, half are wife, and half foolifh. So, if we follow fuch methods of expounding, we muft conclude from the firft of thefe parables, there are three times more bad than good men; from the fecond, that there are twice more good than bad: and from the third, that the good and bad are equal in number.

I mention

comes up, but soon withereth away; the seed sown amongst thorns springs up and grows, and bears no fruit; the seed sown in good ground brings forth fruit in its season, but yet in various degrees, and much more plentiful in some soils than in others.

Ground which disappointeth not the sower, and bringeth forth fruit in its season, is naturally good, and is improved by culture. The heart of every well-disposed person is such. God hath given to all of us abilities, and power to exert them; he hath also to us Christians superadded his revealed will in the Gospel, and what aid is necessary, that he is ever ready to bestow: but a man must put forth his own strength, and seek out and work out his own salvation. The persons therefore here described act like rational creatures; they have a love of knowledge and goodness, and a desire to make improvements in both. Thence they are disposed to inquire into themselves and their duty, and opportunities for this are never wanting; morality and revealed religion lie within their reach, and they may read or hear what God requires from them. They hear the word, and understand it, says our Lord; they lay it to heart, and call it to mind; they meditate upon the benefits arising from it, the danger of neglecting it, the reasonable and amiable nature of it, the dangers, inconveniences and temptations which may arise and assault them, the proper methods of shunning or resisting them, and the wisdom of preferring eternal life to all other considerations. Such is the fair foundation laid for a regular course of life, and an honest discharge of Christian duties.

Some
I mention this, chiefly for the sake of observing to you, that, in the interpretation of parables, care should be taken not to overstrain them, but to distinguish those parts which are merely ornamental from those which are moral and instructive.

Some difficulties will occur, some trials will arise from within and without; some spots and blemishes, some faults and defects, will always accompany men in their religious progress: but they who have an honest mind, and an habitual probity, if they fall, yet rise again, if they transgress, they repent, and in the main are obedient and dutiful, human weaknesses excepted. And this is patience and perseverance, which are mentioned as the distinguishing marks of those who receive the word of God and keep it.

Goodness and wickedness seem not to consist in a fixed and determinate number of right or wrong actions. Men are good or bad in an infinite variety of degrees; and therefore, according to the law of proportions, and the result of causes and effects, their future condition must needs be infinitely various, either as to gain or loss, as to recompence or correction. What is revealed to us concerning it, is only in gross and in general, and it is impossible for us in the present state to form a just and complete notion of it. None but God, all-wise, all-powerful, and perfectly just and good, is capable of dispensing these retributions, and of allotting to each of his creatures his proper situation, and his due measure and proportion, of elevation or depression, of joy or sorrow, of reward or punishment, according to his deeds, and to the dispositions which he has contracted in the days of his mortality. Therefore, in general, it behoves us above all things to be wise and cautious, in this our time of trial and probation, and to secure to ourselves a portion amongst those faithful servants of Christ, whose good deeds shall be found to preponderate, and to surpass their transgressions, and thus to qualify ourselves for a state of peace and rest in some of the happy mansions allotted to the righteous.

Good persons are here described by our Saviour as being so in various degrees, some twice and some thrice

better

better than others, who yet may be called good alſo. This conſiderable difference between righteous perſons ariſes from two cauſes. Firſt it ariſes from an inequality between them to which they do not contribute, from a difference of natural abilities, and of opportunities to receive improvement, and to exert themſelves by doing or ſuffering. This diverſity of talents is the free gift of God, which he diſpenſes according to his own pleaſure: yet there is no partiality in all this, ſince it is ſuitable to perfect wiſdom and goodneſs to make a variety of beings of different ranks and capacities, and to place them accordingly higher or lower both in this world and in the next. But to every one who hath improved his talents, whether they were two, or whether they were ten, it will be ſaid; Well done, good and faithful ſervant, Enter thou into the joy of thy Lord. He who enters into the joy of his Lord, will be rewarded to the full extent of his views and capacity; and that is ſufficient to juſtify the goodneſs of the Lord, and to ſecure the happineſs of the ſervant.

But, ſecondly, the difference between two righteous perſons ariſes more commonly and uſually, not from their natural abilities, or their ſituation in life, but purely from themſelves, and their own endeavours, from the care, caution, aſſiduity, zeal, and induſtry, exerted more or leſs in things pertaining to morality and religion: and in this caſe, a difference of retribution is highly reaſonable. It is fit in the nature of things, that the event ſhould be proportionable to the pains, that no good deed ſhould go unnoticed and unrewarded, but yet that he who ſoweth ſparingly ſhould reap ſparingly, and he who ſoweth plenteouſly ſhould reap plenteouſly; that ſome ſhould be ſaved, ſcarcely and with difficulty, like a brand plucked out of the fire, and others ſhould receive a far more exceeding and abundant weight of glory.

How can we better cloſe our remarks on this ſubject, than with the ſerious and ſolemn admonition with
which

which our Saviour concludes: He that hath ears to hear, let him hear!

Which is, as if our Lord had said; What I have delivered to you, is not a discourse to amuse and entertain you, not a point of curiosity and speculation, not an ordinary and indifferent affair, which will be of small consequence to you, whether you attend to it or disregard it, whether you recollect it or forget it. It is of unspeakable importance, and nothing less than your eternal happiness or misery depends upon it. As you make a good or a bad use of my exhortations and instructions, you will be acquitted or condemned when I come to judgment. Therefore, Be wise, and Remember.

SERMON II.

LUKE xvi. 31.

If they hear not Moses and the Prophets, neither will they be perfuaded, though one rofe from the dead.

OUR Lord tells us that there was a certain rich man, who was clothed in purple and fine linen, and fared fumptuoufly every day. He died, and went into a ftate of punifhment; and ſeeing Abraham afar off, and Lazarus in his bofom, he intreated him to fend Lazarus, that he might dip the tip of his finger in water, and cool his tongue. Abraham replies, that this cannot be done. Remember, fon, fays he, that thou in thy life-time receivedſt thy good things, and likewife Lazarus evil things; but now he is comforted, and thou art tormented.

I. There was a man, fays our Lord, who had great riches; confequently he had leifure hours to fpend in the ftudy of religious truths, and of the duties incumbent on a perfon of his rank; he had prefling motives to gratitude towards God, who had beftowed fo many temporal bleffings upon him; he had power and opportunity of doing confiderable fervice to the public, of encouraging virtue by the authority and influence of his example, of fhewing kindnefs to the unhappy, of being a father to the fatherlefs, a defence to the oppreffed, a rewarder of induftry, a friend and patron to modeft merit. What ufe did he make of thefe advantages?

ges? Why, truly, the history of his life, briefly summed up, was that he eat, and drank, and dressed himself. A poor man, of his own nation, reduced to the utmost distress, lay at his door. Did he assist him? We may suppose that he did not; for it is not said that he took any notice of him, but the contrary seems rather to be intimated through the whole parable. Thus he was one who lived to himself, and did no good to others, his heart was set upon worldly objects, and he removed religion far from his thoughts.

II. The character here drawn of the rich man is not uncommon. What is said of him in the Parable, is true in another sense; He hath many brethren. They behave themselves like him; they kill not, perhaps, they defraud not, they use no scandalous methods to increase their wealth; there are several crimes which they commit not, either because they lie under no provocations to commit them, or because they fear the laws of their country, or because they would avoid ignominy and shame, or because they are too indolent, or too busy. But then they have no desire to excel in any virtue. The business of their lives is to divert themselves, to gratify their senses, to seek out new pleasures and amusements, and thus to waste their days, regardless of God, and useless to mankind.

It was for a warning to all such, that our Lord spake this parable. He sets before them the example of this man, who had received his good things, and who, taking no care to employ them in a proper manner, goes into a state of punishment. Hence they may learn that if God hath committed much to them, he hath much to require from them, and that when they come to give an account of themselves to him, it will be no excuse to be able to say that they are free from this or that fault, that they have not been as wicked as many others, that they have not committed the evil which lay in their power.
The

The question will be, What good they have done, and what returns they have made to God for all the blessings which he hath conferred upon them?

III. Of the rich man it is said expressly, that he fared sumptuously every day. This is the character of a glutton; and hence it may be supposed that as extreme want produced the diseases which sent poor Lazarus out of the world; so what is called *living well* had the same effect upon the rich man, and helped to shorten his days.

Here then it will not be improper to take occasion to recommend to you temperance and abstinence, abstinence exercised with discretion, and free from superstitious and injudicious austerities.

There is, as we may not improperly call it, a perpetual fast, to which we are obliged, as rational creatures and as Christians; namely, a fast from all intemperate affections, turbulent passions, and irregular practices. But there is also an abstinence at particular times from the lawful pleasures of life; and the fitness of such a conduct might easily be proved even upon the principles of human reason, or common sense. I explain myself by a few instances: your own thoughts may suggest more.

A person in health and in good circumstances hath food of various kinds at command. But such is the instability of human affairs, that he may be reduced to a morsel of bread. It is expedient therefore for him, at certain times, to take up with such spare and plain diet as sufficeth to remove pain, and to satisfy the cravings of the body. He will be better able to shift for himself upon any turn of fortune. I need not add that such abstinence will conduce to preserve his health. No one, I presume, will deny it.

Such a person, it may be, hath various diversions and entertainments at command, and may repair to them as often as he thinks fit. But many accidents may deprive him at a stroke of all these beloved amusements.

Let

Let him learn then to live without them, by shunning them more frequently whilst they are in his reach.

Such a person may usually have a variety of company abroad and at home. But various events may reduce him to solitude. Let him then learn before hand to bear solitude at certain times, to converse with sacred and with useful books, with his Maker, and with his own soul: and think himself in good company whilst he is thus engaged.

Whosoever practiseth such abstinence, upon the principles above-mentioned, may be said to keep a moral and philosophical fast: but if what he thus saves in his expences he gives to the needy and the deserving, then, and not till then, he converts his rational into a truly religious and Christian fast.

IV. We may observe that our Lord, both in this parable, and in other discourses, mentions the great dangers which attend wealth and power, and worldly prosperity; and declares it to be difficult for those, who enjoy all these things, to acquire and to preserve the virtues necessary to their salvation. He observes that the Gospel would be preached in vain to such persons, that either they would not receive it, or if they did, would not act conformably to it. As when seed falls among thorns the thorns spring up and choke it; so, says Christ, when the word of God is preached to the rich, the cares of this world, and the deceitfulness of riches choke the word, and it becometh unfruitful. When the young man came to him, and seemed sincerely desirous of receiving instruction, and of performing any action that might recommend him to God's favour, the sudden answer, If thou wilt be perfect, sell that thou hast, and give it to the poor, and follow me, quite disconcerted him, because he had great possessions; and he went away sorrowful. Upon which our Lord observed that it was next to impossible for a rich man to be his disciple.

So it is: The great and wealthy are exposed to various temptations. Riches are often attended with pride,

pride, insolence, indifference for religion, cares about the present, and carelessness about the future state, voluptuousness, intemperance, contempt and neglect of the poor, and the spirit of oppression, vices which lead to perdition.

If this be true, riches, it may be said, seem to be rather a curse than an advantage. How then shall we reconcile this with those declarations in the Scriptures, that even wealth and worldly prosperity are blessings of God? Very easily, if we consider these two things.

First, A wealthy state is exposed to many temptations; but there is no state free from them. Whatsoever our condition be, if we entertain good dispositions, we want neither power nor opportunities to serve God, and recommend ourselves to his favour; and if we indulge evil inclinations, we shall never fail of objects enticing us to sin.

A state of worldly happiness may be accounted dangerous for the reasons above-mentioned. Let us take a state of poverty, and see whether that have not its temptations also.

Poverty often makes a man envy his superiors, and hate and slander them, raises in him restless discontent and resentment, and unbecoming thoughts of divine Providence, and leads him into base or violent practices, to mend his condition.

Let us even take a state between poverty and riches, a state the least exposed to inconvenience and danger, and we shall find, that as ill an use is often made of that as of any other. Many and many persons there are, to whom this desireable lot is fallen, happy if they knew their own happiness, who are so ungrateful as to think that Providence hath not given them enough, who, look with repining uneasiness at those above them, and consider not how many are beneath them, who, placed between indigence and superfluity, partake of the vices to which each of those stations incline us, who are regardless of religion and virtue, and of the improvement

of

SERMON II.

of their minds, but very induſtrious and careful about the things of this life, about riſing, as they call it, in the world, as if they were born for nothing elſe, and as if God had not ſet before them better objects to occupy their thoughts and their views.

Thus if an exalted ſtation be ſurrounded with temptations, yet there is no ſtation ſecured from them, and therefore no bleſſing which a perverſe mind may not abuſe, and no affliction which ſhall be able to correct and amend it. The rich man might have been as poor as Lazarus, and not the more virtuous and religious. It muſt indeed be confeſſed that plenty and proſperity expoſe us to many dangers. Therefore let the advantages of ſuch a ſtate be conſidered, and ſet againſt the perils to which it lies open. To poſſeſs riches, and not to be enſlaved to them; to be juſt when acts of iniquity may be committed with impunity, and would be excuſed or even applauded by flattery; to be humble and condeſcending in the midſt of invitations to pride and inſolence; to be regular and temperate when the oppoſite vices might be indulged without reſtraint; to love and ſerve God, when the World offers many objects to call off the affections from him; to have much power to do good, and to do good to the utmoſt of that power; this is virtue put to the trial, and obtaining a glorious conqueſt. Peace of mind, reſpect and reputation here, and eternal hapineſs hereafter, are the rewards of ſuch a behaviour.

This might have been the caſe of the rich man in the Parable, who is repreſented as ſituated by divine Providence in ſuch a condition, that he might have been happy in both worlds. God gave him large poſſeſſions; and if he had been an example of piety, as he was of proſperity, if he had not meanly confined his good things to his own uſe, but endeavoured to make others alſo happy and virtuous, he might have paſſed his days agreeably, and enjoyed with moderation, which is the only way of enjoying, the rational comforts of life, he had died in peace, after he had lived in credit and honour, and had gone to a happier place, and not to receive the recompence due to his evil deeds.

V. Our Lord, that he might teach those who are in a low state to be contented with it, and reconcile them to poverty, if poverty were their portion, and perfuade them to bear afflictions with patience, hath set before them in the person of Lazarus a man extremely unhappy in the eye of the world, and in as great distress as human nature can well undergo. Yet this very poor man was a good man, and in the favour of God, and was received after death into happy mansions.

The difference between him and the rich man was as wide as could be conceived. One laboured under a wretched variety of calamities, was afflicted with sickness and pain, and had neither food nor house, nor friends, nor any to take pity of him: the other was at ease, and knew no sorrows and disappointments. But how quickly did this difference cease! And it came to pass that the beggar died—the rich man also died and was buried. Both of them have soon run their appointed course; their days are passed as a shadow, as a tale that is told. Thus the hours of our life, and the good and evil which they bring along with them, hasten away; the sorrows and afflictions of men, their joys and pleasures are soon ended, and become as though they had never been.

These are truths, to which none of us are strangers; they are well known, and little considered. Serious reflections upon them would teach us to think and act like immortal beings, to extend our hopes and desires beyond the present scene which will disappear so soon, and to prepare for the eternal state into which we are entering; they would teach us to be patient and resigned under calamities which can be of no long continuance, and which may in the event prove the greatest blessing that God could have bestowed upon us. Instead of repining at our circumstances, if they be not

such

such as we should chuse for ourselves, we ought to consider that if we have not some advantages which we fancy we should find in a higher or happier state, we have not also its inconveniences and dangers; that all these differences are in a manner for a moment, and that we must soon appear before Him, who will reward every one according to his works, who will bestow various degrees of honour and felicity upon his servants, amongst whom it is reasonable to suppose that they shall not be placed lowest, who, having received the fewest temporal blessings from him, yet constantly retained a sincere love towards him, and an unshaken reliance upon him, patiently expecting that all should be made up to them in a future state.

VI. By the example of the rich man our Lord sets before us the fatal issue of a wicked life. He who dwelt at his ease, is delivered over to remorse, sorrow, and pain. The remembrance of his former happiness makes his present state more wretched, whilst he considers what he is, and what he was, and looks back to those days which are gone, and cannot return again.

And to complete his misery, this cruel reflection must arise in his mind, that by his own fault he had brought himself into that sad state, that whilst he lived on the earth he might have been both happy and virtuous at the same time, that he had by the greatest folly chosen rather to be ungrateful to God, and disobedient to his just and reasonable laws, that he was fallen into evils from which he might once have easily secured himself, that he had rejected the opportunities of working out his salvation which had so frequently offered themselves to him, and of breaking off his sins by a timely repentance.

Thus it is that our Saviour, who knew what was in man, and what arguments were most proper to work upon his rebellious heart, that he might deter us from sin, shews us its sad consequences; and sets before us those scenes of horror, to awaken thoughtless and stubborn

born offenders, to give them a sense of their danger, and, by raising their fear, to compel them to those duties, which, if they acted like reasonable creatures, they would make their choice, and their chief delight.

VII. Lazarus is here said to be carried by the Angels to a place of happiness, called Abraham's bosom, that is to a great feast, where he sits next to Abraham, he who, when he lived below, lay upon the ground at the rich man's door; and through the whole Parable, the invisible state after death is described by images borrowed from the present life and from the objects of our senses, and should not be taken according to the letter.

The generality of the Jews in our Saviour's time believed the soul's immortality, and rewards and punishments when this life was ended. They had collected their notions of these things, partly from ancient tradition, partly from some facts and intimations contained in the Old Testament, partly from the light of reason, and partly from conversation with the Greeks, and from Pagan authors. Our Saviour here accommodates himself to their common notions and received ways of speech, which answered his intention, namely, to confirm them still more in the belief of a state of retribution.

The doctrine of future rewards and punishments, in general and at large, is all that we can learn from this parable; for we must not think to draw any certain consequences from particular circumstances mentioned in it, which may be purely ornamental, for any thing that we can prove to the contrary. The parable intimates, that there is a state of happiness or misery after death, and before the resurrection; but there are other passages of Scripture, which seem to be more conclusive for the happiness of the good in the state of separation from the body, than this popular image of Lazarus placed in Abraham's bosom; as for example,

St.

St. Paul's wiſh to be abſent from the body, and preſent with the Lord.

VIII. Laſtly, Abraham declares, that there was no reaſon for which Lazarus could be ſent to the rich man's brethren, to convert them, becauſe they had Moſes and the Prophets, whom they might hear; he adds alſo, that it would be to no purpoſe; for, ſays he, if they hear not Moſes and the Prophets, neither will they be perſuaded, though one roſe from the dead.

This is a point which deſerves particular conſideration, for it ſeems to contain a very ſtrange aſſertion, which we hardly can believe. But much of the apparent difficulty will be removed, if we duly obſerve theſe two things.

Firſt, the Parables of our Saviour are very often prophecies, and theſe words before us are a prophecy declaring how the Jews would behave themſelves; as the event fully ſhewed.

Secondly, To deter men from wickedneſs, the Scriptures frequently uſe very ſtrong, figurative, and lively expreſſions concerning the dangerous nature of bad habits, repreſenting them as incurable, and deſcribe the difficulties of amendment as mere impoſſibilities; in all which places, leſs is to be underſtood than the words naturally and literally imply.

1. The Jews had Moſes and the Prophets, but would not hear them, ſo as to obſerve their moral Precepts. This diſobedience aroſe not from an unbelief of revealed religion; for they acknowledged the divine authority and the miracles of Moſes and the Prophets. Indeed, they had not ſeen thoſe miracles; they only knew them by the teſtimony of former ages. Therefore it might be ſuppoſed that miracles wrought before their eyes would have a more powerful effect upon them.

This evidence was granted to them: Chriſt gave them daily proofs of his authority, by healing all manner of diseases, and by many other wonderful works; yet it did not move them.

But of all miracles the resurrection of a dead person seems the most striking, and the most likely to prevail even upon a stubborn mind. If Lazarus would return from the grave, and testify unto them, they would surely repent. This also was done to convince them. Christ raised a man to life, and a man whose name was Lazarus. After this, Christ himself arose from the grave, and his Apostles restored some dead persons to life; and yet many of the Jews were not converted by these things, but persevered to the last in unbelief.

2. Since the Scriptures often represent things difficult as altogether impossible, the assertion that they who will not hear Moses, would not hear a dead man returned to life, may be supposed to contain in it no more than this general doctrine, that they who have a revealed religion to guide them, and act against the dictates of their own reason, and the testimony of their own conscience, who know what is right, and persist in doing what is wrong, are in a condition extremely dangerous, and that there is little hope of their amendment.

A sinner of this kind often doth things which seem very strange, resists the most pressing motives, and acts in a manner for which we can account no other way than from the prodigious force of bad habits.

He believes a God, a revelation, and a future state, and in defiance of that belief he perversely pursues his own ruin. He trusts to an uncertain repentance, and yet he knows that by being delayed it becomes more difficult to be accomplished, and that he may be suddenly taken out of the world. Such is the tyranny of habit, and the custom of suspending and driving away from time to time all serious thoughts of stifling the reproofs of conscience, and silencing the voice of

reason

reason by the assistance of the noise and follies, the hurry and business, of the world.

He hath, it may be, the dreadful example of wicked companions cut off in the midst of their iniquity. This affects him, and he instantly resolves to amend. Yet the resolution holds only for a short time; his vices return, and not only recover their former dominion, but daily acquire new strength.

At last he is himself surprised by sickness or danger, and Death and Hell are before his eyes. His fears are raised, his conscience is awakened, he mourns, he condemns himself, he is determined to become a new man. The danger ceases; and he not only returns to his former ways, but grows worse than he was before.

So little hope there is, so small a chance, so slender a probability, that such a person shall repent and amend his ways, that in the style of the Scriptures, and in the common way of speaking, it may be said of him, that he is dead in trespasses and sins, dead to all that is good, that it is impossible to bring him to a right mind, that sooner may an Æthiopian change his skin, and a leopard his spots, than he become an example of virtue and piety, that one sent to him from the dead would not reclaim him, and that if he had lived in the time of Christ and of the Apostles, the miracles which they wrought would have had no other influence upon him, than they had upon the unbelieving Jews; all which strong and severe expressions amount in reality only to this, that the condition of such a person is very dangerous, and his recovery scarcely to be expected.

These things were written for our instruction, or, if they fail of producing that effect, for our condemnation. He who can hear this parable of our Saviour, and not be the better for it, more cautious and vigilant, more dutiful to God, and useful to his neighbour, is in danger of becoming one of those upon whom even a miracle would be thrown away.

SERMON III.

MATTH. xxii. 32.

God is not the God of the dead, but of the living.

THESE words being spoken by our Saviour with relation to the Patriarchs, Abraham, Isaac, and Jacob, after they were dead, and with a view to establish the doctrines of the soul's immortality, a future state, and a resurrection; I shall take occasion from them to discuss these two important points:

I. That the soul of man subsists after death, and hath some place of abode allotted to it till the resurrection:

II. That this intermediate state is, in all probability, not a state of insensibility to the souls of the righteous; but of thought and self-consciousness, and consequently of content and of happiness, in a certain degree.

These two propositions I intend to support, not by arguments taken from the light of reason, and from the nature of the soul, considered as an active, simple, uncompounded, immaterial substance; not that I slight those arguments, on the contrary, I think they have much weight and force; but, as they are rather of too refined a nature for common use, I shall at present confine myself to proofs taken from revelation, and to the testimonies of holy Scripture.

There have been Christians, and those serious and good men, who, firmly believing that resurrection, and that life to come which our Saviour hath promised us,

yet

SERMON III.

yet denied the subsistence, or at least the sensibility of the soul after the death of the body. They supposed that when the body is dissolved, the soul is extinguished along with it, or that all its operations are entirely suspended; that it sleeps a sleep without dreams, and is to all intents and purposes as though it were not, till the last day shall awaken the dead man, and restore him to himself again.

This is not a novel notion, and the product of our inquisitive times. It was espoused of old by some Christians, though rejected by a great majority, and condemned as an heretical doctrine, and it hath in later times been revived, and recommended to us by persons of piety and of abilities.

I am far from designing to insult these men, or their notions. The intermediate state between death and the resurrection is a subject of enquiry, upon which the Scriptures have not said so much as perhaps one could wish. The sacred writers have not treated the point directly and fully. Only some things have been said by them occasionally, of which a proper use may be made; and these passages are so favourable to us, that I am persuaded the probability lies on our side of the question.

I could produce some passages from the Old Testament, in support of our opinion; but waving them, I shall consider those which are to be found in the New Testament.

Our Saviour thus admonisheth his disciples; Fear not them who kill the body, but are not able to kill the soul: but rather fear him, who is able to destroy both soul and body in hell.

If the soul hath such a necessary dependence upon the body, that when this dies, that dies with it, then he who kills the body, would with the same stroke kill the soul also. But our Saviour tells us that this is impossible, because the soul remains after the dissolution of the body, and is out of the reach of human or of

created

created power. If it be said that our Saviour only means the utter and eternal destruction of the soul, which no one can effect, because God hath promised us a resurrection to a second life, this would be a mere shift, to avoid the force of a plain text. For in this flat and far-fetched sense, our Lord might as well have denied that men can kill the body, because at the resurrection we shall again consist of soul and body, knowing ourselves to be the same persons that we were before.

Our Saviour himself, at the point of death, said; Father, into thy hands I commend my spirit. And lest we should think this a peculiar privilege belonging to the Son of God, St. Stephen, when dying, having a vision of Jesus Christ standing at God's right hand, addresseth himself to him, and says; Lord Jesus, receive my spirit.

Again; Our Saviour's words to the penitent thief are express; Verily I say unto thee, To-day thou shalt be with me in Paradise. Here, I must inform you that, in order to elude the force of this text, the persons of the contrary opinion alter the stopping, and read it thus; Verily I say unto thee to-day, Thou shalt be with me in Paradise; that is, thou shalt be with me hereafter, some time or other, at the resurrection. But of all such forced interpretations, this seems to be one of the lowest; and what makes it still worse is, that Paradise, as we shall shew, means not the kingdom of heaven, but the place of the good after death, and before the resurrection.

Farther; In the New Testament we read of separate spirits. Of the spirit of good persons departed, the Author of the Epistle to the Hebrews speaks, where he tells us that Christians are joined to the Church Catholic; that is, not only to their brethren upon earth, and to the host of holy angels, but to the invisible society of the spirits of just men made perfect; who

are

SERMON III.

are made perfect, that is, who have finished their course, and accomplished their warfare.

St. Paul also hath informed us that a man, that is, the soul of a man, may be separated from the body, and yet live without it, when he says; We are confident and willing rather to be absent from the body, and to be present with the Lord.

He also speaks of some visions and revelations which he had seen and received in Paradise, and in the third heaven; but declares himself doubtful in what situation his soul was at that time; whether in the body, says he, or whether out of the body, I know not; God knoweth. Now if he had believed that the soul could not subsist or could not act in a state of separation, he might easily have cleared up his own doubts, and have concluded that he was in the body.

In our Saviour's time, the Sadducees and the Pharisees differed greatly concerning the nature of the soul, and its duration and destination. The Sadducees held that the soul was material and mortal, or rather, that a man was nothing more than a living thinking body, who entirely perished when he died. Upon this system of theirs a resurrection was indeed an impossibility, and mere contradiction. It could only be a new creation of a new creature, which could have no relation to the man that was dead and gone. And in this the Sadducees were consistent with themselves, and drew a just conclusion from false premisses. The Pharisees held immaterial and immortal substances, angels good and evil, and human spirits, or souls subsisting after death, and therefore capable of being reunited to an human body. Our Saviour decides the question for the Pharisees and against the Sadducees, from this text of Moses; I am the God of Abraham, of Isaac, and of Jacob, spoken after these holy men were dead; and he builds his argument upon this foundation, God is not the God of the dead, but of the living. If then the souls of these holy men were living, the very foundation

tion of the Sadducean doctrine was overturned, and the doctrine of a resurrection was cleared of the main difficulties, and nothing could be urged by them against it, except one small objection, which our Saviour also condescended to remove. Whose wife, said they, shall the woman be at the resurrection, who had been joined to seven husbands upon earth? In answer to this, he informs them that after the resurrection to life eternal there shall be no such connections, but the righteous shall be in a more exalted condition, clothed with spiritualized bodies, wanting no repairs, and liable to no decay.

This seems to be a plain and true account of our Saviour's reasoning upon that famous text, I am the God of Abraham, &c. which some Interpreters have misunderstood, for want of attending to the principles of the Sadducees, against whom he argues. For if his reasoning had been so subtle as they have made it, the common people who stood by would hardly have felt the force of it. But they perceived clearly from the text, as it was explained by him, that the holy Patriarchs, Abraham, Isaac, and Jacob, were still alive after the dissolution of their bodies; and they knew that this was an effectual confutation of the Sadducean notion that there was no life besides the present, and that death put an end to the whole man. It hath been said of our Lord's argument, that it proves rather the permanency of the same person, and the life of the soul, than the resurrection of a dead man, according to our common notion of that word. But, first, his argument was fully sufficient to confute the Sadducees with whom he had to do; and secondly, another living state of the same person, after this, and besides this present state, may justly be called a resurrection, and is as much as the word * *resurrection*, considered in itself, ever implies.

Thus

---

* Ἀνάστασις.—They who in the text above-mentioned look for a proof of the resurrection of that identical body which died, are seeking what they will not find.

SERMON III.

Thus the subsistence of the soul after the death of the body, appears to be the doctrine of Christ and of his Apostles delivered in the New Testament. To this it should be added, that the Fathers of the Church, who lived in or near the times of the Apostles, were unanimous in this opinion, and persuaded that the soul of every man, upon the dissolution of the body, died not, but had a proper place to go to; and accordingly this doctrine is to be found in the most ancient Christian Liturgies.

This is an argument of weight; for though we are not obliged to adopt all the notions or reasonings which are to be found in the Primitive Fathers; yet a due regard is to be paid to their testimony concerning doctrines which they deliver as received by the Church in their days.

The same opinion was also by a tradition from the remotest antiquity, adopted by all the civilized heathen nations in Greece, and in the East; and indeed in those parts of the world which have been more lately discovered, in the vast regions of America.

II. Now I proceed to the second proposition, to shew that this intermediate state is in all probability not a state of sleep, for the souls of the righteous, but of sensibility, and consequently of content and of happiness in a certain degree.

Under this head I observe, that, as we find many intimations in the Scriptures concerning this state of the good, and hardly any concerning the state of the bad, I shall confine my inquiries to the former: only taking notice of this, that a positive punishment, inflicted by a righteous God, cannot well be supposed to be the lot of wicked souls in their separate state; for the last day being always described to us as the time of trial, sentence, and condemnation to the wicked, this induceth us to think that such actual punishment will not be inflicted upon them before that time. It seems therefore more probable, that their disquiet, if they feel any,
will

will arise, not from punishment, but from the expectation of it, which is the natural result of a guilty conscience, and is indeed a most disconsolate and miserable situation.

The same thing in the New Testament is intimated concerning evil Spirits, or Devils, namely, that they are reserved, as St. Peter says, to the day of judgment, to be punished; and in St. Matthew, they intreat Christ, not to torment them before the time.

And for the same reason, it is likewise to be supposed that the souls of the righteous receive not their proper and intended reward before that day, and that they rest in the joyful expectation of it.

If it be asked how and in what manner the soul acts, whilst it is deprived of the body, whether by its own natural powers, or by more subtile material organs and instruments fitted to its separate state? we must answer with St. Paul, We cannot tell; God knoweth. Even now we are little known to ourselves; and the soul, which is the eye of the mind, is like the eye of the body; it sees other things, but it cannot see itself, its own nature and natural powers. We cannot explain how we see, or hear, or think, or imagine, or understand, or dream, and least of all how we remember; and yet we have a constant experience of all these operations in ourselves. No wonder then that we cannot conceive how our souls can understand and act, when out of the body, since that is a state of which we have had no experience. But the thing itself, that the soul in a state of separation shall have life and perception, this is, as I have shewed, the most obvious and probable sense of some passages in Scripture, and Scripture is our surest guide in this inquiry, and without its help, our best philosophy would be precarious and defective.

Let us therefore hear what the Scripture suggests to us in this matter: and here most of the texts which we have already produced to support the first proposition will serve to support the second.

The

The Scriptures teach us that there are spirits good and evil, who think and act, and yet either are united to no bodies, or have bodies of a quite different kind from ours. Why should not human souls have the same inherent active principle?

St. Paul, who had been taken up into the third heaven, and also into Paradise, declares himself unable to say whether he was in the body, or out of the body; thus manifestly supposing that the soul separated from the body may perceive and know things that are even beyond the apprehensions of living men. For he says, that being thus in Paradise, he heard unspeakable words, which it was not lawful, or rather not possible, for man to utter. So then this paradise is not a place of darkness, silence, and oblivion, where spirits sleep, like some creatures in their winter-quarters; but a place of glory, light, and joy.

The same Apostle, whilst he was in the flesh, tells us that he was very desirous to depart, and to be with Jesus Christ, which is far better. Nevertheless, says he, to abide in the flesh is more needful for you. Now how could the Apostle think it far better to depart from the body than to remain in it, if after that departure he should be deprived of all sense and thought? Is it not better to have our reasoning faculty than to be without it? Is it not better to serve God in a land of the living, than to sink into a state wherein we can do nothing? St. Paul surely doth not desire to die, merely to be free from the persecutions and troubles that he underwent, which is the cold exposition of some Commentators; but he wanted to depart, that he might go to that Paradise again, of which he had been favoured with a sight; or, as he expresses it, to go and be with Christ.

Now certainly a good man hath more communion with Christ, whilst he is serving him here in the flesh, than he would have in a state of insensibility.

Let us hear the same Apostle again. We know, says he, that whilst we are at home, or rather, whilst we dwell in the body, we are abfent from the Lord: we are therefore willing rather to be abfent from the body, and to be prefent, or converfant with the Lord.

He fpeaks here of the ftate of the Faithful, which commenceth after death, and not of that only which follows the refurrection, fince he calls it an abfence from the body. He alfo fpeaks of other Chriftians along with himfelf, that we may not fancy it to be an Apoftolical privilege and recompence. There is no joining thefe declarations to a ftate of fleep and infenfibility, without fome far-fetched reafoning, fome violence offered to the more obvious fenfe.

But let us hear our Lord himfelf. When he was dying, he faid to the penitent Thief, To-day thou fhalt be with me in Paradife. Here Chrift, as a liberal Prince, promifeth more to his humble petitioner, than the man prefumed to afk. The requeft was, Lord, remember me when thou comeft into thy kingdom. The anfwer was to this effect; I will not put thee off till that day cometh; but I will take thee under my protection this very day. Die fecurely; thou fhalt inftantly go along with me to Paradife. To Paradife: What place is that? Our Saviour fpake thefe words to a Jew, and intended to be underftood by him. From the Jews therefore we muft learn the meaning of the word. Paradife originally meant the Garden of Eden, where our firft parents dwelt in a ftate of innocence and happinefs. Hence the Jews ufed this word to reprefent the place where the fouls of the righteous go, when they are feparated from the body. They diftinguifh Paradife from Heaven; and fo doth St. Paul, when he fpeaks of his vifions and revelations.

Again, Our Saviour reprefents Lazarus, as carried after death to Abraham's bofom. This was another name for that ftate of peace and comfort to which the fpirits of the righteous were conveyed.

This doctrine was, as we obferved before, conftantly received in the primitive Church.

In

In procefs of time, fome new notions and practices were introduced. Firft of all, prayers for the dead, which indeed is a practice of no fmall antiquity. But thefe prayers originally were rather a fort of pious wifhes, they were offered in general for all thofe who died in the faith, that they with thofe who were ftill living upon earth might partake together of a joyful and glorious refurrection at the laft day. To fay the truth, this feems to have been a kind of will-worfhip, and a practice not commanded in the New Teftament.

Then came the doctrine of Purgatory, and the doctrine of praying to departed Saints.

The doctrine of Purgatory was founded upon a fuppofition that the fouls of imperfect Chriftians go into a ftate of temporary punifhment, and may be relieved by the prayers and other pious ceremonies of the Church; and then that thofe prayers might be purchafed by pious legacies; which proved an inexhauftible mine of filver and gold to the Romifh Clergy.

Prayers to Saints were founded upon a notion that thofe holy perfons were in heaven, and would there intercede with God for us; of which interceffion there is not a fhadow of a proof in the Scriptures. The only proof was the teftimony of lying miracles, and enthufiaftic vifions.

This doctrine, you may obferve, doth not agree with that of praying for the dead in general, fince fuch prayers for the dead did fuppofe that they were not admitted into heaven before the refurrection.

Here let me add two or three paffages more from the New Teftament, relating to the interval between death and the refurrection.

The firft is the account of Chrift's transfiguration, at which time the Evangelifts inform us that Mofes and Elias came and converfed with Jefus, and were feen and heard by thofe difciples who were prefent. As to Elias, he died not; but, like Enoch before him, was taken up into heaven. But of Mofes it is written that he died

and

and was buried. This account therefore is a fair intimation that good men continue to live and to act after they are released from this mortal body.

The other passage is that in the Revelation, which the Church useth in the burial service; I heard a voice from heaven, saying unto me, Write, Blessed are the dead which die in the Lord, yea, saith the Spirit, that they may rest from their labours, and their works do follow them. There is nothing in a state of insensibility that seems to deserve the title of blessedness or happiness; and if we should grant it to be a blessing, the wicked would have it as much as the good during that interval of inactivity. But in the same Book, the souls of the righteous are described as in a waking condition. I saw, says St. John, under the altar the souls of them that were slain for the word of God; and they cried, How long, O Lord holy and true, dost thou not judge and avenge our blood? And it was said to them, that they should still rest for a little season. This is a visionary scene and transaction; and yet it intimates that these holy Martyrs were in a living state (*b*).

And

(*b*) As to the condition of the wicked, in the interval of the separate state, there is one passage in the New Testament that seems to relate to it, and that is the parable of the rich man and Lazarus, where the former is said, after death and before the resurrection, to go into *Hell*, as we translate it; but the word is not *Gehenna*, it is *Hades*, which means the intermediate state of the dead, and there to be in pain, whilst Lazarus was in Abraham's bosom. This is the only place in the New Testament where *Hades* expressly denotes a state of punishment. But, as it is a Parable, and many things in it cannot well be taken according to the letter, the only conclusion that can be drawn from it with full certainty, is the general doctrine of a future state of retribution.

The Apostles, in the first chapter of the Acts, say of Judas, that he was gone to his own place; but whether that was a place of punishment, or of darkness and silence is not said.

Perhaps the matter might be compounded with those who contend for the sleep of the soul, by allowing that whilst the good enter into a state of peace and comfort, the wicked are probably condemned to an insensible condition till the last day calls them forth.

SERMON III.

And now I shall make application of the foregoing doctrine, and consider it as a matter of hope and consolation to all those who endeavour to obtain and to secure the favour of God.

The reward of eternal life promised to the good at the resurrection, as it is more than the best of men can claim as their due, and the effect of the mere bounty of God, is surely sufficient to encourage and content them. Suppose that when they die they should sleep till the Lord comes and wakes them, yet they should consider that sleep as a rest from trouble, a protection from temptations, a calm repose under the wings of the Almighty. In a sleep without sensation, be it long or short, the interval is as nothing; and in this case a thousand years are as one day, yea as one moment. It is like closing the eyes, and opening them again instantly.

But, as I have been endeavouring to shew you, it is more probable that the interval between death and the resurrection is not a sleep to the servants of Christ, but a removal of the soul to a place called Paradise: it is not a stupid insensible rest, but a rest accompanied with self-consciousness and satisfaction. It is a place of the best society, and the most desirable company; where dwell the spirits of just men, the holy Patriarchs, Apostles, Prophets, Martyrs, Confessors, where the Angels of God go, to and fro, and which probably the son of God himself sometimes favours with his presence. In that safe retirement there are no wicked intruders to corrupt or insult the inhabitants; no evil Spirits to seduce, no temptations of any kind to make their assaults. It is a place whence sin, and sorrow, and fear, are banished; and where there is peace, and love, and hope, and expectation of still greater rewards. If death calls a Christian to such a place, why should he not be willing to go to it, to depart hence, and to be with the Lord?

As to the wicked and impenitent, let them not flatter themselves with the vain hope of sleeping till the day of judgment. If it should be so, the senseless interval, as we observed before, doth not in reality remove that fatal hour, but death and the resurrection will seem to them closely united together.

Upon the supposition that death is a state of lethargy overshadowed with profound darkness, till Christ arises, and shines upon it at the last day; upon this supposition, I say, a Christian might more reasonably desire to continue here a little longer, and a little longer, because here he hath some opportunity of doing good, and of being busy in his vocation. Upon the supposition of the Romish Church, that after death there follows a burning fiery furnace, called Purgatory, a Christian might well be afraid to die. But the Scriptures teach us better things; and therefore let us comfort one another with the words there recorded; and that we may be qualified to enter after death into the regions of peace and hope, and at the general resurrection to meet the Lord, and to enter into his kingdom, let us purify ourselves from evil inclinations and evil practices, that we may find mercy from God, both in the separate state, and at the last day (c).

(c) Some remarks in this Sermon are taken from the Discourses of Bishop Bull on the same subject.

SERMON

SERMON IV.

JEREMIAH xiii. 23.

Can the Æthiopian change his skin, or the leopard his spots? then may ye also do good, that are accustomed to do evil.

THE holy Scriptures, to make us wise unto Salvation, instruct us in our duty, and give us all possible encouragement to the practice of it, particularly by assuring us that what sins soever we have committed, if we repent of them and forsake them, they shall be forgiven. No hour is represented as too late, no time is limited after which our repentance shall not be accepted. But, that this goodness of God, thus always ready to pardon, should not have a bad effect upon us, and encourage us to continue in sin and to put off our reformation to a distant day, the same Scriptures assure us that by long persisting to offend we may make ourselves almost incapable of amending. God continues ever ready to shew mercy to us when we change our evil courses; but no good will thence arise to us, if we adding sin to sin should harden ourselves till we lose all inclination and almost all power to qualify ourselves for receiving his mercy.

This is the doctrine contained in the text: Can the Æthiopian change his skin or the leopard his spots? then may ye also do good who are accustomed to do evil. The meaning of this is that they who are accustomed to do evil will find the work of repentance and reformation to be, not indeed impossible, but extremely difficult.

The

The truth of this may be shewed,

I. From the nature of habits in general, of vicious habits in particular:

II. From experience:

III. From the testimony of Scripture.

I. Concerning habits we may observe that there are many things which we practise at first with difficulty, and which at last, by daily and frequent repetition, we perform not only without labour, but without premeditation and design, and then they are habits.

Habits of the body or of the mind, which at first were indifferent actions, in process of time become almost unavoidable.

Thus it is with the habits of memory. By frequent practice and slow degrees we acquire the use of speech: we retain a surprising variety of words, of arbitrary sounds, which we make the signs of things. These we readily use; and when we want to express our thoughts, words present themselves to us unsought, and our native language sticks by us, and if we once perfectly understand it, we can never forget it.

Thus it is in the habits of the imagination. When we accustom our minds to certain objects, when we call them often before us, view them and reflect upon them continually, these objects, which at first were perhaps as indifferent as any other, become familiar to us, they appear uncalled and force themselves upon us, and though we strive to drive them out, still they will return, and possess the uppermost place in our mind.

Thus also it is with the habits of sin. They are acquired like other habits by repeated acts; they fix themselves upon us in the same manner, and are corrected with the same difficulty.

A sinner by long offending contracts an aversion from his duty, and weakens his power of deliberating and chusing upon wise motives.

By giving way to his passions he has made them ungovernable; they are always solliciting him for the same

same indulgence, and he is ever uneasy till they are satisfied; they rise of themselves, and stay not for his consent, and by every victory over him, they gain new strength, and he grows less able to resist them.

His understanding and reason become unserviceable to him. Sin has always a bad effect upon them, to corrupt and impair them. He endeavours to persuade himself that he is in no danger; perhaps there will be no future judgment, perhaps the threatnings of God will not be executed. Or, if he cannot argue himself out of his belief, he can so consistently employ his thought upon other objects more agreeable to him, that his belief shall be weak and inactive and shall give him no trouble.

At first, when he did amiss, he was ashamed of it; but shame is lost by long offending. At first vice appeared to him delightful for the present, yet unreasonable and detestable; but by degrees this deformity wears off, and he sees nothing in it odious and unnatural. At first he was divided between good and evil, he had intervals when reflection took place, when he saw the beauty of virtue, and had faint wishes at least that it were more suitable to his inclinations, and easier to be practised, and some sorrow that his reason and his passions should be so at variance: at last the desires and the judgment are unhappily united and reconciled, and the whole man uniformly pursues that which is evil.

Add to this, that vicious habits make a deeper impression and gain faster upon us than good habits. Sin recommends itself to our senses by bringing present profit or pleasure, whilst religion consists frequently in renouncing present profit or pleasure for a greater interest at a distance, and so recommends itself, not to our senses, but to our reason; upon which account it is more difficult to be good than to be bad. Thus, in the style of the Scriptures, piety is a victory, which implies labour and contending; sin is a state of slavery, into which it is easy to fall by negligence and indolence, by betraying

and

and tamely giving up those powers which God had bestowed upon us for better purposes.

One being asked, what could be the (a) reason why weeds grew more plentifully than corn; answered, Because the earth was the mother of weeds, but the step-mother of corn; that is, the one she produced of her own accord, the other not till she was compelled to it by man's toil and industry. This may not unfitly be applied to the human mind, which, on account of its intimate union with the body, and commerce with sensible objects, easily and willingly performs the things of the flesh, but will not bring forth the spiritual fruits of piety and virtue, unless cultivated with assiduity and application.

An habitual sinner, before he can be converted, must be sorry and grieved that he has misbehaved himself; but he will find it a hard thing to bring his mind into this temper. He may be sorry indeed, sorry that God is offended at sin, sorry that he cannot be wicked here and happy hereafter; which is not even the beginning of amendment. A sorrow that we ought to repent is a very different thing from repentance.

Such a person, before he can be converted, must be acquainted with his duty. This seems not to be difficult; yet even for this a sinner by long offending becomes often unfit. Years after years have passed away, without any serious reflections upon religious truths: he has never allowed them a place in his thoughts, his thoughts have been all bent another way, to gain, perhaps, to fraud, to malice, to oppression, to revenge, to ambition, to unlawful pleasures, to vanity and trifles. And when the thoughts have thus been long used to run in another course, and have worn for themselves a deep chanel, few persons are able to turn the stream, to apply them to things sacred and serious, to employ them upon such disagreeable meditations; they will force
their

(a) Grotius ad Luc. viii. 7.

their way back again, and purfue their accuftomed courfe.

If thefe difpofitions and actions, which only lead to amendment, may prove fo uneafy and unacceptable to an old offender, we may thence judge what pains and what application it will coft him to proceed to perfect reformation.

Thus the doctrine contained in the text is confirmed from obfervations upon the nature of habits in general, of evil habits in particular.

II. A fecond proof of it may be drawn from experience, which fhews us that there are few who forfake any vice to which they are remarkably addicted, fewer than we ufually imagine. The truth of this may be eafieft obferved in thofe faults where the body feems not to be much concerned, fuch as pride, conceit, levity of mind, rafhnefs in judging and determining, cenforioufnefs, malice, cruelty, wrath, morofenefs, envy, felfifhnefs, avarice. Thefe bad difpofitions feldom forfake a perfon in whom they are fixed; if they have accompanied him from youth to manhood, they will in all probability follow him through the longeft old age, down to the grave, and beyond the grave, to the world of feparate fpirits.

Befides, many of them are of fo deceitful a nature, that the mind entertains them and knows it not; the man thinks himfelf free from faults which to every other perfon are moft vifible; and when this double diftemper is upon him, the danger muft needs be great, and the condition deplorable; for how fhould he feek out and apply a remedy, who knows not that he ftands in need of any?

Since fuch is the malignity of evil habits of the mind, we may fuppofe that thofe vices which are of a groffer kind, and in which the body is more employed, differ little from the former; that intemperance and debauchery are almoft as difficultly corrected as pride and envy. A man may abftain from them for a confiderable time,

or

or quite cease to commit them, only because he wants power and opportunity, and consequently without repentance and reformation: his imagination and inclination may pursue the same evil object, when the body is unable to comply with them.

III. The holy Scriptures concur with reason and experience. Every one who has read them, or heard them read and explained, must know that they perpetually represent to us the unreasonableness, the folly, the baseness, and the bad consequences of sin; whence we should conclude, that if all sin in general and every act of it is so dangerous, repeated and habitual sins must be beyond comparison and beyond expression more dangerous.

When the Scriptures speak of evil habits, they make use of figures as strong and bold as language can utter and the imagination conceive, to set forth their pernious nature. Persons in that condition are said to be inclosed in a snare, to be taken captives, to have sold themselves to work wickedness, to be in a state of slavery. He who is a slave to a bad master has no prospect of liberty; and worse masters can no man serve than the Devil, and his own vile and imperious Lusts. They are said to have lost all their senses and faculties, to be deaf, to be blind, and to walk in darkness, to be hardened and past feeling, to be sick beyond hopes of recovery, to be dead in trespasses and sins.

To part with a beloved vice is called to cut off one's own hand and to pull out one's own eye; to return from a long course of sin to righteousness is a resurrection from the dead and a new creation. Even those passages of Scripture which contain great encouragement and favourable promises to repentance, inform us at the same time of the difficulty of amending. Our Saviour gives a plain and familiar representation of it. A shepherd, says he, rejoices more over one sheep which was lost and is found, than over ninety and nine which went not astray. Why so? For this, amongst other

other reasons; because he could not reasonably expect such good fortune, and had little hopes of finding a creature exposed to a thousand dangers, and unable to shift for itself.

Thus the nature of sin, the usual consequences of it, experience, and the word of God, all concur to establish this melancholy truth, that a change from habitual vice to virtue is seldom made, and not without great difficulty: which doctrine suggests many reflections useful to persons of all ages and of all dispositions.

1. Can the Æthiopian change his skin, or the leopard his spots? then may ye also do good, who are accustomed to do evil. If these words were to be taken rigorously and in the strictest sense, it would be a folly to exhort an habitual sinner to repentance, and an unreasonable thing to expect from him a natural impossibility; but it is certain that they mean no more than an extreme difficulty. The genius of sublime and figurative language requires such lively expressions, and describes things which are hard to be accomplished as quite impossible.

That the text is to be thus understood appears also from the whole chapter, which contains terrible threatnings against the Jews, of evils which should come upon them for their impiety. These threats are mixed with exhortations to repentance, and then follows the text, which must not be taken as a declaration that they could not possibly repent; for then the Prophet ought not to have pressed them in the same discourse to amend their ways, and to give glory to the Lord, before he caused darkness, and before their feet stumbled, and they should fall to rise no more.

The Scriptures continually invite and excite sinners to repentance, they declare perpetually, and suitably to the common notions of mankind, that the destruction of such persons is from themselves, and these plain and easy expressions may help us to understand rightly those few difficult places, where God is said to harden men's hearts,

hearts, by which no more can be meant than that God permits the wicked to be hardened, and to undergo this and other natural confequences of their tranfgreffions.

The Gentiles, who had no juft notions of God's government, ufed to afcribe events to Fate, or to Fortune; that is, to mere names which themfelves underftood not, to things which had no power, no influence, and indeed no being. The Jews, accuftomed to a more religious way of fpeaking, ufed to afcribe all things, all events to God, by which they only intended to acknowledge his providence, and to declare that nothing could come to pafs againft his will, or without either his permiffion or his affiftance; and hence it is that they fometimes afcribe to him actions of which he cannot be the immediate author.

If God could be fuppofed to harden the hearts of finners by an act of his own, and to create in them a hatred of their duty, fuch an interpofition would take off the guilt from them, and make their punifhment unreafonable, and contradict all our notions of his goodnefs and juftice. To which we may add, that he would often exert his power on occafions which required it not. Alas! a wicked man is able to work out his own deftruction, without the affiftance of the Almighty in the unhappy undertaking; and fo pernicious is fin, that of itfelf it is fufficient to produce a fad change for the worfe in thofe who are enflaved to it, to deprive them of their good qualities, and to render their condition almoft defperate.

The difficulty of reforming bad habits, though it may feem to be rather a diffuafive and difcouragement from repentance, is indeed a very proper, and ought to be a moft prevailing motive to it. They who are in this condition fhould confider that as is the difficulty, fo is the danger. Heaven and happinefs retire from them, and are removed to a prodigious diftance; ruin and mifery have almoft overtaken them; they ftand upon the brink of deftruction, and every moment
expofed

exposed to the worst of evils, from which they cannot save themselves without uncommon pains and resolution, and a diligence greater than they exerted before upon any occasion in the whole course of their lives.

The divine Wisdom has thought proper to set these terrors before obstinate offenders, not to drive them to despair, but to awaken in them those powers of the soul which are stupified and weakened, but not destroyed by sin. He who can be made fully sensible of these truths may force his way through a thousand obstacles, exert himself in a surprising manner, and perform things which could scarcely be expected, may be one of those happy persons who was dead and is alive again, who was lost and is found, who causes joy in heaven and on earth by his unexpected reformation. An attempt to grow better is a laudable endeavour; and he who does one virtuous action may proceed to do more, and may hope for the blessing and assistance of God, who loves every thing that is good.

2. There are persons who sincerely profess the Christian religion, who fear God and desire to be in his favour; but whose lives are not so conformable to their belief as they ought to be, who are sorry for their faults, and fall into them again, who make not the progress in goodness which they acknowledge to be justly expected from them, and who have not that command over their passions which by a little more resolution and self-denial they might acquire. Such persons should seriously consider the difficulty of reforming bad habits, and the extreme danger of that state: for though it be not their present condition, yet if they use not timely caution, sad effects may ensue: if they improve not, they will degenerate; if they indulge themselves in smaller offences, they will be insensibly led on to a settled carelessness and disobedience. Such as they now are, were also those who are the most devoted slaves to their vices, for no one is very wicked on a sudden. They whose amendment is represented in the text as
almost

almost impossible were once divided between good and evil, and pursued neither steddily, and when they did amiss condemned themselves for it, and approved those things which they had not the heart to practise, and entertained a shame and felt a remorse for their offences, and proposed to amend their lives. Thus it was with them at the first, till by degrees the deceitfulness of sin infatuated them, and left them in no disposition to righteousness.

3. These sad examples should be a warning to those whose obedience is so incomplete and sullied with so many defects, whose love of virtue is not equal and uniform, and whose affections are placed sometimes on God and religion, and sometimes on the follies and vanities of the world. The tyranny of evil habits, and the easy descent from an unsteddy virtue to those habits, should incite them to correct in themselves every thing that their conscience condemns, to set about it instantly, to-day whilst it is called to-day, whilst they may hope to have time and strength to complete the undertaking, whilst piety appears amiable to them, whilst the passage to it is short, and the impediments easily removed. These considerations are more particularly to be recommended to young persons, who are entering into a state of trial, to whose choice Virtue and Vice present themselves, and who have as yet no habits of uprightness or of guilt.

4. There are Christians who abstain from known and deliberate transgressions, who strive to make a daily progress in goodness, and to perform an acceptable service to God. The difficulty of reforming vicious habits is a proper subject to be set before these also.

Reflections upon this subject may warn them to be upon their guard, and after they have set out well and proceeded well, they fail not at last, nor lose a reward near at hand. The best persons may find benefit from all kind of motives to religion, even from those which seem only designed for the profligate. Whilst they are here,

here, they are liable to be seduced, and never quite out of the reach of danger till they have finished their course: they have just cause to hope that they shall never forsake God, and they have reason to work out their salvation with pious fear, and to remember what is threatened, when the righteous man turneth away from his righteousness.

5. They who have wisely and happily preserved themselves from evil habits ought to be very thankful to God, by whose blessing they are free from that heavy bondage, and strangers to the sad train of evils which attend it.

When they see the deplorable condition of those who are accustomed to do evil, and whose amendment is so necessary, and yet so difficult, they will pity the case of such persons; but to this compassionate concern will (*b*) naturally be added a great satisfaction, when they look in upon the state of their own mind; and consider what misery they have avoided, and what advantages they have secured.

6. Lastly, from the doctrine of the text we may find this singular encouragement to well-doing, that by a perseverance in our duty we may make righteousness habitual to us, and not less pleasant than profitable. God has not so dealt with us, that whilst the passage from vice to virtue is difficult, the passage from virtue to vice should be easy. There is, in this respect, not much difference in habits; and if it be not altogether, it is almost, as hard to turn from righteousness to sin, as it is to turn from sin to righteousness.

The enemies of religion have sometimes represented it as consisting altogether in self-denial and pain, and have said that piety is no piety, except it cross our inclinations, that justice and charity and purity and temperance, and every thing that is good, deserves no praise, when we are, as it were, unavoidably disposed to it,

---

(*b*) Suave mari magno, turbantibus æquora ventis, &c.

it, when we take a pleasure in it, and could not act in a contrary manner without great uneasiness. But this is a false and a foolish notion. Some cases will happen to the best of men, in which duty and desire will be at variance, and then obedience is self-denial and mortification; but in general he who is accustomed to serve God, will serve him by choice and with ease and satisfaction. To be good against the bent of the heart and by violence continually offered to the passions, is the condition of one who has contracted vicious habits, and begins to get the better of them, and this laborious conquest is greatly to be commended. To be good by temper and disposition, is the consequence of a regular and constant obedience, and is much more excellent: nor indeed is this temper to be acquired without diligent care and long application; for as we are not born wicked, so neither are we born good; and we must not expect to delight in virtue, till we have made it habitual by a right use of reason, and by a power over the affections gradually obtained.

Thus from the pernicious nature of sinful habits every Christian may draw inferences suited to his own state, may find motives to repentance and improvement, or encouragement to perseverance, or a timely warning to set out wisely, and chuse the good part which shall not easily be taken from him.

SERMON V.

Prov. x. 9.

He that walketh uprightly, walketh surely; but he that perverteth his ways shall be known.

Happiness is the favourite wish and the alluring object which every living creature pursues; but through the ignorance and the corruption which is so prevalent in the world, it unfortunately comes to pass that many persons fall into mistakes in their notions both of happiness itself, and of the best and surest methods to obtain it. In pursuing the end they are agreed, but in the ways of securing the end they differ widely. The choice of these means shews a man to be wise or foolish, religious or wicked. Every one would be happy, but every one will not take the proper course to secure that share of happiness for which he was designed, and which he is capable of obtaining.

The case is this: Every one would be happy if he could, not only upon the whole, but in each instant of his existence; he would enjoy perpetual pleasure and satisfaction without any pain, any loss or disappointment, any uneasiness of body or of mind. These are natural desires, and they seem in some measure to be common to all living creatures. But man, besides this innate appetite, hath a superior principle in him, which is reason; and reason will inform him that a happiness of this kind, all pleasure and no pain, all joy and no sorrow, all good and no evil, is unattainable and impossible, and as much out of the course of things as all light and no shade, all day and no night, all spring and no winter; and that, discarding such foolish hopes, he must consider what method will secure to him the most satisfaction and the least disquiet upon the whole, during his passage through this world, and beyond that period, even through the endless ages of futurity.

The only way to obtain this much desired and most desireable blessing is, as Solomon says, to walk uprightly. Solomon stands distinguished for great abilities both natural and acquired, and for great experience of good and evil, and one might safely take his word, and trust to his judgment. But in this point, we want not the sanction of his authority; and every man may be as wise as Solomon, and see the truth of the assertion, if he will make a due use of his understanding. He that walketh uprightly, walketh surely.

It is proper to be mentioned, but not necessary to be proved, that ways and paths, in the language of the Scriptures, are the courses and the manner of action. These expressions are become familiar to us, and every one knows that to walk signifies our usual course of dealing, and our common practice. So then, walking uprightly means goodness, righteousness, integrity, piety, religion in general. He may be said to walk uprightly, who hath good principles, and whose thoughts, words, and actions, are conformable to those principles; and such a person walketh surely, safe from danger and certain of success upon the whole. Here then is the duty, and here is the encouragement and the reward.

But, that we may set this exhortation of the wise man in such a light as to make it of general use and application, we will endeavour, before we proceed any farther, to remove a discouraging objection which may be made to it.

For

For it may be faid that, although the pofition in the text fhould be allowed to be true, yet it contains a truth of very little ufe or comfort to us, and a promife which none of us can apply to his own perfon. If he who is in every refpect righteous and religious may fairly prefume that he fhall enjoy a perfect fecurity upon the whole, what is that to finners? And finners we all are in various degrees. If Solomon's perfectly good man is found at laft to be an imaginary man, an accomplifhed creature which no where exifts, it fignifies little to us what recompence fuch a behaviour may expect and receive.

Two obfervations I have to offer, which will take off the force of the objection.

Firft, Although uprightnefs, in the ufual ftyle of the Scriptures and in the common acceptation of the word, means goodnefs in general, and an upright man is a perfect and a righteous man, yet this feems not to be the character which Solomon here intends to reprefent. It feems rather that he takes uprightnefs in a more limited fenfe, and confiders it as a focial virtue producing a good conduct towards others. And then his meaning will be, that he who in all his dealings is honeft, fincere, charitable, candid, and friendly, will in return receive good ufage, and efcape ill ufage. What induces me to fuppofe that this is the virtue which Solomon hath more particularly in view, is the contraft between the former and the latter part of the fentence. He that walketh uprightly, fays he, walketh furely: but he that perverteth his ways fhall be known. Shall be known of whom? why certainly, fhall be known of men. As to his being known of God, that is true, but is rather foreign from the purpofe. A wicked man is always known of God, from whom nothing is hidden, and who feeth the fecret purpofes of an evil heart, before they break out into action. But when Solomon fays that he fhall be known, it is as much as to fay, he fhall be difcovered and expofed,

in

in spite of all his dissimulation and caution, and then men will abhor him, and treat him as he deserves.

Now consequently, if the upright man is the man who performs his duty to his neighbour, and behaves himself well in civil society, we must suppose the promised reward of safety to be also of the social kind, namely security and peace, honour and reputation, esteem and favour, encouragement and assistance, rather than the future rewards of righteousness, which come not properly here into consideration.

Admitting this interpretation, we have an encouragement to well-doing, which any person may apply to himself upon conditions which are by no means impracticable, or even difficult, or uncommon, but which have been and are tolerably well performed by many, and of which performance he may find examples without going far to seek them.

For if we consider the threefold duty of man, to God, to his neighbour, and to himself, we shall find, I think, upon a due enquiry, that men who are not reprobates, who have good-nature and honour, and a sense of religion and morality, do usually perform their duty to their neighbour better upon the whole than their duty to God, and to themselves.

For, as to our duty to God, which is represented as nothing less than to love him with all our heart and soul, even religious people must condemn themselves for many omissions and commissions, for deficiencies in that piety, zeal, and activity, gratitude, resignation, reliance, faith, and devotion, which are due to our great Creator and Benefactor.

And as to our duty to ourselves, which consists in spending our time in the most rational and useful way, in improving our understanding, in purity and temperance, in regulating all our thoughts, inclinations, desires, affections, and passions, even religious persons must be conscious how frequently they fall short of
observing

observing the important and the difficult law of self-government.

But as to the civil and social behaviour, good persons approach nearer to regularity in this branch of duty, and usually endeavour in a tolerable manner to do to others as they would be done by, to be just, and to be charitable.

This is the first consideration which I have to offer, to shew that a man, though far from perfection, may apply Solomon's promise of safety to himself.

Another remark tending to the same purpose is this, that though we should suppose the uprightness mentioned in the text to mean goodness in general, and a goodness to which we cannot pretend, yet we may hope to make some advances towards it, and consequently may hope to come in for some share of the reward. If he who walketh uprightly in all respects, walketh surely in all respects, he who endeavours to do so, and on several occasions doth walk uprightly, will obtain some degree of safety and security, proportionable to his moral improvements.

Having thus shewed that the reward proposed by Solomon may be considered as attainable, more or less, by those who are not despisers of their duty and void of good qualities, we will now take his words in their full latitude, though perhaps in a greater latitude than he intended, and suppose that uprightness means goodness in general, and that safety means security in every sense and in every respect.

He that walketh uprightly, walketh safely; but he that perverteth his ways, shall be known.

The truth of these assertions will appear from the following considerations.

1. In the language of the Scriptures, the ways of the righteous are called (a) plain, direct, even ways, which may be found even by the ignorant, and where the

(a) Barrow, *Serm.* on the Text.

the simple paſſenger ſhall not err. Nothing is leſs difficult than to know our duty, and our intereſt alſo, if there be a ſincerity of intention and an integrity of heart. Our duty is graven in our minds and conſciences, and we may eaſily read it there. It is alſo written in the holy Scriptures, and there ſo plainly expreſſed and ſo frequently inculcated, that without wilful negligence or ſtubborn perverſeneſs we cannot fail to diſcover it. The Scriptures were calculated for general uſe, they were intended to make wiſe the ſimple, to give the young man knowledge and diſcretion, and to direct inquirers of all ranks and conditions in their duty, and towards their happineſs.

Such are both Chriſtian faith and Chriſtian practice, plain and perſpicuous ſo far as they are of univerſal importance, and of abſolute neceſſity. If any teachers have delivered them in a dark and abſtruſe, an inconſiſtent or incomprehenſible way, they are teachers who wanted to be taught themſelves, and who drew their notions, not from the fountain itſelf, but from muddy ciſterns.

The Scriptures indeed have their obſcurities and their difficulties; but then they relate to the knowledge of ancient languages, hiſtories, prophecies, facts, cuſtoms, ceremonies, controverſies, errors, and hereſies; and ſo they are properly the allotment of the ſtudious, of perſons who have learning and leiſure, and a man may know very little of them, and yet be wiſe unto ſalvation.

As the ways of the upright are plain and direct, ſo on the contrary, the ways of the unrighteous are repreſented in the Scriptures as dark, crooked, rough, and ſlippery ways. Wicked projects and unlawful methods of purſuing the objects of our vain deſires are various and uncertain, dangerous and deceitful. He who ſets out with ſuch bad proſpects, and ſuch pernicious guides, often falls and periſhes in the midſt of his courſe, or, if he get to the end of it, and to the

poſſeſſion

possession of the thing pursued, he finds himself disappointed at last. He sought pleasure and peace, and he receives trouble and vexation, shame and remorse.

For take a survey of an evil course of life, and it will appear that a sinner at his first setting out proposes to himself either the enjoyment of criminal pleasures, or the attainment of wealth and of power by unjustifiable methods.

What is to be done, and what is to be paid beforehand, for the obtaining all this? No less than labour and toil, cares and anxiety, fraud, rapine, extortion, violence, hypocrisy, lying, flattery, submission to the fantastical humours, the unreasonable demands, and the intolerable insolence of great and powerful men, an intimacy with the wicked, danger, distress, envy, malice, perpetual quarrels, and innumerable inconveniences.

And, as much is to be given, so much is to be given up, namely, reputation, peace, quiet, and security.

And what are the usual consequences of such proceedings? A distempered body, and a distracted mind, and very often the loss of temporal prosperity, and of all that is valuable even in this world.

And what are the hopes upon which such a person relies? They are the hopes, either that there is no God and no future state, or that God will not execute his threatenings, or that a late repentance may atone for all the irregularities of a vicious life. But he will find at last that hopes are no certainties, and wishes are no demonstrations.

Such is the deplorable situation of every one who lives in contradiction to Nature, and in defiance to Grace.

2. He that walketh uprightly acts upon good moral principles, which will stand the test of the strictest scrutiny, and appear to the more advantage, the more closely they are viewed, and which afford the firmest security.

security. They are recommended to us by the holy Scriptures, they have often been visibly rewarded by Providence, they are justified by experience, chosen by the wise and good, generally allowed to be agreeable to reason, and profitable in the end, and they have the approbation not only of the good, but of the bad likewise, who in their melancholy hours, in time of danger, trouble, or sickness, and at the close of life, usually condemn themselves, and bear testimony to the prudence of a conduct which they once used to blame or to deride.

The belief of these principles is absolutely necessary even for upholding civil government and preserving human society. No obligation upon the consciences of men, no faith and reliance between them, no friendship and peace, no common honesty, can subsist without it. Therefore Princes and Governors though they should be void of morality and religion, ought at least to pretend to it, and to save appearances, even for the sake of their own lives and fortunes, of their own present welfare; they should, as far as they prudently can, discountenance and repress all attempts to recommend vice, to ridicule virtue, and to overset the belief of a God, a providence, and a future state. Differences of religion are as unavoidable as differences of face and shape; and no man should be molested for his sentiments, when conscience can be fairly and honestly pleaded: but Vice and Atheism have no claims of this kind; and where there is no conscience at all, there can be no plea of conscience. It is ridiculous and unpardonable for such persons to plead liberty of conscience, and scruples of conscience; it is adding insult to disobedience, and impudence to iniquity.

All other springs and motives of action, besides reason and religion, are fickle and various. Humour, passion, interest, are perpetually changeable, and depend upon opportunities, casualties, different states and dispositions of body or of mind, and the ceaseless
vicissitudes

vicissitudes of worldly things. Thence it comes to pass, that he who is conducted by such guides, and governed by such masters, must be unstable in all his ways, and scarcely know whither he goes, and enjoy no settled rest of mind. But an upright person in all cases, and in all conditions is the same person, and goes the same way. By this he is secured from diffidence and self-distrust, and distraction of mind, from leading an unequal and inconsistent life, to his own dissatisfaction and uneasiness, and to the disappointment and detriment of others.

3. He that walketh uprightly walketh surely, even as to the present time, because he hath taken the proper way to attain all that a man can reasonably hope and desire in this world. The things which he aims at here are honour and reputation, and the friendship of virtuous persons, and temporal conveniences, so far as they are consistent with the more valuable blessings which God hath promised to those who love him.

And this way to success in these views and undertakings is that which the Scriptures call the strait and the plain way, namely, the way of diligence and benevolence, of honour, honesty, and integrity, which may seem to be slow, but is both sure and speedy also; whilst guile and fraud, extortion and oppression, over-reaching and supplanting others, are of all methods the most precarious and dangerous, and terminate in every thing that is scandalous, contemptible, and disastrous.

" Therefore, as a good (*b*) Writer hath observed, God seems in great wisdom to have hid from men of false and dishonest minds the wonderful advantages of truth and integrity to the prosperity even of our worldly affairs. These men are so blinded by their covetousness and ambition, that they cannot look beyond a present advantage, nor forbear to seize upon it,

(*b*) Tillotson.

it, though by ways never so indirect; they cannot see so far as to the remote consequences of a steady integrity, and the vast benefits and advantages which it will bring a man at last. Were but this sort of men wise and clear-sighted enough to discern this, they would be honest out of very knavery, not out of any love to honesty and virtue, but with a crafty design to promote and advance more effectually their own interests; and therefore the justice of the divine Providence hath hid this truest point of wisdom from their eyes, that bad men might not be upon equal terms with the just and upright, and serve their own wicked designs by honest and lawful means."

4. He who designs only what is just and reasonable, and prosecutes those designs fairly and innocently, can run no great hazard, can fall into no extreme disaster, and cannot be utterly disappointed.

In all probability he will not receive any great injury from intriguing men, or trouble from the vain and busy world. The world has its occupations, and so has he; the world has its pleasures, and so has he. But as he means well and deals inoffensively, as he gives no just provocation to others, so he is in less danger of meeting with obstructions. He can scarcely raise up adversaries, at least such as are very formidable.

The way of the upright is pleasant; serenity, satisfaction, and a just confidence, always attend upon him; and in that sense also he walketh surely. He is conscious to himself that his intentions are honest, and that he prosecutes them by lawful and honourable means. He is thoroughly satisfied and pleased with all that he undertakes, his judgment acquiesces in it, and approves of it as worthy of himself, agreeable to his reason, and conformable to his duty. He is secure of this, that the better he is known, the better he will be liked.

SERMON V.

It is observable that good (c) dispositions of the heart, like great abilities of the mind, are open, free, unsuspicious, courageous, and liberal; they are of a tame and familiar nature; the possessor of them is easy of access, and suffers himself to be approached, viewed, and surveyed. If you (d) want his opinion, his advice, his direction, and his assistance, you may have them for asking. But the designing Knave and the assuming Hypocrite, who pretends to accomplishments and excellences which he hath not, is reserved and formal solemn and important, and keeps you at a distance, if not from his outward, yet from his inward man; looks upon you as upon a cheat or a spy, and is afraid lest you should discern something or other which he wants to hide.

The upright person is constant and consistent with himself; his heart and his face, his mind and his speech, his professions and his deeds agree together. He uses no tricks to serve a present turn, he draws no one into mischief for the furtherance of his own ends; he never hath recourse to detraction, dissimulation, flattery, fawning and crouching: his wisdom is tempered with humanity, meekness, and charity; he lies not under perpetual constraint, engaged to keep a constant guard upon himself, to watch his memory, to curb his tongue, to manage his very looks, lest they should betray his intentions. Men do not shun his commerce, but readily place a confidence in him. He therefore undisturbedly partakes of the benefits of society, and passeth his days with safety, quiet, and reputation.

He

(c) La fausse grandeur est farouche & inaccessible; comme elle sent son foible, elle se cache, ou du moins ne se montre pas de front, & ne se fait voir qu'autant qu'il faut pour imposer.—La veritable grandeur est libre, douce, familiere, populaire; elle se laisse toucher & manier; elle ne perd rien à être vûë de près. *Bruyere.*

(d) "Ἄφθονοι Μυσῶν θύραι.

He is secure as to the final result of affairs, the main end and the considerable purposes of human life. So that if prosperity consists in a satisfaction of mind upon the whole, he cannot fail of being prosperous. No good and wise person will pursue worldly and private interest as an object which he hath a right to obtain, but will ask and seek it under condition, and with this reserve, if it seem good to the divine wisdom; and then the pains which are employed on any honest purpose, and in an honest way, are not misemployed, if they terminate in acquiescence and submission to God's will. When a man is able to meet temporal and transient disappointments with such a temper, his loss is a gain to him, just as on the contrary to one of evil dispositions his success is his undoing. Events which are seemingly undesirable often produce something incomparably more excellent to the righteous than any worldly profit; as humility, patience, meekness, moderation, contentedness, and a hope of obtaining a place in God's kingdom, a small degree of which is worth all the wealth, all the power, and all the pleasure, in the world.

5. To conclude: Either there is a future state, or there is not. Put the case that there is not. Religion then is a fable, and the hopes of immortality are fond and flattering illusions. But what hath the upright person lost by his error? Very little, if any thing. Upon the whole, he hath rather had the advantage over the ungodly. However that be, the wicked and he are at last upon the level: they are gone together to the land where there will be none to insult or deride others, and none to be insulted or derided, for having made a wrong choice in the days of their existence.

But if there be a future state, as Nature, Reason, Revelation, all most positively affirm, then it is that the Righteous and the Wicked are distinguished indeed. It is this great event, this final and unchangeable

able issue of things, that determines the wisdom or the folly of human actions.

I shall only make one short inference. If these things be so, then they who endeavour to do their duty, and to act a decent and an honest part upon this stage, should beware of a weakness to which they are too prone, that is, of grieving and repining at the seeming prosperity of those wicked or worthless sons of Fortune, who obtain a greater affluence of worldly favours than many persons far better than themselves. Why should we envy those with whom we would not make an exchange, and accept of their condition together with their heart and understanding? or why should we set so high a value upon such poor advantages? He who hath not God and his own Conscience for his friends, wheresoever placed, or howsoever furnished with externals, is wretched and miserable, an object not of emulation or envy, but to speak in a Philosophical style, of scorn and contempt, or rather, to speak in a Christian style, of pity and compassion.

SERMON VI.

MATT. xxii. 35.

Then one of them—asked him a question—saying, Master, which is the great commandment in the Law?

IT is probable that the question which this Jewish Doctor put to our Saviour was a point contested amongst the Jews; but it is certain from our Saviour's answer, that it was a proper question, that there was some commandment greater than the rest, that some duties were more important than others, and that it concerns us to know which they are. If that had not been the case, our Lord would have told him so; and if it had been a matter of mere curiosity, he would have put it off without a direct reply; for it was his constant method not to answer improper questions, or, instead of resolving them, to teach the inquirers something that might be of use to themselves. When they asked him, with a wicked intent, whether they should pay tribute to Cæsar, he gave them an oblique answer, intimating that they ought to pay it, but not affirming it. Render unto Cæsar, says he, the things that are Cæsar's; the justice of which sentence neither party could deny. When Peter asked him concerning his fellow-disciple John, how it should fare with him? Christ answers, What is that to thee? follow thou me. When the Disciples inquired, whether few should be saved, he says, Strive to enter in, and take heed that yourselves be of that number. When they inquired

SERMON VI.

quired who should be greatest in the kingdom of heaven? he tells them, Unless ye be meek and humble, ye shall not enter there at all.

A religion which hath God for its author, ought to be observed entirely and without exception, because God the Maker and Ruler of all hath an undoubted right to our whole obedience; because he who is most wise and good, can command nothing which is not fit and reasonable; because it is our own profit to comply in all things with his will; and because a stubborn and contemptuous neglect of any of his ordinances must receive its due punishment, unless we prevent it by repentance and amendment.

Yet when the precepts of religion are examined by religion, and compared together, some will be found more excellent, more useful, and more important than others; and therefore a more particular regard must be paid to them.

The revelation which God made to the Jews, and their religion, as it is contained in the Law and the Prophets, may be divided into three parts, of which the first is more important than the second, and the second is above the third.

Under the first and principal part we must place whatsoever is of its own nature eternally and unalterably good, namely, morality, righteousness, virtue. Under the second division may be ranged every action which hath a direct tendency to promote moral virtue, as prayer, and reading the Scriptures, and other good books, with a view to religious instruction. To the third and lowest part belong all rites and ceremonies which have no intrinsic goodness, but, when they are appointed of God, must be supposed to be intended for wise ends and purposes. These we commonly call positive duties, in opposition to moral duties.

Of the Jewish rites some were plainly conducing to righteousness, as the eating of the Passover in remembrance of a signal and miraculous deliverance; for this was proper to remind them of God's power and goodness, and to excite faith and gratitude and obedience. Other rites there were, which had no such visible connection with righteousness, as abstinence from particular meats, and were only so far good, as they were acts of obedience to divine commands.

An exact compliance with all these things was required of the Jews, and a wilful transgression of the smallest of them was to receive punishment; and God himself miraculously inflicted it at different times, and on particular occasions. Many instances of that kind are recorded in the Old Testament.

But though God required this entire and uniform respect to all his precepts, though he sometimes punished offences against the ceremonial law with more rigour than some transgressions of the moral and everlasting law, yet the Prophets have carefully and constantly distinguished the several duties of men in the same manner and order which hath been mentioned. They set morality above ceremonies, they prefer prayer to sacrifice, and righteousness to both of them. And our Saviour hath done the same. Ye tithe all manner of herbs, says he, and pass over judgment and the love of God, and have omitted the weightier matters of the Law, judgment, mercy, and faith: these ought ye to have done, and not to leave the others undone. When he was asked, which was the great commandment? he said that it was the love of God and our neighbour. And when the Apostles speak of the principal duties of Christianity, they mention sobriety, righteousness, godliness, purity, charity, and faith working by love.

There have been writers, who, notwithstanding all this, have set positive duties upon the level with moral actions, and in some sense have even given them

the

SERMON VI.

the preference, as being acts of greater compliance and submission.

A short answer, I think, will suffice, and an example upon a supposed case may set the matter in a true light.

The Jews, we know, often neglected the duties of morality, whilst they adhered to the ritual law. Upon this, they stand rebuked in the following manner: To what purpose are your sacrifices and your solemn fasts to me? saith the lord. I delight not in them; my soul hates them; I am weary to bear them. Cease to do evil; learn to do well; and so forth.

Now let us suppose the contrary case to have happened: that the Jews had neglected the ceremonial, and observed the moral part of the Law. It is impossible to imagine that they could have been rebuked in the following manner: To what purpose is your piety to me? saith the Lord. I delight not in righteousness. Bring me no more of your morality. Charity is an abomination to me: your just dealing I cannot away with: your mercy and your chastity my soul hateth. Wash your clothes, and make your outside clean, and bring me your rams and your bullocks. If this be most absurd, it is the genuine consequence of equalling ceremonies to moral virtues.

I shall now lay before you the duties of man, and the several parts into which religion may be distributed, beginning with those which are most important, and proceeding to those which are of an inferior nature, and placing them in their proper order; after which I shall consider the uses which may be made of this distinction of our duties, and of the inequality which is to be found in them.

The things of the most importance are undoubtedly contained in those places of Scripture which have been just now mentioned.

The love of God is a grateful sense of his goodness, a desire to obtain and to secure his favour, and an endea-

endeavour to imitate his perfections, and to observe his will.

The love of our neighbour is an endeavour to promote the welfare of mankind, by which we shall at the same time promote our own.

Sobriety, righteousness, and godliness, are represented by St. Paul, as the great duties which the Gospel requires of us. Sobriety contains our duty to ourselves, and consists in the regulation of our appetites, passions, and desires, that our souls and bodies may be fit for the exercise of the functions for which they were intended. Righteousness comprehends our duty to our neighbour, its two principal branches, justice and charity, particular acts of which are veracity, sincerity, faithfulness, integrity, long-suffering, patience, forgiveness of injuries, liberality, and disinterestedness. Godliness is that part of our duty which relates to God, and shews itself in love and faith, reliance, resignation, gratitude, pious fear, and humility.

To love God, to love our neighbour, to delight in doing good to others, to make a right use of our reason and understanding, and of all the powers committed to us, that we may fulfil the purposes for which we were created, these are the great duties and the chief commandments, these were discoverable by the light of reason, these are required of all intelligent creatures, of the highest Angel, and of every man upon earth; these were the principal precepts of the Law, these were more especially inculcated by the Prophets, these are the most important part of the Gospel, and these shall be the religion of Saints in heaven, when other duties and acts of obedience shall cease, as impracticable or unnecessary.

The Christian revelation teacheth these moral virtues clearly, and affords the best helps and encouragements to the practice of them: for the Gospel lays before us the following doctrines, as conducing to our present and future welfare:

That

That man is made to love God above all things, to love his neighbour as himself, and to love himself with a prudent and rational affection, and to remember that goodness is the only way to happiness:

That man is a weak and imperfect creature, who in many things offends; but that God is merciful, and willing to accept repentance and careful endeavours to do well, instead of unsinning righteousness and unerring discretion; and ready also to afford aid to all who sincerely desire and humbly seek it. So that men, whilst they exert their own natural powers in the performance of their duty, should address themselves to God in prayer, acknowledging their offences, desiring forgiveness, requesting his assistance, and returning thanks for his benefits:

That there shall be a resurrection of the dead, and a day of judgment, when all shall receive according to their works, and rewards and punishments shall be dispensed with justice and with mercy:

That there is a person called the Word of God, and the Son of God, who before time and the world dwelt with the Father; that God made all things by him, and afterwards sent him into the world, to teach these doctrines to men, and by his sufferings and death to redeem those who should repent and obey the Gospel:

That the same divine person is appointed of God to dispense the rewards and punishments of the next age, at the consummation of all things:

That there is a divine Spirit present in all times and places, who inspired the Prophets, who assisted the Apostles, who was the Author of the miracles by which the Christian religion was confirmed, and who is ready to comfort succour and direct those who are willing to be guided by him.

These are the principal parts of Christian faith and practice; and Christ required of all to whom the Gospel should be preached, first, that they should observe the moral duties; secondly, that they should believe

those

those doctrines and truths which are proper incitements and encouragements to virtue and piety; and thirdly, that they should openly profess this faith, and own themselves his disciples, whatsoever should be the consequence.

As the Christian religion is a system which plainly and necessarily supposes and requires society, as it is contained in the Scriptures, hence arise two other consequential duties; first, that we should, if we possibly can, join ourselves to some Christian society; and secondly, that, according to our abilities and opportunities, we should use the proper means and helps to understand the Scriptures, particularly the Gospel, and the will of our Saviour declared in it.

Lastly, upon an examination of the books of the New Testament, and of Christian antiquity, we find two and only two positive duties belonging to our religion, Baptism and the Lord's Supper. These may be called the ritual part of the Gospel, the Ceremonial Law of Christianity. By the first we enter into the Christian covenant; by the second we declare our desire and resolution to continue in it. The first is performed once, and repeated no more; and the times of celebrating the second are left in a good measure to our own convenience and discretion. We cannot therefore account it grievous to comply with institutions so easy, so plain, so significant, and so well adapted to improve us in goodness; and we ought not to slight and undervalue them under a pretence that they are ritual and positive, and in nature and importance inferior to morality. Wilful transgressions under the Law against the ceremonial part of it, often brought down divine judgments upon the offenders: and under the Gospel, we find that the Corinthian Christians, because they behaved themselves irreverently at the Lord's Supper, were chastised with sickness and death. But on the other hand we should take care not to place either of these institutions upon the level with the weightier parts of the Gospel,

with

with the love of God and the love of our neighbour, nor to think that the bare action or sign is of itself of any efficacy without the things signified, which are faith, and repentance, and obedience.

I come now to consider the uses which are to be made of this division of our duty into its several parts, according to their order and importance.

Moral goodness, or virtue, or righteousness, is the main of all, the principal part of religion; the next to it is faith, or a belief of Christianity; and thirdly, a right use of the means and helps which may strengthen our faith in Christ, and promote the practice of righteousness, namely, repentance, prayer, an acquaintance with the Scriptures, pious meditation, an open profession of our religion, and a partaking of the Lord's Supper.

By giving heed to this we may preserve ourselves free from an illusion into which corrupt minds in all times are always falling, and that is, a hope to make amends for deficiences in morality by things which are good indeed, but of an inferior order to morality, or by a partial and incomplete obedience.

Men, who assent to the Gospel, and yet will not pay a due obedience to the moral part of it, invent several expedients, by which they may quiet their consciences, and excuse themselves.

As first a zeal for religion, or rather for certain controverted points and religious speculations. When this zeal is without knowledge, it cannot be good for much, but when it is without the moral virtues, it is good for nothing.

A second method, by which men hope to compound for their faults, is to attend the public worship of God, to pray to him, and to receive the communion. But these actions are only then acceptable to God, when they serve the purposes for which they were appointed. These actions are not virtue and righteousness, but helps to produce virtue and righteousness; and when they produce no good effects, they are of no value.

How

How good and commendable foever they may be, yet as they are means, they muſt be inferior to the end; and therefore they are not named by our Lord and his diſciples, where they briefly ſum up the main parts of our duty.

Another expedient, by which ſome may hope to ſupply their moral defects, is the ſtudy of religious knowledge. Such occupations are indeed commendable; but if they do not improve a man's heart, they will be to him of no benefit.

Many, ſays our Saviour, will ſay to me in the day of judgment, Lord, Lord, have we not propheſied in thy name? and in thy name have caſt out Devils? and in thy name done many wonderful works? And then I will profeſs unto them, I never knew ye: depart from me, ye that work iniquity.

And St. Paul obſerves, that if it were poſſible for a man to have the gift of ſpeaking all languages, and the power of working miracles, and prophecy, and religious knowledge, and faith: yet without moral virtues it would be of no profit to him.

Laſtly, another expedient is, to practiſe ſome moral duties, ſuch as juſtice, temperance, patience, almſgiving. Theſe things doubtleſs are good and praiſeworthy; but it is a dangerous illuſion to expect that God will accept a partial obedience, and the obſervance of certain virtues, from thoſe who deliberately and conſtantly offend againſt ſome known duty.

Another uſe, which ariſeth from right notions of the moſt important parts of religion, is that we ſhall be enabled to judge truly of faults and errors, as being more or leſs dangerous and miſchievous, according as they are more or leſs hurtful to virtue and morality. This will teach us to be ſtrict upon ſome occaſions in which we are too remiſs and careleſs; and to be candid and favourable in ſome caſes in which we are inclined to be too ſevere and uncharitable.

For

SERMON VI.

For example; Every thing that is lewd, vicious, immoral, profane; every thing that makes us flight virtue, and account vice to be genteel, polite, safe, or not very dangerous; every thing that renders us thoughtless about our future condition, slaves to bad customs and evil inclinations, cold to religion, and immoderately fond of the vanities of this present world; every thing of this kind, and attended with these effects, should be detested by us. In shunning these things more care and caution, more labour and resolution, is requisite than we usually imagine, and are willing to exert. We should beware that the love of riches, honours, and pleasures possess not the best place, in our hearts, we should not waste our time in folly and idleness, we should avoid the familiarity of wicked persons, of all those who make a mock of sin, and speak irreverently of God and of religion; we should shun them, unless absolute necessity requires us to converse with them, or charity and a reasonable hope of reclaiming them: nor should we converse with those books which are incentives to looseness and immorality; nor should we give ourselves up to amusements and diversions, which, though perhaps harmless in themselves, and harmless to some other persons, yet are not so to us, but lead us into temptation, and weaken our good resolutions.

These are faults which we cannot too much disapprove and discourage on all occasions. On these points our zeal cannot be too active. Our love cannot be too strong and sincere for the things on which all that is valuable depends, nor our aversion too violent from the things which would separate us from God, and from future happiness.

And yet here we are disposed to make unreasonable allowances to persons and to vices, to ourselves and to others, and to reserve our indignation and zeal for occasions where compassion and charity and forbearance would better become us.

The

The Christian religion hath spread itself over the world; many nations have received it; many ages are elapsed since the days of the Apostles, some of which were ages of the greatest depravity and the grossest ignorance; many difficulties attend the interpretation of the Scriptures in speculative, and controverted points; many erroneous and false doctrines have in all times found approvers and abettors; nor doth there seem any probability that errors of this kind will ever be banished from the Christian world, unless the Divine Providence should interpose once again in a visible and miraculous manner.

(*a*) There have been (*b*) persons, who endeavoured to procure a reconcilement of all Churches, and an union in one common faith. Their honest intentions, and their learned and pious labours, deserved commendation; but the attempt proved vain, as men of lesser abilities than they might easily have foreseen. Of many impediments which make the thing impracticable, I shall only mention one; The Church of Rome will never hold communion with other Christian societies, except upon her own terms, that is, upon a total submission on their side. She claims infallibility, and so stands bound in haughty ignorance, and for fear of self-contradiction, to give up nothing, to reform nothing, to maintain all the old abuses which she hath consecrated and sanctified by the unerring decrees of Popes and Councils. In this case, the condition of learned men in that Communion is really hard; for they are obliged to toil and drudge and exert all their powers in palliating and defending all the absurdities, which in darker ages were invented by crafty, or wild enthusiasts.

An union between Protestants, and especially between Protestants inhabiting the same country, as it may seem more practicable, so it would be much more desireable. But to this also there are many impediments, which
arise.

(*a*) See Jer. Taylor, Serm. VI. p. 101.
(*b*) Of whom Grotius was one.

arise perhaps from faults on all sides, and which wise and good men would gladly remove, if they were able.

Fourteen hundred years ago, the first Christian Emperor earnestly endeavoured to compose the unhappy differences between Christians; but with all his interest, and with all his authority, he could not accomplish it.

The only thing that we can do, in the present general situation of Christianity, is to be united in charity, though not in opinion, with our fellow-Christians, and not to pass a rash and a hard sentence on those errors, which have not a manifest connection with immorality, and no plain tendency to make a man dishonest and profane, cruel and imperious, turbulent and seditious. Of all religious errors, those are by far the worst, which encourage inhumanity, rebellion, perjury, and persecution. As to other speculative mistakes, we ought carefully to shun and reject them; but we may hope that God will forgive them, and that at the great day, when truth shall be made manifest, not only they who found it and knew it, but they who loved and sought it, shall be accepted; the false opinion shall burn, and the man himself shall escape.

Thus should we endeavour to entertain sentiments of moderation, and to form candid judgments concerning persons or societies professing the religion of Jesus Christ; which temper and behaviour may be very consistent with a superior love and esteem, and a preference given to the Church of which we declare ourselves members.

SERMON VII.

LUKE xxiii. 42, 43.

And he said unto Jesus; Lord, remember me, when thou comest into thy kingdom. And Jesus said unto him, Verily I say unto thee, to-day shalt thou be with me in Paradise.

THE history of the penitent thief, recorded by St. Luke, is very remarkable, singular and affecting; and there are two religious and practical inferences to be made from it. The first is the encouragement which it affords, even after great misdemeanors, to repenting sinners, who if they will sincerely perform all that is in their power, ought by no means to think it a lost labour, and to give themselves up to despair, but to entertain honourable sentiments and humble hopes of God's placability and mercy. The second use of the text, which ought always to be joined with the first, is to dissuade men from habitual vices and a delay of reformation, by shewing them how little reason such offenders have to expect that they shall ever so qualify themselves, as to become fit to obtain the favour which was extended to this man.

I. The example of the penitent thief is adapted to excite even in great offenders a reliance on the goodness and compassion of God, if they will return to him and to their duty.

It was prophesied of our Saviour, that he should not break the bruised reed, nor quench the smoaking flax; that he should be a comforter of the mourners, and a

preacher

preacher of glad tidings to the penitent; that he should not afflict the afflicted, nor deal harshly with those who condemned themselves, and had a due sense of their faults; that, on the contrary, where he should find any dispositions to amendment, he would cherish them with the utmost tenderness, and not cast a damp on the smallest spark of spiritual life.

Accordingly, it was his constant declaration, that he came to call sinners to repentance. He suffered such to have a free access to his sacred person; he never reproached them with that which was past, but only commanded them to do so no more. In his discourses and parables he gave such kind encouragement to the penitent, and took so much care to secure them from despondency, and to quiet and compose their troubled minds, that he seemed almost to represent them as better than those whose conduct had been more regular, and less blameable. He observed, that they to whom he had forgiven most, would in all probability love him most. On account of his affability and condescension to such persons, he was called by his enemies, The friend and companion of sinners: but he disdained neither the name nor the office; he owned, that he came for that kind and compassionate purpose, to seek and to save that which was lost.

If he shewed any rigour and severity, it was towards those who were full of spiritual pride, and conceited of their own righteousness, and who, instead of correcting their own faults, were ever censuring and exaggerating those of others. Of such arrogant hypocrites he speaks with so much indignation, that he seems to have had no hopes of their amendment. He chose for his disciples and followers, says an (*a*) old Christian writer, men who were sinners above all sinners. The expression surely is too strong, and not true without great amendments. But thus far it seems probable, that few of his disciples

---

(*a*) Who goes under the name of Barnabas.

disciples had been eminent in goodness before he called them. And indeed, after he had called them, they were guilty of several follies, indiscretions, and weaknesses; they all forsook him, and one of them basely denied him; and we know that the Apostle who was the most active and successful in his service, had been before his conversion a persecutor of the Church. Such persons he chose, who, being conscious of their own former defects, and fully sensible of God's signal mercy towards them, might be the more disposed to support the weak, and bear with the infirm, and deal gently with the penitent, and encourage the desponding. Therefore Christ, forewarning Peter of his fall, said to him, When thou art converted, strengthen thy brethren. And St. Paul tells the Galatians; Brethren, if a man be overtaken in a fault, ye who are spiritual, restore such an one in the spirit of meekness; lest thou also be tempted.

This mild behaviour in our Saviour appeared the more remarkable, as it might have been expected that he, who was himself without sin, would be more severe and less affable towards sinners. Amongst men, they who, by a good disposition, and a good education, and by being happily situated out of the reach of violent temptations and pressing opportunities, have avoided evil habits, and kept themselves free from grosser offences, are too often inclined rather to rigour than to clemency towards repenting transgressors. In the earlier ages of Christianity, when in time of persecution some had fallen from the faith through fear of suffering, and afterwards repented, and begged to be re-admitted, there were several who declared that they ought never to be received; and this produced much contention, and a pernicious schism in the Church. But the majority were more moderate, and determined that such rigid proceedings were unlawful, and that the examples of Christ and his Apostles recommended more lenity to

those

those unhappy persons, who, all things considered, had been more weak than wicked.

Such was the clemency of our Lord during the course of his ministry; and as he began, so he ended it, and had a signal opportunity of exercising his charity at the close of his life. For his impenitent murderers, he offered up prayers to his Father; and, to shew what the penitent might hope from him, it was so ordered by divine providence, that a malefactor should suffer along with him, whose change for the better made him a proper object of mercy. From the cross he sealed this criminal's pardon, and gave him a place in the kingdom of heaven.

Here is a man who had committed a crime for which by his own confession he deserved to die. He had no opportunity of leading a new life, and of proving his amendment by a regular course of virtuous actions. His faith, and the manner in which he shewed it, were doubtless very commendable; and yet they seem to have been rather too highly extolled by some writers, and somewhat beyond measure. The behaviour of Christ under his sufferings, and the wonderful circumstances attending his crucifixion, might easily induce an unprejudiced man to think that he could be no ordinary person, much less a malefactor; and these things, joined to the knowledge which this man, being of the Jewish nation, might have had before of Christ and of his ministry, might well induce him to acknowledge him for the Messias. He did so; he rebuked his companion for his hardened impiety, and he proclaimed the innocence and holiness of Jesus, when the Jews were reviling him, and the Disciples had in a manner deserted him. But then it is likewise to be considered that he ran no risque, as to his worldly concerns, in so doing: the world could not use him worse; and his miseries had placed him beyond earthly fear and hope, beyond the reach of malice and cruelty. To his repentance then is to be ascribed the gracious reception which he found: his re-

pentance

pentance was sincere, and God was pleased to accept the will for the deed.

Therefore, by way of inference, Why should not any sinner, who sincerely repents, hope that God will have mercy on him likewise? For since God is no respecter of persons, where the same dispositions are found, the favour will be extended. The consequence thus far seems to be just. As repentance is the duty of all who have offended, so it is a duty which can at no time be unfit and unprofitable; as it is an act of religion reasonable in itself, and agreeable to God, it must needs, like other good actions, produce some beneficial effects. Whatsoever tends to diminish the guilt, must tend to diminish the punishment of guilt, to say the least of it. And this is a sufficient ground and motive to exhort all sorts of persons at all times to repentance, to encourage it whensoever it appears, to think and speak honourably of the divine mercy, to cherish and favour the first signs of amendment, and to defend it from that despondence which is very apt to attend it in guilty and melancholy minds.

But then, lest any should make perverse inferences from these premises, and fatally delude themselves upon groundless hopes, and draw false conclusions from the doctrine of the divine goodness, and think that they may safely sin on, because a reformation, though ever so late, will reinstate them in God's favour, and save them from final ruin, it may be very proper to consider the example of the Penitent Thief in another light, since is is an example which appears the most favourable to long and notorious offenders, and to shew that it contains little comfort and little encouragement to such sort of offenders.

In general then, the delay of amendment to a future time is one of those follies which carries its own conviction along with it, and stands condemned upon the plainest and most obvious reasons.

For,

For, first, To abuse and provoke the lenity and long suffering of God in this manner, to be wicked because he is good, is monstrously base and perverse, and shews a very dangerous depravity. There is nothing in this that gives any prospect of a future reformation. To sin by surprize, or through the influence of some violent temptation, seems not to be so great a fault as to entertain a fixed and deliberate purpose to transgress now, and hereafter to return to our duty, because God is merciful, and will then receive us. In the dealings of men with each other, such a behaviour would be thought very exasperating. If a man were to injure his best friend, and to continue to use him ill, and to give this reason for it, that he knew him to be very goodnatured, and so might be reconciled to him easily, and at his own leisure, and when he thought fit, he would probably lose his friend for ever by the base experiment, and none would justify him, or even pity him.

Secondly, Sin, if it be not resisted, grows daily upon us, and makes the return to righteousness more and more difficult and improbable; and he who cannot find in his heart to amend, even whilst he is a novice in iniquity, will be less disposed to it, when time and custom have hardened him.

Thirdly, Sin is of a most infatuating nature, and corrupts not only the heart, but the understanding; and who knows where it may end? He who proposed at first to reform his ways after some time, and to return to God, may come to doubt whether there be a God; and if he cannot quite exclude him, and finds himself forced to acknowledge a first Cause, and a Mind that rules the world, he will strip the Deity of his moral perfections, he will frame to himself a God who keeps up the order and course of things by a natural necessity, and who hath neither good nor ill will towards any creature, nor any regard for the actions of men. This kind of atheism is far more common amongst wicked people than we usually imagine. Some of the Devil's

Agents have induſtriouſly recommended it to the Public; wretches who hate men as much as they hate God, and would fain deprive them of one of the greateſt comforts of this life, the belief of a good and gracious Providence.

Now when a man is come to this way of thinking, and imagines himſelf a man of ſingular penetration for having made this great diſcovery, there is not even a diſtant probability of his repentance and amendment; and it is not at all unlikely that he ſhould fall into ſuch profane ſentiments, ſince a long courſe of offending induces a man to wiſh that there were no God; and from wiſhing to believing, the diſtance, we know, is not great. True it is, that an immediate ſenſe of danger and death may bring back the ancient and more natural fear of God; and from wiſhing to believing, the diſtance, we know, is not great. True it is, that an immediate ſenſe of danger and death may bring back the ancient and more natural fear of God; but this fear may come too late, and produce deſpair inſtead of reformation.

Fourthly, as all other habits can no other way be removed than by introducing contrary habits, which is the work of patience, reſolution, and repeated attempts; the ſame muſt hold true concerning ſinful habits. So that though a change of mind, and a purpoſe of amendment may be wrought ſoon and ſuddenly, yet a change of behaviour which is the only ſure proof of amendment, requires time and labour; and it is hard to conceive how a late repentance can change bad habits, unleſs we ſuppoſe that the alteration for the better, which is juſt beginning in this world, may be carried on and compleated in the next. But concerning this the Scriptures are ſilent; and who would riſque his ſoul upon conjectural hopes?

Fifthly, Since ſinners have perhaps often deſigned and purpoſed, and reſolved, without performing, they will have too much reaſon to ſuſpect the ſincerity of
their

SERMON VII.

their own hearts, and to rely but little on a change of purpose which present and pressing danger extorts from them.

Add to this, that a sinner may be removed out of this world suddenly, and without any warning, or that many infirmities of body or mind may deprive him in a great measure of his understanding, and render him incapable of performing any rational act of any kind, and consequently, the act of repenting.

Again: The Gospel requires from all men improvement and perseverance. A late repentance, such as it is, at the close of a bad life, can seldom exert the first of these duties, and never the second.

Lastly; An intention to do just enough to save ourselves from perdition, and no more, is putting ourselves in a very dangerous situation. A cold and faint attempt to enter in must be attended with the hazard of being shut out.

We will now consider the case of the penitent Thief. To-day shalt thou be with me in Paradise, said our Lord to him. His reward was great; and thence we may conclude that there was something particular in him that qualified him for such a favour.

Many (*b*) strange things have been supposed concerning this man; as that he had been very wicked, that he continued so till his crucifixion, that even then he joined at first with the other thief, and profanely railed at Jesus Christ; when a flood of light from above burst in upon him, and divine grace with omnipotent force took sudden possession of his hard heart, and transformed him from a sinner into a Saint in an instant.

All this may be easily said, and to a heated imagination it may furnish copious matter for popular rhetoric, about sudden conversions, and irresistible inward calls.

But

(*b*) See the injudicious things which Tillemont hath collected and approved, upon this subject. *Hist. Eccl.* T. i. p. 42.

But when we examine it sedately, we find many supposals taken for granted which can never be proved.

The man is called a thief or a robber; and this seems to carry with it the notion of a person, who after having led a dissolute life, is driven by his vices and by his necessities to these vile courses, and betakes himself to the high-ways; but even amongst thieves and robbers some are sometimes to be found, whose fault is attended with circumstances that extenuate the guilt, and render them in some measure objects of compassion. It is very reasonable to imagine that this malefactor was such an one, and that several things unknown to us might be pleaded in his behalf.

But upon the whole it seems most probable that he had joined in some revolt against the Romans.

For, first, in ancient writers the word *thief* or *robber* is often given to those who were engaged in insurrections.

Secondly, at that time there had been seditions in Judæa; and Barabbas had been active in one, whose pardon the Jews had obtained of the Governor.

Thirdly, His punishment was crucifixion, a punishment not in use amongst the Jews, but often inflicted by the Romans upon slaves, and foreigners, who had rebelled against them.

Lastly, Christ himself suffered under the unjust imputation of rebellion, and was condemned for it by the Roman Magistrate, else he could not have been crucified; and it is probable that the two who were crucified with him, suffered for rebellion.

The man then may be supposed to have been guilty of sedition against the Roman government. This was a crime; and yet it was a crime into which a person might have fallen, who had his good qualities, and who had led a regular life.

The Jews were designed by divine Providence to continue for a considerable time a separate and independent people, and to be governed by their own laws,

laws, and by Magistrates or Kings of their own nation. As long as they had power and jurisdiction, they were expresly forbidden to take a foreigner for their King. One from among thy brethren, says Moses, shalt thou set king over thee thou mayest not set a stranger over thee, who is not thy brother. Upon their transgressions, God had from time to time given them up into the hands of their adversaries, and had suffered other nations and other Lords to rule over them. At this season God's peculiar providence was in a great measure withdrawn, and they were in subjection to the Romans. It is no wonder that they wished and sighed for their liberties again; and though, after they had submitted, they were obliged in general to obedience, and obliged in mere prudence, as they had not strength enough to resist; yet how far this obligation extended itself, and how far they were to bear ill usage, was not altogether so clear a case, in which an honest man might not mistake. The Roman Governors were usually bad rulers of the provinces. Their principal care and occupation was to beggar the people, and to enrich themselves and their creatures; and if they were contented with extorting and pillaging, and did not add to it cruelty and murders, and massacres, they might pass, as the world then went, for tolerable Magistrates. As to Pontius Pilate, he is delivered down to us by History as a cruel, stubborn, insolent tyrant, and a shedder of blood. So that the innocence of Jesus Christ, and his amiable and venerable character, must have been extremely manifest to all honest persons, since even this man, bad as he was, made repeated attempts to save him from his malicious enemies, and gave him up with great reluctance.

Now who knows what provocations this penitent Thief might have received, in such times and from such Governors? Oppression will make a wise man mad. So says Solomon, who was a wise man, and a king too. Or he might have been influenced by his relations and
friends,

friends, and over-perſuaded, and drawn in unawares; or he might have had little hand in the ſedition.

He had committed a fault; and in ſuch a caſe, what ſays even ſtrict Juſtice? No more than this, that puniſhment ſhould enſue. If he treſpaſſed, he paid dearly for it; and if he was only guilty of robbery, he was puniſhed more ſeverely than the law of Moſes permitted. It ſeems to have been a prevailing opinion, not only amongſt the Jews, but every where elſe, that offences might in ſome meaſure be expiated, might obtain the divine pardon by temporal ſufferings, if the offender ſubmitted to them patiently, and ſorrowfully owned his guilt: and St. Paul repreſents the chaſtiſements, which tranſgreſſing Chriſtians ſometimes underwent in the world, as merciful corrections, and means to avoid worſe. He delivered over a notorious offender to Satan, for the deſtruction of the fleſh; that is, he delivered him up to ſorrow of mind and pain of body, to mortify his irregular affections, that the ſpirit, ſays he, might be ſaved in the day of the Lord. And he tells the Corinthians, that, by behaving themſelves indecently at the Lord's table, they had eaten and drunk their own damnation or condemnation. And what was the condemnation? It was, that diſeaſes and untimely deaths had enſued. For this cauſe many are weak and ſickly amongſt you, and many ſleep. But, ſays he, when ye are thus judged, ye are chaſtened of the Lord, that ye ſhould not be condemned with the world; Chriſt corrects you now, that he may not reject you hereafter.

We read in the Acts of the Apoſtles that Ananias and Sapphira were guilty of a deliberate fraud, an attempt to impoſe upon the Church of Chriſt, and the Apoſtles, by giving a falſe account of the money which they had paid into the common ſtock. It was an attempt to deceive not only men, but the ſpirit of God which was in the Apoſtles, and it is called, Lying unto God; and for this crime, they were puniſhed with ſudden death. Sudden death after ſuch an offence, left no
room

SERMON VII.

room for religious sorrow and repentance; and looked like an eternal condemnation. And yet some of the ancient (c) Fathers were inclined to the charitable hope that those persons received their correction in this world, and were spared in the next.

Consider then the case of the man on whom we are discoursing. As soon as he was taken, he knew that the most cruel death would ensue, and under this sad prospect he continued till his crucifixion; so that his sufferings were as great as can easily be conceived, and nothing worse can befall a man here below. If he had escaped this calamity, he would probably have joined himself to the first Christians, and been as ready to do and to suffer for the sake of the Gospel as any of the disciples. When he came to die, he expressed no desire to live and to escape punishment; he seems to have possessed himself, and to have suffered with constancy and resignation. He thought Christ to be the Messias, he knew that the Prophets had foretold his everlasting kingdom, and he saw him perishing like a malefactor, and in all appearance forsaken of God as much as of men. But he had faith, and it was a great degree of faith at such a juncture, to believe that God would still make good his promises to this very person, and that he should still in God's appointed time receive power and majesty and dominion; and he humbly and modestly besought him to think of his poor fellow-sufferer, though unworthy of such a favour, when that glorious time should come. He received a gracious answer; and Christ from his cross, as from his throne, granted him more than his request.

Now what hopes can an habitual offender build upon a case so singular, and attended with so many extraordinary circumstances? what comfort can he find from the example of a man, who probably was not so guilty as he, and who received so severe a correction in this world?

(c) Origen, in Matt. p. 383. Augustin, in Parmen. iii. i.

world? Great things are said in Scripture in favour of repentance and reformation, and they are constantly represented as certain means to appease the divine pleasure. But when this repentance is delayed till no reformation can appear, what shall we say of it? How far it may profit, God only knows. It becomes not us to set bounds to his goodness: but this we must say, that these are favours which can only proceed from his hidden mercies, and which he hath not expresly promised in his Gospel. One would willingly indulge the pleasing hope that there may be undiscovered treasures of compassion in the secret counsels of God, without which the condition of so many would be so deplorable. But then let us live, as if we had no such hopes; lest by presuming too much, and performing too little, and proposing to enter into peace and rest upon the cheapest terms, we should at last find ourselves deluded and excluded.

SERMON VIII.

Coloss. iii. 8.

But now you also put off all these; anger, wrath, malice.

THE ancient moralists had great disputes amongst themselves concerning anger, whether it were agreeable to nature, or in other words, whether it were in any degree lawful, and therefore whether it were the part of a wise man to moderate and restrain it, or to root it entirely out of his mind. As this controversy turned upon words, and nice inquiries, and subtle distinctions, it was not easy for the learned, and impossible for the unlearned, to judge which side was in the right. In one thing they all agreed, that the excesses of anger were to be avoided, and that this passion ought to be in good measure under the guidance of reason.

The holy Scriptures were written to make us wise unto salvation, and not to instruct us in nice and abstruse and difficult points, which have little connection with practice, and are of small consequence to the conduct of our lives; and therefore they enter not into an accurate discussion of the nature of anger, nor have they any where given us a definition of it; but, supposing that we already know what it is, they bid us carefully avoid it, and restrain it if ever we be overtaken and surprised by it.

To know then what anger is, the anger against which we must guard ourselves, we need not have recourse

recourse to the learned for instruction. Common experience will sufficiently teach us what it is, and will set it in a true light. What is the reason why men are angry? We shall usually find it to be, because they think that another hath injured them. And what is it that their anger prompts them to do? It prompts them to return evil for evil, to revenge themselves, and to make the offender suffer for his ill behaviour. Anger then is an (*a*) offence taken at a real or supposed injury, attended with a desire of revenging it.

But here it is to be observed that though anger is forbidden in the text as unlawful, which appears both because we are commanded to put it off, to be free from it, and because it is joined to malice and evil-speaking, which are certainly unlawful, yet there are other passages in Scripture whence it may be concluded that anger is not always a sin. For example:

First; it is recorded of our Saviour, in whom no sin was found, that he was angry. He looked round on the Jews with anger, being grieved for the hardness of their hearts.

Secondly; God is frequently said to be angry. Every one who hath read the Scriptures knows that perpetual mention is made of his wrath and indignation, though not in the same sense in which our Lord is said to have been angry. Christ, who took our nature upon him, took with it our natural affections: God, who is a pure spirit, hath no human passions. Anger, jealousy, grief, joy, and change of mind, belong no more truly and literally to him, than the eyes and

---

(*a*) In Seneca's Books *De Ira*, his definition of anger is lost: but from many places in that treatise, and from Lactantius, we may gather that it was much like this which I have proposed. Aristotle, Cicero, and Zeno in Diogenes Laertius, admit a desire of revenge or punishing in their definitions of anger. Concerning the disputes of the Stoics and Peripatetics on this subject, see Cicero *De Offic.* i 25. and Muretus there.

and the ears, the hands and the feet, the sleeping and the waking, which are also attributed to him in the sacred writings. But we may observe, that though the Scriptures, condescending to our capacities and to our language, ascribe human actions and human passions to God, yet no where do they ascribe human vices to him; whence we may also conclude that anger is not always sinful.

These things may be reconciled by considering that anger is at first, an (*b*) offence taken at an ill behaviour, an emotion of mind raised at the sense of injuries done to us or to others. This is a passion belonging to our nature, and no sin, viewed in this light, and confined to this description; but when this offence leads us to intentions of revenge as it frequently doth, when it is raised upon slight provocation and without just cause, when it hurries us into indecencies, when it is suffered to lodge in our minds, and to turn to a confirmed hatred and malice, it becomes a fault. Our passions were implanted in us for good purposes: they seem to be necessary to us as springs of action, and without them the mind would be dull and stupid, and given up to indolence.

The use of anger is to stir us up to self-preservation, and to put us upon our guard against injuries. When it hath done this, it hath performed all that belongs to it; for what measures we may take to effect this, how we may secure ourselves, and how we should behave towards those who offend us, these are points concerning which we must not consult our *passions*,
but

(*b*) Seneca distinguisheth much in the same manner. He absolutely condemns anger; but he adds that there is, *primus ictus animi, qui nos post opinionem injuriæ movet; agitatio animi, quam species injuriæ incussit.* This emotion of mind, says he, is natural and necessary. But, *ira est concitatio animi ad ultionem voluntate et judicio pergentis;* and this is blameable. *De Ira*, ii. 2, 3.

but our *reason*, which was given us to (c) moderate our passions, and to prescribe laws for our actions.

What I have to offer further upon this subject, will be contained,

I. In shewing the ill effects and consequences of sinful anger:

II. In giving some directions how we may restrain it.

1. Amongst many motives, which should induce us to moderate and restrain our passions, this is one, that whensoever we suffer them to exceed their bounds, they constantly put us to pain; so that for our own interest we find it necessary to keep them in subjection.

This is plainly the case of anger, which whilst it lasts is a most uneasy passion. They who are under its dominion are like the troubled sea; their thoughts are in an unnatural violent commotion, they can take no satisfaction in any thing, they can apply themselves to no business, and to no amusement, they are forced to dwell upon those objects only which disturb and torment them. A painful memory of injuries received, a violent abhorrence of those who have offended them, a fierce desire of revenge, an anxious impatience till it be accomplished, all join together to afflict them. Thus do they use themselves as ill as even their worst enemies could wish.

2. As anger makes us very uneasy, so doth it no less disgrace us by its deformity, by a strange alteration which it produces in the whole man, and by a thousand follies and indecences obvious even to the observation of a child.

It

(c) ——— celsa sedet arce,
Sceptra tenens, mollitque animos, et temperat iras.
Ni faceret, &c.

Virgil.

It makes us also contemptible or odious to thofe with whom we converfe. This paffion is difficult to be concealed and diffembled; and he who is fubject to it frequently difcovers it to all who come in his way. He will therefore be flighted and fhunned by thofe who have no particular obligations to him; for anger, with the follies, the rudenefs, the noife, the malice, and the impertinence, which attend it, is highly difagreeable to us. We diflike it in others, though we can overlook and excufe it in ourfelves. The paffionate perfon will foon weary out thofe over whom he has no authority. They who are dependent upon him, who neither can leave him, nor dare to flight him, will be forced to fubmit and to bear as well as they can the ill treatment which they daily receive from him; they will fear him, and they will perhaps obey him more than they ought, and comply with any thing that he propofes, though abfurd and unreafonable, and carefully conceal their diflike; but friendfhip and efteem and love he muft not expect from them.

3. By anger men are often incited to acts of vile injuftice and unmerciful feverity. Anger defires immediate revenge; it blots out of their minds all notions of right and wrong; it frequently extinguifheth every fentiment of humanity, and fometimes, overcoming the dread of fhame and of fuffering, it hurries them on to deeds of violence, which are punifhed by human laws, or if they efcape that punifhment, are feverely condemned by confcience and reafon, when they return and refume their loft authority. Or if by fear and felf-intereft they are kept from running into fuch enormities, they take another fort of revenge, fpeaking evil of thofe at whom they are offended, endeavouring to blaft their reputation, and to raife them up enemies, aggravating their faults, detracting from their good qualities, purfuing them with lies and flanders, and opprobrious language, with all the fecret ill offices

and

and little arts of mischief which malice ever fruitful in invention can suggest.

This behaviour not only corrupts the mind, and robs it of its peace, and spoils the temper, but produces returns of ill-will and malice, and establishes mutual hatred and uncharitableness.

How often by outrageous and frantic anger persons are hurried on to murder others, or to lay violent hands upon themselves, is a thing as lamentable as it is common and notorious.

Under this head we may observe, that anger leads directly and almost unavoidably not only to slandering and reviling, but to profane conversation, to oaths and curses and blasphemies. These are the usual effects of this furious passion, and the manner in which it gives itself vent and present relief.

4. Another bad consequence of anger is that it produces an irreligious impious temper. Such persons will be angry not only with men, but with the course of things and with the dispensations of providence, that is, with God himself. When trouble, or loss, or disappointments befall them, they will lose all patience, and entertain injurious thoughts even of their Maker.

The calamities which befall us are often of such a nature, that they render us incapable of exerting the active and social duties. In such a situation all that we are able to do is to be as little troublesome to others as we possibly can, to acknowledge the goodness of God, to love him, and to trust in him, and to set an example of faith and patience and resignation to all about us.

These, if they are less honourable in the sight of men, and less admired than some other shining virtues, yet are not less valuable in themselves, nor less profitable to us. God highly approves them, and a great reward is due to them. They are never found in furious and passionate minds. Such persons therefore,
when

when they are in adversity, add to the weight of their sorrows, and become at that time the most useless of creatures, neither serving God, nor their neighbour, nor themselves.

5. Lastly, if the evil habits, which the soul contracts whilst it is united to the body, continue after its separation from it, which there is reason to fear, a mind easily provoked and full of resentment, always discomposed and dissatisfied, must be unfit for the society of spirits who have no such turbulent passions, and for a place in the mansions of love and peace.

These are the ill effects and pernicious consequences of sinful anger: whence it is evident, that, if we value our ease and reputation here, or our future happiness, we must strive against it, and keep it in subjection; which was the second point to be considered.

II. In general we may observe that the excess of this passion is to be cured by no other way than by a resolution to restrain it, which must arise from a persuasion that it is our duty and our interest so to act. A right use of reason therefore is the only remedy. It may perhaps be said that this is a remedy which seems good, but is found to be useless upon trial. Such persons in their cooler hours know the evil and the pernicious nature of anger, see it plainly, and acknowledge it readily; but upon sudden provocations, anger takes sudden possession of them, and banishes all reason from their minds, and thus when they want it most they have it least.

In this objection there is something true and something false. It is true that in persons who have lost all government of their passions, fits of anger are scarcely different from fits of madness, and that at those times they can make no use of their reason. To this deplorable condition they may bring themselves at last. But that the passions may be kept in due bounds by a right and timely use of reason is true both in appearance and in fact, and also that by the same

means

means they may be restrained though they have formerly been unlawfully indulged. Whosoever begins early to exert his dominion over them, will rule them without great difficulty. When they have been long uncontrolled, it is very hard to regulate them, and much labour and resolution are requisite. But labour and resolution will conquer stubborn difficulties, and men ought not to be discouraged in such cases, if they find the progress to be slow.

Let us apply this to anger. They who are even greatly subject to it, yet have many intervals in which they are free from it; for no one is always angry. When therefore their understanding is sedate and untroubled, they should consult their own reason; and reason, if they hearken patiently to it, will offer them the following remedies:

1. A serious consideration of the ill effects and consequences of sinful anger, what a restless, fretful, and tormenting passion it is, how much it disgraces them by its deformity, and renders them more like beasts than men, how it causes them to be either scorned, or slighted, or shunned, or feared, or hated by their acquaintance and friends, how it produces injurious language, malicious calumny, and acts of violence, how contrary it is to that benevolent disposition which the gospel requires from every Christian. These things, if they are frequently called to mind, and seriously considered, will certainly restrain immoderate anger, because such reflections will awaken in us passions which are contrary to anger, and not consistent with it; they will raise the fear of disgrace, the fear of disobliging our friends, and of making enemies, the fear of offending God, the fear of present detriment or future punishment. Fear and shame and self-love will all oppose themselves to anger, and deter us from it. The passions may be considered as so many unruly subjects, over whom the Mind is placed; but this advantage the Mind hath, that it can oppose the one
to

to the other, and by setting them at variance, govern them the more easily. Thus, if anger suggests revenge, fear will suggest many reasons why we should not make ourselves miserable by foolishly indulging a perverse and spiteful humour.

' 2. Another remedy for anger is the study of ourselves, an intimate acquaintance with our defects, especially with those which concern others. We should be wise and happy indeed if we never gave any person just cause of uneasiness. But we are not so perfect. Through levity, inadvertence, hastiness, and self-love, we misbehave ourselves on many occasions, and stand in need of pardon. The remembrance of this ought to check our anger. We know that we likewise offend, and would willingly have our faults overlooked and excused. Why then should any one expect more from others than he would give them leave to require from him?

3. The imperfections of men, and the necessity of making proper allowances for those imperfections, should induce us to moderate our anger.

We are quick to observe and prone to censure the follies and vices of the world. Hence the complaints that virtue is unfashionable and antiquated, that friendship and charity and benevolence are rarely found, that censure and detraction have taken their place, that trifles set us at variance, that the great end which most persons have in view is their own interest, and that when advantage offers itself, they fear not God, nor regard their neighbour. These and the like reproaches are cast upon the age, reproaches in which there is some truth, mixed, it is to be hoped, with some exaggeration.

But if men think thus in general concerning the imperfections of mankind, and the great corruption which is in the world, they should not expect to be treated according to the rules of equity and humanity, as if they lived in a (*d*) society of philosophers, or of true Christians, and should not lose all patience upon an injury or provocation, as if some unusual evil had befallen them, and as if any one who hath (*e*) seen thirty years could wonder at any thing of that sort. We should learn to restrain our anger by banishing the foolish hope of escaping rudeness, ingratitude, and ill usage, by expecting that men will be men, and by pitying rather than resenting those faults at least which produce no great mischief. The world is an (*f*) hospital of infirm creatures labouring under various diseases of the mind; and we should bear with their follies and defects, as with the frowardness of persons in pain.

4. Another remedy for anger, which reason suggests to us, is to resolve with ourselves not to give way to it upon trifling provocations.

It is with this as it is with our other passions. When they are often suffered to rise and take possession of the mind, they gather strength and grow more impetuous; when they have never been very violent and are seldom troublesome to us, they are easily restrained. We may hope to govern this passion without great difficulty, if we can suppress it, when the cause which excites it is little and insignificant. If we could upon all such occasions be masters of our temper, we should not often be provoked; for they who are frequently angry are so because they are disturbed at very trifles. By learning thus to resist smaller temptations to anger we shall be able at last to receive greater injuries, not
unmoved

(*d*) In Platonis Republica, non in fæce Romuli.

(*e*) —— Stupet hæc, qui jam post terga reliquit
    Sexaginta annos; &c.
                                            Juvenal.

(*f*) Νοσοκομεῖον.
Num quis irascitur pueris, &c. *Seneca* De Ira, ii. 9.
Οὐκ ὀλίγω, ὡσεί με γυνὴ βάλοι, ἢ παῖς ἄφρων.

unmoved indeed and unconcerned, but neither seeking nor wishing for revenge, nor losing our peace of mind, nor making ourselves miserable.

And if we could consider calmly and seriously, without prejudice and partiality, what are those offences which ought to be esteemed small and unworthy of our notice and unfit to raise our wrath, we should find that the greater part of affronts, wrongs, and indignities, as we call them, are of this nature; that we make them grievous by thinking too well of ourselves and too ill of others, and setting too high a value upon things on which our happiness depends not, or ought not to depend. He who could exercise his reason in forming just judgments of things, who could love and esteem, or fear and shun them, as upon a careful survey he found them to be valuable or pernicious, such a person would be seldom provoked and disturbed, and would be placed almost out of the reach of injuries.

5. Lastly, they who would govern their anger, must resist and restrain it at the first, in its beginnings, before it acquires strength and breaks out into extravagances. Anger at its first rise is an involuntary unavoidable passion. Be it so; yet we can refrain from speaking, knowing that we shall talk indiscreetly, if we give a loose to our tongue; we can shun those who have offended us, knowing that the sight of them may overpower our better resolutions; we can deprive ourselves of the means and opportunities of revenge, by change of place and by endeavouring to employ and divert ourselves some other way, and thus we can give our passion time to cool, and go out, (*g*) for want of fuel.

H 2

When

(*g*) Maximum est iræ remedium mora, nec ab illa pete initio ut ignoscat, sed ut judicet. Desinet si expectat; nec universam illam tentaveris tollere; graves habet impetus primos; tota vincetur, dum partibus carpitur. *Seneca* De Ira, ii. 28.

When we are so far superior to this passion, that we can stop it in its rise from breaking out into acts of violence, or injurious language, when no ill effect is produced by it, when it is only a light without heat, which is perceived but not felt, we have made no small progress in the government of ourselves, and may hope by care and resolution to become masters of our temper.

These are the means which reason discovers and recommends as proper to assist us in subduing sinful anger. The holy Scriptures lay before us many motives to excite us to gain this victory over ourselves.

By teaching us the little value of temporal good things in comparison with those which are promised to us in a better world, they shew us plainly that what raises anger and strife and malice and animosities amongst men, is generally beneath the notice of a Christian.

By revealing the love and mercy of God to us sinners, they remind us that we should not entertain in our minds spite and hatred and revenge, but forgive one another, even as God for Christ's sake hath forgiven us.

By informing us that we are all servants of the same Master, that we have all the same calling, and the same hopes, they shew us that we ought to live together as brethren, in a mutual exchange of good offices, as it becomes those who expect to live together for ever hereafter.

By assuring us that the future recompence consists chiefly in an improvement of our good dispositions, and in a resemblance to God, they discover to us the absolute necessity of not suffering anger, or any other disorderly affection, to bring us into bondage. Such bad habits will leave a deep and lasting impression upon the soul, and make it not fit to dwell in the presence of God, nor capable of enjoying the rewards of virtue.

What

SERMON VIII.

What hath been said of anger may in a great measure be applied to all our other inclinations. They have all their use; but they are only then useful when they are under the dominion of reason. When they are suffered to break loose from that state of subjection, they promise pleasure, but they always give pain.

The art of governing the passions is more useful and more important than many things in the search and pursuit of which we spend our days. Without this art, riches and health and skill and knowledge will give us little satisfaction; and whatsoever else we be, we can be neither happy, nor wise, nor good.

SERMON IX.

1 Sam. ii. 30.

For them that honour me, I will honour.

THESE are the words of God to Eli, who was the most considerable person in all Israel, being Judge and high Priest, who also seems to have been a good man, one great fault excepted. His two sons were oppressors and corrupters of the nation, and given up to wickedness: he reproved them for it, and intreated them to mend their manners; but he proceeded no farther, and upon the whole it is certain that he had not taken due care to check and correct them. His sons, says God, made themselves vile, and he restrained them not. Therefore God denounces heavy judgments against him, and his sons, and all his posterity: I said indeed that thy house, and the house of thy father should walk before me for ever; but now the Lord saith, Be it far from me; for them that honour me I will honour, and they that despise me shall be lightly esteemed.

The desire of honour, credit, reputation, soon arises in us, because the usefulness of it soon appears to us; for as we live in society and continually converse with others, and stand in need of them, we see how necessary it is that others should think and speak well of us, that they should be willing to serve and oblige us, that they should like our acquaintance and seek our friendship.

This

This defire of honour, which is common to us all, is very profitable to fociety, of fingular ufe to keep men in order, to deter them from wickednefs, and to excite them to many virtues. He who is generally efteemed may be much more ferviceable to mankind than he could elfe be.

The facred writers have alfo reprefented honour as defirable, and in fome meafure worthy to be fought and loved. We do therefore nothing mifbecoming our nature when we value it, if we be not over-fond of it, and make it not the chief end of our actions. In the words of the text, God propofes it as a reward and a blefling coming from him, which he will beftow on thofe who honour him. In difcourfing on which words, I fhall,

I. Inquire in what manner we can honour God.

II. I fhall fhew how and in what fenfe we difhonour him.

III. I will prove that to honour God is the beft method by which we may obtain honour ourfelves.

I. Let us explain what it is to honour God.

As the fear of God, the love of God, and other parts of our duty, are frequently put for the whole, fo by honouring God may be meant in general all religion. If we honour God as we ought, we fhall endeavour to ferve him in all things; and if we prefumptuoufly difobey any of his commandments, it is impoffible that we fhould truly honour him. But though univerfal obedience be included in this expreffion, there are fome particular acts in which the honouring of God may be faid moft eminently to appear. More diftinctly therefore, to honour God is to have an efteem and reverence for him, and to fhew it to the world in a manner which may promote virtue and religion, to let our light fo fhine before men, that they may fee our good works, and glorify our Father which is in heaven.

To honour God is to frame to ourfelves juft and worthy notions of him, of his perfections, of his power, wifdom, wisdom, justice, goodness, and mercy, to reflect upon them with pleasure and respect, to love him, to trust in him, to desire to resemble him as nearly as our nature permits, and in all things to consult his will as the rule of our life. This is the honour which we must pay to God, which he who sees all that passes within us expects from us, and without which all bodily service is unacceptable and indeed abominable in his sight.

To honour God is to declare openly before men by our behaviour that we reverence him, and would chuse above all things to approve ourselves to him, and that neither fear, nor shame, nor custom, nor interest, have any power over us to discourage us from the practice of our duty.

To honour God is to be constant in the performance of all public acts of religion, to profess in an open and solemn manner our Christian faith, and to set a good example to others. So, to worship God, to return praise and thanks to him for mercies received, to acknowledge his supreme dominion over all, to confess our sins, to repent and amend, are, in the language of the Scriptures, to give glory to God, to give him the honour due unto his name, to give glory and honour to the King of heaven.

To honour God is to improve our abilities, and to discharge the duties of our station in a manner which shall procure respect to the religion which we profess, and advantage to the country to which we belong. He who has wealth, honours God when with it he relieves the indigent, encourages honest industry and useful knowledge, which is called in Scripture to honour God with our substance. He who has learning, wit, and judgment, honours God when he applies them to recommend and set off what in itself is praise-worthy, and to kindle in men's hearts an ambition of excelling in goodness. He who has power, honours God when he discourages profaneness and immorality, and by his own illustrious example endeavours to invite others to well-doing, when he protects the deserving, and administers

ministers impartial justice to all. He who has credit and reputation, honours God when he employs it to bring virtue into credit and reputation, and to make vice unfashionable and contemptible, and to do friendly offices to good men. He who has others committed to his care, honours God when he instils into them religious principles. He who is in the lowest station, honours God, when he performs the duties of it, and in his little sphere shines an example to the poorer sort, of honesty, humility, diligence, and sobriety, of contentment and reliance upon God.

II. We have seen what it is to honour God, and hence we may know what on the contrary is meant by dishonouring him.

God is dishonoured, in general, by all kind of moral evil, which is a contempt of his authority, an abuse of his gifts, and a disobedience to his will. But more particularly;

God is dishonoured by atheism and unbelief. They who have senses and reason, by which they may perceive the boundless extent, the infinite variety, the exact order, the regular motions, the beauty, and the conspiring harmony of the several parts which compose the visible world, and also the wonderful operations of the human and invisible mind, and can ascribe it all to chance or to necessity, that is to mere names, to nothings, dishonour their own understanding, and dishonour God who has impressed such manifest characters of himself, of his power, wisdom, and goodness, in every thing that we behold and contemplate.

God is dishonoured by that kind of idolatry, in which, instead of him, many false Gods are worshipped, which was the folly and fault of the Gentiles: for the same proofs which shew that there is any God, shew that there is one supreme God.

God is dishonoured by that kind of idolatry, in which he is worshipped by images. Of this fault the kingdoms of Israel and Judah were often guilty; and the Church of Rome hath fallen either into it, or into
some-

something very like it. The second commandment strictly forbids it; and it is frequently represented in the old Testament as most odious and detestable, because it directly tends to fill the minds of men with mean and unworthy notions of the divine nature.

God is dishonoured by a doctrine which once prevailed much, that there were two rulers of all things, the one a good, the other an evil being. Into this error men were betrayed, because they could not conceive how so much evil could otherwise have found entrance into the world. But even now there are undeniable proofs of God's supreme goodness, power, and wisdom; we ought therefore with faith and humility to wait for the world to come, for the future state, when these divine perfections shall appear still more evidently, and the difficulties concerning God's providence and government shall be cleared up.

God is dishonoured by those who, pretending to acknowledge him, deny a providence or a future state, which is little better than atheism, is not consistent with a belief of his perfections, and utterly destroys faith and reliance, and love towards him.

God is dishonoured by those who reject the Gospel of Christ; for he has done what could be performed on his part to convince them, unless he should offer violence to their liberty, and compel them by such overbearing evidence as would destroy the nature of faith.

Amongst those who profess the Christian religion, God is dishonoured by such as live not suitably to it: for as the virtue of good men allures and incites others to honour God; so a vicious behaviour often brings a reproach upon religion, and in that sense dishonours God. The sons of Eli by their wickedness dishonoured God, making men to abhor the offering of the Lord. David by his sin is said to have given occasion to the enemies of the Lord to blaspheme. Wicked and oppressive men are said to cause the name of God to be blasphemed; and

SERMON IX.

and by St. Paul they who break God's laws are said to dishonour him, to cause his name and his word to be blasphemed.

Thus God is said to be dishonoured by sinners, because they refuse to pay him that veneration which is due to him from all his creatures; because by their bad example they spread vice and discourage piety; because by pretending, as they often do, to be religious, they give occasion to unbelievers to think and to say that the religion must be bad which is chosen by bad men, and which produces nothing in them that is commendable; and because, when they suffer no evils here proportionable to their offences, they make profane and injudicious persons conclude that God takes no notice and care of human affairs, since he suffers such profligates to pass unpunished.

God is dishonoured by two sorts of hypocrisy, which are directly opposite to each other; by the one men pretend to be better, and by the other to be worse than they are.

On some occasions, and with some people, devotion, or the appearance of it, is the only way to get credit and reputation; and then they who have little regard for goodness in their hearts, take care in their words and outward carriage to seem very pious. This behaviour gives offence to those who are of a loose and gay and inconsiderate temper: they compare the wicked actions of such men with their religious demeanour, and godly professions, and they proceed often to despise and dislike and suspect every thing that looks like piety.

Again; in some situations, an indifference for religion is more fashionable; and then many fear to be thought the servants of God, and by a most detestable dissimulation would seem more loose in principles and practice than they are; which vice is rather worse than a mere form of godliness; for to

pretend

pretend to goodness is to pay some outward homage at least to it, some shadow of respect: but this perverse and wicked shame is a silent acknowledgment that religion is deformed and odious, mean and ridiculous.

III. Let us now proceed to consider the reward promised to those who honour God. Them that honour me, I will honour.

And here we must repeat the observation which was made before, that to honour God means all religion in general, and the whole of our duty; and therefore the sense of the text is, that they who are good and righteous, and honour God by their obedience and upright conduct, shall be honoured themselves. Honour then is proposed to us in the Scriptures as a reward of well-doing, and it is promised in both Testaments. In the Old Testament riches and honour are often said to come from God, to be gifts which he bestows upon his servants. In the Gospel, there is an honour which is said to come from God, and which we are exhorted to seek; glory and honour is there promised to every one that doth well. If any man serve me, says our Saviour, him will my Father honour.

By the honour thus promised to the righteous, the same thing is not altogether meant in the Old Testament, and in the New; for because, under the Law, future rewards were not so clearly propounded, the honour there mentioned relates principally to this world, though honour in the world to come is not excluded: on the contrary, in the New Testament, where eternal life is more fully taught, the honour promised relates principally to that honour which the good shall hereafter receive, though honour even for the present is not to be excluded.

It is moreover to be remembered, that the promises of temporal rewards made in the Scriptures to particular persons, must always be understood with
proper

proper restrictions and limitations, as usually and frequently, but not constantly and invariably fulfilled; else they could not be reconciled with the dispensations of providence, nor with the nature of things, and the liberty of free beings. As this is generally the case in all worldly blessings and conveniencies, it is particularly so as to honour and reputation; for honour is the regard which is paid to us by others on account of our good and useful qualities; all therefore that we can do towards obtaining it, is to deserve it. Whether others will bestow it upon us or no, is uncertain: it depends upon their opinion and inclinations, which cannot be compelled. We must not therefore expect to receive it always, and to receive it from all persons with whom we converse. God himself hath it not in this manner. He who has all perfections, who alone has them, upon whom all depend, who ought to be honoured above all things by all rational beings, is continually dishonoured by multitudes of ungrateful and rebellious creatures, who deny his very being and providence, disobey his laws, and abuse the blessings which he bestows upon them. If therefore, as our Saviour says, they have called the master of the house Beelzebub, much more will they do the same to those of his household. The disciple must not expect to be above his master, nor the servant to be above his Lord: the most upright person, the most useful to mankind, the most beneficent and inoffensive must not hope for honour from men without some abatement, without some slanders and insults from ignorance, envy, and malice.

The promise therefore contained in the text may be fairly restrained and reduced to this, that the good shall be rewarded with honour, usually in this world, and certainly in the world to come. They will be usually honoured in this life, because their virtues naturally tend to produce this effect, and because the
favour

favour and the blessing of God is often visibly and remarkably extended to them. Goodness is the plain and direct way to honour and respect; but there are by-paths, which men fancy to be more easy and compendious, and through which they hope to find or make their way to it. Certain things there are, upon which the world sets a value, and which fall to the share of few; and if they possess these, they foolishly suppose that honour must follow of course.

Thus riches, high stations, nobility, titles, power, courage, and great abilities, natural and acquired, are all accounted by many persons sure and easy means of gaining honour: and so far it is true, that they afford extraordinary helps to obtain it, because they place men in the eye and observation of the world, and put it in their power to do many good offices. If therefore these accomplishments and advantages are joined to sober unaffected piety, humility, industry, justice, mercy, clemency, and liberality, they will infallibly procure honour and respect to the possessor; but if they are perverted and abused, they will make him detested: and the greater his power and his possessions, and his station and his abilities are, the wider will his infamy be spread. He may be honoured by those who are like himself, and he may receive outward, ceremonious, insincere, and insignificant respect from those who approach him, and who perhaps revile him in all other times and places; and he who can call this honour, and be contented with it, knows not, nor can be taught to know and comprehend what honour is.

Honour is not to be obtained by those who do nothing to deserve it. All the gifts which this world can bestow upon us will not secure it. Kings are called fountains of honour, and can bestow it where they please. The people have the absolute disposal of their own applause, and can bestow that as they think fit: but neither the one nor the other can confer

SERMON IX.

fer reputation in the true sense of the word. There must be something intrinsic to support it; something that will bear a near inspection and a strict examination.

A good person will always be useful to society, as far as his station and abilities permit; he will not despise and wrong others, and he will do them all the services that lie in his power. So far therefore as he is known, he will probably be esteemed. All honest and wise men will be glad to assist him, will place confidence in him, will rejoice at his prosperity, and will approve his conduct; and even they who are not so religious as they should be, and on many accounts may be reckoned amongst the bad, will often respect him; for one of the last good qualities which we lose is an esteem for virtue and virtuous persons. As to those profligates who can dislike and deride a man for his blameless and upright behaviour, their voices are of no moment in bestowing or denying reputation, and to be censured by them is a kind of honour. The world is bad enough, but yet it rarely happens that worthy persons fall into general contempt; for Virtue is majestic and venerable; and it is easier even to hate it than to despise it. In our other temporal pursuits, we are exposed to various disappointments, and in other temporal recompences there is much uncertainty, which have produced perpetual complaints of the arbitrary and fantastical humour of Time, Fate, Chance, Fortune, who were supposed by ignorant men to preside here below: but in the distribution of reputation, there is a tolerable degree of impartiality, and a good character secured by good deeds is usually a treasure laid up in a sacred fortress, where neither Detraction can corrupt, nor pilfering Envy break through and steal.

Thus respect and honour is the natural consequence of goodness, and in the common course of things must attend it. But there is, over and above all this,
a promise

a promise of God that it shall be so, and we must not suppose that he leaves the issues of things altogether to second causes, and never interposeth himself. In the Scriptures of the old Testament, we find in how extraordinary a manner God honoured those who honoured him. To some persons remarkable for goodness he afforded great deliverances; to others he testified his approbation by working miracles in their behalf; to others he granted their requests when they made prayers and intercessions for their own nation; to others he fulfilled illustriously the promise that he would shew mercy to a thousand generations of them that love him and keep his commandments, shewing great favour to their progeny for their sakes; to others he gave power and dignity, raising them from the lowest to the highest stations.

If we descend to the times when piety most flourished, and yet was attended with the fewest temporal recompences, to the first age of Christianity, we find that the disciples of Christ, and other eminent persons in the Church, though persecuted, scorned, and slandered by the Gentiles and the unbelieving Jews, received great authority and miraculous powers from God, and the utmost duty, love, and respect, from their numerous brethren in the faith; and since their death, their names and memory have been more honoured than those of any of the princes and conquerors and disturbers of this world.

It must be acknowledged that a good man may unjustly suffer in his reputation, or that he may be poor and neglected, and covered with obscurity, and hardly known even to his neighbours; but God has promised to honour those who honour him; and they shall be honoured; nor can a malicious and ungrateful world deprive them of this recompence.

The

SERMON IX.

The truth of this will manifestly appear, when we have considered the nature of real and complete honour.

The most perfect honour that we can conceive is the esteem which a person obtains from many who excel in wisdom and power and goodness, and which shall continue for ever.

Of all creatures who possess understanding and reason, we seem to be the lowest in rank; superior to us are innumerable beings, inhabitants of other and better worlds, the least of whom surpass us in knowledge, power and virtue, who possess these excellencies in various degrees, according to their several orders.

Such are all who have gone before us in the ways of righteousness, and have put off their mortal bodies, and the host of Angels, whom Gods sends forth to minister unto them who shall be heirs of salvation.

Every good man therefore, howsoever slighted and overlooked by those amongst whom he dwells, acts in a great theatre, and has numberless spectators and applauders of his conduct. To be approved and commended by these holy and wise and impartial judges, this is true honour; and this honour every righteous person enjoys, who like those blessed Spirits is performing the will of God, and filling up with integrity and dignity the offices of his station. His honour indeed is not perfect in the present short life, for he is not acquainted with these superior beings, and knows not when they observe him, and what they think of him. But as soon as he departs hence, he goes to the invisible world, and converses with the Spirits of just men made perfect, and with the Angels, who congratulate him upon his deliverance from mortality, and his constancy in running the course set before him. Then he enters into the possession of true and eternal honour, which shall be en-

Vol. II.   I   creased

creased in the great day, when he shall receive the approbation of Christ the judge of the world, and of the God and Father of all. This is honour in the strictest sense, or rather this alone deserves to be called honour. The marks of distinction which mortal creatures confer upon each other, when compared to this, appear vain and trifling and contemptible beyond expression.

SERMON

SERMON X.

DEUTER. xxix. 29.

The secret things belong unto the Lord our God, but those things which are revealed belong unto us, and to our children for ever, that we may do all the works of this law.

MOSES in this chapter, and in many other places of this Book, earnestly exhorts the people to keep the covenant which they had made with God, and to serve him with their whole heart, promising them every kind of blessing if they would be obedient, and denouncing the severest punishments, personal and national, if they transgressed. After these threatnings, he adds in the words of the text; The secret things belong unto the Lord our God: but those things which are revealed belong unto us, and to our children for ever, that we may do all the words of this law: which hath no manifest connection with the foregoing or the following discourse. It seems to be an answer to an inquiry which the people of Israel might naturally have made. Shall we ever be so wicked, they might have said to Moses, after all the corrections we have undergone, and all the mercies which we have received, and all the miracles which we have seen, as to provoke God to destroy us? shall our posterity become so profligate as to bring down upon itself such terrible punishments, such unexampled calamities, as thou hast described? To a question of this kind the words of the text would have been a proper reply; The secret things belong unto the Lord our God. Such events are hidden in the dark recesses of futurity, and it concerns you not to know them. It is enough for you to know this, that both you and your posterity, if you do well, shall be rewarded; and if you do ill shall be punished. The promises and threatnings of God are conditional, and it is in your power to deserve the one or the other; the execution of them depends upon your own behaviour and upon your own choice.

The text, considered by itself, contains in it this doctrine, that there are things which a man ought to know, namely, the truths which God hath revealed, and the duties which he requires; and that there are things which men cannot discover, or ought not to know, and that they must not busy themselves in inquiries after them.

The love of knowledge is one of our natural affections: we all delight in knowledge, and we all seek it, with this difference, that some pursue useful and commendable, others trifling, or vicious, or unlawful, or unattainable knowledge. As God hath implanted in us all a desire of knowledge, so he hath set a vast variety of alluring truths within our reach, and has furnished us abundantly with objects on which we may employ our searches. The knowledge of religion, both natural and revealed, the study of Nature, of the works of God, of ourselves, and of mankind, of all the arts and sciences which are cultivated in civilized countries, of the laws of our own and other nations, and of those things which belong to our own particular profession or occupation, all this is more than sufficient to employ our leisure hours; for even of each single branch of knowledge it may truly be said that Art is long, and Life is short, so that we need never sit down and lament that we have no more worlds of knowledge to conquer. As he who should set out from home with a desire to see every part of this habitable world, would end his days before he

had

had ended his journey ; so the mind of man in its pursuit of truth can make only a small and inconsiderable progress, and therefore should shun all vain and unprofitable inquiries, and not spend time and pains to no purpose, much less to an evil purpose.

1. Amongst the things which are secret, may be placed a complete knowledge of nature, of the visible world, and of the effects of matter and motion.

Natural philosophy is a branch of knowledge, which hath been extremely improved in this and in the last century, and, which is still better, it has been successfully applied to the confirmation of natural religion, and to the confutation of Atheism.

Many farther improvements may probably be made in this extensive subject: but there are bounds to it, beyond which we cannot pass. Several in this part of knowledge have employed their time and pains to find out or to perform what is (*a*) impossible ; but this is not so much an immorality, as a want of judgment ; and they who thus seek in vain, yet sometimes accidentally discover things which they did not seek. There are also, it may be, many natural effects of matter and motion, within the reach of human skill and sagacity, which yet by the wise counsels of Providence shall be hidden from us, because by misapplication they would produce more evil than good in the world, and furnish us with new means of hurting the peace of society, and of destroying one another.

2. Amongst the things pertaining to religion which have occupied the minds of men to no purpose, we may reckon what has been called absolute predestination, or the everlasting decrees of God concerning the salvation and destruction of particular persons. If there were such a decree, it must certainly be one of those secret things which belong to the Lord our God, because the knowledge

---

(*a*) As a perpetual motion, the transmutation of metals, the making of gold, the art of flying, of travelling in the air, &c.

ledge of it could not produce any possible good to mankind; and would undoubtedly produce bad effects, and therefore it would never have been revealed. But it is evident that no such doctrine is contained in the holy Scriptures. All the decrees of God relating to our future state are conditional; for God hath made us free, and consequently hath made our doom to depend upon our own choice. True it is that his foreknowledge extends to all things that are the objects of knowledge, and that we are at a loss clearly to apprehend how the actions of free beings can be foreseen: but since we are as sure of our liberty as we are of our very being, and have the same inward sense of the one as of the other, whilst we cannot form to ourselves just conceptions how the things which are not as yet, and which depend upon man's choice, are present to the divine knowledge, we must be contented with that which is evident, and look upon the other as upon one of those hidden things with which we are not concerned.

3. Another secret is an accurate knowledge of God, of his nature and perfections. He is incomprehensible to us, and the reason is evident, because he is perfect and we are imperfect, and the lesser cannot contain the greater; because he is infinite and eternal, and we are limited both in time and place, and there is something in infinity, eternity, and absolute perfection, which perplexes us and involves us in its difficulties. But then we know that God is, though we know not how he is, and the certainty and truth of many incomprehensibles may be proved; for reason and imagination are two distinct powers, and our reason perceives evidently that things are and must be, of which our imagination can frame no just and clear conception. Thus reason assures us, beyond a possibility of doubting that something has been from all eternity, but imagination cannot comprehend a past eternity.

We

We have likewife a fufficient notion of the perfections of God, fo far as they concern us. We underftand very well what power is, and wifdom, and juftice, and goodnefs: they are the fame in kind and in nature with human power, wifdom, juftice, and goodnefs, but the fupreme Being muft poffefs them in a degree infinitely fuperior.

In this manner we may know God; and this is a very valuable knowledge, when it produces fuitable effects. Concerning this knowledge the prophet Jeremiah fays, Thus faith the Lord, Let not the wife man glory in his wifdom, neither let the mighty man glory in his might, let not the rich man glory in his riches. But let him that glorieth, glory in this, that he underftandeth and knoweth me, that I am the Lord which exercifeth loving-kindnefs, judgment, and righteoufnefs in the earth. Let no man glory in wifdom, power, and riches: Why fo? Becaufe they may be loft, they may be abufed, they may be of fmall fervice to the poffeffor. But happy is he who underftandeth and knoweth me. He fays not, who underftandeth my nature, and knoweth all my perfections, for that is impoffible; but he inftances in thofe divine qualities in which men are concerned, and which they are beft able to apprehend, the juftice, the equity, the holinefs, and the mercy of God. He who has a lively fenfe, and a practical knowledge of thefe perfections, which will caufe him to love and honour his Maker; poffeffes what is more glorious and advantageous than all the wifdom, and power, and wealth in the world.

4. Amongft the things which we muft not expect thoroughly to underftand, is God's providence, the manner in which he prefides over rational beings, the reafons of his conduct, the ends which he propofes, and the methods by which he accomplifhes them, and how far he is affifting, hindering, or permitting, in all events. In this divine government there muft be much hidden knowledge, to which may be applied the words of St. Paul;

Paul; O the depth of the riches both of the wisdom and knowledge of God! how unsearchable are his judgments, and his ways past finding out! For who hath known the mind of the Lord? or who hath been his counsellor?

The difficulties concerning the divine providence and government of the universe arise principally from the evil which is the creation, namely, sin and misery. But we know and can prove by a multitude of arguments, that God is good, and that if he were an evil being, there could be no such thing as good in the world. This must satisfy us, and thence we must conclude, that all is ordered for the best, and would so appear to us, if we were able to comprehend the whole plan of divine providence.

5. Under this head which concerns the mysteries of providence, may be placed the reasons for which God bestows prosperity upon one person, and adversity upon another. In this there is something of which we are not competent judges. Thus much we know in general, that prosperity and adversity both serve to good and wise purposes, and that the one may be granted, and the other inflicted, for useful and beneficial ends. But we must not pretend to say that temporal advantages are given to this person as a recompence for his goodness, or that affliction befalls another as a punishment for some particular offence. As to worldly happiness, we are not over-forward to ascribe it to piety, for it is an old and a common complaint, that many enjoy more than they deserve: but as to calamities there have been always censorious people, who have ascribed them to the sins of the suffering person. If any evil befalls those of whom they have a hard opinion, they call it a judgment; if it befalls themselves or their friends, they give it a more civil and gentle name, and call it a trial.

This way of thinking and talking our Saviour has reprimanded more than once, whence we may conclude that the Jews in his time were much addicted to it.

SERMON X.

Suppose ye, says he, that these men were sinners above all men, because they suffered such things? I tell you nay; but except ye repent, ye shall all likewise perish.

The promises and threatnings of temporal blessings and punishments, which were so frequent in their Law, and had been so frequently fulfilled, might incline them to these hard surmises; and yet they had instances enough to the contrary, to warn them not to account adversity any sure mark of divine pleasure. But if this was a fault in them, it was much worse in Christians, who have been fully instructed upon this subject. There are indeed some sufferings which naturally result from some follies and vices; but it is very rash and unfair to suppose such a connection where we can see none.

6. The future condition of the righteous and of the wicked is one of those things of which we cannot have a distinct and particular knowledge. The Scriptures have taught us enough concerning it to excite our hopes, and to raise our fears, and to put us upon more serious endeavours, more zeal, more care and caution to save ourselves, and to provide for eternity, than we usually exert. The Scriptures assure us in general, that the Judge of all the earth will do what is right and just, and that every one shall receive suitably to his conduct and disposition, in a vast variety of degrees. Therefore we must be contented with this general knowledge, which answers all good and religious purposes, and take care to avoid the two extremes of ascribing to God either a lenity which is not consistent with justice and order, or a severity which is not reconcileable with goodness; for these errors must be attended with very bad effects, and produce either remissness, or presumption, or despair, or unbelief.

7. Amongst those things which are hidden from us, we may place many difficult parts of the Scriptures. Not that the study of them is unlawful or vain: far from

from it; but as they afford occasion to many discoveries, they give rise to many mistakes; so that modesty and diffidence are necessary qualifications in all those who exercise their thoughts that way. There are also many parts of Scripture which may seem to contain rather matter of mere curiosity than of Christian instruction: but there is scarcely any historical fact or truth which is useless; there is a secret connection between all kind of knowledge; all Arts and Sciences are Sisters, and upon many occasions lend one another a friendly aid. Much more do the holy Scriptures in general, and every part of them in particular deserve our study and meditation, as giving light to each other where one would not expect it. The difficulties in the sacred Books are not without their use, they have employed the sagacity and industry of many persons, and by their labours much light hath been thrown upon many passages, which were little understood, or safely interpreted; and in this respect the later ages have manifestly improved upon the former, as it is natural to suppose. But these things concern not the bulk of mankind, nor doth the present or future happiness of Christians depend upon them, nor ought they to be made matter of strife and censure, or suffered to extinguish the moral virtues, candour, meekness, compassion, forbearance, and charity, which are of more value than all the knowledge in the world. It is a general opinion amongst Protestants, that the Scriptures are not difficult in points of universal use and importance, though even in these points skill and integrity is requisite in the teacher, and a good disposition in the learner, and diligence and application in them both. The things which the Apostles of our Lord propounded to mankind as necessary to be believed were plain and simple, and easily apprehended, and the duties which they enjoined were manly and rational. In process of time Christianity was altered much for the worse, nor hath she yet recovered her ancient simplicity.

8. There

8. There are some parts of Scripture which seem to be designedly concealed from us, and they are those prophecies which are as yet unfulfilled; for which many reasons might be assigned. As the prophecies concerning Christ were never perfectly understood, till he came and fulfilled them; so those predictions which relate to future ages, and have not received their completion, are dark to us, and will continue so, until the day itself unfolds them; and all attempts to interpret them have been unsuccessful. Indeed it concerns us very little to know what shall be done upon earth after we are gone from it, and we might as well be solicitous to learn what passed a thousand years before man was created.

9. Lastly; the knowledge of things to come, of the good and evil which will befall us in this life, and of the time when our life will end, are secrets which God hath concealed from us. We may add, that with great wisdom and kindness he hath concealed them, since such knowledge could do us no service, and might make us very uneasy. Our Saviour's words may be justly adapted to this purpose: Take no thought for the morrow, for the morrow shall take thought for the things of itself: sufficient for the day is the evil thereof.

David says; Lord, let me know my end, and the number of my days, that I may be certified how long I have to live. We must not suppose from these words that David wanted exactly to know how many years he should live, which had been an indiscreet petition; nor are we to suppose that the end of man's life is fixed by any decree, so that it cannot be prolonged or shortened: but the meaning is plainly this; Grant, O Lord, that I may have a practical knowledge and a due sense of the shortness and uncertainty of human life, which may teach me to make a wise use of it, and preserve me from folly and iniquity.

If there were any arts and methods by which we could discover future events, every one who was wise and valued his own ease and quiet would desire to be ignorant of them; and if there were any persons who could inform us of such things, they would deserve to be shunned as dangerous enemies. And yet such hath been the infatuation of mankind in almost all ages, that many have had an intemperate desire of this forbidden and pernicious knowledge, which gave rise and encouragement to wicked arts and to vile impostures. In favour of the age in which we live, we may say that these wicked arts and foolish notions were never in lower esteem, never more neglected, than at present; so that if we were as wise and as commendable in other respects, we should be better than we are.

These are the several things which are hidden in obscurity and removed far from us, so that either we cannot discover them at all, or can apprehend them only in a confused and superficial way. And here our curiosity is to be repressed, and turned to better and more suitable objects. Besides these which lie out of our knowledge, there are several things discoverable in their own nature and not placed beyond the reach of the human understanding, which yet must be hidden from many persons, and known only to those who have the means and opportunities and capacities requisite for that purpose. Every one therefore should suit his desires of knowledge to his condition, and neither seek what he has not power to attain, nor yet fancy himself knowing where he is ignorant, nor be contentious and positive about things which he understands not.

The secret things belong unto the Lord our God: but those things which are revealed belong unto us, and to our children for ever, that we may do all the words of this law. Here the knowledge of God's revealed will is represented as of the greatest use and importance, but it is represented as an active knowledge influencing the behaviour. The things revealed belong to us. As how? He says not, that we may know, but, that we may

may do all the words of this law. Our Saviour, though he was the greatest encourager and the most assiduous teacher of useful knowledge, yet always discouraged and disappointed inquiries of mere curiosity. When he was asked at what time his second coming should be, and the kingdom should be restored to Israel, and how long one of his disciples should live? when these and other questions of the like nature were put to him, his answer was, It is not for you to know these things. What is that to thee? Follow thou me. But when he was asked, What shall I do, that I may obtain eternal life? he gave a direct answer.

The knowledge of our duty then is knowledge in the truest and most excellent sense; and it is a practical knowledge, and consists in action more than in speculation. It may be obtained by every one who seeks it; we have all of us natural abilities to acquire it in such a degree as is necessary for us; we were made for this end and purpose, and besides our inward powers, we have God's revealed will, and assistance. These important things which we must know and do, and which belong to us and to our children, may be comprised in a few words. We are the offspring of a Parent infinitely wise and good, to whom we have unspeakable obligations; him we must love and honour and endeavour to resemble. We are placed by him here to live in society with our fellow-creatures; we must do them all the good and all the service that we can. We have each of us a little society within ourselves, in which our powers, capacities, passions, and inclinations, are so many subjects, and often unruly subjects, which must be guided and governed by the Mind: the powers must be well employed, the capacities improved, the passions kept within due bounds, and the inclinations directed to proper objects. This is our duty, this is our business; business sufficient to keep us in constant occupation. Our days are few, and then follows eternity; and such as our behaviour is here, such will our condition be hereafter. The thought of this should ever be present with us, it should awake with us, and lie down with us; it should haunt us, if we may use the expression, in all times and places, and give us no peace and no quiet, till we have provided for our great change, and our everlasting welfare.

SERMON

SERMON XI.

MATTH. xii. 31.

All manner of sin and blasphemy shall be forgiven unto men: but the blasphemy against the holy Ghost shall not be forgiven unto men.

THE occasion of these words was this: They brought to our Saviour one possessed with a Devil, blind and dumb, and he healed him, insomuch that the blind and dumb both spake and saw; upon which the people who were present acknowledged Christ to be the son of David, the promised Messias.

But when the Pharisees heard it, they said, This man doth not cast out Devils, but by Beelzebub the prince of the Devils.

These Pharisees, being resolved never to believe in Christ, what evidence soever he gave of his authority, and to do their utmost to keep others from believing in him, and yet not able to deny that he had wrought this miracle, endeavoured to persuade the people that he was a magician, who cast out evil spirits by the assistance of the Prince of the Devils.

Jesus knew their thoughts, and said to them; Every kingdom divided against itself is brought to desolation, and every city or house divided against itself shall not stand. And if Satan cast out Satan, he is divided against himself; how then shall his kingdom stand? And if I by Beelzebub cast out Devils, by whom do your

your children cast them out? therefore shall they be your judges. But if I cast out Devils by the Spirit of God, then the kingdom of God is come unto you. Or else how can one enter into a strong man's house, and spoil his goods, except he first bind the strong man? and then he will spoil his house. He that is not with me, is against me; and he that gathereth not with me, scattereth abroad.

In these words are contained four arguments against the wicked suggestion of those Pharisees, that he acted by a compact with the Devil.

First: If I by Beelzebub cast out Devils, by whom do your sons cast them out?

There were amongst the Jews certain persons who took upon them to cast out Devils. These persons were probably of the sect of the Pharisees; and their method was, to call upon the name of God, the God of Abraham, of Isaac, and of Jacob. The argument then is this: There are persons of whom you have a good opinion, and who are said by you to cast out evil spirits. By whom do they cast them out? by the name of God, or by the power of the Devil? you must acknowledge that it is by the former. I also act in the name of God, I profess to receive all my powers from him, ascribe all my works to him, and I perform far more miracles even of this sort than all your exorcists. Therefore you are guilty of a most malicious and wicked obstinacy, when you dare thus to pass two contrary judgments upon actions which are alike.

Here perhaps you would ask, Did these Exorcists really cast out Devils or no? to which I answer; It is not material to our Saviour's argument whether their attempts were or were not successful; and we have not light enough given to us in the Gospel, or in the history of those times, to determine this question with any certainty.

Another

SERMON XI.

Another argument used by our Lord is this: You say that I by the assistance of the prince of the Devils cast out evil Spirits. The Devils have cunning and wisdom enough to prosecute their purposes by the most proper methods, and to know that union amongst themselves is absolutely necessary. No kingdom, no society, divided against itself, can stand: it must be brought to desolation. I cast out Devils, rebuking them, treating them as wicked Spirits, and commanding them with all authority. To suppose that I do this by the assistance of the Devil, is to suppose that one evil Spirit insults another, and makes him appear contemptible in the sight of men. Such can never be the behaviour of beings united to support the same bad cause, confederates in iniquity, and by no means void of subtilty and wicked prudence.

To this argument a Pharisee would perhaps have replied, that the Devils might exercise this real or seeming authority over each other, with a view to establish the kingdom of Satan, because the evil Spirit, by whose assistance another Devil was cast out, would receive honour from it, and so the cause of impiety would still be advanced.

But our Lord has obviated this, by adding to the former another argument in confirmation of it, which cannot be eluded. It is contained in these words; How can one enter into a strong man's house and spoil his goods, except he first bind the strong man? and then he will spoil his house. That is, in other word; A man enters by force into the house of a bold and resolute enemy, binds him, and spoils his goods, and reduces him to the deplorable state of indigence and captivity. In such a case will any one pretend to affirm that the conquered person submitted to this willingly, that he was pleased with the success of his adversary, and that he contributed designedly to his own destruction? Without question he used all his force and skill to defend himself, and was overpowered by a superior strength.

This, says our Lord, is an exact image of all that passeth between me and Satan. I am his great and constant enemy; the business of my life hath been to oppose him and destroy his dominion. My doctrine deters men from vice, and encourages them to well-doing, and consequently tends to make them wise unto salvation. His study is to corrupt men, and to make them miserable. Since this is undeniable, how wicked is it to say that I have his assistance, and how absurd to think that he would assist me, and deliberately contribute to the destruction of his own power! It is plain that I cast out Devils because I am mightier than they, and that they obey my commands not out of choice, but necessity.

A fourth argument, though strictly speaking it is not so much a new argument as an illustration of the foregoing, is contained in these words; He that is not with me is against me, and he that gathereth not with me scattereth abroad. This is a proverbial saying, and the sense of it is, He who is not my friend is my enemy. That we may understand how it is applied, we must observe that Christ had just before represented Satan under the image of a strong man, and himself under the image of a mightier man, who fights with him, and conquers and enslaves him. Our Lord continues in the same way of speaking, and alludes to a state of war between two powerful and irreconcileable enemies. At such a time, whosoever is able to assist either side and stands neuter, will usually be reputed an enemy by them both, according to the Proverb, Whoso is not my friend is my foe.

The cause of vice and the cause of virtue are opposite, and Satan is at irreconcileable war with the Servants of God. Were I only to stand neuter, says Christ, Satan would esteem me as his enemy: how much

much more, when I do so much to weaken his power, and to destroy his kingdom?

But, as proverbial sayings are applicable to various purposes, our Saviour might also have himself in view when he said, He that is not with me is against me; and then the sense will be, He who is convinced that I am sent from God, and that my miracles prove it, and yet dares not own it, for fear of worldly inconveniences, deserves to be esteemed my enemy; and if such a man is no better than an enemy, how much worse is he who dares to ascribe my miracles to evil Spirits? Then follow the words of the text: Wherefore I say unto you, All manner of sin and blasphemy shall be forgiven unto men; but the blasphemy against the holy Ghost shall not be forgiven unto men; and whosoever speaketh a word against the Son of man, it shall be forgiven him; but whosoever speaketh against the holy Ghost, it shall not be forgiven him, neither in this world, neither in the world to come. St Mark adds, because they said, He hath an unclean spirit.

The meaning of the words is this; Since it is evident that I am sent from God, and that the works which I do, are performed by his authority, and by the assistance of his holy Spirit, and yet you Pharisees ascribe these works to the Devil, therefore I say unto you that an obstinacy so malicious shall never be forgiven. All other blasphemies and sins may be forgiven. Even he who speaks against the Son of man, that is, me as I am the Messias, he who says that I am not that great person foretold by the prophets, such an one may afterwards be convinced of his error, and receive pardon; but he who reviles these mighty works, wrought by the Spirit of God, shall not be pardoned. It shall not be forgiven him, neither in this world, neither in the world to come; that is, it shall never be forgiven. In St. Mark it is, he hath never forgiveness, but is in danger of eternal damnation;

tion; the meaning is, he is obnoxious to it, he commits a crime of which such condemnation is the punishment.

He who calls himself a prophet, and says that he is commanded to instruct men in their duty, and to require their obedience, and who works miracles in the name of God, and who teaches nothing contradictory to common sense, produces as clear evidence of his authority as can reasonably be desired.

Miracles were in a particular manner the best proof which could be offered to the Jews. Their religion stood upon the evidence of miracles. By many signs and wonders was their law confirmed, and the mission of Moses their Law-giver; after which God had from time to time sent them prophets, who either foretold future events, or wrought miracles. A prophet, giving such signs, had a right, according to the laws of God, to require their obedience, unless he enticed them to idolatry, which was the only exception to a general rule. These Pharisees therefore acted very wickedly in ascribing the miracles of Christ to the power of Satan; and their wickedness was the greater, because the casting out Devils was more particularly a proof that Christ was the Messias, who should destroy the power and the works of the Devil, and establish a kingdom directly opposite to his; and because, as they could not pretend to say that Christ had ever preached idolatry, and endeavoured to seduce the people from worshipping the Lord their God, they were by their own law, no less than by reason, obliged to receive him as a prophet, and had the same motives to obey him which they had to believe that the law of Moses was the law of God.

Besides this, there were other circumstances increasing the guilt of these blasphemers. They were not poor and rude and ignorant, but the most learned persons of the nation, who pretended to great holiness, who were acquainted with the Scriptures, and esteemed

SERMON XI.

ed by the people, of whom they were guides and teachers. Malicious slanders uttered by them were very pernicious and inexcusable.

From these observations, added to the answers of our Lord in which he confutes the Pharisees, we see that their offence was great; and yet we have hitherto seen only a part of it. This disposition of their mind rendered it still more heinous. The same evil action committed by two persons shall be more criminal in one than in another, according as they offend more or less against knowledge. We may reasonably suppose, we ought indeed to suppose, that all the circumstances which can aggravate a crime were to be found in these Pharisees, since our Lord passed so terrible a sentence upon them. It is plain that Christ had a view to those circumstances, which to men could not appear perfectly, but were known to him, to whom all hearts were open; for St. Matthew tells us, that Jesus, knowing their hearts and their thoughts, answered them so and so; and when he had declared in the words of the text that their crime should not be forgiven, he adds, Either make the tree good and his fruit good, or else make the tree corrupt and his fruit corrupt; for the tree is known by his fruit. O generation of vipers, how can ye, being evil, speak good things? for out of the abundance of the heart the mouth speaketh. He intimates that their blasphemy was owing to an incorrigible wickedness, and that therefore not so much for the single act of reviling his miracles as for the cause whence it sprang, they were incapable of amendment. Hence we may infer;

First, that these Pharisees were prompted to this blasphemy by envy and hatred and malice and pride and worldly interest; that, giving way to their passions, they were furiously carried on to oppose Christ, and allowed not themselves leisure to examine sedately whether he was a true prophet; and that they reviled

viled him without a serious persuasion that they did right.

Secondly, that perhaps their (*a*) own conscience condemned them, and that they acted in some degree against conviction, chusing to say any thing rather than to lose their authority over the people, and to suffer them to entertain a good opinion of Christ.

Here arises a question: Is it possible that men should maliciously oppose the truth, when they know and are convinced that it is the truth? (*b*) Some have thought it is impossible, and that human nature is not capable of it.

It seems indeed not to be in the power of a man to oppose the truth, when he is satisfied and convinced that it is the truth, and is also persuaded that such opposition shall not be forgiven; nor could a Pharisee say that the miracles of Christ were the works of the Devil, if he believed both that Christ was a true prophet, and that they who opposed him should certainly suffer for it. But a Pharisee might believe in his heart that Christ wrought miracles by a divine power, at least, he might not be persuaded of the contrary, and yet ascribe those miracles to evil spirits, if he was prompted to say so by his wicked disposition and unruly passions, and if he thought that he might escape divine vengeance one way or other. The Jews had a notion that all sins should be forgiven to the children of Abraham, except apostacy, and some particular crimes which they specified.

The Pharisees are said to have blasphemed against the Holy Ghost, because they ascribed to an evil Spirit miracles which were wrought by the Spirit of God.

Yet it did not consist barely in this, but in a great measure in the baseness, malice, and obstinacy which accompanied

(*a*) Grotius on Matt. xii. 31.
(*b*) Tillotson, Vol. I. Serm. xvii.

accompanied it. One might call Chrift a falfe prophet, might perfecute him and his difciples, and yet not offend fo much as another who did the fame; for though the offence in outward appearance would be the fame in both, the circumftances aggravating or leffening it might be very different. Thus the Jews who crucified Chrift were all finners, but finners in various degrees. Some did it in ignorance, through prejudices of education, mifled by their rulers and teachers for whom they had great refpect, and perfuaded that God approved their behaviour. Thefe might obtain mercy, and probably were afterwards converted to Chriftianity. Others perfecuted Chrift out of malice and revenge, fwayed by worldly intereft, ftifling the reproofs of confcience, urged by vile and fhameful motives. Such had no difpofitions leading to repentance, and fuch we may fuppofe them to have been who continued all their days contradicting and blafpheming, and enemies to the Gofpel.

A blafphemer againft the Holy Ghoft was therefore one who faw the miracles of Chrift, and by fome very wicked motive malicioufly afcribed them to Satan, and who probably finned againft confcience.

Let us confider the fentence which our Saviour pronounced againft this crime: It fhall never be forgiven.

All manner of fin and blafphemy, fays our Saviour, fhall be forgiven. All manner of fin, that is, all fins of this kind, fuch as lying, flandering, and reviling. Blafphemy againft the Holy Ghoft is not here compared with apoftacy, atheifm, murder, tyranny, perfecution, inceft, adultery, nor can we fuppofe that it is a greater crime than thefe ufually are: but the meaning feems to be that of all evil fpeech proceeding from an evil heart, this is the worft and the moft heinous.

It fhall never be forgiven.

Since

Since according to the doctrine of the Gospel, all sinners are invited to repentance, and forgiveness of sins is promised to all who repent, we must not so interpret the text, and two or three other passages in Scripture, as to conclude either that there is any sin so heinous as not to be pardoned upon repentance, or that any person, how wicked soever, may lose his natural power of repenting and amending. A few difficult or severe expressions in the sacred writings ought to be explained by those which are clear, express, merciful, and more in number. Rather than to infer from the words before us that any man cannot repent, or by repentance cannot please God, it would be better to suppose that, though no exception is made in the text, there is one to be understood; as if our Lord had said, of all sins of this kind which a man can commit there is none of so criminal a nature as blasphemy against the holy Ghost. It is very improbable that he who is guilty of it will be reformed, and it is certain that he will not be forgiven unless he exercise a solemn and a serious repentance.

In behalf of this favourable intrepretation two things may be said.

First; the language of the Scriptures is such that very often more is expressed than is to be understood. In the interpretation of such passages the rules of reason, justice, equity, good sense, should be consulted. To mention one passage only, and one suitable to our subject; Jeremiah says, Can the Æthiopian change his skin, or the leopard his spots? then may ye also do good, who are accustomed to do evil. That is; the amendment of an habitual sinner is difficult and unfrequent. The Prophet could not mean more than this, because at the same time he exhorts these sinners to repentance.

Secondly, and which is also parallel to our subject, when the Scriptures affirm one thing and deny another, command this and forbid that, such expressions are

often

SERMON XI.

often to be underſtood, not abſolutely but comparatively, and only a preference is given of the one to the other; as, Labour not for the meat that periſheth, but for the meat which endureth unto everlaſting life; that is, not ſo much for the one as for the other.

According to this way of interpreting, two ſenſes may be given to the words before us, which amount nearly to the ſame thing.

All other ſins of the tongue may be forſaken and forgiven; but there is little reaſon to hope and expect this of blaſphemy againſt the holy Ghoſt.

Or: ſooner ſhall any kind of evil ſpeaking be corrected and find pardon than this.

But ſince the words of the text may imply that this offence would not be pardoned, if we take them in this rigid ſenſe, we muſt ſuppoſe the reaſon, and the only reaſon to be, that they who then offended, and who at any time ſhould offend in that particular manner, would never be changed for the better; which, like other events, was known to Chriſt, and therefore he made no exception in caſe of amendment, but ſpake as a prophet who foreſaw what would come to paſs, and beheld the preſent and the future behaviour of ſuch ſinners.

I conclude with a few obſervations on the ſubject.

1. From the account which hath been given of this crime, it appears how little reaſon ſome melancholy perſons have to fancy themſelves guilty of it, ſince they neither are nor can be in the circumſtances of thoſe who are condemned in the text.

2. We may obſerve that blaſphemy againſt the Holy Ghoſt is not named in the New Teſtament upon any other occaſion, and that the Apoſtles in their Epiſtles have not cautioned men againſt it. There is a crime mentioned by them which approaches near

to

to it, and against which like threatnings are denounced. That crime is a lawful and total apostacy from the profession or practice of Christianity; and these apostates were persons who had either received extraordinary powers themselves from the holy Ghost, or who had seen the miracles wrought by the Apostles in confirmation of the Gospel. Of these it is said, that it is impossible, extremely difficult, to renew them to repentance, that that there remaineth no more sacrifice for their sin, that it is a sin unto death, and there is no reasonable hope and prospect of their recovery.

What hath been observed concerning blasphemy against the holy Ghost, may be said of this sin, that a Christian now cannot fall into it, because he cannot offend against the same evidence.

But though Christians cannot, in these ages and in their present situation, become guilty of the very same faults; they may so far abandon themselves to vice, that their recovery may be highly improbable.

God invites to repentance, and to repentance annexes forgiveness: but, that sinners may not pursue their evil courses upon the fallacious prospect of a future uncertain repentance, he hath in the Scriptures warned us to take timely care that we be not hardened through the deceitfulness of sin.

As by patient continuance in well-doing men will be enabled to perform their duty with ease and cheerfulness, so by complicated and repeated offences they will enter into the condition of those who are represented in the Scriptures as slaves and captives, mortally wounded, deprived of all their senses and powers, and of life itself, and whose amendment is compared to contradictions and natural

ral impossibilities; by which expressions, though they ought not to be interpreted rigorously according to the letter, less cannot be understood than this, that the reformation of such offenders is attended with the greatest difficulty, and that their state is extremely dangerous.

SERMON

SERMON XII.

1 JOHN ii. 15.

Love not the world, neither the things that are in the world.

IF by the world, we understand the earth which we inhabit, and all those who dwell with us, and all the things which surround us, and all that we can possess during our abode here, all the conveniencies of life, and all the objects of our senses, we must suppose that when we are commanded in a general and unlimited manner not to love these things, the meaning is that we must not love these things, too much: for there is a frequent way of speaking in Scripture, according to which, things are forbidden absolutely, which are only to be understood comparatively. Love not the world, that is, Love it not immoderately, and so as to prefer things transitory to things eternal.

If by the world, we understand the vicious world, with all its idle follies and unlawful pleasures, the prohibition is to be understood strictly, and without exception; Love it not at all.

Let us therefore examine how far, and in what sense, the love of the world is forbidden, or when we may be said to love the world too much.

1. We love the world too much, when, for the sake of any profit or pleasure, we wilfully and knowingly, and deliberately, transgress the commandments of God, and become openly and habitually wicked and vicious, and live addicted to sensuality, to intemperance, to fraud,

fraud, to extortion, to injuſtice. Love not the world, neither the things that are in the world: if any man love the world, the love of the Father is not in him: for all that is in the world, the luſt of fleſh, and the luſt of the eyes, and the pride of life, is not of the Father, but is of the world.

By the luſt of the fleſh, is meant ſenſuality and intemperance, unruly appetites, and irregular pleaſures.

By the luſt of the eyes, is meant the love of vain magnificence and ſuperfluous wealth, an eager purſuit and exceſſive fondneſs of it. The deſire of riches is called the luſt of the eyes, becauſe in ſuperfluous and miſapplied wealth, there is nothing to be found, beſides feeding the eyes with an unprofitable object. In ſuch treaſures, ſays Solomon, what good is there to the owners thereof, ſaving the beholding them with their eyes? Speaking of covetouſneſs, he ſays, The eye is never ſatisfied with riches. And hence covetouſneſs, or coveting what belongs to others, is ſometimes called, an evil eye.

By the pride of life, is meant power, power obtained by unlawful means, or exerciſed in an imperious and oppreſſive manner.

Thus the vices, which the Apoſtle compriſes under the love of the wicked world, are theſe; ſenſuality and intemperance, covetouſneſs and rapaciouſneſs, ambition and overbearing inſolence.

That they who are addicted to theſe crimes, love the world too much, and that their love of it cannot be conſiſtent with the love of God, are truths plain and undeniable. They themſelves either renounce all pretences to religion; or, if they call themſelves Chriſtians, are ſelf-condemned, and know that they have no right to that name; or elſe are ignorant in the higheſt degree of the nature and ſpirit of Chriſtianity.

Let us proceed to conſider the **caſe of perſons, who are not ſo guilty as thoſe before mentioned, who have**

have not cast off all regard to God, and to piety, and to virtue, and to their own souls; but are too much addicted to the things of the present life; who love the world more than they ought, and yet sometimes are not sensible of it, and delude themselves, and think that they do nothing amiss.

2. We may therefore, secondly, be said to love the world too much, when we take more pains to obtain and secure the conveniences of this life, than to qualify ourselves for the rewards of the next.

We were made without question for this world, and this world for us; and the good things, the comforts and conveniencies which it contains, are usually placed in our view, and within our reach, as both an incitement and a recompence of our honest industry. They are called in Scripture, gifts of God, which, when he sees proper, he bestows upon his servants. They may therefore be lawfully sought, and lawfully possessed; else they would be pernicious blessings, the gifts of an enemy, and not the favours of our best friend. This we know well enough; and we can practise all that is suitable to this knowledge in providing for our subsistence, and seldom fail in it for want of inclination: but often we forget a much more important truth, that this world is a passage to the next; that our present state lasts a few days, and the next for ever; that in the future, the eternal and unchangeable state, we cannot be happy, unless we carry hence with us, a mind purified from evil inclinations, and capable of delighting in goodness. Forgetting these truths, and suffering the objects of the senses to take possession of our hearts, we are perpetually occupied in pursuing things temporal and transitory, as if there were no hereafter, as if we were to live here for ever, as if our soul were the only safe and the only trifling thing about us. We allot scanty portions and small fragments of our time to subjects sacred and serious, we meditate upon them seldom, and that with too much coldness,

SERMON XII.

coldness, indifference, and dissipation; we stand in need of calamities and disappointments, and such like severe instructors, to take us off from our vain pursuits and foolish occupations. This is to have an undue affection for the world, and not to regard the precepts of our Master, who hath directed us to seek in the first place the kingdom of God, and the righteousness thereof.

3. We love the world too much, when we cannot be contented, or patient and resigned, under low or inconvenient circumstances.

We can readily and cheerfully submit, in our temporal concerns, to present loss or hardship, and forego a present good, when we are encouraged by the prospect of a considerable advantage, which may be thus, and which cannot be otherways, obtained. If therefore we repine, and murmur, and afflict ourselves beyond measure, when things fall not out according to our expectation, we plainly shew that we account temporal prosperity to be the greatest of all blessings; we behave ourselves as if we imagined that God himself could not make us amends, and repay these disappointments with more valuable favours. And yet the Religion which we profess, if it hath any due influence upon us, will teach us to account the light of his countenance, and the remission of sins, and peace of mind, and the hopes of eternal life, to be infinitely superior to all that this fleeting world can bestow; will teach us to seek them with the utmost assiduity, and then if our present situation and state be not such as we perhaps should chuse for ourselves, to bear it decently, remembering that this hath often been the condition of the worthiest persons, of the best servants of God; that to them it is rather an earnest of future happiness, than a mark of divine displeasure; that almost all the great men recorded in sacred and secular history were such as were ennobled by their calamities; and that Christ bequeathed distress and

slights

slights and affronts, as a legacy to his disciples. A Christian therefore in the lowest condition may find resources of support and consolation, and may say to himself; I am not poorer and more afflicted, more despised, or calumniated, than the Son of God was. It can be no intolerable evil, and no real disgrace, to resemble him: he hath given a kind of dignity and lustre to adversity, by condescending to adopt and undergo it.

4. We love the world too much, when we cannot part with any thing that we possess to those who want it, who deserve it, and who have indeed a right to it. This is also to set an immoderate value upon the superfluities of this life, and to act as if we thought that there were no treasures in heaven, no recompence for our kindness to our fellow-creatures, and that God could not exceed us in liberality. This is to forget that we have not an absolute right over our fortunes, or possessions of any kind, which are not given, but lent to us, upon terms and conditions which we must not presume to violate. They who cannot comply with such a duty, a duty to which we have a kind of natural propensity, may judge how they would have behaved themselves, if they had lived in the times of the Apostles, when it frequently happened that all was to be forsaken for the Gospel; or how they would act, if such times should again return: and they may consider whether it be reasonable to suppose that Christ will confess and acknowledge them hereafter for his servants, who would not confess him, if any loss or inconvenience were to follow the confession, and who will part with nothing upon his account, and at his command.

These are the reasons for which our Saviour represented the danger of wealth in such strong expressions as startled his hearers. The evil effects which riches often produce, are the love of riches, and the love of those pernicious pleasures which riches can command,
together

together with many mean cares and immoral practices; and then the man proceeds from bad to worse, and is lost to all that is good and great. Piety and charity can find no room in his breast; Mammon hath taken possession of it, and brings with him other spirits as wicked as himself, and they enter in, and dwell there.

5. We love the world too much, when we envy those who are more fortunate and more favoured by the world than we are, and cannot behold their success without repining; when at the same time we can see others better and wiser, more knowing, more virtuous, and more religious, if they be in a lower state than ourselves, without the least uneasiness, without emulation, and a desire to equal them. This amounts, though perhaps we know it not, to an acknowledgment that we account temporal prosperity to be superior to all endowments of the heart and mind, producing greater complacency and pleasure, the first thing to be pursued, and the last thing to be resigned. But whosoever can entertain such opinions, deserves not that immortal soul, and that understanding which God hath bestowed upon him, and should not have been born a rational creature. Reason improved by Christianity shews us our own dignity, and our own weakness; and these teach a lowliness and a greatness of mind, which agree perfectly together, and neither of which will suffer us to envy the external and trifling and transitory distinctions and advantages possessed by others.

6. We love the world too much, when we honour and esteem and favour persons purely according to their birth, fortunes, and success, measuring our judgment and approbation, by their outward appearance and situation in life. To lawful power, obedience is due; to persons of rank and distinction, that respect which custom hath appointed and established; affability, civility, and courtesy to all: but the esteem which

we have for others, the honour which we pay them in our thoughts and judgment, should be founded on better things, and arise from those good qualities which make them useful to society, and recommend them to the favour of God. Where these good qualities are wanting, and where bad ones supply their place, whatsoever the person be, no more respect is due to him than his station requires. Indeed the respect is paid to the station: the man himself deserves nothing besides contempt or pity.

7. We love the world too much, when we dislike and slight, and despise others, only because the world favours them not, because they are in a low condition; and thus suffer our affections, our judgment, and our behaviour, to be guided and regulated by the notions and customs of men, and indeed of the worst or silliest sort of men, of men who estimate their own and other people's abilities purely by their income, and fancy that a poor man cannot say a good thing, or do a wise one.

8. We love the world too much, when worldly prosperity makes us proud and vain and arrogant, and we expect to be greatly honoured and reverenced by others, only because they are placed beneath us, though in other respects, in valuable qualities, they may surpass us; and when we resent any little failure of homage as a real injury: for if we had a true sense of things, and esteemed them according to their intrinsic value, we should desire no more respect and submission than the laws of order and the welfare of society demand, and we should be more solicitous about securing our rank in the future state, than maintaining it in this.

9. Lastly; We love the world too much, when we omit no opportunity of enjoying the good things of this life, when our great business and serious employment is to amuse and divert ourselves, till we contract an indifference for manly and rational occupations,

ons, deceiving ourselves all the while, and fancying that we are in a safe condition, because we are not so bad as several whom we could name, nor guilty of such and such vices with which the world abounds. The character and state of this sort of persons is described by our Saviour in his parable of the Rich man, whose ground brought forth plentifully. In him we may behold a man, who can boast of a knowledge which few rich persons ever attain, for he knows at least when he hath enough. He lays no projects for improving his great fortunes, either by injustice, fraud, rapine, and oppression, or by anxious care and sordid sparing: he entertains no envy, no hatred, no bad designs against his neighbours: he only proposes to live well, as it is called, and to enjoy himself. But God said unto him: Thou fool, this night thy soul shall be required of thee; then whose shall those things be, which thou hast provided? So is he that layeth up treasure for himself, and is not rich towards God.

Of all the dispositions, which are not directly vicious, there is none of a more deceitful and dangerous nature than a prevalent inclination to diversions and amusements, none which is to be governed with a stricter hand. If this temper be indulged and suffered to grow to a settled habit, it produces a sad variety of inconveniences and evils; it often calls for large expences, and contracts debts and an incapacity to pay them, and this brings on a shameless and hardened dishonesty; it wastes the time, and leaves no leisure, and no taste for piety and industry; it fills the head with a loose train of unprofitable and unconnected fancies; it keeps the imagination awake, and the understanding asleep; it unbends and softens all the powers of the mind, so that the least cross event discomposes it, the slightest calamity wounds it; just as, on the contrary, hardships, and labour, and rational discreet self-denial, strengthen the body, and arm the soul with patience and courage. Thus the better years steal away; worse succeed; no provision is laid up for the evil days; the soul departs hence, and leaves the body, in which she hath trifled so long, enters into the visible world of spirits, naked, disconsolate, deprived of all that was her delight, and weeps for her children, for her sensual pleasures, and refuseth to be comforted, because they are not.

I have shewed when and in what degrees and circumstances our love of the world is unlawful, whence we learn what the duty of a Christian is, and what the disposition of his mind ought to be, with relation to the world. The corrupted world, with its vicious maxims and loose practices, he is to renounce, to have no fellowship or compliance with it, and no regard and esteem for it. His affections must be fixed on no unlawful objects. Nor is this prohibition to be accounted grievous and severe. It deprives us only of those things which for our own sake we ought to shun, though God had given us no command concerning them. The pleasures of society and of friendship, and the things which conduce to our present ease and satisfaction, to the improvement of our minds, and to the support of our body; and even riches and honours and power, when they are not bought too dear, at the expence of something more valuable, and when we employ them as we ought, are not forbidden by the precept which enjoins us, not to love the world. There are things relating to the present life, which we call good things, and which deserve that name, things convenient for us during our abode here below, such as liberty, and health, and food, and raiment, and a state of independency, and reputation, and friends, and relations. The love of these things is natural; nor doth Religion absolutely forbid this love, but only limits and moderates it. It commands us to love them rationally, and with a due subordination to objects more excellent, and of greater concern to us; and to prefer the favour of God, the cause of virtue, the good of mankind, and our own eternal welfare, to all these precarious possessions.

SERMON XII.

ons. He who hath such dispositions may be truly said, not to love the world overmuch.

Such dispositions therefore we must endeavour to acquire; and if our endeavours be sincere, they will certainly be succesful; for God hath abundantly enabled us to overcome an immoderate love of the world, and hath so dealt with us, and so ordered the course of things, that we shall never want powerful motives and incitements to set our affections more on things above than on things below.

The doctrine of a future state should seem even alone to be sufficient for this purpose. Rewards are proposed to us which surpass beyond comparison the most valuable things of this life, and the loss of which cannot be compensated by gaining the whole world. One might therefore suppose that whosoever firmly believes this revelation of immortality, cannot love in any degree any thing that tends to deprive him of this inestimable reward, and cannot love immoderately temporal and transitory objects.

But because this recompence of well-doing is unseen and future, and for that reason affects us more faintly, whilst worldly objects strike immediately upon our senses, and worldly temptations press upon us from all sides; that we might not be seduced by these allurements, God hath with great wisdom and kindness so ordered things, that there should be nothing here below, fit to engross and enslave our hearts.

Happy it is for us, that it is so; for (a) how should we dote on the world, if it always favoured us, when we love it still, false and ungrateful as it is! With all its imperfections it is too dear to us, though we seen them, and feel them, and resent them. We behave ourselves in this respect, as we do sometimes to those

for

(a) O Munde, teneri, vis pergens: quid faceris, si remaneres? quam non deciperes dulcis, si amarus alimenta mentiris?

for whom we have a strong affection: we love them best, when we complain of them most.

Lest the wicked world should seduce us, such is the appointed course of causes and effects, that all extravavant desires, all vicious dispositions, all unlawful pleasures, bring with them, or draw after them, innumerable evils, bodily distempers, uneasiness of mind, poverty, shame, remorse, disgrace, hatred, and enmity.

The objects which worldly-minded persons so eagerly pursue, cannot be obtained, or not without great difficulty. What the Scripture saith of Charity, is in some degree applicable to Ambition or Worldly-mindedness; It suffereth long, beareth all things, hopeth all things, endureth all things; and all this to a very poor purpose, or to no purpose. Wealth, and power, and intemperate pleasures, lie often beyond the reach of their adorers; and though a man be willing to purchase them at any rate, and even to sell his country, his honour, his soul, or his Saviour for them, he is frequently disappointed, and hath the toil and the guilt without success. He lives in a corrupted world, amidst innumerable competitors, all as bad as himself, and all pursuing the same end; and as he will not stick to deceive and injure them, if he can gratify his passions by it, so are they ready to do the same to him. In the paths of virtue and religion there is room for all, and they may be good without any inconvenience to each other: but it is not so in the kingdom of vice, in which every one hath innumerable wants, and insatiable cravings. The vicious World is not wide enough for all those who would be eminent in it; and therefore a wicked man is in continual danger of suffering by the ill offices of those who are like himself, of being supplanted by their superior diligence, subtilty, and success. Even they whom he calls his friends, may prove his enemies; for such men usually have no friends, in the true sense of the word, but only partners in iniquity.

And

And should he be so fortunate as to obtain his heart's desire, it may come too late; for if remorse of mind, or pain, or sickness, and a decay of the senses, come along with it, these will make every thing disagreeable or indifferent to him.

Add to this, that he will find all vain and sinful objects of the affections, all irregular pleasures, in their own nature empty and illusive. They appear best at a distance; familiarity discovers to him their defects; and experience, the only instructor of fools, teaches him the inconveniencies which attend them; and then perhaps he finds out some other trifle to love and pursue, and runs the same circle over again of desire and discontent.

Every vicious person finds himself at last far from happiness, hath fears which nothing can remove, and wants which nothing can satisfy; whence he might learn, if it were not perhaps too late, that religion is not so severe and morose in its commands and prohibitions as he imagines; that, even setting aside the consideration of a future state, virtue in most cases is to be sought for her own sake; and that the most probable way to pass our days in quiet, is to have few, and those moderate, desires.

Lastly; Not only the vicious, but even the innocent pleasures of this world are empty and deceitful in some respects. Life itself, the fountain and foundation of them all, is most uncertain. Health, without which life is not life, is soon and easily, and irretrievably lost. The days of our abode here are few; the days of our youth and strength are fewer. The public welfare, and our own private possessions are precarious and exposed to many dangers. Our friends and relations sometimes are removed far from us, sometimes fall into calamities from which we cannot deliver them, sometimes die before us, sometimes prove ungrateful and undutiful.

These

SERMON XII.

These are undoubtedly evils out of which good may arise; they are harsh and severe instructors, but they teach useful knowledge; they are distasteful remedies, but they remove dangerous distempers. They are designed to make us modest and humble in prosperity, and patient in adversity, careful to secure ourselves an inheritance in heaven, and indifferent to every thing that of its own nature is changeable and transitory. When these profitable effects are produced in us, we are not only disposed and qualified to live hereafter with God and good beings, but to enjoy at present all the happiness that ought to be expected in this state of trial and disorder.

SERMON

SERMON XIII.

PSALM ciii. 15, 16.

As for man, his days are as grass; as a flower of the field, so he flourisheth; for the wind passeth over it, and it is gone, and the place thereof shall know it no more.

THIS is the season in which our Church calls upon us to contemplate the last scene of our Saviour's sufferings; and amongst the various uses which may be made of this solemn and affecting subject, one is, to be reminded by it of our own transitory condition, and of our approaching latter end. The Lessons, the Epistle, and the Gospel for the day, are so many Lectures upon mortality, and a sort of Funeral Discourses.

Our Lord was a man like unto us, and to him as well as to us may properly be applied the words of the Text. He was a Flower, which flourisheth for a little time, and then fades and falls. His days were few and evil; there he was like us: but none of those days were lost or misemployed; there we are not like him. Count his life by his mornings and evenings; it was a short one. Count it by his acts of industry and charity, and by the great works which he accomplished; and it will seem a long one, a life of ages. Let us then turn our thoughts upon ourselves, and upon our own mortality.

When our first parent had trespassed, he and in him all his posterity were condemned to sojourn here for a time, and then to lie down in the grave, and return to the earth out of which they were taken.

If

If we consider ourselves as offenders in many things, which we all are, death is a just consequence of our transgressions; for it is fit and reasonable that disobedient creatures should be deprived of the powers which they pervert and abuse. If we consider life in its most favourable view, as affording variety of satisfaction, as the first thing which we love, and the last thing which we would forsake, death is the loss of that much beloved blessing, an eternal farewell to this earth, and to all its objects with which we are so well acquainted, and in which we so much delight. If we spend our days here in a wicked manner, death becomes still more formidable, not only as a deprivation of life and of its pleasures, but as the beginning of woe, and an entrance into a state of horror and despair. If we take a view of life on its disagreeable side, as abounding with disappointment and sorrow, and such it is to many of us, death is a refuge from all those evils, a deep and a quiet repose (*a*), which human calamities cannot approach and disturb. If we consider ourselves as Christians, and live suitably to our profession, death is in no small measure disarmed of its terrors, it becomes in some sort a favour and a blessing, it is a short and a safe passage to holiness and to happiness in our Father's house.

Many are the descriptions of the shortness and uncertainty of life in the holy Scriptures. They compare our present state to clouds dispersed by the wind, to a dream, to a shadow, to the flowers and the grass of the field, which flourish in the morning, and in the evening are cut down and withered, to smoke, to a vapour which appeareth for a little time and vanisheth away, to a tale that is told, to the remembrance of a guest who tarrieth but a day, to the path of a ship through the waves, to the flight of a bird, and of an arrow through the air.

Other celebrated writers have exercised themselves upon the same subject; and their expressions are usually

---

(*a*) Dulcis et alta quies, placidoque simillima somno.

ally true and pathetic. They are true, because life, when compared to eternity, is such a trifle that the wit of man cannot find out images which shall represent it more fleeting, and less considerable, than it is. They are pathetic, because grief is eloquent; and few have turned their thoughts this way who have not a melancholy temper, or who have not been acquainted with disappointments and afflictions. They who live at their ease seldom care to meditate upon death, or to read or to hear any thing that relates to mortality, or to see any thing that puts them in mind of it. And if indeed by avoiding to think upon death we could escape it, it might seem best to employ our minds in other contemplations and occupations; but since it will overtake us, and fall heaviest upon those who have considered it least, it is not possible to be duly prepared for it without frequent reflections upon it in our better days, and during the whole course of our life.

Complaints of those many disasters and sufferings which take off so much from the satisfaction of human life, and bring on decay and dissolution, serve to no good purpose, and tend rather to relax and weaken the mind, and to make us discontented and dispirited. But there is a way of considering this subject, which is manly, and rational, and philosophical, and religious; which justifies these dispensations of providence, and arms us with fortitude and patience against all events, and teaches us to possess our souls in peace;

I. By proving that our present state of mortality is convenient and useful to us upon many accounts:

II. By pointing out to us the most proper means which we can use, to cure ourselves of an immoderate fear of death.

I. Let us then, first, endeavour to prove that our present state of mortality is upon many accounts convenient and useful.

It is convenient that we should die, because this world is a state of trial.

God

God hath given us an immortal soul, he clothes it with a body, and he first places us here, where we feel a succession of pain and pleasure, of satisfaction and uneasiness. From the uneasiness we are taught to desire a better state; and from the satisfaction we are warned to fear lest we should fall into a worse. Thus is our condition neither completely good nor bad, but suitable to a time of probation, inciting us to hope more happiness and to dread more evil than we have hitherto experienced.

The end for which we are sent into this world is, to serve God, to be useful to mankind, to cultivate and improve our mind, and to make a constant progress in knowledge and in virtuous habits; which if we do, God will reward us; if we do not, we must expect to lose his favour, and consequently to be miserable. This is our business, this is our work, a work of the utmost importance, and a work of some difficulty, because there are obstacles and temptations which lie in our way, and interpose between us and our duty, and conspire to deprive us of our recompence, and to draw upon us a future punishment. Such are our own inclinations and passions, which unless discreetly governed, degenerate so as to become vices, and persuade us to make an ill use of the good things of this world; such is bad example, with which we are constantly surrounded; the seeming prosperity of many wicked persons, and their endeavours to corrupt us by persuasion, flattery, or rewards, and to discourage us from virtue by ridicule or ill usage.

In this state and situation, whilst these affections are within us, and these objects round about us, if we were not subject to mortality, and to bodily infirmities which accompany it, we should probably be more prone to evil than we now are; so that, amongst the assistances which God affords us to conquer the enemies to our salvation, we may reckon death as none of the least.

SERMON XIII.

least. There are seducing infatuating pleasures in vice, and there are sometimes inconveniences and hardships in virtue; but there is such a thing as death, and in that one word are contained many motives to us to despise those pleasures, and not to be disheartened at those inconveniences.

Again; as the consideration of death hath a tendency to deter us from vice, it consequently prevents some disorders, and makes us live together in society better than we else should pass our days.

As it is, though we are weak and infirm creatures, and through pain and sickness and decays often dead to this world before we leave it, though our stay here be always uncertain, and short at the very longest, yet, forgetting the future state to which we are hastening, and fixed upon the follies of the present, we multiply transgressions against God and our neighbour, and are no less deficient in our duty to ourselves. Hence we may (*b*) conjecture that the behaviour of men would be worse, if the fear of pain and death, and of other evils, to which mortality exposes us, did not restrain many, upon whose stubborn and base tempers gentler methods and more generous motives would prove ineffectual. This may keep several from some enormities, which their inclinations would teach them to commit, if they were sure to continue here for ever in health and vigour, or even to have their life protracted to a considerable length.

As many persons have perverse and unsociable dispositions, and take little delight in performing acts of humanity, it is in some respects a favour and a blessing that such are parted so soon, and called away

from

(*b*) Si mors certæ constituta esset ætati, fieret homo insolentissimus, et humanitate omni careret. Nam fere omnia jura humanittais, quibus inter nos cohæremus, ex metu & conscientia fragilitatis oriuntur, &c. *Lactantius*, De Opif. Dei.

from plaguing and injuring each other, and from disturbing the common peace. We read in Genesis, that before the flood the wickedness of men was exceeding great, and the thoughts of their hearts only evil continually; that the earth was filled with violence, and that Noah and his small family were the only persons who escaped destruction. By the extraordinary punishment with which God visited that generation, we may conclude that their offences were as extraordinary; and this excess of impiety might perhaps be partly occasioned by the usual length of life at that time, which so far surpassed the present period.

It is also convenient that we should die, because the future recompences of obedience are of a spiritual nature.

If we perform our duty here, God promiseth us a great reward in the kingdom of heaven; but this is a reward in the expectation or possession of which none besides a virtuous person can take delight. It consists in love and friendship, and in the society of good beings, in a great improvement in knowledge, in a release from evil affections and temptations to sin, in praising and serving God. Now let it be considered that our senses here are employed before our understanding, that outward objects get the first possession of our minds, and engross too large a share of our affections; and that some, who abstain from heinous offences, and have many virtues and good qualities, are often too fond of the things of this life, too careful about them, too unwilling to leave or lose them. Hence it evidently appears, that when such is the disposition of our mind, death and the usual forerunners of death are useful to us. The world appears too amiable, and steals upon our hearts. Here we would willingly stay; here we would fix our abode if we might. But the pains of a body tending to dissolution, decays, and infirmities, reminding

us

SERMON XIII.

us that we must think of going hence, and lessening the satisfaction which we take in temporal blessings, and in all earthly things, unloose by gentle degrees the bonds that hold us too fast to outward objects, teach the mind to look out for something else, on which it may fix its desires, and from things sensible and transitory raise it to things spiritual and eternal.

Another reason why it is convenient that we should die, is, that our obedience at best being defective, death prepares us for the next state, and excites in the soul thoughts and inclinations which ought to accompany it at its entrance into the world of spirits, and into the presence of its Maker.

If we consider God, how just he is, how great, how holy and pure, and ourselves how imperfect and unworthy to stand before him; how numerous our offences have been, and how many spots our soul hath contracted during its union with the body, we shall find many reasons to fear him, to be filled with a religious dread and confusion at the thought of appearing in his presence, and of giving an account of ourselves to our great judge.

It is therefore very reasonable that we sinful creatures should enter into our future state through the dark and melancholy and humbling passage of death and the grave; that we should lie down in our Mother's bosom, and mix with the dust from which we were taken, and where we should lie for ever, if God were not as merciful as he is powerful. Death is a kind of Purgatory, which it is expedient for us to undergo, before we return to Him who made us. It may be observed of those who through the course of their lives have preserved a sober regard to their duty, and a desire of pleasing God, and who therefore may entertain a reasonable hope of forgiveness, that their good dispositions exert themselves most at the close of their days, and that the last acts of religion

gion are usually the best performed. When the time of their departure approaches, they are more perfectly sensible of the vanity of all earthly things, and of the value of God's favour; they humbly acknowledge their trespasses, they put their whole trust in the mercy of God, and in the mediation of Christ; they submit to the divine will with a pious resignation, and depart hence with thoughts and dispositions acceptable in the sight of God.

The Jews had a notion, that death was an expiation for the sins of life. This opinion, with a few restrictions, is not so absurd as it may seem to some. If we disclaim all merit arising from our imperfect virtues, and allow no expiation, strictly so called, besides that of our Saviour, thus much we may suppose, that meekly to acknowledge ourselves sinners, who as such ought to die, and to undergo this dissolution as a chastisement which we deserve, without repining and murmuring, and with a decent submission, is an act of piety and obedience, which shall by no means lose its reward.

It is not only convenient, but indeed it is desirable and profitable that we should die, if death conducts us to life eternal. Death at first was inflicted as a punishment; but our Lord hath considerably mitigated it, hath in a great measure disarmed it of its terrors, and, having first conquered it himself, puts it in our power to follow his triumph, and to partake of his victory. We may therefore, if we be wise and good, so spend our few days here, that death shall be to us the end of trouble, and the beginning of peace and happiness.

Lastly, if by obedience and perseverance we secure to ourselves an inheritance in the kingdom of God, when that promised time shall come, and this corruptible shall put on incorruption, the remembrance of our former earthly state, and of all its inconveniences, may probably add to our happiness; and then it will be good for us that we once were mortal creatures.

tures. Certain it is, that we are now difpofed to receive pleafure from thinking of the evils through which we have paffed after we have efcaped them. There is not a perfon living, who, to make his fortunes, or to perform his duty, hath taken great pains, and expofed himfelf to many dangers, and endured great hardfhips, and whofe honeft labours have been rewarded with fuccefs, who is not alfo delighted with the (c) recollection of the toil and peril which he has undergone in thofe days. Such may be our temper hereafter; and they who, having overcome the vices and temptations of the world, are fafely arrived at thofe bleffed manfions where no evil of any kind is permitted to enter, may find no fmall fatisfaction in remembering their troublefome paffage through this vale of tears, and in comparing the vain world, which is paffed away, and is no more, with the eternal kingdom into which God hath gracioufly received them.

II. Let us now, fecondly, confider the methods which we muft ufe to allay and reftrain thofe immoderate fears of death, which are blameable, and which alfo render life itfelf, with all its conveniences, dull and comfortlefs.

Frequent thoughts of our latter end will affift to produce this good effect.

As timorous perfons are obferved in danger to fhut their eyes, and fhun the fight of the evil which they dread, though thereby they often only expofe themfelves the more, and lofe the opportunity of faving their lives; fo it is with thofe who greatly fear death. They induftrioufly fly the thoughts of it at all times, and thereby they only increafe that natural dread, and make death infupportable, whenfoever it comes. And as courage is improved by repeated approaches to danger, and a long familiarity with it; fo, if we have death often in our minds, and contract as it were an intimacy with

(c) See Grangæus on Juvenal, xii. 81.

with it, we lessen the abhorrence of it. Therefore, if we would quit our present being with decency, and without great consternation, we should always look upon the hour of departure as at hand, and think with ourselves, as often as we go forth to our worldly affairs, that we may never return home again; and as often as we lie down to rest, that we may wake no more to this world.

Another way of reconciling ourselves to death, is to consider it as unavoidable. That we ought to meet with boldness what we cannot shun, and endure it with all the constancy which human nature can summon, and that it is folly to act otherwise, is one of the plainest dictates of reason. Though it must be confessed that this consideration affords little comfort under extreme pain, or extraordinary afflictions, yet in many evils it hath its use, and in particular it may help us to lessen the fears of death. It has been observed of many persons in great danger, that, so long as there remained hopes and possibility of escaping it, they have been timorous; but, when all hopes were cut off, they have grown bold, and despair itself has given them courage.

Another consideration tending to make us more willing to die is, that it is (*d*) common to all.

God hath created beings who never die, as the Angels; but they live in another world, and have seldom shewed themselves to men. And it is best that it should be so. If they and we had frequently conversed together, we might perhaps envy their immortality, and die with more reluctance, beholding so many happy and glorious creatures free from that change. But now we inhabit a place where we see all about us subject to the same fate, and may teach and learn resignation to a law from which nothing here is exempted. Not only the powerful and the wise, but the most righteous, must undergo it. We read of only two who died not, Enoch and Elias; and we may justly suppose that, not for their righteousness

---

(*d*) See *Seneca* Consol. ad Polyb. c. 21.

SERMON XIII.

righteousness did God deliver them from death, but rather to confirm men in the belief of another life; for though they were very good men, yet in the holy Scriptures there are persons recorded as good as they, and as much in the favour of God.

The troubles of life, rightly considered, may help to remove a great dislike of death. The same good and wise Providence, which hath appointed us so few days for our abode here, hath made that abode inconvenient in many respects, that we might be the better disposed to leave it; and to those who are not so disposed, Providence seems to say; Can you bear neither the disease, nor the remedy? You are unwilling to suffer; you are unwilling to be released. What can be done for you.

Through how many troubles we pass, I need not say, nor reckon up those disagreeable and inseparable attendants on frail mortality. Every one knows them, every one feels them, more or less. Even they who meet with the fewest causes of uneasiness, have often the unhappy art of creating them, and of becoming more wretched than they need to be. I shall therefore only observe, that, in our progress here, the evils of life commonly increase upon us, and its pleasures diminish, till we come to a declining age, which has for the most part, to many of us at least, so much to make it unacceptable, that the fear of it, if we have not yet reached it, or the burden of it, if we lie under it, might teach us more indifference to the present world. What Solomon says of knowledge, may as truly be said of life; In much of it is much grief, and he who increaseth days, increaseth sorrow. To outlive our dearest friends and relations, our health, our strength, our memory, in short, every thing except perhaps some follies and weaknesses, this is the prospect upon which he who is greedy of many days sets his heart; this is the state which he who experiences, and is still in love with life,

may

may be said to be born again, not in the Christian sense, but as one who enters into a second childhood.

Another remedy against immoderate fears of death is a good life. This I mention as the last and best, and indeed the only one to which we can trust; and I barely mention it, because it is an evident truth, which wants no confirmation.

I have shewed, that on many accounts it is fit and reasonable, and may be advantageous to us, that we should be mortal creatures, and that there are various motives which should dispose us to depart with decency and resignation. If they have no effect at all upon us, the reason is that our faith and obedience are defective. Either we suspect that death is the utter destruction of soul and body, or we fear to go into a state worse than that which we leave. From both these causes of consternation a Christian life will secure us. He who believes the Gospel, and endeavours to conform himself to it, will find in his faith, and in the testimony of his conscience, consolations against the terrors of death. It must not be said or expected, that he will intirely overcome the fear of it, because some persons are by constitution and temper less resolute than others, and even the most resolute would probably prefer life to death, if they had their choice. But most assuredly he will not have that dread of it which he would have felt, if he had spent his days in folly and iniquity.

SERMON XIV.

MATTH. v. 5.

Blessed are the meek.

MEEKNESS by writers of Morality is called a virtue which is exercised in restraining and moderating our anger. According to this description, a meek man is one who with an even temper can bear misfortunes and injuries, which would raise the violent wrath of an impatient person.

But in the Scriptures meekness is a more extensive virtue.

Sometimes it signifies a courteous and peaceable disposition. Sometimes it denotes humility, lowliness, and a modest opinion of ourselves; sometimes patience under ill usage or bad circumstances. Sometimes by it seems to be understood a pliable and teachable temper. Sometimes, as one virtue is put for all, and a part of religion for the whole, it may mean any or every kind of righteousness. Sometimes also it stands opposed to wickedness in general, and then likewise it means the same as goodness.

Again; as meekness, strictly speaking, is opposed to excessive anger, and as men are often angry, not only at men, but at God himself, and under hard circumstances repine at providence, there is no reason why meekness may not also mean a patient submission to the calamities which fall upon us, from the consideration
that

that they are permitted by a wife and good Mind directing and overuling all things.

I shall at present consider meekness as a social virtue, and as a virtue opposed not only to wrath, but to pride, stubbornness, moroseness, austerity, peevishness, and ill-nature; and as it may be called a quiet and gentle temper producing a mild behaviour towards others.

Meekness and good-nature are nearly alike; and the difference seems to be only this, that good-nature, as the word implies, is an original propensity; but meekness is an habit acquired and preserved by a right use of reason.

The nature of meekness is best discovered by descending into particulars, and considering the several relations which we bear to different persons, and the conduct towards them which meekness produces.

As we are members of civil society, we live under laws and magistrates appointed to enforce them. Now meekness produces a dutiful submission to those who are set in authority over us, a willing obedience to them in all things lawful, particularly in things which conduce to the common good, and a respect to them in our outward behaviour, in our words and actions, for the sake of the public character which they bear, though their personal qualities should be such, that it may be impossible to esteem them.

To the laws of our country meekness teaches us a quiet submission, as we are private persons, even though they may prove inconvenient to us, and lay us under hardships, or though through the licentiousness of the times it may be in our power to violate them with impunity.

Meekness towards our parents and instructors disposes us to be modest, obliging and tractable, to obey them in all things which contradict not our duty to God and to the Public; and if at any time we are bound to dissent from them, and to plead our reasons for it, to take care that we do it with due civility and submission; to

bear

bear with their weaknesses, and especially with those which arise from the infirmities of old age.

Much deference and honour is due to the aged: and has been usually paid to them by wise and polite nations. We ought to be courteous to those who have so short a time to stay with us, and to make the burden of years as easy, and the evening of life as comfortable to them as we can. Hereby we gain the love and friendship of persons, who through observation and experience are often enabled to repay our kindness with good advice and instruction, and we may reasonably hope to find that respect ourselves hereafter which we have shewed to our elders.

A great part of the behaviour which meekness requires from children to parents, is also due from servants to masters. For, as every master should account himself the parent of his family, and consider in some sort his servants as his children; so every servant should love and honour and assist such a master, as if he were his parent, and pay him a ready and a chearful obedience. The Apostles, in very strong terms, both set forth the duty of masters to servants, and enjoin servants to obey their masters with diligence, willingness, humility, and patience, even under ill usage. But it ought to be observed, that as their condition, so their duty now is not altogether the same that it was in ancient times, in the times of the Apostles. Servants then usually were slaves; now their service is no more than what arises from contract and agreement.

Meekness discovers itself in courtesy and condescension to our inferiors. Such a person, in his intercourse with those of a lower station, will conceal his superiority as much as he can, will seem to have forgotten it, or to be ignorant of it; he will place them as nearly upon the level with himself as the laws of good order permit, though possibly custom authorised by pride and vanity may not greatly favour such condescension.

Meekness

Meekness consists in shewing humanity and mercy towards our enemies, in moderating our wrath when we are provoked, and in the forgiveness of injuries. Herein is this virtue chiefly tried and exerted; and by our behaviour upon such occasions we may best know whether we possess it.

As also by our behaviour towards those who are in error, if we undertake to reclaim or to confute them; for meekness will incline us to contend for a good cause with calmness and candour, especially with those who act with decency and civility. They who in such contests have recourse to ridiculing, railing, insulting, and reviling, may call it pious warmth and zeal for religion; but in this they either deceive or are deceived. He who loves the Truth, will never do all that lies in his power to make his brother hate it. But this is what every one does, who treats another with rudeness and insolence on account of his mistakes.

Meekness towards sinners is accompanied with endeavours to lead them to repentance and amendment by gentle methods, whilst there is any hope that lenity may have a due effect, and in rebuking and restraining them in a manner which may shew that we desire their temporal and eternal welfare, and that we hate the vice, not the person.

Meekness, as it relates to those who are committed to our care, and placed under our government, will dispose us to make their state of subjection easy to them, never to have recourse to rigour and severity when it can be avoided, to excuse smaller faults which proceed not from a bad mind, to persuade them rather than to compel them, to conduct them like rational creatures by reason and encouragement, that their inclinations may go along with their actions, and that they may take a delight in their duty.

Meekness, as it is exercised towards all persons in general, is shewed in studying to live peaceably with them, in complying with them in things indifferent, in

observing

SERMON XIV.

observing whatsoever innocent custom and fashion have established, and in yielding sometimes and departing from our right, especially in smaller matters, for the sake of quiet.

Such is the nature of meekness, and the behaviour which it produces in all stations, upon all occasions, and towards all persons. The most plain and artless description of this virtue is at the same time the recommendation of it; and to persuade any reasonable person to love and esteem it, it is sufficient to shew him what it is, and what actions it produces. But the good effects arising from it will more fully and distinctly appear, if we consider,

I. The usefulness of it to society.
II. Its usefulness to ourselves.

I. As to the first; The end of society is the benefit of every person belonging to it. Men formed themselves into communities, that they might enjoy their rights, and the fruits of their industry, and mutually support and assist each other; and if all men would steddily pursue the end for which society is instituted, and do all the good to others that was within their power, they would escape a multitude of evils, and enjoy as much tranquillity and satisfaction as this world can afford.

But men are men; they have usually a mixture of good and bad qualities, and in some of them the evil outweighs the good; and when such beings enter into society, each contributes to the whole, to the common stock, not only his labour, his skill, his understanding, his abilities, his possessions, but his imperfections, his follies, and his vices. In all societies several will be found, who are often swayed in their actions, not by justice and benevolence, but by unruly passions and private interest. Hence there arises a necessity that Laws should be made, to restrain such unreasonable and ill-disposed persons, and that the laws should appoint and require a punishment suitable to the offence.

Yet

Yet human laws are and must be liable to two defects, which meekness alone can supply, and which, if it were more exercised, it would in a great measure remove.

One defect in human laws is, that they cannot possibly be extended to all offences against our neighbour. There are many breaches of our social duties, which produce much mischief in society, and yet must be out of the reach of laws, because it is impracticable to call every such offender to account, to pass a just judgment upon his fault, and to assign proper punishments of it. Human laws can only take cognisance of the more notorious crimes; they cannot, for example, conveniently punish uncharitableness, covetousness, selfishness, insincerity, lying, stubbornness, pride, moroseness, rudeness, ingratitude, and such unsocial qualities.

We (*a*) read that some (*b*) nations had laws against ingratitude. But (*c*) gratitude is a voluntary recompence

(*a*) Grotius de Jur. B. II. xxv. p. 261. Ed. Gronov.
(*b*) The Persians, the Athenians, and the Romans also; though Seneca speaks as if he were not acquainted with the Statutes of his own nation concerning it. It is true that between equals there could be no Action for Ingratitude; but there are laws against the ingratitude of freedmen, and of sons and daughters, which are to be found in the *Digests*.

Ingratos, de quibus patroni quererentur, revocavit [Claudius] in servitutem. *Suetonius* Claud. 25.

(*c*) *Athenis*—adversus ingratos actio constituta est. Et recte; quia dandi et accipiendi beneficii commercium, sine quo vix vita hominum constat, perdit et tollit quisquis benemerito parem referre gratiam negligit. *Valer. Maximus*, V. iii. 3.

But Seneca is of another opinion, and says,

Hoc tam invisum vitium, an impunitum esse debeat, quæritur: et an hæc lex, quæ in scholis exercetur, etiam in civitate ponenda sit, qua ingrati datur actio.—Magnum hoc argumentum dandam non fuisse; quia adversus maleficium omne consensimus, et homicidii, veneficii, parricidii, violatarum religionum, aliubi atque aliubi diversa pœna est; sed ubique aliqua. Hoc frequentissimum crimen nusquam punitur, ubique improbatur. Neque absolvimus illud: sed cum difficilis esset incertæ rei æstimatio, tantum odio damnavimus, et inter ea reliquimus quæ ad judices Deos mittimus. Rationes autem multæ mihi occurrunt, propter quas crimen hoc in legem cadere non debeat, &c. *De Benef.* iii. 6.

SERMON XIV.

pence for benefits voluntarily bestowed. In acts of generosity and kindness, it is supposed that the person who confers a favour, confers it without requiring a promise of a return; else it would not be giving, but trading and selling. In acts of gratitude, the obliged person requites according to his inclination and abilities. He is often the best judge of the value of the kindness which he has received, and of the circumstances increasing or lessening it; and he returns good offices, favours, and services; perhaps he hath nothing to give besides his heart, he repays benefits with love, honour, and respect, which are no contemptible returns, and prove him to be truly grateful. But human Courts cannot measure the degrees of love and honour which are due to a benefactor, or the manner in which they should be expressed. These and other reasons may be given, to shew that such laws should not be made, and cannot be executed.

National laws being thus necessarily imperfect, and incapable of securing the public tranquillity; men, to supply this defect, have added to them another law, the law of Civility or Good-manners. This is a law of custom, established by common consent; and the violation of it is punished by the general disapprobation and contempt which the offenders against it usually undergo. But this law also is insufficient for the purposes for which it is designed; as may be known, if we consider that civility for the most part is outside shew, dwells upon the tongue and in the carriage, and is not required to extend itself to acts of real beneficence towards others, especially towards those who have offended us; so that one may observe the laws of civility and decency, and yet be deficient in his duty to his neighbour.

But, in those (*d*) cases in which the laws fall short of their

---

(*d*) Quam angusta innocentia est, ad legem bonum esse! quanto latius officiorum patet, quam juris regula! quam multa pietas, humanitas, liberalitas, justitia, fides exigunt, quæ omnia extra publicas tabula sunt! *Seneca* De Ira, ii. 27.

their design, a meek person will be a law to himself, and shew more courtesy, humanity, and condescension, than they require of him.

Another imperfection in human laws is, that sometimes they will be too severe, and consequently will give ill-disposed men an opportunity of treating others with inhumanity, and of exercising that strict justice which is no better than injustice. For this reason a power is usually vested in the Supreme Magistrate to mitigate the asperity of the laws, when equity requires it.

Reputation is valuable upon several accounts, and often brings great advantage, besides great satisfaction, to the possessor; the loss of it may grievously hurt the mind, the body, and the fortunes, of the sufferer. A detracting calumniating liar is sometimes more pernicious and more detestable than a thief and a robber. It is therefore expedient that the Law should endeavour to secure to us our character from injury no less than other things to which we have a right, and that it should punish defamation. But if a person should revenge every slight offence of that kind which hath been heedlessly and rashly committed against him, and require legal satisfaction, he might himself in so doing be almost as blameable as those who had wronged him.

To deter men from laziness, extravagance, and injustice, there is a necessity that the laws should guard the property of the subject, and enable him to recover it from those who are indebted to him. But sometimes a person, by severely requiring his own, may do nothing which the Law of his country forbids, and yet may offend against the sacred and everlasting law of Mercy. Several like cases there are, in which we must consider, not what the Public permits, but what becomes us, as men and as Christians, to do to our fellow-creature and to our brother.

Our Saviour declared to his hearers, that in courtesy and good offices they were bound to exceed the rules which custom had established amongst them; and that it it was their duty in many inſtances to depart from their right, and not to inſiſt upon thoſe puniſhments and payments which the laws of retaliation and of reſtitution enjoined.

On all theſe occaſions a meek perſon carries in his own breaſt a law of equity, to conſult, and is guided by it, and will paſs over ſlighter offences, though ſtrict juſtice would give him leave to take harſher methods.

From the foregoing obſervations it appears that meekneſs is in a moſt eminent manner a ſocial virtue, a virtue which, if generally practiſed, would cauſe men to live peaceably together, endeavouring to excel in humanity, ſupplying what is deficient, and ſoftening what is ſevere, in the national laws by which they are governed.

II. Let us now, ſecondly, conſider the uſefulneſs of this virtue to ourſelves.

Every virtue is profitable, as it is a behaviour ſuitable to right reaſon, and an act of obedience paid to the commands of God, and as it conduces to our ſalvation. But beſides theſe, meekneſs hath ſome peculiar advantages and recompences.

To receive returns of humanity, to be eſteemed for our good qualities, and not cenſured ſeverely for our failings, to meet with kindneſs from thoſe with whom we converſe, will contribute much to our preſent happineſs, and is what we all would willingly obtain, and what is uſually an object of our deſires. Thoſe deſires would ſeldom be diſappointed if we were ſuch ourſelves towards others as we would have others be towards us. Men unjuſt in many things, and blind to their own failings, yet can eaſily diſcover and readily cenſure the faults of their neighbour. Pride, if grounded upon ſuperiority, is deteſted; if accompanied with no merit, is deſpiſed. An implacable, fierce, contentious, and inhuman temper is expoſed to the reproaches and averſion even of thoſe in whom the ſame evil diſpoſitions are to be found. But many perſons, who are proud, envious,

envious, and contentious, will often shew more courtesy and favour to those who are free from those faults, than to those who are like themselves. Pride will frequently conceal itself from the humble, and content itself with a secret applause and preference. Anger grows cool when it is not provoked by opposition. Envy will scarcely find an object for its aversion in the meek and gentle. He who is adorned with these qualities, which can so often make insolence and wrath and strife disappear at their appearance, and be ashamed to shew themselves, hath the best prospect of enjoying peace in this world, and of finding a present reward in his meekness; at least, he hath the satisfaction of knowing that he deserves it.

By possessing this virtue he possesses also an inward calm, unknown to perverse, insolent and turbulent tempers. He is not disquieted with pride and envy, nor distracted with anger, and hatred, and desires of revenge. To see the prosperity of others, gives him no pain; to be overlooked and disregarded, gives him no uneasiness. Whilst he is at peace with others, he is at peace with himself, and keeps those raging passions composed, which, at the same time that they disturb the world, and are seeking whom they may devour, are no less tyrants at home, and torment the heart from which they spring.

Men, whether they be courteous and meek themselves, or whether they be not, yet approve such a temper and conduct in others, and expect it from them; whether they forgive or no, yet would be forgiven. If they have offended another, they would have him pass it over, especially if they be sorry for it, and own the fault. If by submission they cannot regain his favour, they then begin to think themselves the injured persons, and conclude that he deserves ill usage who cannot by any methods be persuaded to excuse it.

He therefore, who will overlook no incivility and inadvertence, who will endure no affront, who
will

will bear and pardon no injury who infifts, upon his whole right, who for no confideration will give up any thing to which he has a title; fuch an one takes the method to deftroy, at leaft to leffen, his repofe and his fortunes, to have many enemies, and thofe violent and implacable, and to lofe his friends. The Precept of Chrift; If any one will take away thy cloak, let him have thy coat alfo: that is, If any one wrongs thee in fmaller matters, bear with it rather than contend about it; this precept is agreeable not only to religious (e), but to worldly wifdom. Many have been fufferers by rigidly infifting upon their due; many by ftubbornly refifting oppreffion armed with authority; others, refufing to fit down with a trifling lofs, have brought upon themfelves a greater, by feeking (f) legal redrefs, and fo have fallen into inconveniences from which a peaceable temper would have fecured them.

Bleffed are the meek, fays our Lord, for they fhall inherit the earth. Yet a little while, fays David, and the wicked fhall not be; but the meek fhall inherit the earth, and fhall delight themfelves in the abundance of peace. The meaning feems to be this:

Men who are factious, rebellious, contentious, and violent, ufually fuffer for it, and bring many calamities upon themfelves. Sometimes they come to an untimely end, and fall by the hand of their enemies; or captivity or imprifonment is their portion; or they are forced to fly their country and go into banifhment; or they lofe their fortunes, and are reduced to poverty, or at leaft they are continually involved in quarrels, ever hating and hated, doing and receiving injuries. But the meek fhall inherit the earth, fhall dwell in fecurity and reputation, expofed to none of thefe hardfhips

---

(e) Conveniet—effe equum et facilem; multa multis de jure fuo cedentem: a litibus vero, quantum liceat, et nefcio an paullo plus etiam quam liceat, abhorrentem. *Cicero* De Offic. II. 18.

(f) "Ἀνευθε χρυσῶν ἡ Θέμις ἐ μαντεύεται.

ships and disasters. They, by the providence of God, and according to the common course of things, will probably find friends and protectors, escape injuries, and quietly enjoy their possessions, and the fruits of their honest industry.

Since then meekness is upon so many accounts commendable and profitable, we should strive to acquire and retain this virtue; strive, I say; for without some pains many persons will scarcely attain or preserve it, because there are impediments to be removed, and temptations to be subdued.

For, first, temporal blessings, as reputation, power, wealth, honours, as also great abilities, too often make men vain, insolent, overbearing, impatient of opposition, and easily provoked.

Secondly, a low state and a course of disappointments frequently sours the mind, and introduces habits of envy and spite, of stubbornness and detraction.

Thirdly, the original temper itself is sometimes contrary to meekness. The mind of each person seems to have certain distinguishing characters impressed upon it, certain predominant passions and prevailing inclinations, which we call natural propensities, because they shew themselves early, and before reason exerts its power. Thus some are confident, bold, and daring, others bashful, cautious, and diffident; some are free and open, others shy and reserved; some are inquisitive, others careless; some are good-natured, others froward, from their very childhood.

But there are none of these difficulties which may not be mastered by pains, and care, and resolution. Others have done it, have obtained this victory over themselves. The Pagan world affords (*h*) some, and the Christian world many examples. When the Gospel was first preached, several received it, who before
had

(*h*) Socrates. Vid. *Cicero* de Fato V. p. 275. Ed. Davis.

had lived, as St. Paul fays, hateful and hating one another, in malice and envy, and who then acquired a peaceable temper, and became the fervants and the imitators of Chrift. The prophecy of Ifaiah, that the wolf fhould dwell with the lamb, and the leopard lie down with the kid, was fulfilled in the wonderful change of thofe fierce and turbulent fpirits, which humbly fubmitted to the precepts of lowlinefs and meeknefs, of courtefy and condefcenfion.

SERMON XV.

MATTH. xiv. 23.

And when he had sent away the multitudes, he went up into a mountain apart to pray.

SINCE our Saviour came into the world to instruct us by his doctrines and by his life, the Writers of the Gospels have carefully recorded not only his words, but his actions, that we, setting both frequently before us, and meditating seriously upon them, might, as far as human infirmity permits, obey his precepts and imitate his example.

In the chapter whence the text is taken, we read that our Saviour, after he had spent the day in acts of charity, in relieving and instructing the people, withdrew to a secret place, where he spent the evening alone in prayer and contemplation.

From his behaviour, as it is here described, we may draw these observations for our own use:

I. That we ought to set apart some portions of our time for private and silent acts of religion, for conversation with God and our own hearts. Our Lord went up into a mountain apart to pray:

II. That we ought to employ all the powers and abilities which God has conferred upon us, to the glory of their author and to the benefit of mankind, and lose no opportunity of doing good. Our Saviour spent the day in feeding and teaching the people.

III. That

III. That the active and social duties are more valuable and important than the contemplative virtues, which are of a private and solitary nature. Our Saviour left not the people till the evening came on; and the hours which he passed in solitude and retirement were few, compared with those which he spent in the discharge of his ministry.

IV. That, as our Saviour had, so we also have, time enough for the one and for the other, for the exercise of public and private duties and virtues; and that therefore neither should be admitted.

I. I observe that we ought to set apart certain portions of our time for private and silent acts of religion, for conversation with God and our own hearts, after the example of our Saviour, who sent away the multitudes, and retired into a mountain to pray.

The duty of which I now speak seems to consist in the following things:

In a recollection (*a*) of our past transgressions, in resolutions of amendment and improvement, and in prayers to God to forgive and assist us.

In a review of the favours and mercies which we have received from him, and in a grateful acknowledgment of them.

In meditations on the shortness and uncertainty of life, on the duties which more particularly belong to our station, on the abilities and opportunities which we have of improving our heart and understanding, and of doing the work of him who has sent us into the world.

Lastly, and in general, in a study of religious truths.

It is not difficult to prove that some hours of life ought to be employed in this manner, that we shall find great benefit from such a way of exercising our thoughts and memories, and that very bad consequences arise from the neglect of it.

(*a*) See Seneca *de Ira*, iii. 36.

In all times and places there are many who pass a thoughtless life in a perpetual unconcern for religion, who are entirely taken up with the follies, the amusements, the hurry and business of the world, who banish all serious reflections as a melancholy employment, and make an art of forgetting themselves. Let us endeavour to trace out the causes of this unreasonable conduct.

1. One great cause of it seems to be a bad education. The instruction which is given to young persons of the lower and middle sort is frequently an instruction which relates chiefly, if not solely, to this life. If they are dissuaded from idleness or extravagance or any other vice, or if they are exhorted to any thing praiseworthy, it is often by no other arguments than those which are drawn from the bare present advantage or disadvantage arising from a good or a bad behaviour. They are taught to set too great a value upon the conveniences, and to fear too much the evils, which are confined to this transitory state; they are taught too little concerning the duties of a Christian, and that little is rendered the less useful by the examples which they often see at home. They are soon able to observe that their instructors live as if the chief good of man consisted in profit and pleasure, and a small refuse of time were sufficient for the service of God.

Young persons of a higher rank and station may too often learn from the example, if not from the mouth of their parents, that people of fashion enter into this world to take their pastime therein; that a great part of their life is to be spent in fashionable amusements, the rest in polite learning, or in political wisdom, and in other temporal concerns; and that religion is either not to be minded, or that a few acts of it are to be now and then performed for the sake of decency, and in civil compliance with custom.

By such means it comes to pass that many young persons have their senses much and their understanding

little

SERMON XV.

little employed, or not to good purpose; that external objects take firm possession of their minds, and are hardly made to give place to those of more importance which reason and revelation suggest; and that they are disposed to fly from these to the world, with which they have contracted an early familiarity.

2. The common practice of the world, when we are grown up, has the same bad effect that a wrong education and the contagion of domestic faults produce in our earlier days. When young persons become their own masters, they find themselves surrounded with multitudes employed in vain diversions, or in business almost as vain. Some they see pursuing wealth, honour, and power, with as much industry as if they were to live here for ever, and with as little conscience as if there were no future state: others they see contriving how to amuse and entertain themselves in the most agreeable manner, according to their depraved taste, and placing all happiness in the pleasures of the senses. From the one sort they learn to be most diligent about the things of the least value, and not scrupulous concerning the methods to obtain them; from the other, they learn to fill up all their vacant hours with foolish and wicked diversions; from both, to compose their minds into a false security, to go, (*b*) not where Wisdom directs, but where custom leads, to imagine that it is safe enough to follow a multitude, and to live like others, and that what is so common cannot be dangerous.

3. But man is by nature a rational creature; understanding and conscience he carries about with him, whether he will or no; and though the one be uncultivated and abused, and the other discouraged and depressed, yet they will sometimes rebel, and fly in his face, and tell him disagreeable truths. Therefore, when he is sensible of his defects and deviations from righteousness, and of the necessity of amendment, and yet find no inclination to act this rational part, he hates his

(*b*) Non qua eundum est, sed qua itur. *Seneca.*

(c) his own company, and is afraid of himself, because, when he is retired from his usual diversions, from the noise and hurry of society, serious reflections will sometimes force in upon him. This makes him take the readiest way to avoid such unwelcome guests, that is, never to be at home, or never at leisure to receive them.

Thus men learn of others to forget themselves and their duty, and are ready to return them the same uncharitable offices; and thus, whilst they converse together under the appearance of friends, they are in truth not seldom the worst of enemies, and a society of robbers depriving each other of all that is valuable.

These are the causes of that thoughtless unconcern in which man passeth away his days, his days given him for other ends, and employments more noble and more suitable to the dignity of his nature: his life is spent in a circle of vanities, or in a creditable sort of idleness, in employments which make him neither wiser nor better.

To avoid these ill effects of conversing with the world, to lessen our indiscreet fondness for it, and to make us more diligent in our great concern, we should set apart some hours for serious meditations. Self-love, indolence, levity of mind, frailness, the love of diversions, the hurry of business, and the persuasive force of bad example, all conspire to amuse and deceive us, to keep us in ignorance, and to draw us into sin. It is expedient therefore at certain

---

(c) "Ἔνιοι τὸν ἴδιον βίον, ὡς ἀτερπέστατον θέαμα προσιδεῖν ἐκ ὑπομένουσιν, οὐδ᾽ ἀνακλάσαι τὸν λογισμὸν, ὡς φῶς ἐφ᾽ ἑαυτοὺς ἢ περιαγαγεῖν· ἀλλ᾽ ἡ ψυχὴ γέμουσα κακῶν παντοδαπῶν, ᾗ φριττούσα, ᾗ φοβουμένη τὰ ἔνδον, ἐκπηδᾷ θύραζε. *Plutarch.* de Curios. p. 516.

———Adde quod idem
Non horam tecum esse potes, non otia recte
Ponere; teque ipsum vitas fugitivus et erro.
Horat. Serm. ii. 7.

tain times to compare our duty with our practice, and to get acquainted with our own deceitful hearts and with religious truths.

For this knowledge is not to be acquired without application, nor can we apply ourselves to the search of it, unless we have quiet, and leisure, and silence, and retirement, and shut up the usual entrances to vanity and sin.

By this method we may hope to keep ourselves free from vicious habits, which are confirmed by thoughtless indolence, and which dwell not with consideration.

We shall learn what the defects are to which we are prone, which usually escape our notice when we seldom look in upon ourselves; and thus we shall be better able to watch over them, and to correct them.

We shall learn how to rule our passions whom by our own fault we often make our masters and our worst enemies, and amidst whom the soul dwells, as amidst a wicked and rebellious people; but which, directed by reason, may prove as useful to us, as they are pernicious when too much indulged.

We shall know what abilities God has given us, which else we should perhaps suffer to be buried in slothful obscurity, and which, improved and brightened by use, may possibly be applied to excellent purposes, and become public benefits.

We shall take the most proper method to learn our duty, and to confirm in ourselves good dispositions and a resolution to act suitably to our knowledge. Sometimes we offend against the conviction of our own mind and the reproofs of conscience; and sometimes we err through wrong judgment, whilst our reason is biassed by prejudice, misled by hastiness and levity, or clouded and corrupted by irregular passions. Serious reflection and meditation are the best means to prevent or remove both these evils,

evils, to improve and strengthen our reason, and at the same time to subdue and reform the heart.

We shall then be able to converse in safety with the world, which hath so many arts to seduce us, and in which we so difficultly maintain our innocence. We cannot be too well guarded against the dangers which there surround us, nor consider with ourselves too often and too carefully how we may perform our part in public life with uprightness and a stedfast integrity.

Thus should all reserve a portion of their time to converse with God and with their own hearts, having great reason to expect these advantages from it. They especially whose time is their own, and whose education has opened to them a nearer way to knowledge, are altogether inexcusable if they employ not themselves in religious thoughts and useful inquiries; if they will not allow themselves leisure to search after truths of the utmost importance, which shun the noise of folly, and are only to be found in retirement.

II. My second observation upon the text is, that we ought to employ all the powers and abilities which God has conferred upon us to the glory of their Author, and to the benefit of mankind, and to lose no opportunity of doing good, after the example of our Saviour, who spent the day in feeding and teaching the people.

I shall not prove that we are obliged to this conduct, and that our religion strictly requires it. It is well known. Instead of endeavouring to clear up an evident truth, I shall lay before you, in few words, the several ways of doing good and of serving our neighbour, from which it will appear that every person is able in some measure to perform this duty.

The actions and the behaviour by which we can be useful to others are,

Liberality,

Liberality, by which we relieve the wants of the poor and the deserving:

Justice, by which we render to every one his due, protect the defenceless, and redress the injured:

Instruction, by which we convey truth and skill and knowledge to the young, the ignorant, and those who stand in need of it:

Counsel and advice, by which we direct those who stand in need of it:

Reproof and correction, tempered with moderation and prudence, by which we restrain and discourage vice:

Commendation and encouragement, by which we animate ingenuous tempers to excel in things profitable and praise-worthy:

Patience and meekness, by which we are enabled to forgive injuries, and to overlook and excuse faults and imperfections:

Compassion, which both incites and fits us to comfort the miserable, and to use the best means to compose their passions, and to mitigate their sorrows:

Condescension, courteousness, and affability, by which we are agreeable to all those with whom we converse, especially to our inferiors, to those who depend upon us, to those who are obliged to serve and attend us:

Lastly, and in general, a life suitable to the religion which we profess, by which we set a good example, and allure others to imitation.

III. The third thing to be observed from the text is, that our Saviour did not leave the people till the evening came on; and that the hours which he passed in retirement were few compared with those which he spent in the discharge of his ministry; whence we may learn that the active and social duties are more valuable and important than the
con-

contemplative virtues, which are of a private and solitary nature. The reason why they are more valuable and important is because they are more beneficial. This is a plain, a short, a full, and a sufficient reason; and therefore they ought to be preferred to the other, when it ever happens that one of them must be left undone. Private acts of piety must be deferred, when we have an opportunity of doing good to the souls or to the bodies of others, and when they want our assistance. A neglect of our duty to our friends and families, to any person who may justly expect it from us, cannot be excused by allotting those hours to meditation, to prayer, to religious studies, which belong properly to society, and to the exercise of social virtues.

This leads me to observe, that from very ancient times many Christians, either weary of the world, or fearing its temptations, or flying from its persecution, or aspiring to a sublime degree of holiness, or intending to afflict themselves for their sins, forsook all, parted with their possessions, and retired into solitary places, and afterwards into religious houses. This humour increased along with ignorance and superstition, and grew so prevalent and contagious, that at last one fourth part perhaps of the Christian world consisted of such recluses.

Some have magnified these acts of self-denial, and this silent and secret way of life; others have resolved it all into folly, enthusiasm, and weakness or perverseness of judgment. I shall endeavour to give a fair representation of the case.

First, Man, who is not sufficient to his own happiness, finds himself made for society, to which his wants, his imperfections, and his desires incline him; it cannot therefore be his duty to check and overrule these innocent desires, and against his inclinations to quit the world and hide himself from his fellow-creatures.

Secondly,

Secondly, By society we are assisted not only in the conveniences of life, but in the improvement of our understanding and in the performance of our duty. These are benefits which we should repay to the utmost of our power. One who by natural and acquired abilities can be serviceable to the public, or who has relations and dependents for whom he ought to provide, is not at liberty to leave them under the frivolous pretence of serving God in secret.

Thirdly, Of two persons who live soberly and righteously, the one in a public station, the other in retirement, the former must be allowed to be the more excellent person, and the brighter example of virtue; for it is more commendable, because more useful, to be a burning light in the midst of a crooked and perverse generation, than in a desart, in a solitude, where it is in a great measure lost to the world, and shines almost only to itself.

Fourthly, The account which we have of the old solitary Saints, though written by their admirers and adorers, is often little to their advantage, or to the credit of Christianity. If Time, which hath destroyed so many excellent records and monuments, had swept away those histories, the loss had been inconsiderable. We find that their retired situation and moping and musing way of life threw them frequently into melancholy and enthusiasm, and sometimes into frenzy and madness: and indeed there are few heads strong enough to bear perpetual solitude, and a confinement to the same place, the same objects, the same occupations, and the same little circle of action; and when to all this is added want of proper food and of sleep, it is no wonder if a man loses his senses.

One would not censure without distinction all those who retired from the world. Their design might be honest, and their piety sincere; but, whilst we make proper allowances for their good intention, we cannot

compliment

compliment their prudence and commend their choice, especially when these institutions became a public nuisance, and called aloud for a reformation. Several evils arose from this injudicious devotion: young persons were sometimes seduced from their parents, and sometimes confined against their inclinations; they engaged themselves by vows never to change their way of life, which exposed them to innumerable temptations; a blind and slavish obedience was required to their governors; the public was deprived of many useful citizens, and great sums were misemployed by the indiscreet charity of simple persons, who gave away their possessions to such societies. Vice also and works of darkness found their way into some of these religious houses, which seemed to be only bolted and barred against charity and true piety.

One of the general weaknesses of mankind, is to run into extremes; and, in truth, there is a middle way between a quite solitary life, and a life of gaiety, hurry, and dissipation, which consists in so laying out and dividing our time, and chusing our friends and acquaintance, that we may give to every laborious or studious occupation, and to every innocent amusement, its proper season, and find leisure for every thing that is good and reasonable: and this may be done in populous cities as well as in cloisters, and perhaps much better.

IV. The last observation which I have to offer to you upon the text, is that as our Saviour had, so we also may have, sufficient time and proper opportunities for the exercise of public and private duties and virtues, and that therefore neither should be omitted.

We were not made to consume our time in sloth, in folly, and impertinence; much less in vice. If there were no state besides this, we might with a better grace trifle away our days, for life itself would then be a trifle with all its concerns. But we are the offspring of God,

we

we are born for eternity, and we pass our infancy in this lower world to prepare ourselves for a better. We are by nature active beings, and we have business enough relating both to the present and the future state to keep us employed. Our business here is, to be industrious in our station and calling, that we may be able to live decently, and to provide for those whom divine and human laws have committed to our care; to be useful to our country, to improve our understanding, to correct our bad dispositions, and to make a daily progress in virtue. This cannot be done, unless, like our Saviour, we lay hold on every occasion of honouring God and serving mankind, and at certain times retire to perform those duties, and to obtain that skill and knowledge, which require leisure and silence, and a mind free from other thoughts and occupations.

Every person, who is not hardened in iniquity, and has not lost the common notions of right and wrong, must and will acknowledge that such a conduct is reasonable and commendable, that we cannot act more prudently, and that if we act so we shall be wife and happy. But many will object, that they must live like others, and that consequently they cannot find time to spare for a regular performance of all these things; that the example of our Lord, in this as in other respects, is too bright and too excellent, that at the most they can only adore it, and follow it at a great distance: that those few who have passed their days in this manner were extraordinary persons; and that every one cannot hope to be a Saint.

The excuse then is want of time, an excuse which is false and frivolous, and will appear to be so, though we should make large allowances, and not examine it by rigid rules. It shall be acknowledged that we were not born only for contemplation and severer studies, nor yet to be always employed in that which is most wife and right. Human nature is not capable of this
perfection.

perfection. Sometimes we may be allowed to do nothing, or things (*d*) of no consequence. Relaxation and diversion are in a certain degree innocent, and indeed necessary. But many persons should be reminded, that they carry these amusements to excess, and sacrifice to them too large a portion of this short and uncertain life. I speak not of those or to those who waste their days, and, along with their days, their strength, their health, their fortunes, and their understanding, in dissolute practices: for such persons not only throw away their time, but their (*e*) souls too, which is the greater loss. Setting aside the case of these, we may say of those who have better dispositions, that they would have more leisure for the improvement of their mind and their heart, if they were more discreet and frugal in the management of their time, too much of which is stolen from them either by business, or by conversation, or by diversion, or by all the three.

By business I mean unnecessary and unprofitable business. Many persons are not unemployed, but they are employed to no purpose, by vanity, or a bad taste, or an over-officious and meddling temper, or by a disposition to strife and contention, or by a love of power, honour, and superfluous abundance.

Others pass hours after hours in the company of persons whom they neither love nor esteem, and from whom they can learn nothing, and this purely because they hate to think, and be alone.

Others pursue diversion so earnestly and constantly, that they contract, if not poverty and debts, yet laziness, levity of mind, an unsettled temper, and a distaste for virtuous and manly occupations.

It

(*d*) Desipere in loco. *Horat.*
(*e*) Ego quoque una pereo, quod mi est carius. *Terent.*

It is our duty to draw into a moderate compass the time which we bestow upon diversions, conversation, and unprofitable business, and not to be over fond of them, that we may be able without reluctance and disquiet to set them aside when better affairs require our attention.

SERMON XVI.

Matth. xiii. 43.

Then shall the righteous shine forth as the sun in the kingdom of their father.

Every serious and considerate person is desirous of knowing what shall become of him, when the few days are passed which are allotted to him in this world, and what he may expect hereafter if he takes care to live virtuously here.

The holy Scriptures have given us a view of the future state of the good; if not a view sufficient to afford full satisfaction to the inquisitive mind of man, yet a view sufficient to remove that disquiet which attends uncertainty. They assure us often that the good shall be perfectly happy; they say little of the particulars in which that happiness shall consist. They inform us, that in heaven is reserved for the righteous an inheritance incorruptible and undefiled, which fadeth not away, an eternal weight of glory, a kingdom which cannot be moved, a city whose builder and maker is God, where rust and moth do not corrupt, and where thieves do not break through and steal; where the just shall shine forth as the sun in the kingdom of their Father, where God hath prepared, for those who love him, things which the eye hath not seen, nor ear heard, nor hath it entered into the heart of man to conceive. But though the Scriptures descend

SERMON XVI.

not into a distinct and particular account of these future rewards, yet we cannot say that they are silent. Some discovery they have made to us of that state, and reveal as much of it as is necessary to be known to us, as much as perhaps we are able to comprehend, and enough to raise our hopes and encourage us to contend earnestly for the recompence set before us. What they have delivered upon this subject I shall set before you, and then shew the effect which it ought to have upon you.

1. The good will hereafter be free from all the pain and all the evils of life. Of this we are assured in the Scriptures, which tell us that they who die in the Lord, immediately rest from their labours, and enter into peace, and that at the resurrection Christ shall change their vile bodies into the likeness of his own glorious body, shall clothe them with bodies pure and bright, and active and incorruptible, subject to no imperfections, and united for ever to the soul.

To be free from pain, and fear, and uneasiness of mind, is undoubtedly a most desirable acquisition. Happiness consists not indeed in this alone; but it is a considerable part of happiness, to those beings especially who have felt such evils, which, more or less, is the case of human creatures, who are all born to suffer. Our bodies are so framed as to lie open to injuries from every thing that surrounds us; and every object, that can make disagreeable or hurtful impressions upon them, is able through them to wound the mind. Our souls, besides the evils to which they are exposed from the assault of things external, are liable to many distempers arising from internal causes, from ignorance, from error, and from irregular passions. Our possessions are so precarious, that they can scarcely be called our own. Society, which was designed for our benefit and comfort, is often so far from answering those excellent ends, that it is worse than solitude, and hath given just cause to many to join in that melancholy wish of the prophet Jeremiah; Oh that I had in the wilderness a lodging place of wayfaring men, that I might leave my people, and go from them! Even in better times and places than those of which the Prophet complains, a hope of escaping ill usage and slight and injuries is mere folly, whilst there are such enemies to our repose as pride, and insolence, and ambition, and ingratitude, and covetousness, and treachery, and slander, and fraud, and malice, and envy. Our friends and relations sometimes forsake us, sometimes give us sorrow for their afflictions which we cannot remove, sometimes are unable to serve us when we stand most in need of their assistance, sometimes die before us, sometimes take ill courses and disappoint our hopes. Our country, which justly claims our service and our affection, and whose interest is inseparably connected with our own, is not seldom exposed to great calamities. These are inconveniences and distresses which attend upon human nature, upon frail mortality; this is the patrimony and estate which we inherit from our first parent. They have indeed their use in a state of probation, and the Christian religion teaches us the important art of turning them to our spiritual profit. But the benefits which thus arise from them do not alter their nature. Evils they are; but they are evils of a short continuance, which cannot follow the good beyond the grave, nor enter with them into heaven; and this is one of the advantages which that eternal day will bring forth. An advantage it is which we can very well understand and conceive, better perhaps than an Angel, better than any creature of a superior order, who hath not like us experienced the nature of evil. (*a*) None take so much satisfaction in health as they who are recovered

(*a*) ―― μετὰ γάρ τε ἄλγεσι τέρπεται ἀνήρ,
Ὅστις δὴ μάλα πολλὰ πάθῃ.

Homer *Odyss.* O. 399. &c. &c.

vered from sickness; none receive more pleasure from kind offices of humanity and civility than they who have been oppressed and persecuted; none enjoy the conveniences of life with a truer taste than they who have felt the extremes of poverty; none know the value of liberty so well as they who are released from bondage. If therefore it may reasonably be supposed that the remembrance of this life will not be obliterated, and swallowed up in the happiness of the next, it must be a pleasing reflection to the good, to cast a thought back upon their ancient condition, and to consider that they have exchanged imperfection and misery for every desireable blessing. In the Revelation it is said of the righteous; They are before the throne of God, and serve him day and night in his temple; and he that sitteth on the throne shall dwell among them; they shall hunger no more, neither thirst any more, neither shall the sun light on them nor any heat; for the Lamb who is in the midst of the throne shall feed them, and shall lead them unto living fountains of waters; and God shall wipe away all tears from their eyes, and there shall be no more death, neither sorrow nor crying; for the former things are passed away.

These words may relate to a temporal prosperity which the Church of Christ should enjoy at a certain time, and which is thus magnified by the sublime and and majestic style of prophecy; but surely they are well adapted to express the consummate bliss which ought not to be expected and will never be found in the present world, and they are justly applicable to the future condition of the servants of God.

2. The good will be happy in the encrease of knowledge.

For this we have the testimony of St. Paul, who in his first epistle to the Corinthians describes the future state of rewards as a state in which error and doubt and suspence, and faith itself, as it is the belief of things not seen, shall give place to truth and certainty. He tells us that the knowledge which the righteous can now acquire, compared to the improvements which they shall then receive, resembles the trifling and vain fancies of a child, compared to the reasonings of a man arrived to maturity of judgment. He says that they now know in part, but that they shall then know, even as also they are known, even as they are known of God. He could not have chosen stronger words to express the extensive views and the enlarged faculties of the human understanding, when it shall be so wonderfully exalted and enlightened, and the discoveries which it shall make concerning its own powers, and the works of the creation, and the ways of Providence, and the nature of God.

It is probable that of these discoveries and improvements there will be no end. Perfection of any kind belongs to God alone, and from him alone nothing is concealed. The wisdom, and the knowledge of all created and limited beings must be limited; but we may reasonably suppose that they will be for ever increasing in beings who shall for ever be good and happy.

They who have employed themselves in searching for truth, are very sensible that there is much satisfaction in discovering it, that many difficulties attend the enquiries after it, and that little of it can be obtained. The soul, which is an active and reflecting being, and formed by nature to love and pursue knowledge, enjoys a serious and rational pleasure in possessing it; but the pursuit of knowledge is laborious, and exposed to many discouragements; the imperfections and diseases of the body affecting the mind, and the disorders and distempers of the mind itself, are continual impediments in our way to it.

By a right use of our own understanding we may at last be so wise and so learned as to know our ignorance, and to be sensible that in many things we cannot

not advance beyond probability and conjecture; and that for want of leisure and opportunity we must be unskilled in several things which the mind by the exercise of its powers is capable of discerning. Such is our present state of infancy, to be delivered from which will make no small part of the felicity of the good.

Under this head we may add those declarations in Scripture concerning them, that they shall see God. When the Apostle observes that without obedience none can enter into heaven, he thus expresses it; Without holiness no man shall see the Lord. Our Saviour says of the pure in heart, that they shall see God; and St. John, that they shall see his face, and his name shall be in their foreheads.

Concerning this phrase of seeing God, it may be observed that it seems designed to represent in general the happiness of heaven. To see God is to dwell in his courts and kingdom, in that place where is the most glorious manifestation of his presence, and to enjoy that fulness of satisfaction which must be found there. But to see God, as it implies something more distinct and particular, is probably, to know him, to see him with the eye of the understanding, to have clearer and juster notions than we can now attain of his nature and of his works, and consequently of his power, and wisdom, and justice, and goodness, and mercy. Thus the good will see God; and with their knowledge of the all-perfect Being, their veneration, their gratitude, and love towards him, will increase.

3. The good will be happy, in being free from sin.

To account for which perfection, we need not suppose that they shall lose the natural power of committing evil, which seems to be inseparable from rational creatures. But being placed in a state remote from any allurements to sin, they will be secured from ever offending God, and from losing their reward. Even here upon earth, in this state of imperfection, there are persons who will not, and who indeed cannot be guilty of some particular vices, both because they have contracted virtuous habits, and because they have a strong detestation of those crimes, and could not fall into them without much uneasiness and violence offered to their inclinations. Much more may the inhabitants of heaven be confirmed in upright dispositions, when their wisdom and knowledge, their love of God and of holiness, will be abundantly increased, and they shall be exposed to none of those temptations which we now experience, and which arise from the constitution of our body, from the objects which present themselves to us, from our wants and desires, from our hopes and fears.

4. The good will be happy in the society of beings like themselves. St Paul, in the account which he has given us of charity, or the love of our fellow-creatures, tells us that it is everlasting, and a virtue to be exercised by the righteous not only in their present, but in their future state. And indeed without it heaven would not be heaven, not that region of peace and joy that it is said to be. Of all the pleasures which this world can afford, there are none more rational, more uniform, and more agreeable, than those which arise from conversing and dwelling with persons for whom we have a just esteem. Yet is this pleasure by no means sincere, and something will interpose to allay and lessen it, or to deprive us of it. The imperfections and the inequalities of temper from which none is exempt, the calamities to which our friends are exposed, and the loss of them, when we outlive them, are evils which attend a social life, and take away part of the satisfaction which we owe to it. But in heaven will be found all that can be valuable in society; without any of these inconveniences.

niences. The righteous will there converse with the best and the wisest beings; and, as they may reasonably hope, with those whom they loved here below for their good qualities. Our Saviour had his friends when he dwelt here; and when he saw them deeply afflicted at the thoughts of losing him, he pitied their distress, and applied a suitable consolation. I only go, says he, to prepare a place for you, that where I am, there ye may be also. He says not to them, as a just Master, ye shall be happy; but he says, as an affectionate Friend, you shall be where I am, along with me; intimating possibly that such alliances are immortal, and that Death, which breaks all other bonds, dissolves not the union between virtuous minds.

5. The occupations of the good in their future state are not revealed to us. We may conclude that they will be suitable to their dignity and dispositions. The Scriptures have informed us that the Angels are ministring spirits, that they execute the will and the commands of God, that they are employed in the government of the world, to succour the good, and to correct the bad; and it is said of the righteous, that hereafter they shall be like the Angels; they shall be like to them in glory and abilities; and they shall perhaps be like to them in office, and have the care of other creatures in other worlds committed to them. Employment they can never want; for the works of God in the visible and invisible creation can in all probability neither be summoned up by numbers, nor contained within any limits, and the objects with which a wise and good mind may entertain itself can never be exhausted, and will administer new pleasure and improvement through all ages.

6. The happiness of the good will in many respects surpass any description which we can make of it. The truth of this assertion appears from the very silence of the Scriptures upon the particulars of their future reward, and from the reason which is given of that

silence;

silence; namely, that it is so far superior to our apprehensions, that words cannot express it, nor the imagination reach it. If a brute could try to form a judgment concerning the powers and properties of human nature, that judgment would be mixed with much error. When a man endeavours to represent to himself the perfections of God, or even of an Angel, the representation is obscure, superficial, and defective; for the lesser cannot contain the greater. He who never had sight or hearing is utterly incapable of attaining a notion of that sense and of its objects. Nor are we able to comprehend the future rewards of the righteous, since they shall receive new excellencies, and since there may be a variety of senses with which we are not acquainted, and through which knowledge and happiness may be conveyed to the soul.

7. I have had occasion already to observe that the recompence which God will bestow upon his servants shall be everlasting; and I need not endeavour to shew how much happiness must arise from a certainty of never losing it. Every one who considers it will feel it and know it, and will know at the same time that no words can express it.

8. Lastly, though the good will be freed from the evils of this life, and placed in a condition agreeable to their desires and inclinations, and in no danger of being deprived of it, yet this excludes not a wide inequality between them. The Scriptures frequently assure us that every one shall receive proportionable to the improvements which he has made, to the trials which he has undergone, to the proofs which he has given of his virtue; and this is perfectly agreeable to all our notions of justice and equity. It is a truth upon which every humble and contrite heart may reflect with much satisfaction. To the obstinate indeed and the impenitent neither this nor any other truth revealed in Scripture, or discoverable by Reason, can afford the least comfort. But there are persons who, conscious

scious to themselves of many omissions and transgressions, sincerely and industriously endeavour to reform whatsoever is amiss in their inclinations and behaviour, and so to live for the time to come, that their bad dispositions may die before them. To such it must be a pleasing consideration that a great variety of rewards will be distributed, some of which they may humbly hope to obtain.

Thus much the Scriptures have made known to us concerning the future state of the good; not to entertain and amuse our imagination, but to affect our heart, and to mend our lives. We should therefore consider, and so consider as to become better by it, that we cannot lose this reward without being extremely miserable, nor obtain it by any other method than by serving God to the utmost of our power. As in our Father's house are many mansions, so doubtless in those unhappy regions to which evil Spirits and wicked men will be confined, are various abodes suited to the several degrees of depravity and guilt which they shall have contracted. But alas, the least punishment which we can suppose allotted to those who end their days under God's displeasure, is such, that none, who knew what he was doing, would gain the whole world to undergo it. Wretched must be the condition of an immortal being, who, after having rejected the means and opportunities of securing a place in the kingdom of heaven, must bitterly reproach himself for his folly and madness, and perpetually converse with the worst of companions, even with his own uneasy thoughts.

The Scripture tells us, that without holiness we shall not see God, and dwell in his presence; and our own understanding will assure us that this must be true. Sin renders us in all respects unlike to him who is the fountain of happiness, and in a resemblance to whom all happiness must have its foundation. Whilst we are in subjection to evil habits, we cannot love him, nor

can

can he love us; nor can we lose his favour without the loss of every thing that is valuable. Besides; Virtue, in one sense, is certainly its own reward; virtue is rewarded with virtue both here and hereafter. For example; If we endeavour to imitate God, we shall continually approach nearer to his perfections; if we love him, that love will continually increase; if we are careful to abstain from every thing that is evil, all temptations to it will be lessened daily here, and quite removed hereafter. A sinner therefore may deceive himself in this, as in many other points: he may fancy, that he would gladly receive everlasting life, but whatsoever he may imagine, he undoubtedly hath not the least desire of obtaining the recompence which God hath promised to the good. To dwell here for ever, to indulge his inclinations for ever without controul, for ever to be the same vain and perverse creature that he now is, this would be the utmost felicity that he can conceive. If he would willingly go to heaven, it is only that he may avoid pain and punishment. Heaven is a place whence sensual enjoyments, whence wealth and titles, and earthly pomp and splendor, and the power and respect which they procure, are all excluded. The pleasures which it affords, are serious pleasures, arising from wisdom, and knowledge, and purity, and holy love. All this is most unwelcome and insipid to a depraved heart.

Hence we may learn that it is our duty and our interest, not only to preserve ourselves free from vicious habits, from grosser acts of iniquity, but to contract no excessive fondness for those lawful and innocent objects, which, though convenient and useful to us in our present circumstances, cease with this world, and cannot follow us into the next. If we make it the business of our lives to employ and gratify our senses, and take no care to exercise and improve our understanding, if we have a dislike for serious thoughts and reflections, if we cannot endure to meditate upon truth

and

and virtue, upon the perfections of the works of God, and our own nature and capacities, and the ends for which we were made; what will become of us when we shall have no more to do with this earth, and with the objects which are so dear to us, and so necessary to our contentment? But if we can delight in conversing with ourselves, in honouring and obeying God, in growing wiser and better, in enlarging our knowledge and in contracting our wants and desires, we shall by acquiring these good habits secure to ourselves lasting and rational pleasures, when these frail bodies shall be no more, or shall put on a pure and a brighter form.

SERMON XVII.

1 Cor. xiii. 13.

And now abideth faith, hope, charity, these three; but the greatest of these is charity.

IN this chapter St. Paul recommends the duty of charity, or the love of our neighbour. He shews wherein it consists, he sets forth the necessity of observing it, and he concludes with remarks upon its excellence.

The Christians of Corinth, to whom he addresses this Epistle, were at that time unhappily divided by dissentions, and some foul errors and corruptions had crept in amongst them. Therefore in this letter he corrects their mistaken notions of religion, and their deficiencies in morality, exhorts them to unity and brotherly love, and answers several questions which they had proposed to him.

In the chapter before this, mention is made of several spiritual and extraordinary gifts which God in those early times conferred upon Christians.

But we find that even these excellent gifts of the holy Spirit, the Spirit of love and peace and order, did not altogether produce in the Corinthian Church the fruits which might have been expected; that there were persons who misapplied the gifts of tongues; that some were guilty of pride and ostentation, others of jealousy and envy. St. Paul therefore

fore puts them in mind that these gifts, various and variously distributed, though unequal in their use and excellence, yet all proceeded from one and the same holy Spirit, and all conspired to the same good end; being designed by him for the edification of the Church, and to preserve unity and concord amongst its members, though unhappily perverted by some of them. Hence he takes occasion to exhort them to put away all strife and vain-glory, and envy, and contempt, to love and esteem and serve each other, and to apply the powers which they had received from God to the public good, and to the glory of their author. Covet earnestly, says he, the best gifts; and yet shew I unto you a more excellent way. That is; You may beg of God that he would confer upon you those gifts which are most useful; for to serve him in this manner is an honourable employment, and to desire it is a laudable ambition; but remember that there is a grace of more value in the sight of God, and more beneficial to men, more glorious therefore, and more desireable, than all these extraordinary gifts, than all the abilities of the mind, and that is, Charity.

Hence we may learn not to regret the withdrawing of those gifts, nor to think ourselves on that account less regarded of God, in these later ages. If any one amongst us hath charity in its due extent, he will surpass some of the earliest Christians, who seem to have been deficient in this most excellent virtue. We are apt to think highly of them, because of the miraculous powers which they possessed: but a judicious examiner will judge that nothing is more to be admired in the primitive Christians, than the charity, the zeal, the patience, and the perseverance, which so eminently appeared in so many of them.

St. Paul proceeds to shew the nature of charity, and the effects which it produces; and says of it, that it suffereth long, and is kind, envieth not, vaunt-
cth

eth not itself, doth not behave itself unseemly, seeketh not its own, is not easily provoked, thinketh no evil, rejoiceth not in iniquity, but rejoiceth in the truth, beareth all things, believeth all things, hopeth all things, endureth all things.

In this description of charity there are a few words of uncertain signification, with an enquiry into which I shall not detain you, but observe that the charitable man, as he is represented by St. Paul, is one who in all his behaviour hath the convenience and welfare of his neighbour as much in his view and at heart as his own. He bears with gentleness, meekness, and patience, the defects and faults of others, and is willing to conceal them, though himself is the sufferer; nor doth he expose them, unless justice and the public good absolutely require it. He allows those who have offended against him time and leisure to become sensible of it and to amend their manners. He is inclined to entertain hopes of their reformation, and to give credit to favourable reports of it, when there is any reason to suppose them true. Free from suspicious malice, rashness and censoriousness, he had much rather be mistaken in thinking too kindly than too hardly. He is never hurried away and overcome by anger; never loses his prudence, and becomes unable to govern himself. He always tempers this passion, and restrains it from breaking out into any indecencies of words and actions. He is courteous and civil, void of austerity, ill-humour, and moroseness; liberal and ready to the utmost of his power to relieve and assist all who stand in need of his aid. He envieth not the prosperity of his neighbour; he sincerely desires it, and rejoiceth at it, as if he were a gainer by it; and indeed he is; for by this benevolent temper he in some sort partakes of it, and makes it his own, without any loss to the proprietor. He is free from
that

that pride, conceit, and arrogance, which is always attended with a difregard and contempt of others. He never mifbehaves himfelf through vain-glory; but, feems rather ignorant of his own good qualities, than an admirer and a proclaimer of them. He is willing to fubmit to the loweft offices for the benefit of his fellow Chriftians, not thinking it beneath his dignity to be thus employed. His zeal for the glory of God and for the advancement of religion is ftrong and active, but joined with difcretion and goodnature. He is difinterefted and public-fpirited, and prefers the common welfare to his private advantage and convenience. Thus he thinks, and thus he acts, not by fits and ftarts, but uniformly and through the whole courfe of his life.

Let us now proceed to confider what St. Paul advances concerning the neceffity of practifing this virtue.

Though I fpeak, fays he, with the tongues of men and of Angels, and have not charity, I am become as founding brafs, or a tinkling cymbal (a); and though I have the gift of prophecy, and underftand all myfteries and all knowledge, and though I have all faith, fo that I could remove mountains, and have no charity, I am nothing: and though I beftow all my goods to feed the poor, and though I give my body to be burned, and have not charity, it profiteth me nothing.

That

(a) St. Paul ufeth here the cymbal, and the χαλκὸς ἠχῶν, whatfoever inftrument it may be, for emblems of a vain, noify, ufelefs talker. Apion, who was a conceited pedant, was called *Cymbalum mundi* by Tiberius. So χρόταλον ftands for a noify fellow, in Ariftophanes, *Nub.* 447. Κρόταλον εὔσομος ἢ εὔγλωτ]ος, ὡς τὰ κρόταλα. Schol.

Οἶδ' ἄνδρα κρόταλον, δριμὺ Σιούφε γένος.
Euripides, *Cycl.*

Τὸ χαλκίον τὸ Δωδωναῖον was ufed proverbially of a prater. *Alenander*, p. 24, and Bentley's note.

That is; if I had the gift of tongues, a gift which you earneſtly covet, and ſometimes miſapply, if I had it in the utmoſt extent, ſo that I could ſpeak all languages, yet if I have not charity alſo, which would direct me to uſe it properly at all times, for the good of the Church, and which would keep me from exalting myſelf above others upon that account, I ſhould be only a vain and uſeleſs talker, and ſhould ſound forth my own praiſe, not the glory of God,

And though I have the ſpirit of prophecy, a gift ſuperior to the former, by which I can expound the Scriptures, and teach the Goſpel, and ſometimes foretel things to come; and though I underſtand and can explain all the figures and myſteries of the Old Teſtament accompliſhed in Chriſt; and though I am perfect in the knowledge of divine truths; and though I have the higheſt degree of that faith by which we are enabled to work miracles, ſo that I can perform the moſt wonderful works; if I have not Charity, I am nothing, nothing worth in the ſight of God, nor to be compared with thoſe who have this virtue, but am far from Chriſtian perfection.

And though I give alms to the needy, till by relieving them I become as poor as they; though I lay down my life when I might ſave it by renouncing my religion, yet if I have not Charity, it availeth me nothing. If I think by thoſe ſplendid acts of ſelf-denial and conſtancy to pleaſe God, and at the ſame time violate the duty of Charity, I deceive myſelf in imagining that God will accept ſo incomplete an obedience.

It is not neceſſary to ſuppoſe, that St. Paul here puts a caſe which ever yet happened; that any Chriſtian ever had ſo many ſupernatural gifts, ſo much faith, ſo much liberality, ſo much religious knowledge, and ſuch a perſevering zeal, as to die

SERMON XVII.

for the Gospel; and yet was void of Charity. But it is no uncommon thing to make extraordinary, or even impossible, suppositions or concessions, with a view to strengthen the argument: as when it is said by our Saviour: If a man should gain the whole world, and lose his own soul, he would make a bad exchange. St. Paul hath an impetuous kind of eloquence, he is vehement and lively in his style, and expresses himself with warmth and energy. His meaning in the passage before us, and the doctrine delivered by him, is plain enough. It is this: If a man have not Charity, whatsoever he may do that appears great and commendable, and whatsoever gifts of the holy Spirit he may possess, he cannot deserve the name of a good man.

Thus St. Paul, in a few words, but those the most striking and expressive that could be chosen, declares the necessity of performing this great duty. He proceeds to make some observations upon the excellence of charity in the following manner:

Charity never faileth; but whether there be prophecies, they shall fail; whether there be tongues, they shall cease; whether there be knowledge, it shall vanish away.

That is; Herein Charity exceeds these gifts, that its use and duration are endless, but these must cease, at the end of the world, if not sooner. At this time they have their use, and according to it they are to be esteemed; but hereafter, the gift of tongues shall cease; and prophecy, whether it be the knowledge of divine truths, or the prediction of future events, shall become unnecessary.

For we know in part, and we prophesy in part; but when that which is perfect is come, then that which is in part shall be done away.

Our knowledge of God and of religious truths is confined in narrow bounds; and the prediction of future events extends itself not to many things, and is not without obscurity, and will have its completion in this world. These gifts are bestowed upon us as helps suitable to our present imperfect state, and must become useless hereafter, when we shall arrive at a state of perfection.

When I was a child, I spake as a child, I understood as a child, I thought as a child: but when I became a man, I put away childish things.

That is; Whilst we are children, our thoughts are low and trifling, our manner of expressing them suitable to such thoughts, our reasoning weak and inconclusive; but as we advance in years, we advance in understanding. Such, and far greater, is the difference between our knowledge here in this life, and that which we shall attain hereafter. This is our state of childhood, and we now reason of divine things imperfectly, and suitably to our obscure apprehensions of them: but in the next world all difficulties will vanish, and these things will be clear to us.

For now we see (*b*) through a glass darkly, but then face to face: now I know in part, but then shall I know even as also I am known.

Divine truths are at present seen by us but obscurely and imperfectly. Our knowledge of God, of his nature and properties, of the scheme of his providence and the method of his government, is short and incomplete. But in heaven we shall not be less wise than happy; we shall then know many things, which are now in a great measure hidden from us; we shall know them,

---

(*b*) The sense may be; We see δι' ἐσόπτρου, per *specular*, vel *speculare*, through a glass, or pellucid stone, which perhaps was not so clear and transparent as our glass. See Lambert Bos, *Exerc. Phil.* p. 147.

We see δι' ἐσόπτρου, and we see ἐν αἰνίγματι. Perhaps it should be ἐν ἀνεώγματι or ἐν ἀνοίγματι, through, or at a door, a wicket, or a chink. "Ἀνοιγμα is used in the LXX. 3. *Reg.* xiv. 6. Others have made this conjecture also.

SERMON XVII.

them, as we ourselves are known of God, that is, clearly and perfectly.

And now abideth faith, hope, charity, these three; but the greatest of these is Charity.

That is; Above all the miraculous gifts of the Spirit, are these three Christian graces; faith, or a belief in God, and in the truths which he hath revealed to us by his Son; hope of receiving from God those rewards which he hath promised to the obedient; and Charity, or a love and good-will to all men: but of these three, the last mentioned is the first in dignity, being the most perfect, the most useful, and the most durable.

In this place, the word faith, being distinguished from hope and charity, is used by St. Paul in a limited sense, as barely a belief of Christianity. It cannot be the justifying faith, of which he speaks in other places; for as to the faith here mentioned, St. Paul prefers charity to it; and without charity it is so far from justifying, that it signifies nothing. But the faith which justifies, is believing, receiving, and obeying the Gospel; that is, it is faith, and hope, and charity altogether; or, which amounts, to the same thing, it is faith producing hope and charity, and working by love. For it is as hard to comprehend how a man can be justified, or, which is the same thing, how he can be a good man, by believing without obeying, as how he can be sick and well, or alive and dead, at the same time.

Having examined and endeavoured to explain the several parts of the Apostle's discourse upon the duty of charity, we will now review the doctrine contained in it.

The design of St. Paul is, to shew the nature and the importance of charity. By the word charity we often mean alms-giving: but St. Paul distinguisheth alms-giving from charity; though I bestow all my goods, says he, to feed the poor, and have not charity, it profiteth me nothing. The word charity, or love, is constantly used in the New Testament in a more extensive manner, and means that benevolent disposition which rejoices in doing what is good and right, and is earnestly bent upon promoting the happiness of mankind. And yet relieving the bodily wants of our fellow-creatures is both by our Saviour and by his Apostles represented as a considerable part of charity; and such it plainly is, as not only the spirit of Christianity, but the social nature and inclinations of man, the unequal distribution of things, the uncertainty of worldly possessions, and the public welfare, evidently prove.

Charity, according to St. Paul's description, with relation to our conduct towards those who offend us, is long-suffering, abstains from revenge, is inclined to forgive, is slow to wrath, and decent and moderate in reproving.

With relation to our behaviour towards men in general, it is free from envy, vanity, insolence, pride, self-interest, suspiciousness, censoriousness; is condescending, courteous, kind, compassionate, merciful, and liberal; judges candidly and favourably; is disposed to think well and hope well of others, as far as reason will permit; and rejoiceth at their temporal and spitual welfare.

He who possesseth this virtue in its full extent, and who is incited to the practice of it by Christian principles, by faith in God and in our Saviour, and by hope of living hereafter in that state of happiness which is promised to the obedient, is supposed by St. Paul to be a good Christian, human infirmities excepted, and to love God and man. And indeed the word charity, in its largest sense, means not only the love of man, but the love of God also; and there is no reason to exclude this sense of it from the text: although the Apostle in his description of charity seems to consider it principally as a social duty, and as influencing and directing our conduct towards our neighbour.

Con-

SERMON XVII.

Concerning charity St. Paul obferves that without it all natural or fupernatural gifts are nothing, and all hopes of pleafing God groundlefs and vain. The end for which extraordinary gifts were conferred upon the firft Chriftians, and to which every accomplifhment and power, natural and acquired, fhould tend, is the increafing of virtue, peace, and happinefs in the world. A man who hath not this end in view, let him have all the abilities that can be conceived, is a bad man; and fo much the worfe, by how much the greater are the means of doing good which are committed to him, and of which he makes an ill ufe.

St. Paul placed charity above the knowledge of divine things and the extraordinary gift of the Spirit. The reafon was plain; becaufe it was a Chriftian virtue, and they were not; becaufe by it men might judge whether they were in the favour of God, by them they could not; and becaufe it was more excellent than they, knowledge lying within narrow limits, and the uncommon gifts of the Spirit not being intended to continue long.

The higheft degree of knowledge which we can acquire at prefent is very imperfect, though fully fufficient to conduct us to a better ftate; and then they who fhall be found worthy of a bleffed immortality, fhall know even as they are known of God, and receive improvements to which the difcoveries of the wifeft men bear no proportion.

Above all knowledge, and all the extraordinary powers given by the holy Spirit to the firft believers, above thefe ftand the moral and Chriftian virtues, as faith in God, and hope of eternal life grounded upon that faith: but above thefe alfo is charity, as in ufefulnefs, fo likewife in duration. For faith fhall ceafe, when we fhall have put off thefe immortal bodies, and fee the completion of God's promifes; and hope fhall ceafe when there fhall be no room for expectation or fear of difappointappointment. Faith and Hope accompany a Christian through his state of trial, inspiring him with constancy and courage, giving him peace of mind, lessening the evils incident to this life by placing before him the reward for which he contends.

When he hath finished his course, and is admitted into the joy of his Lord, they seem to have performed their part. But charity, universal benevolence, follows him into heaven, there to be exercised by him for ever. Indeed it may be that some parts of charity shall then cease, as those which consist in relieving the needy, instructing the ignorant, reclaiming the bad, protecting the oppressed, forgiving injuries, and bearing with the weakness and follies and frowardness of others; for the kingdom of heaven is represented as a place where none of these imperfections and evils will be found. But if God should employ the Saints hereafter as ministering spirits to inferior creatures, they may perhaps have occasion to exert some of these acts of kindness and patience, no less than the holy Angels, who now do us service, who doubtless surpass us in charity as well as in other perfections. Of this we may be certain, that an affectionate regard for all, a desire that they may serve their Maker, and act suitably to their several stations, and an endeavour to promote the general good, shall be part of the occupation of the righteous in the life which is to come. And in that age, if we may judge from some expressions in Scripture, the most distinguished and glorious reward shall be given, not to the wise, not to the learned, not to the prophet, not to the worker of miracles; but to him who hath been the best friend to mankind, the most assiduously employed in the labour of love, in endeavouring to make others happier and wiser.

Such is charity, as described by St. Paul, and such its extent, its excellence, and importance. We might now

now proceed to confider how much happier men would be, if this virtue were more generally practifed, how venerable and amiable it is, and how many prefent advantages it procures to thofe who by exercifing it ufe the moft probable means of paffing through this world with quiet and dignity. We might obferve how by it we may form no bad judgment of the religion of Chriftian focieties, or of particular perfons; and that, according as their doctrines and behaviour agree with it, or contradict it, they may not unreafonably be fuppofed to have retained or quitted the ancient faith or practice.

To banifh, imprifon, plunder, ftarve, hang, and burn men for religion, is not the Gofpel of Chrift; it is the Gofpel of the Devil. Where perfecution begins, Chriftianity ends; and if the name of it remains, the fpirit is gone. Chrift never ufed any thing that looked like force or violence, except once; and that was, to drive bad men out of the Temple, and not to drive them in.

Paffing over the farther confideration of thefe things, I fhall at prefent only juft remind you of fome faults contrary to this virtue of charity.

And they are covetoufnefs and felfifhnefs, which make us hard-hearted and infenfible to the diftrefs of our neighbour; injuftice of all forts, not only that which deprives him of any part of his poffeffions by force or fraud, but that which takes from him by flander his honour and good name; and, an infolent pride and difdain in our behaviour to others. Thefe vices are not confiftent with the loweft degree of Chriftian benevolence: and to thefe we may add two other faults, which are as oppofite to each other as they are to charity.

The firft is a cold indifference about religion and virtue. He in whom this carelefs indolence prevails, hath no regard and affection for truth, no concern whether

whether it prospers or not, and whether men be good or bad. He neither promotes piety, nor discountenances vice, nor shuns, as far as prudence permits, persons of wicked lives and debauched principles.

The other is a zeal for things not essential to religion, which exerts itself in an eager fierceness about doubtful and disputable points, in judging unmercifully of those who, being sober and religious people, have a different way of thinking from ourselves, in making no allowances for the various degrees of understanding, and the imperious force of education, and the obscurity perhaps of the controverted subjects. Such a litigious Christian, if he be right in his opinions, which is much to be doubted, is wrong in his way of defending them: he keeps a doctrine, and breaks a commandment.

True religion consists more in doing than in prating, more in practice than in speculation. A man who hath got an orthodox faith, and never learned to lead an orthodox life, proclaims his own folly and madness. He lays a strong foundation, and then raises a rotten building on it.

We cannot endure a state of doubt and suspense; we love to get at certainty. For this we are not to be blamed. But we love to be positive and dogmatical, and are seldom sensible how little at present it is given to us to know. Paganism was thick darkness; Christianity, in some respects, is only a twilight. For now we talk like children, now we know in part, now we see through a glass darkly; unless we be wiser than St. Paul, who says this of himself, as well as of other Christians.

Let us above all so live as to be able to entertain hopes of living with God hereafter, and then often suspending our judgment and content of some things to be quite ignorant, and some things to know obscurely and in part, and united, if not in opinion,

yet

yet in charity with our brethren; let us wait with humble patience for that blessed time when we shall know even also as we are known. If goodness dwell in us, knowledge will not stay long behind. Yet a few days, and the (c) cloud shall be removed from our eyes, and truth shall shine upon us in its full splendor.

(c) ——ἀλλὰ συ ῥῦ σαι ὑπ' ἠέρος——
Ποίησον δ' αἴθρην, δὸς δ' ὀφθαλμοῖσιν ἰδέσθαι.

Il. p. 645.

Ἀχλὺν δ' αὖ τοι ἀπ' ὀφθαλμῶν ἕλον, ἣ πρὶν ἐπῆεν.

Il. ε. 217.

SERMON

SERMON XVIII.

ROM. xii. 18.

If it be possible, as much as lieth in you, live peaceably with all men.

THAT it is a pleasant and desirable thing to live peaceably with all men, and to be esteemed by those with whom we have dealings and to whom we are known, is an assertion which wants no proof, and is generally acknowledged even by those whose temper and behaviour would incline one to think that they abhorred such a state, and that they could no more live without daily quarrels, than without daily bread. Even they will always complain loudly of injuries received, and will sometimes declare that, for their part, they would willingly be at peace with all the world, by which they mean that they should be very well pleased if all the world would bear with their humours, and submit to their insolence, and forgive their rudeness, and excuse their defects, and think and speak well of them. Thus we all desire the good-will and esteem of mankind, though many of us deserve it not, and though it be absurd and ridiculous to expect it, whilst we commit those very faults which we dislike and blame in others.

It is evident that we were created to live together in a peaceable way, and in a friendly manner. It appears from the frame of our body, and the powers of our mind, from our natural inclinations and defires, from our wants and from the methods of fupplying and removing them, from the good offices which we can receive and return. Thus a ftate of mutual kindnefs and charity is a ftate for which Providence plainly intended us: but fin, blinding the underftanding, corrupting the hearts, and inflaming the paffions of men, fet them at variance, and made them as much enemies to each other as to God.

Our Lord came to put an end to thefe evils, and to reftore peace amongft us. His doctrine and his example fhew that he had nothing more conftantly in view; the behaviour of his difciples, and of many whom they converted, fhew the happy effects of his doctrine in promoting humanity and brotherly love; and if Chriftians enjoy not this peace, the fault is in them, and not in their religion.

The world abounds with perverfe difpofitions which are ever bufy in difturbing and vexing others. Hence it comes to pafs that they who, by natural temper, and by Chriftian principles, defire and endeavour to live quietly, and to give no offence, often cannot obtain the end which they feek. Friends will be envious, captious, and fickle, and enemies will fpring up in an unaccountable manner; they are weeds which will grow of themfelves, without our planting or watering. A man fhall be blamed and hated becaufe he has not performed things which he cannot do, or which he ought not to do; becaufe he has not gratified unreafonable expectations, and facrificed his fortunes, his health, his reputation, his confcience, his liberty, his honour, to the humours of this and that perfon. The Apoftle feems to have had this in view, when he gave Chriftians the precept in the text accompanied with a reftriction: Live peaceably, fays he, with all men, if it be poffible, and as much as lieth in you. Endeavour to have no enemies. Perhaps the endeavour will be unfuccefsful,

cefsful, and you may meet with perſons who will not live at peace with you, and whoſe favourable opinion you cannot obtain. Your duty is, to take care that the fault lie not on your ſide, and that none ſhould have juſt cauſe to complain of your conduct.

St. Paul knew that Chriſtians could not enjoy peace at that time with a great part of the world. They lived amongſt men who entertained an ill opinion of them, who either perſecuted, or hated, or deſpiſed them. Several lies had been raiſed concerning the belief and the behaviour of Chriſtians, to blacken them, and to make them odious; and theſe calumnies had been received as truths by many credulous and malicious Pagans. Chriſtians were thought by them to be men of a moroſe and unſociable temper, men of no learning, no judgment, and no abilities, men who loved each other, but hated every one elſe, men who avoided the company of all except their brethren, that they might keep their crimes concealed from the public, men who rejected the religion of their anceſtors, and the eſtabliſhed rites and ceremonies, through ſtupidity and obſtinate prejudice and ſenſeleſs ſcruple. St. Paul therefore commands Chriſtians to uſe their endeavours to live peaceably both amongſt themſelves, and with the Pagans, with whom they had the misfortune to be joined in civil ſociety, and to procure the good opinion of every one, even of their ſlanderers and perſecutors, by all acts of prudence and affability, of meekneſs and charity, by all methods which were conſiſtent with their character and with the Goſpel of Chriſt. But it was not permitted to them to do more than this, to uſe any ſinful compliances, to deny or diſſemble their religion, to neglect any Chriſtian duty, or to join in idolatrous practices. So the author of the Epiſtle to the Hebrews gives them theſe two precepts joined together; Follow peace with all men, and holineſs without which no man ſhall

ſee

see the Lord; which by some is understood to be an advice to them, that they should use all lawful methods to live peaceably with Christians, with Jews, and with Gentiles, but be careful, whilst they sought peace, to preserve a good conscience, and not offend God to obtain any present advantage. The admonition was necessary; for when the Gospel was first preached, some of those who received it pursued peace and the favour of the world by unjustifiable methods. It is probable that they who, in the Epistle to the Hebrews, are said to have forsaken the assembling themselves together, acted this part out of fear, or with a view to preserve the esteem of unbelievers. The Corinthians, to make themselves agreeable to their Pagan friends, partook of the feasts which they celebrated when they sacrificed to Idols. Soon after the death of the Apostles some arose, who, to preserve themselves from danger, to avoid the displeasure, and to secure the favour of the Heathen, made no scruple of sacrificing to Idols, and even of denying and renouncing Jesus Christ, when they were brought before Magistrates.

Though we in this age are not exposed to the same trials, and in danger of committing the same faults; yet we dwell with many wicked and unreasonable persons, and may often find it impossible to serve and please God, and to oblige them at the same time. In these cases the precept given to us is plain and full and strict, and not to be evaded: He who loveth his relations, his friends, his companions, his ease and repose, his pleasures, his fortunes, his vices, or his life, more than his Saviour, is not worthy of him; and he who fears the scorn, the censure, and the malice of profane persons more than the wrath of God, must seek his reward, if he can obtain it, from those to whom he pays an unrighteous and slavish obedience. Peace is a most valuable thing; but it may be purchased at too dear a rate.

I pro-

I proceed to lay down some directions and rules of conduct, which we ought to follow if we would live peaceably with all men.

1. If we would live peaceably with all men, it is necessary that we be at peace within, with ourselves, and that we be not under the tyrannical government of our own turbulent vices. Whosoever is a slave to these bad masters will never be a friend to mankind, or live quietly with his fellow-creatures: he will lie under violent temptations to hate, to envy, to censure, to slander, to wrong others, and to promote his own interest, and pursue his selfish views, at their expence. If he is not actually engaged in quarrels, yet he is not, properly speaking, in a state of peace with others: at the best, it is a cessation of hostilities, a short suspension of arms, a precarious truce, and a smothered fire which will burst out when the least wind fans it. But he who is not troubled with impetuous passions, who is easily contented, and whose views are fixed upon better things than are to be found here below, will not disturb the peace of his neighbour; and, as he will not be envied by worldly-minded persons, he will probably escape their ill offices, and be overlooked by them as one who interferes not with their projects.

2. They who would live peaceably with all men will find prudence a necessary quality; for an honest and well-meaning person may by indiscretion be extremely troublesome to other, and make himself odious. Of this there are many instances.

It is rashness to throw ourselves into danger in a good cause, when we can avoid it without sin, and when the command of God is not clear and express. A man ought to love his neighbour as himself; his country, and religion, and truth, and virtue, more than himself, that is, more than his temporal interests; and should be willing to expose himself to inconvenience and peril for their sake. But there is a

SERMON XVIII.

perverse zeal and frantic courage, which seeks out trouble and hazard, and defends truth itself in a rude and insolent manner; which refuses to submit to the lawful arts of courtesy and insinuation, by which our adversaries might be softened and brought to a better temper.

The same kind of indiscretion hath also shewed itself in fierce and turbulent endeavours to reform smaller errors and abuses, when there was little hope of succeeding, and when even the good which could be supposed to be gained by such amendments could not compensate the animosities and disturbances raised about it.

They act indiscreetly, who, having no particular obligation to it, take upon them to (*a*) reprimand offenders, and do it without good temper and civility, without a due attention to the circumstances of time and place, of persons and dispositions.

It is also an indiscretion to contradict those who are mistaken, and to endeavour to convince them of their beloved errors, when there is reason to think that they will only despise, or hate, or slander, and misrepresent us for it. There are persons who seem to be doomed by a kind of fatality to think absurdly and judge perversly, who are as fond of their prejudices as Job was of his righteousness and integrity, and hold them fast, and will not let them go as long as they live. In contending with such persons we shall lose always our pains and our time, and perhaps our temper too.

In general, before we enter into any disputes and contentions, religious or political, and, as Solomon represents it, let out a water whose course we cannot stop

---

(*a*) Illum liberius admonuisti quam debebas: itaque non emendasti, sed offendisti: de cætero vide, non tantum an verum sit quod dicis, sed an ille cui dicitur, veri patiens sit. *Seneca* de Ira, iii. 36.

stop when we will, we should carefully consider what may be the end of it, and whether it will serve to any wise and profitable purpose; and we should beware that we exercise not intemperately the liberty of judging and speaking and writing; we should beware of this, even for the sake of liberty, which is never in more danger of being quite lost than when it is greatly abused.

3. They who desire to live peaceably with all men, must refrain from slander and evil speaking. Though the Scripture commands the forgiveness of injuries, yet so apt are men to forget or to explain away this precept, that he would be not only a wicked, but a weak person, who should hope to censure and calumniate others, and to find them ready to excuse it. He would soon learn by experience that resentment is stronger than charity. An infallible method therefore of losing friends, and adding to the number of our enemies, and making their enmity perpetual, is to be busy-bodies, tale-bearers, and evil-speakers. The observation in the Gospel, that with what measure we mete, it shall be measured to us again, will be more than fulfilled in this case; full measure, and heaped up, and running over, will those who have been injured by us, return into our bosom; for men, who are weak in other respects, are (b) strong to do an evil turn. Indignation will sometimes perform what Nature never seemed to promise: It will make even the dull and stupid quick to discover, and skilful to expose, the faults of an enemy.

These are evils which they have a very probable prospect of escaping, who set a watch over their words, who concern themselves as little as may be with the affairs and conduct and character of others, who bear with their imperfections, who, when they hear any person defamed, are either silent, or, if a

proper

(b) Ad nocendum potentes sumus. *Seneca*, de Ira, i. 3.

proper opportunity offers itself, say what may be justly said in their vindication and excuse.

Such persons will usually find their reward even in this world, will live honoured by those to whom they are known, and spared by the morose and censorious, who can often see the amiableness of a quiet and candid disposition, and pay it an aukward kind of reverence. Slander is ungenerous, and pernicious to our present interest; nor should we give up ourselves to it, if bad example and custom, and inadvertence, added to some irregular passions and mean views, did not lead us on thus to do mischief often to others, and always to ourselves.

This is one of the faults which should be corrected and restrained betimes, since, instead of decreasing, it is apt to grow upon us with our years; because, feeling our infirmities and decays, and suspecting that we are slighted by the rising generation, we are tempted more and more to peevishness and censoriousness.

One of the best methods to avoid evil speaking and its bad consequences, is the Apostle's direction, to study to be quiet and to mind our own business. Tale-bearers, censurers, and calumniators, often belong to the Lazy Order, and are persons whose time hangs heavily upon their hands, and who cannot bear to be alone, or to be employed in any thing that is useful.

4. Another rule to be observed by those who would live peaceably, is to avoid the familiarity of malicious, quarrelsome, and censorious persons. The reason is evident. We imitate those with whom we frequently converse, and insensibly conform ourselves to their behaviour. As our understanding is improved by the instruction of the wise, the learned, and the judicious; as the discourse and the example of the good incite us to the practice of virtue; so the defects of those with whom we are intimate have a bad influence upon us, and corrupt our minds, which are too

much disposed to receive and retain evil impressions. Even they who are naturally gentle and peaceable, by associating with those who are unlike themselves, are often led into faults which they once abhorred. When these unequal alliances are made between contrary tempers, the usual consequence is, that the evil temper spoils the good, and that the good produces no change in the evil. If we keep up friendships with such people, we shall probably comply with them more than we ought, judge partially in their behalf, enter into their quarrels, engage in their animosities, and entertain an ill opinion of those whom they continually misrepresent. If we could be wary and discreet masters of our own hearts and passions, and able to converse with such persons frequently and to preserve ourselves uncorrupted, which is not at all likely, yet we act imprudently, whilst we lead ourselves into such temptations; we expose our virtue to a dangerous trial; we run the risque of forfeiting our reputation; and we may expect to be accounted as bad as those with whom we chuse to spend our time, because a likeness of disposition is commonly and reasonably suppose to beget and preserve intimacies and friendships. We may indeed and we must often converse with people of all tempers; else, as the Apostle says, must we needs go out of the world; but in the choice of our friends we should be circumspect, and avoid those who have the unhappy art of making themselves enemies.

5. They who would live peaceably with all men, must be patient and long-suffering, must overlook and forgive injuries. Therefore St. Paul, after he had given the precept in the text of living peaceably, subjoins, Bless those who persecute you; Recompense to no man evil for evil; Avenge not yourselves; Overcome evil with good. Men are frail and imperfect: difference of opinions, difference of interests, credulity, anger, pride, and vanity, will produce a

behaviour

SERMON XVIII.

behaviour towards us which may offend us, but should not highly provoke and discompose us. If they who trespass against us acknowledge the fault, and promise amendment, we should be easily pacified; and though they persist obstinately, hatred and malice and revenge are unlawful returns. It was said in praise of a certain Roman, that he was a man of strict honour and probity, and one (*c*) who could neither offer nor put up an injury; but the Gospel requires of us more than this. If we could preserve ourselves free from every thought, word, and action, contrary to justice, we should be obliged to add to those good qualities the forgiveness of injuries. But since we have all of us (*d*) faults of our own, and failings to be excused by those with whom we converse, we are bound upon that account to return the forbearance of which we stand in need. He who will excuse no faults, must be at variance with many persons, and must be at variance, without hope or prospect of reconcilement; whence we may see that our Lord justly requires us to pardon those who trespass against us. It is a precept which the impetuous passions of men may render hard and disagreeable; but it conduces most evidently to the common good and interest of all societies, and is therefore profitable to all the members of society. In all wise nations it has been taught and believed, that it was the duty of every man to forgive an injury, and to receive an enemy into favour, when the good of his country required it; and examples of persons who have remarkably fulfilled this duty, are recorded in history.

(*c*) Seneca, the father, says of Albutius; *Homo summæ probitatis, qui nec facere injuriam, nec pati sciret.* Controv. iii. Præfat. But the resentment, which Albutius is there said to have shewed, had nothing unlawful in it.

(*d*) Nemo invenitur, qui se possit absolvere: et innocentem quisque se dicit, respiciens testem, non conscientiam. *Seneca* de Ira, i. 14.

This rule will be found very extenſive, and comprehending moſt caſes; for, if every perſon in ſociety ſhould forgive no offences, univerſal hatred would be eſtabliſhed, and a total diſorder would enſue. The ſad effects of this implacable temper have been felt in many places, where quarrels have been hereditary, and deſcending like a patrimony through many generations, and thouſands have been ruined or deſtroyed through the fault of one or two. For the ſake therefore of the public, every one ſhould conſent to entertain no rancour and malice in his heart, and to leave the avenging of injuries to God and to the laws of his country, paſſing over all the faults committed againſt him, which the welfare of the community will ſuffer to be excuſed.

6. Another good quality, which produces and preſerves peace, is what is called civility or manners. I know not whether we may reckon it a virtue; but ſurely it belongs to the family of virtues, and is nearly related to them. Many offences are committed againſt it, not perhaps by malignity of heart, but by capriciouſneſs, haſtineſs, inattention, and want of breeding; and yet it is an accompliſhment highly neceſſary upon ſeveral accounts. Though goodneſs of heart be the main thing, yet external forms are not to be neglected. As men cannot ſee one another's minds, and read one another's thoughts, they judge uſually by the outſide, by the appearance, as it happens to be taking or diſguſting. A rough and forbidding manner is ſuppoſed to ariſe from pride and contempt; and contempt is of all ill uſage what we can leaſt endure and excuſe.

7. Again; another quality, neceſſary for the cultivation of peace, is modeſty or humility, as nothing is more contrary to our own repoſe and to that of others than haughtineſs and preſumption, the expectation of receiving a large ſhare of reſpect, homage, deference, and

and services from others, and a resentment when these hopes are disappointed. Every one dislikes these overbearing people, these petty tyrants in civil society, who would exact from others a reverence which we chuse not to pay as a debt, but to give as a favour, freely and without constraint, and to give it to those who deserve it best, and require it least.

8. Lastly, They who would live peaceably with all, should do good to all, to the utmost of their power. To be masters of our affections, to be wise and prudent, to set a watch over our lips, to abstain from evil speaking, to chuse for our friends and companions persons who are virtuous and of a peaceable disposition, to forgive injuries, to be civil and courteous, modest and humble, all this will not be sufficient to produce the desired effect, unless we add to these a beneficent temper, and an endeavour to promote the happiness and prosperity of others. Without this amiable quality we cannot expect to be loved and esteemed. We were certainly made to do kind offices; and every one has a right to expect and require them, if he deserves them, and unless he has forfeited it by his crimes, a right founded in nature and religion. Human laws cannot easily fix this mutual claim, nor punish those who are deficient in this duty: but men will supply this defect of the laws, by slighting and censuring such offenders. They must not hope to be well spoken of, living or dead; but he who loves his neighbour and shews it by his actions will probably secure that general love and regard, which power, and riches, and dignity, and knowledge, and great abilities, cannot command, and daily fail of obtaining.

There is nothing which will more enable us to live peaceably, than a due sense of the shortness and uncertainty of human life, and the small value of those possessions which end with it, if not before it. An immoderate love of pleasure, of wealth, of power, of
popular

popular applause, are the chief causes of the misunderstanding, the rudeness, the contention, the hatred, the malice, the spite, the envy, the cruelty, the detraction, the fraud, the faction, and the violence, which disturb the world. That is, in other words, Men are old children, and quarrel eagerly for trifles; whilst they have them not, they are miserable; and when they have obtained them, they find them unsatisfactory.

The wise and the good have also many objects of desire; but then they desire and pursue things, which the vain, the covetous, the proud, the ignorant, and the vicious, neither understand nor esteem; and therefore, unenvied and unmolested, they often find a safe and a quiet passage from this world to a better.

SERMON XIX.

PSALM cxix. 71.

It is good for me that I have been afflicted.

THAT man is born to trouble, is a general assertion, to which so few exceptions are to be found, that the foolishest hope which we can entertain is, that we shall pass our lives in uninterrupted prosperity; and know the nature of trouble and disappointment, not by experience, but by observation.

Yet they who are in a state of prosperity are often inclined to indulge this vain hope, and to flatter themselves with the expectation of many days to come, all as fair as those which they at present enjoy.

There is another illusion as common as this, and more dangerous; namely, a persuasion that adversity is the greatest evil which can befall us. The Scriptures frequently affirm the contrary; and though, out of respect to their sacred authority, we admit in general all to be true which is contained in them; yet in this point, we believe as though we believed not, our faith is imperfect, and its influence upon our passions is small and superficial.

And yet the doctrine of the Scriptures upon this subject is agreeable to general experience, and to plain common sense. The Scriptures have no refined and subtle notions about the nature of adversity, nor do they endeavour to persuade us that we may take pleasure in it; but, acknowledging that it is irksome and

contrary

contrary to our inclinations, they assure us that it produces many excellent effects. No chastning, say they, for the present seemeth to be joyous, but grievous; nevertheless afterwards it yieldeth the peaceable fruit of righteousness unto them that are exercised thereby. It is good for me, says David, in the words of the text, that I have been afflicted. He doth not say, that afflictions, whilst he endured them, were agreeable to him; but that he had found them profitable, and that they had made him a better man, a more careful observer of the laws of God. It is good for me that I have been afflicted, that I might learn thy statutes. He confesseth that prosperity had been prejudicial to him; that it had conduced to make him negligent of his duty; that, whilst he seemed to be happy, his soul was in no good condition, though he perhaps was not sensible of it, till adversity taught him his danger, and the necessity of amendment. Before I was afflicted, says he in this Psalm, I went astray: but now have I kept thy word.

The good which afflictions have an aptness and a tendency to produce, is reformation and improvement. It will be proper to shew this, and to shew it in particular instances.

One use then of afflictions is, that they often make us better members of society, by giving us a compassionate disposition towards those who are unhappy, and a proneness to relieve and assist them.

Experience shews that they who have been acquainted with trouble are the most inclined to pity a person who is in the same condition. They have been in the like hard circumstances; they then wanted the friendly advice and the good offices of others; they then more especially were displeased, if they found themselves neglected and slighted, and their reasonable requests refused. They are consequently the more disposed to make the case of others their own, and to have a strong sense of the beauty of that divine precept, which directs

SERMON XIX.

rects us to do to our neighbour what we would that he should do to us. The sacred writers have not omitted this obfervation, when, to encourage us to truft in our Mediator, they remind us that he, having borne our nature and its weakneffes, is confequently the more ready to affift us; for in that himfelf hath fuffered, being tempted, he is able to fuccour them that are tempted.

We feem to be naturally difpofed to pity thofe who fuffer: but this difpofition may be weakened, deftroyed, preferved, or ftrengthened. It is often weakened by temporal profperity, which raifes in us a thoughtlefs, carelefs gaiety, a great love of amufements and pleafure, and an averfion from all objects which may create any melancholy and uneafinefs; and it is as frequently preferved and increafed by calamities, which foften the heart, and give it a tafte for the ferious pleafures arifing from benevolence and humanity.

It is a thing of far lefs importance, and yet it is not altogether unworthy of obfervation, that afflictions have a tendency to improve not only a man's moral difpofitions, but his natural abilities alfo, his fentiments and his expreffions, his thoughts and his ftyle.

Here then is a particular and a general ufe of afflictions. They are certainly profitable to thofe, whofe temper and underftanding they have improved; and they are of general ufe to focieties, by raifing up among them public benefactors.

Afflictions have alfo a tendency either to prevent, or to remove from us, pride and infolence, and a difregard of our fellow-creatures.

They who live at their eafe, who have experienced no difappointments, who enjoy health and plenty and power, learn to imagine that health and plenty and power contain in them all perfections of body and mind, or at leaft fupply all the defects of either; they learn too eafily to forget themfelves, and to flight thofe who are beneath them. But trouble, like death, equals

all,

all, and at its approach the frivolous marks of worldly distinction shew their emptiness. Calamities befall the poor and friendless; they visit also the rich and the powerful; and when they come to those whom prosperity hath spoiled, they bring this instruction along with them, that all states are exposed to the evils of life, that all persons stand in need of each other's assistance, and that the most considerable difference between us is that which is made by virtue and vice.

Again: Afflictions are useful, as they wean us from too great a love for this world.

Since men are fond of life, and of all that conduces to its conveniences, and since this fondness is very much increased by the possession of the good things belonging to the present state; it is fit, upon the whole, that man, who is born to die, should also be born to trouble, and meet with disappointments, and see the disagreeable part of life, that he may be contented to submit to a decree which he cannot reverse, and learn to retire decently from a state, which the law of mortality will force him to quit, whether he be willing or no.

It hath been thought by some, that, if we lived long enough, we might and we should learn all this, without the assistance of afflictions, those rigid instructors. (a) We are satiated, say they, as of other things, so of life itself. A constant return of the same occupations and of the same amusements will grow unwelcome and insipid at the last; and we shall desire a release, and receive it as a favour.

A certain mixture of sprightliness and melancholy might lead some persons into this way of thinking; but

---

(a) Habet natura, ut et aliarum rerum omnium, sic et vivendi satietatem. *Cicero.*

Quosdam subit eadem faciendi videndique satietas, et vitæ non odium, sed fastidium: in quod prolabimur ipsa impellente philosophia, dum dicimus: Quousque eadem? ———Multi

but the greater part of men are so (*b*) attached to their present state, that much stronger causes are requisite to give them an indifference towards this world; nor would a long life grow tiresome to them, unless it were attended with worse inconveniencies than a review of the same objects, and a repetition of the same actions.

Afflictions therefore come seasonably to those who would willingly take up their abode in a place which was not designed for their home, and give them a sense of the many defects which render that place undesireable; and then the mind, dissatisfied with its present condition, and ever desirous of finding rest and peace, looks forward, and turns its views towards heaven.

This is another use of troubles, and one of the ends for which they are permitted or appointed by Providence. They are designed for our amendment, and they naturally conduce to it.

Men, living in a neglect of their duty, find ways to compose their conscience, and to drive away the thoughts of their offences, whilst their condition here is easy and prosperous. The variety of amusements and occupations, to which they have recourse, employ and divert

―――

―Multi sunt qui non acerbum judicent vivere, sed superfluum. *Seneca*, Ep. 24. 77. et De Tranquill. 2.

 Cur non, ut vitæ plenus conviva, recedis? &c.
 Nam tibi præterea quod machiner, inveniamque
 Quod placeat, nihil est; eadem sunt omnia semper, &c.
Lucretius iii. 951.

 Τέτον εὐτυχέστατον λέγω,
 Ὅστις θεωρήσας ἀλύπως, Παρμένων,
 Τὰ σεμνὰ ταῦτ', ἀπῆλθεν ὅθεν ἦλθεν ταχύ.
Menander, p. 184. et Not.

(*b*) *Inde* illud Mæcenatis turpissimum votum——
 Debilem facito manu,
 Debilem pede, coxa:
 Tuber adstrue gibberum;
 Lubricos quate dentes.
 Vita dum superest, bene est.
 Hanc mihi, vel acuta
 Si sedeam cruce, sustine.
Seneca, Epist. 101.

divert them, and keep off serious and sorrowful reflections. It was the observation of a Pagan, that (c) Altars were made for the unhappy, and that other people seldom approached them.

But when the scene is changed, and things fall out contrary to their expectation, and trouble overtakes them, a new course of thoughts takes place. They seek relief and assistance, and they see that worldly objects can give them no ease and no comfort: they then begin to know the nature of such objects, and to look upon them with more indifference. When they have lost the things which they most valued, or when they find them deceitful, useless, and unsatisfactory, they learn to pass a new and a better judgment upon them.

At the same time they perceive the beauty of virtue, the excellence of piety, the many advantages of a religious life, and the inestimable value of the future rewards promised to the obedient; and they see the folly of preferring the transitory pleasures of sin to these substantial and durable blessings.

They will then be sensible that God alone can be a refuge to them, that he can many ways assist them, that he can remove or lessen the evils which oppress them, or give them strength of mind to bear them, or make those calamities turn to their temporal or eternal welfare.

Then their past offences will rise up before them, and shame and sorrow that they had not served God better in the days of prosperity: then resolutions of amendment will follow, and of working out their own salvation with care and diligence.

Lastly, afflictions give us an opportunity of recommending ourselves to the favour of God, by exercising the virtues suitable to that state.

In

(c) —— raro fumant felicibus aræ.

In this view they are trials, trials of our patience and conſtancy and faith and reſignation and reliance; and therefore great benefits, when they anſwer the end for which they were deſigned. To be contented, when every thing ſucceeds according to our deſires; to think that God has given us what is neceſſary for our well-being, when we abound with all conveniences of life, is no virtue. But to believe that a ſtate of affliction is proper for us, becauſe God thinks fit to try us with it, to ſubmit to it with meekneſs and patience, to be willing to undergo any thing here, if by it we may ſecure his approbation and a place in his kingdom, is a diſpoſition moſt acceptable to him. The behaviour of ſuch a perſon recommends conſtancy and piety to all who converſe with him, more than the moſt elaborate diſcourſes upon the ſubject. It hath been ſaid, that a good man contending with ill fortune, and ſuperior to it, is a ſpectacle which God himſelf may delight to behold: he is certainly an example from which men by beholding may receive inſtruction and improvement.

I have mentioned ſeveral deſireable effects, which afflictions have a tendency to procure. It is true that they have not always theſe happy conſequences. There are, and there have been, many to whom calamities have done no good, but the contrary. Hence thoſe expoſtulations and complaints in the Prophets; For all this his anger is not turned away, but his hand is ſtretched out ſtill; for the people turneth not to him that ſmiteth them, neither do they ſeek the Lord of hoſts. Why ſhould they be ſtricken any more? they will revolt more and more. Strangers have devoured the ſtrength of Ephraim—but they do not return to the Lord, nor ſeek him for all this. Afflictions produce in ſome a diſtruſt of God's goodneſs, hardneſs of heart, deſpair, injurious thoughts againſt Providence: in others they excite humility, repentance, charity, humanity, and all good works. To be made worſe by ſufferings, is a ſign of a corrupt and profligate mind,

and,

and muſt ariſe from a diſbelief of all religion, or from a very wicked conduct; but they who are in a middle ſtate between groſs impiety and Chriſtian holineſs, who have virtuous inclinations and good principles mixed with many frailties and faults, are often improved by ſufferings.

We may obſerve that in the New Teſtament the afflictions which befall Chriſtians are repreſented not as puniſhments, but as corrections, as the chaſtnings of a father and a friend, as acts of God's kindneſs to us, intended to make us better and happier.

We may alſo obſerve that afflictions will be more or leſs heavy and grievous to us, according to the bad or good effect which they produce in us. Very grievous they muſt be to thoſe who account God to be their enemy, and neither ſeek nor expect his favour and aſſiſtance: but to thoſe who are amended by them, they will not prove inſupportable. Trouble leads them to repentance; and repentance is a kind of pleaſing grief, a remorſe attended and allayed with hopes of being reconciled to our Father, and of ſeeing one time or other an end of ſorrows.

And beſides this, God hath told us that ſuch as our behaviour is when we are thus viſited by him, ſuch will his conduct be towards us. If we turn to him, and receive his corrections with ſubmiſſion and humility, and by the reformation of our lives ſhew that we have a due ſenſe of our faults, and of the kind end for which thoſe corrections were inflicted, God will make them eaſy to us, and in due time relieve or releaſe us: but if we harden our hearts, and ſin on in defiance of his judgments, we may expect that God will deal with us as he declared that he would deal with the people of Iſrael, when, having denounced terrible evils which ſhould overtake them if they forſook him, he tells them; If you will not be reformed by all this, I will puniſh you ſeven times more, and again ſeven times more for your ſins.

I ſhall

SERMON XIX.

I shall now consider the use which is to be made of this doctrine.

There is a pretty fable related by an ancient Pagan Writer, that the Deity, who formed the first man out of the ground, reflecting at the same time on the calamities which the unhappy creature was to undergo, wept over his work, and tempered it with tears; that man, whose heart should be so often overcharged with grief, might not want a way to give it vent.

This Writer hath considered afflictions in a desponding and melancholy way; but there is a more manly and a more rational way of considering them; and it is thus:

Since we have no reason to expect that we shall pass our days in an uninterrupted enjoyment of temporal happiness, since affliction seems on the contrary to be a man's patrimony, his birthright and inheritance, since troubles are also intended for our benefit, and when they produce proper effects become more easy to be endured, it is our duty and our interest to prepare ourselves to meet them, and to acquire the methods of softening their harsh nature, and of improving their good tendency.

Therefore, if we are in an easy condition, we should preserve ourselves free from the faults which often accompany that state, such as pride, uncharitableness, irreligion, a pursuit of unlawful pleasures, and an unreasonable fondness for the world. We should remember that there is nothing besides our virtue that we can call our own, and that almost every thing else is vanity or uncertainty.

There is a thoughtfulness about future evils, which makes us dissatisfied and uneasy before-hand, and raises apprehensions of troubles which may never befall us; and this is a weakness, or rather a folly: but there is a meditation upon these subjects which is pleasant and profitable, which teaches us moderation in the best state, and arms us with courage and constancy against the worst.

Happy circumstances incline us to seek out variety of amusements, to keep much company, to indulge our appetites; in a word, to create to ourselves many wants, to make many things necessary to us, which several persons in lower life never possessed, and never desired. Thus we lay ourselves open to grief and misery upon any change of circumstances, and become unfit to act a rational part in any other station. This evil would not befall us, if we used the pleasures and conveniences of this world, as things which we may lose, and ought to resign decently. If we can gratify our appetites in all things, we should sometimes cross and contradict them, that we may live contented upon a little, if poverty should ever overtake us; if we have friends, and relations, and affairs, and diversions, we should at certain times withdraw from them all, that we may know how to bear retirement and solitude, if need should require it; that we may secure to ourselves good company within our own breast, and be able to converse agreeably with God and our own thoughts.

By acting thus in prosperity, we shall escape those evils which others draw upon themselves, and those which God inflicts upon sinners to bring them to a better mind; and we shall not be overcome by those which befall us.

If our days have been and are prosperous, we have great reason to add to our gratitude an uncommon care of our behaviour, and to work out our own salvation with fear and trembling. God hath often declared that he corrects those whom he loves best: we must therefore beware that we be not of the number of those who receive good things only in this state. If that should be our case, our present happiness would be our heaviest misfortune. But the favours, the temporal favours of Providence, are no curses, unless we make them such. We may be successful and virtuous too.

Indeed

Indeed it requires no small wisdom and caution to join these two blessings, which men almost always put asunder; and the difficulty of doing this should teach us a distrust of ourselves, a moderate esteem of our possessions, and a religious fear lest we should miss our reward in heaven.

If we have endeavoured to behave ourselves like men, and like Christians, then have we many motives to bear adversity with patience and resignation, and not to be quite cast down; then we have a refuge, and may apply to Him who hath told us that all things shall work together for good to them that love him, that he will not suffer them to be tried above their strength, but will with the temptation make a way, that they may escape; and that blessed are they who are trained up by these short hardships to glory and immortality. If our days are evil, they are few, and then follows a state of peace for the righteous, then various rewards will be distributed, and probably none of the smallest to those who have been exercised and improved by afflictions. We judge persons fortunate or wretched according to their present outward circumstances. How uncertain must that judgment be! If God should enable us to see what passeth in the hearts of men, or if he should remove the cloud from our eyes, and give us a view of the state which is to succeed this, how desireable would the condition appear of several whom the World now is disposed to pity, or to despise!

If the evil days come upon us, before we be prepared to meet them, before we have reformed our conduct, it is our duty to consider the purposes for which it pleaseth God to visit us. If we give ourselves up to sullen discontent, or despair, or if we have no sorrow for our past offences, but only for our present calamities, we make not a right use of his corrections, we offend him still more, we add to the weight of the burden which he hath laid upon us. His corrections are calls to repentance; and we should be thankful that he took us not off at a time when death would have been the destruction both of soul and body; and whilst we endeavour to reform our lives, we should trust in the promises of God, that he will be found of those who thus seek him.

Lastly; If we have passed through troubles, and seen an end of them, our behaviour should be such, that we may be able to say with David, It is good for us that we have known afflictions. We may reflect upon them with pleasure, if we are sensible that they weakened our depraved appetites and vain desires, and strengthened our good dispositions, and adorned our minds with new graces. If they have left us no better than they found us, our condition is bad. In honest and generous tempers the blessings of God produce gratitude and love; in those which are less tractable, afflictions often create amendment; but there is no hope of those, upon whom nothing can work, upon whom both severity and kindness are thrown away.

To conclude;

As we profess ourselves to be Christians, we should always bear in mind the declaration of our Lord, that His kingdom is not of this world. We are taught in the Gospel, that we must not expect temporal prosperity, that we are only strangers and sojourners, that we must fix our views upon sublimer objects, and set our affections upon better mansions where Christ is gone before us, where there will be no more pain, no more sorrow, no more violence, and no more vice, but an everlasting calm, and an uninterrupted state of peace and righteousness. What a supreme happiness will it be to be released from such a world as this, and to be admitted into such a world as that! Our hopes, our wishes, our prayers, and our endeavours, should be all bent towards procuring that inestimable blessing.

SERMON XX.

1 Cor. xiii. 4.

Charity envieth not.

CONCERNING envy it may be proper to consider, first, the object; secondly, the causes; thirdly, the effects; and fourthly, the cure of it.

I. As to the object of envy. Envy is an uneasiness arising from the happiness and prosperity of another, from the advantages and the conveniences which he possesseth.

The good things in possession of another, which thus disturb the envious person, are hardly ever those things which best deserve the name of good, and which are of the greatest value.

Thus; piety, righteousness, virtue, are not the objects of envy. A man, when he contemplates the holiness and goodness of another, may indeed feel a painful uneasiness at his own inferiority, and a strong desire of possessing these excellent qualities in as eminent a degree: but this is not envy; this is emulation, a very useful and commendable disposition.

A man indeed may envy a righteous person; but then it is not properly upon account of his righteousness, but on account of the advantages which his integrity procures him, as love, respect, reputation, and the like. And as Christian and moral virtues, so likewise the endowments and abilities of the mind are seldom,

dom, strictly speaking, objects of envy. Envy is usually accompanied with no small degree of self-sufficiency and self-love; so that an envious person seldom thinks meanly of his own capacity and accomplishments, and is little disposed to account others superior to himself in that respect.

A man may envy a person of great knowledge, learning, sagacity, and judgment, skill and dexterity; but it is not so much on account of his natural and improved abilities, as for the recompence, the profit, the credit, and the reputation, which may sometimes attend them.

A man, when he considers the abilities and accomplishments of another person, may be grieved that he hath not acquired these accomplishments himself, and may vehemently wish to equal that person; but this, as we said before, is emulation.

Again; a man seldom envies another for those advantages which he himself possesseth. A rich or fortunate person rarely envies another who is in no respect above him. Not our equals but our superiors are the objects of our envy.

Therefore envy is an uneasiness or grief arising from the temporal and transitory advantages which another enjoys, and which the envious person enjoys not.

The persons who produce this uneasiness in the envious man are usually those whom he has frequent opportunities of seeing, and who are known to him, or at least who dwell in the same country with himself; nor does envy often extend itself farther. But sometimes, when this perversity has taken full possession of the mind, a man shall envy those who are dead and gone, if they be highly esteemed, and if he thinks himself equal to them in merit, and yet not equally honoured.

II. These observations will direct us, secondly, to assign the

the causes of envy, or the reason why persons fall into this vice.

The great cause of it is plainly a mind set upon the things of this world, and very cold and indifferent to virtue and goodness. When a person has represented to himself temporal prosperity and the pleasures of the senses as the greatest blessing and the most desireable possession, they become the constant objects of his wishes, and when he sees others better accommodated than himself, he looks upon them with uneasiness, as persons who engross those things to which he hath naturally as just a right and title as they; and he cannot bear to think upon it with any patience.

The second cause is indolence and laziness. Temporal advantages are usually neither obtained nor secured without industry and application, and idleness is commonly joined to indigence and disappointments; and then, partly for want of better occupation, and partly through want of conveniences, a man envies those who prosper in the world and feel none of his sorrows.

To this may be added pride, an high conceit of one's own merit and capacity, and an opinion that no respect can be too great and no reward too good for them. This temper, especially if joined to low circumstances and obscurity, usually begets envy.

Another cause is a natural propensity to peevishness, fretfulness, frowardness, spleen, and melancholy. They who are of this temper are seldom stupid, but have a quick succession of thoughts and a fertile imagination, and, if they be crossed and disappointed, are easily disposed to envy other people whose defects they quickly spy out, and whose good fortune they judge to be beyond their deserts.

And here a provoking scene lies open to a busy, lively, dissatisfied mind; for in this disorderly state, this confused mixture of good and evil, there are persons

sons who either by birth or alliances possess outward blessings to which they have small pretensions: others are raised from a low condition, not by their good and useful qualities, but by a prostituted conscience, by a never-blushing assurance, by flattering some and calumniating others, by the mere want of abilities, which is sometimes a great recommendation, by sacrificing the valuable hours of life to trifling amusements, by what is commonly called chance and fortune, that is, by means which lie out of sight. And then, as to reputation on account of distinguishing endowments, though that seems to be somewhat more impartially distributed than the good things of this life, yet there is often a strange perverseness and want of judgment in the opinions of the Many, who extol some, as they depress others, altogether without reason. These things strike forcibly upon those who are not destitute of vivacity and good sense, who spend too much time in looking about them, and too little in minding their own concerns, who have strong desires, and few friends, and slender fortunes, and a disposition to censoriousness; and such persons are soon and easily and insensibly led into indignation, resentment, and envy, and never want objects to offend them.

III. The effects which envy produces are many in number, and in quality and consequences very pernicious.

When it is habitual, it makes the mind miserable which harbours it. This I barely mention; the observation is too common to be insisted upon.

Envy, accompanied with ill-nature and spleen, makes a man as uneasy to himself as he can be to others, and displeased with every object that presents itself to his view and consideration. There is hardly any thing in the person, the appearance, the behaviour, the management, the inventions, the works, and the writings of others, that he can find in his heart to approve:

approve: his thoughts are chiefly exercised in seeking out defects, real or imaginary.

When envy becomes predominant, it disturbs a man so that he cannot regularly pursue his business: it takes off the attention and application, and then what is done imperfectly, and by halves, and with an absent mind, turns to no good account, and produces neither credit nor profit.

Envy makes a man hate his neighbour; and here it begins to be an abominable vice, directly opposite to a Christian temper, and to the great commandment of our Saviour. If envy produced nothing besides uneasiness, grief, indolence, dejection, fretfulness, and unsuccessful wishes, and were only an impediment to useful occupations and laudable attempts, it would really be a pitiable distemper, and deserve to be treated with gentleness and kind advice; but as it produces hatred, it becomes black and odious, and merits rougher usage.

Hatred is an active and industrious vice: he who hates others, sets his thoughts to work how he shall do them an ill turn, and vent his spleen upon them; and this he will do by various bad ways. He will catch hold of any flying rumour that tends to their discredit, and spread and improve it; he will censure their actions, aggravate their faults and failings, and detract from their good qualities, give the worst construction to all that they say and do, endeavour to deprive them of their reputation, to raise them up enemies, and to draw away their friends. If any disappointment or calamity befall them, he will rejoice at it, and represent it as a judgment, or as an evil which they well deserve. If they die, his hatred dies not; it will pursue them beyond the grave, and exert itself in acts of hostility against their memory, their friends and family. These are the usual effects of envy towards the hated person. But this is not all; for

envy

envy sins directly against God as well as against man.

Religion teaches us that the world is conducted and ruled by divine providence; and that all things fall out either according to the appointment or by the permission of the most High, that the unequal dispensation of good and evil, the prosperity of sinners, and the adversity of the righteous, and the seeming disorder of the present state, is continued and allowed for wise ends; and that God will be clearly justified when the present scene passes away, and the age of retribution takes place. Now no envious person believes this, certainly he has no sincere and practical belief of it. He is out of humour with the course of things, that is, with the providence of God; and thinks that if he had the ordering of affairs, and the distribution of blessings, all would be much better; he cannot be contented to act the part, and to fill the station allotted to him, but wants what he has not, and ungratefully overlooks what he has. And now we may enlarge the definition which we before gave of envy, and call it a grief arising from the temporal advantages which others enjoy, producing hatred towards them, and hard thoughts of the divine providence. So that such a person is incapable of observing the two great commandments, which are called the sum and substance of religion, and cannot either love God or his neighbour, or indeed himself, with a rational affection.

IV. It therefore greatly concerns us to avoid or to subdue a vice so troublesome in itself, and so bad in its effects, to which men have often many temptations, and sometimes a natural bent; and this leads us to consider, fourthly, the cure of envy.

Now it seems very plain, that if a person can improve his fortunes, his understanding, and his heart, and secure to himself contentment and peace of mind, he will not only be free from envy, but will be placed in a manner above all possible motives and inducements to envy.

The first thing therefore to be recommended is industry in our worldly affairs. As to the conveniences of life, the desires of men are usually suitable to their education and station; and if they have as much as the generality of their own rank and condition and calling, they are not often dejected and dissatisfied. Now thus much industry seldom fails to obtain and to secure: nothing more naturally protects a man from indigence, dependence, contempt, and insults; and what a person acquires by his own labour and contrivance he enjoys with double pleasure; and whilst he is thus occupied, and in an active state of body and mind, he shuts out those repining envious thoughts, which are the unhappy offspring of indolent laziness. Such are the ordinary good effects of business honestly and closely pursued. But since, through various accidents, the gain is not always answerable to the pains and dexterity employed in the pursuit of it, to this kind of industry is to be added another of an higher sort, which is occupied in cultivating the understanding. This particularly concerns those who are in a middle situation, and whose success in life depends more upon the head than upon the hands. These persons are likewise under more temptations to envy, than those of a lower class, because their views and desires are more extensive; and therefore they should guard against it, by applying themselves to those studies and occupations which improve the mind, and render the man serviceable, and acceptable to the public. This kind of labour is attended usually with the same advantages which are obtained by diligence in lower business, and besides it opens a way to esteem and reputation, to the favour and protection of worthy persons. But here also there is some uncertainty, and room for disappointment, according to the melancholy observation

vation of the wife King; I returned, and faw under the fun that the race is not to the fwift, nor the battle to the ftrong, nor yet bread to the wife, nor yet riches to men of underftanding, nor yet favour to men of fkill.—From thefe uncomfortable reflections can any ufeful inference be made? can any peace of mind and fatisfaction arife? Yes. According to the fame Inftructor, Let us hear the conclufion of the whole matter, Fear God and keep his commandments;—for he who does that, fhall never be difappointed.

V. Since in every labour and in every project there is fome uncertainty, we fhould apply ourfelves more earneftly to the improvement of the heart, where never-failing fuccefs fmiles upon our honeft endeavours. A man may be good in fpite of the world and all its frowns; no fraud or violence can take away from virtue its amiable nature and its profitable effects; the peftilent breath of calumny cannot blaft it; it will thrive, if duly cultivated, in every foil, and under every influence; it is fixed as the throne of God, and durable as the days of eternity. Goodnefs fecures to us the favour of God, peace of mind, and the hopes of immortal life; goodnefs compofes and moderates the paffions and defires, and teaches a man to be fatisfied with a little, and inures him to patience and refignation; goodnefs is alfo, according to the common courfe of things, the beft method to procure goodwill, and refpect, and at leaft the neceffaries though not the fuperfluities of life; and what can fuch a perfon difcover in another, that he can look at with an envious eye and an aching heart? I am endeavouring to prove a point, which of itfelf is fufficiently clear, namely, that an induftrious virtuous and religious perfon will not be under the dominion of envy. I proceed therefore to mention fome other confiderations which have a tendency to reftrain this evil difpofition.

1. Then

SERMON XX.

1. Then: the things which excite envy are the good things relating to the present life, as wealth and power and respect, and the pleasures which they can procure. These are things which fall to the share of a few persons, compared with the number of those who possess them not. It is usual for the bulk of mankind to have a slender provision of these external and temporal blessings; it always was so, and it always will be so. And this is a great reason why a man should rest satisfied with his lot, and consequently not envy the flourishing state and gay appearance of others, since nothing strange and unusual befalls him, since thousands who deserve as much as he are as ill accommodated in all respects. If he suffers inconveniences, and disappointments, he suffers in good company, and should bear with decent patience what is so very common.

2. The things which excite envy are things temporal and transitory, and consequently things of small value. Since life itself is so very precarious, and of so short a duration, the conveniences belonging to it partake of the same imperfections, or rather still are more imperfect, because they often cease before life itself. So that an envious person, if he duly considered this, must appear contemptible in his own eyes, for passing so foolish a judgment upon such fleeting advantages. The person who possesses them, cannot secure them and ensure them for an hour; and the person who possesses them not, may soon have no occasion for them; numberless accidents may put an end to him and to his wants, or render every thing useless and insignificant to him.

3. There is in envy a very ugly and base quality, namely, a spiteful pleasure at the calamities of others. Christianity bids us rejoice with those who rejoice, and mourn with those who mourn. Envy bids us do the reverse: It bids us mourn when others rejoice, and rejoice when they mourn. But there is a way of

contemplating

contemplating the evils natural and moral abounding in all times and places, which may be very useful to us, and about which we may employ our thoughts, without taking delight in the faults or the sufferings of others. And this consideration seems to be of great service towards the suppressing of envy: for in truth there are very few people who deserve to be envied, since there are very few so happy as they are imagined to be by injudicious by-standers. Of those who have the honour to be envied, the far greater part deserve much better to be pitied, and would be pitied by any good-natured person who knew them thoroughly.

To a person therefore who is troubled with this fretful distemper, and hates those who have more wealth, or power, or honour, or reputation than himself, it is a seasonable advice to bid him consider that happiness consists not in these things, and that a man may possess them, and be unhappy upon the whole. Thus; if the envied person has ill health or sickness, all external advantages signify little, and the mind cannot enjoy itself, whilst the body is out of order. If he is old, every thing is upon the decline with him, as to satisfaction, and he must soon take leave of all his possessions. If he be proud and ambitious, he receives more uneasiness from the things which he wants, than pleasure from the things which he has obtained. If he be covetous, he uses himself as ill as his worst enemies could wish, and undergoes many fears, and much ungodly self-denial; and one might as well envy the earth and the sea the riches which they hide within their bosom. If he be unhappy in his family, though he were surrounded with pleasures, they would all be insipid. If he loses and outlives those whom he loves, nothing which this world can give will compensate the loss. If he be debauched and profligate, his body, his understanding, his heart, his fortunes, will in all probability suffer for it, and even in this life he will pay dear for his vices. If he be good and virtuous, he
uses

SERMON XX.

uses the things which God hath given him with decency and moderation, and is willing and ready to serve others, and does nothing that can provoke hatred and malice and slander. In a word, be he what he will, he is a man, and cannot avoid human infirmities and human calamities, and has such a mixture of pain and sorrow and disappointments blended with his blessings, that there is nothing in his condition to be envied, except his good qualities, which, as we before observed, are seldom the objects of envy.

It is a truth generally admitted, that a wicked man cannot be happy, that either the reproofs of his mind, or his turbulent passions, or his foolish wants, or the enemies whom he makes, or the fears to which he is exposed, or a violent apprehension of death, will break in upon his repose from time to time. But history will inform us of many princes and great persons, whose character upon the whole was good, and who had many amiable dispositions, together with an affluence of all things which men are wont to desire, and who consequently appeared to others to be in a happy state, who yet have frequently and seriously declared to their intimate friends, that they found all things to be emptiness, vanity, and vexation, and that they were weary of the world, and very willing to leave it.

4. It becomes those who feel a tendency and proneness to envious thoughts, not only to consider the inconveniences which often surround a flourishing state, and the uneasiness which lies concealed under a gay appearance, but also to look in upon themselves, and examine what blessings they enjoy, or may enjoy, which might compensate the wants and deficiencies of which they are apt to complain; for there are often many such things, which we have at home, and yet over-look, such as health, and strength, and a good capacity, and daily bread, and friends, and relations, and hours which we call our own, and which may be employed

employed sometimes in innocent amusements, and sometimes in honest labour. It is a shame for a man to possess these things, and yet to repine, and hate his neighbours, because they live in more splendor than himself; and yet these are advantages which the greatest part of envious persons receive from Providence; for in extreme distress and sore calamities envy seldom exerts itself: it is then excluded by other passions and other cares. Great sorrows rather give the mind a religious turn, and send it to beg relief of God who alone can afford it. But envious persons are usually those who are situated in all respects in that middle state which is an easy and a pleasant state, if a man knew how to make a right use of it.

Thus much concerning envy and envious persons. I shall only add a word or two concerning those whose lot it is to be envied upon account of their superiority and better success.

It becomes all such so to behave themselves as to give no person cause of dissatisfaction. Envy is an odious fault; but there is a fault which is worse, and that is, to excite spleen and jealousy by insolence and scorn, and by refusing reasonable requests, and to take a detestable pleasure in making another uneasy. Such have the sins of others to answer for, besides their own, and act the part of the Devil by drawing them into temptation.

Envy, they will say, is a vice, and consequently no man ought to envy them and to say those things of them which envy suggests. It is true; and yet it is true also that they deserve such usage, and no pity when they receive it. The Providence of God permits that one bad man should punish and plague another, though both are guilty in his sight.

Decency, affability, courtesy, moderation, condescension, and humanity in deeds and words, should accompany and adorn a prosperous state;
and

and then, if such a person should be envied, slandered, and misrepresented, he ought to bear it, and probably he will bear it with much patience, as a thing beneath his notice and resentment.

SERMON

SERMON XXI.

ACTS x. 22.

And they said, Cornelius the centurion, a just man, and one that feareth God, and of good report among all the nation of the Jews, was warned from God by an holy Angel to send for thee into his house, and to hear words of thee.

THE Jews by crucifying Christ were guilty of a most heinous offence, aggravated by many odious circumstances.

First, it was murder; a crime for which death was the unavoidable punishment by their law, and for which no expiatory sacrifice was appointed, or could be accepted. God gave this law to the sons of Noah, Whosoever sheddeth man's blood, by man shall his blood be shed. And afterwards to the people of Israel; He that slayeth a man shall surely be put to death; thou shalt take him even from my altar, that he may die. Ye shall take no satisfaction for the life of a murderer, who is guilty of death: but he shall surely be put to death.

If the murder of a man was so heinous in the sight of God, of a man who perhaps was a great sinner, and a worthless member of society; the crime was enhanced, if he was an innocent and righteous person, and on many accounts useful to his country.

If

If he was a prophet, the offence was still greater. God himself was insulted when his servant and his messenger was thus used. His majesty and honour, and the reverence due to his government and laws, seemed to require that such insolent and provoking guilt should be punished in an exemplary manner.

If he was not only a prophet, but one who was endued with preternatural powers, and who employed them constantly in doing kind and compassionate offices to the people, if all his miracles were of the generous and merciful sort, if he gave them even eyes to see his wonders, and ears to hear his divine doctrines, if his ease and quiet were sacrificed to their benefit; if his life were spent in relieving and removing the wants and diseases of their bodies and minds, if he bestowed upon them both instruction and food, both knowledge and health; to murder such a person was an acts of unspeakable baseness and ingratitude.

But the crime was considerably increased, as it was committed against the Messias, the king of Israel, whose reign had been foretold by the prophets, and to whom they were obliged to pay the exactest obedience. This was rebellion, and high treason; this was a crime for which no legal expiation could be made, and no atonement could be sufficient; none but the blood of Him whom they with wicked hands had crucified and slain.

The only plea which they could offer in their own behalf, to mitigate God's judgments, was their ignorance. This was some kind of excuse; and yet, all things considered, a weak one, because it was mixed with so much ingratitude, stubbornness, perverseness, insolence, and cruelty.

Thus the Jews who consented to the death of Christ were all so far guilty, that they most justly deserved to die themselves for their crime. Yet they were not all equally guilty: some were misled more by prejudice and ignorance than by viler paſſions and baſer motives. And therefore God, who is ever ready to ſhew mercy where there is any opportunity to diſplay it, was willing to paſs over this great iniquity in all thoſe who ſhould repent of it, and receive the Goſpel. This favour he ſhewed them for the ſake of his injured Son, who begged it in his dying words; Father, forgive them, for they know not what they do. Therefore after Chriſt was riſen from the dead, his Apoſtles and Miniſters were ſent to offer him once more to them, if they would even then receive him as their Meſſias and Redeemer. The Apoſtles aſſured them, that what they had done to Chriſt, God would forgive, as committed by miſtake on their part. They alledge all that compaſſion and charity could ſuggeſt in their behalf. And now, brethren, ſays St. Peter, I know that through ignorance ye did it, as did alſo your rulers. Repent therefore, for there is room for reconciliation and amendment. Unto you firſt, you who have been the betrayers and murderers of Chriſt, unto you firſt, unworthy as you are, God having raiſed up his Son Jeſus, ſent him to bleſs you, in turning every one of you from his iniquities.

This gracious offer had its effect in ſome meaſure; it prevailed upon ſeveral well-diſpoſed minds; and it is probable, that they who were then called and converted, were ſuch as had been miſled by falſe repreſentations, and had been the leaſt active in that baſe conſpiracy.

But when the greater part of the nation, notwithſtanding this ſecond offer, not only perſevered in their obſtinacy, and refuſed to accept of Chriſt for their Meſſias, but alſo inſulted and perſecuted his embaſſadors ſent unto them, this their repeated ingratitude was ſo black and odious in the ſight of God, that he could bear with them no longer, but reſolved thence-

thenceforth to caſt them off, and to raiſe up to himſelf a Church amongſt the Gentiles.

To prepare the way for this great event, he ſent a viſion much about the ſame time both to St. Peter, and to Cornelius, captain of the Italian Band, living at Cæſarea, ordaining Peter to be the meſſenger and the preacher, and Cornelius to be the firſt Gentile who ſhould be called to the faith of Chriſt. Therefore the viſion ſent to Peter was intended to admoniſh him that he ſhould not ſcruple, as the Jews then did, to converſe with a Gentile, as with an unclean perſon. This was ſignified to him by a ſheet let down from heaven, wherein were all manner of four-footed beaſts of the earth, and wild beaſts, and creeping things, and fowls of the air, that is, of all, both clean and unclean; with which came alſo a voice, bidding him kill and eat. Peter anſwered; Not ſo, Lord; for I have never eaten any thing that is common or unclean. The voice replied; What God hath cleanſed, that call not thou common. Now as this viſion was to give Peter commiſſion to go to Cornelius; ſo was the viſion of Cornelius to command him to ſend for Peter; for he ſaw evidently at the ninth hour of the day an Angel of the Lord coming to him, and ſaying, Thy prayers and thine alms are come up for a memorial, that is, are had in remembrance before God. And now ſend to Joppa, and call for one Simon, whoſe ſurname is Peter, and he ſhall tell thee what thou haſt to do.

The man to whom the Angel came, was Cornelius, a Gentile, dwelling at Cæſarea, captain of the Italian Band, and without queſtion a Roman; a man in an honourable poſt, and who probably was, as appears from his name, of an ancient and illuſtrious family amongſt the Romans. It is to be obſerved, that at this time, the land of Judæa, as many other nations, was under the Roman empire, and ruled by a Preſident of their appointing. This President was stationed at Cæsarea, a considerable city, two or three days journey from Jerusalem, where there was continually a guard of soldiers, for the Governor's safety, and to keep the Jews in order; and amongst these was this Cornelius, a commander, and a captain of the Italian Band. But though by race and education he was a Gentile, yet as to religion he was not an Idolater, but a worshipper of the true God, the God of Israel, the Creator of heaven and earth; for the Scripture tells us, that he was a devout man, one that feared God with all his house, one who kept only religious servants, who gave much alms to the people, and prayed to God always: which implies, that he was a Proselyte; for so were those converted Gentiles called, who left their false Gods, and worshipped the true God. Yet he was not circumcised, nor had taken upon him to observe the whole Law of Moses, and so was not accounted a member of the Jewish Church. Therefore, according to the ordinances of the Law, and the decisions of the Doctors, he was still esteemed unclean; and so it was not lawful for Peter, or any circumcised person, to keep company with him, if God had not given his Apostle a direction, that he should thenceforth call no man unclean, since that mark of separation was now removed.

The animals of all sorts, clean and unclean, which Peter saw in a vision, represented the Jews and the Gentiles; and the vessel in which they were enclosed, which was let down from heaven, and drawn up again, was an image of the Church whose origin was celestial, and which should be received at last into heavenly mansions.

Whilst the Legal worship stood, and the Jews were God's peculiar people, there were two sorts of Proselytes, or converted Gentiles. One sort were such as were circumcised and took upon them the observance of the whole Law. These came into
that

that part of the temple which was called the Court of Ifrael, to worfhip, being accounted as adopted Jews, and the Jews converfed as freely with them as with one another. But there was a fecond fort of Profelytes, inferior to thefe, who were not circumcifed, nor conformed to the Mofaical rites and ordinances. Only they were bound to the obfervance of thofe commandments which the Jews ufed to call the precepts given to Noah and to his fons, and which by them were fuppofed to be thefe; To worfhip one God, the maker of heaven and earth; To renounce Idolatry; To abftain from blood; that is, from fhedding man's blood, or murder, and from eating the flefh with the blood in it; To refrain from fornication, and the like impurities: To adminifter impartial juftice; To commit no robbery; Laftly, To do as they would be done by.

Thefe Profelytes were indeed confidered in fome refpects as Gentiles, and avoided as fuch. But the Jews, although they fcrupled to eat with them, and to converfe with them, yet, with great prudence, made no fcruple to accept of their money, and never accounted that unclean, but commended their charity and liberality, when themfelves were the objects of it. The Jewifh Doctors alfo allowed, that thefe Profelytes were in the favour of God, and fhould partake of the life to come. Such a Profelyte was Naaman the Syrian; and of fuch there were many of all nations in our Saviour's time, and fuch an one was Cornelius, of whom we are now fpeaking.

Hence it was, that when afterwards there arofe a controverfy in the Chriftian Church, whether the Gentiles, who had received the Gofpel, were to be circumcifed, and confequently bound to obferve the ordinances and rites of Mofes, St. Peter, in the Council of the Apoftles at Jerufalem, determined, It was the will of God, that they fhould be free from fuch impofitions; and he gives this reafon for it, Becaufe

Cornelius,

Cornelius, the first believing Gentile, was no circumcised Proselyte; and yet nevertheless, when I was sent to him, says he, to preach the Gospel of Christ to him, and to his house, the holy Ghost came down upon them, as well as upon those of the circumcision. Whereby it was manifest, that God would have the rest of the Gentiles who believed to have no more imposed upon them than was required of Cornelius. And accordingly the Council concluded, that no other burthen should be laid upon them than only those precepts given to the sons of Noah, to abstain from pollutions of Idols, from blood, from things strangled, and from fornication, together with such directions as they had received already when they became Christians, and so needed not to be expresly mentioned.

From this history of Cornelius some useful inferences may be deduced.

The first observation which offers itself to us is that which St. Peter himself immediately made upon it: Of a truth I perceive that God is no respecter of persons; but in every nation he that feareth him, and worketh righteousness, is accepted with him.

The Jews had the highest thoughts of themselves, as if the sun rose and set only for them, as if all God's blessings were designed for them alone. Of all other nations they entertained the meanest opinion, as if God had no regard for them. Thou madest the world for our sakes, says Apocryphal Esdras; as for the other people, thou hast said, they are nothing, but to be like to spittle, and they have ever been reputed as nothing. The Jews imagined that the Messias should make them a glorious and prosperous people, and destroy or subdue and enslave all their enemies. They believed that God would finally save all the children of Abraham, and give them a portion in the world to come; but that the rest

SERMON XXI. 263

rest of the world, except them and their Proselytes, should be cast away. Hence, in the Acts of the Apostles, the believing Jews greatly wonder that the holy Ghost should descend upon the family of Cornelius, and that God should grant to the Gentiles repentance unto life.

This shews what mean sentiments not only the ignorant, but even the better part of that nation entertained concerning the divine nature and benignity. It shews, that the Jews were never qualified like the Christians to recommend their religion to the world; for the wiser Gentiles must needs have disliked such narrow notions, and such insolent teachers. It is not indeed to be expected, that the writers of the New Testament should say much concerning the possibility of serving God without the knowledge of Christianity; for their business was, to recommend it as a gift of the utmost importance, to press men to accept it, and to shew them the fatal consequences of rejecting it. But concerning the Gentiles, who never heard the Gospel, and who had no revealed Law, St. Paul says of them, that they sometimes did by nature and conscience the things contained in the law, and by so doing performed an acceptable duty; and consequently they were not without those assistances, external or internal, which may save a man from final destruction. And the ancient Christians with a general consent speak favourably of the wise and good Gentiles, who made a proper use of their reason, and say that the Gospel, in one sense, was as old as mankind, and that its main duties had ever been practised by the lovers of truth and virtue.

God is no respecter of persons; but in every nation he that feareth him, and worketh righteousness, is accepted with him.

So long then as we be careful to remember and acknowledge that Christ is the only Redeemer by
whom

whom wo have accefs to the Divine mercy and favour, and that there is no other name under heaven given to men, by which they may be faved, we may fairly allow to thefe words an extenfive fignification; and we may be permitted to fay that God, the univerfal Father of all, hath put it in the power of every one who comes into the world to perform his duty; that he requires no more than he hath given; that he will extend his mercy to all thofe who act a fober and rational part to the beft of their underftanding and ability; and that to fuch Chrift is a Saviour, though they never had the opportunity and the happinefs of knowing him.

This feems founded on the known and unchangeable perfections of God, on his equity and goodnefs. This feems to be matter of juftice, whilft the knowledge of Chriftianity feems to be a matter of favour, which the Almighty beftows upon one, and withholds from another. Concerning divine favours no reafon fhould be required befides the will of God. That one fhould have the law of nature, and another the Gofpel given him for his guide, this is to be refolved into the good pleafure of God; and to thofe who fhould prefume to object to it, the reply is; Shall not I do what I will with my own?

Greater degrees of knowledge are free gifts of God, and gifts which ought to excite the utmoft gratitude and thankfulnefs in the receiver; which leads me to the fecond obfervation, namely, that from the example of Cornelius we may fee how valuable a favour and blefling of God it is, to be placed where opportunity of improvement, and the means of acquiring religious truths are to be found. Cornelius might have been fo fituated and fo occupied, as to have lived and died in Pagan ignorance. But by being ftationed at Cæfarea, near the Jews, where the oracles and the worfhip of the moft High were read and profeffed, he learned and he embraced the truth,

truth, and with all his family he honoured and served God in an exemplary and an acceptable manner.

If this be so, then should we ourselves learn to be more thankful to God than we usually are, for that condition wherein by his Providence we are placed. For we might, if it had pleased him, have had our birth and education amongst those who are strangers to his word and promises, and detained under the bondage of gross idolatry; and in such a state this nation of ours once was. To this goodness it is to be ascribed, that we descend from Christian parents, and dwell in a Christian country, and so are partakers of the benefits of the Gospel from our very infancy. Nay, we might have belonged even to some Christian nations, and yet have had a very imperfect knowledge of religion, and have set in the dim twilight of ignorant and sordid superstition. But we are born and placed in a land where there are more opportunities of learning our duty, and more liberty to perform it, than in most parts of the Christian world. Thankfulness for the first benefits is the best way to obtain more and greater; to acknowledge and value God's favour towards us, in giving us the means of salvation, is the way to obtain grace to use those means to our eternal advantage; as, on the contrary, our neglect of gratitude for the former, may cause God in his just judgment to deprive us of the latter.

A third remark which offers itself to our consideration, is that a good disposition, an honest heart, is the best help to understand religion, and that the practice of morality leads to the practice of our revealed duty. For a love of truth and of virtue, an equitable, fair, and charitable spirit, and a just sense of the necessity and reasonableness of conforming to the will of God, is the first principle and beginning of religion,

religion, the fure and great preparative to open the underftanding, to make men ftudy facred truths with pleafure, and comprehend them with eafe, and judge of them with a full difcernment; and he who practifes what he knows, increafes his knowledge continually by that practice; and, by good actions, more than by fpeculation, is the heart enlightened and improved. Add to which, that God will take care, by the fecret or vifible difpenfations of his providence, that honeft and pioufly difpofed perfons fhall difcover as much as is neceffary for their own wants and for their falvation.

Cornelius by birth and education was a Pagan. But, being of a ferious and inquifitive temper, he examined the religion of his anceftors and of his nation, and on the examination found it weak and abfurd in all its parts. If he had been fo fituated as never to have heard of a divine revelation, it is probable that he would have ufed the beft means of information that he could procure; he would have applied himfelf to the ftudy of morality, and have regulated his belief and conduct upon the moft reafonable notions that were to be gathered from the writings and the doctrines of the Philofophers. But God, who faw the uprightnefs of his heart, fo appointed it, that his ftation of life called him to refide at Cæfarea. There he had an opportunity of being acquainted with the Jews, with the Law, and the Prophets; and there he found a religion grounded on good proofs, and reafonable evidence, on miracles and prophecies, a religion which contained better notions of the divine nature and perfections, and a better morality than any other. To this religion he became a profelyte, and not only a profelyte, but a credit and an honour; for the Scripture bears him this teftimony, that even then he was a devout man, and one that feared God with all his houfe, who

gave

gave much alms to the people, and prayed to God alway.

The same good sense and good disposition, which led him to prefer Judaism to Paganism, shewed him, in all probability that the Jewish religion was not without some defects and imperfections, which should be removed when the Messias, mentioned in the Prophets, should come. And as the Gospel then began to be preached by the Apostles, and opposed by the Jews, he knew not what judgment to form about it; and therefore he applied himself to God in devout supplication, and besought him to remove his doubts, and to direct him to the truth. Upon which an Angel was sent, who thus addressed himself to him; Cornelius, thy prayer is heard.

Fourthly; The Gospel, as it was preached to the poor, so was it embraced by the poor, and people of middle and lower stations of life made up the chief number of the primitive Christians. This the Jews and the Pagans objected to them; but yet unreasonably: for, first, they who had the fewest motives to set their affections on this world, were the best disposed to receive Christianity; and, secondly, the reproach was not altogether true; for though the greater part of Christians were such, yet they had amongst them persons eminent for birth, or station, or authority, or learning, amongst whom may be reckoned this Centurion.

Lastly, The conversion of Cornelius was sudden and miraculous, and a favour was shewed to him which was granted to very few. But it is to be observed how well qualified he was for the reception of the Gospel. He had overcome the prejudices of education, he had preserved himself free from the reigning vices of his country, and of the age in which he lived, an age extremely wicked and debauched. His military life exposed him undoubtedly to various temptations, and he had in the Roman army examples of all iniquity. His character in the Scriptures is, that he was pious and charitable; he loved God with all his heart, and his neighbour as himself. No wonder that he, who was so near to the kingdom of heaven, entered into it so quickly and so easily.

SERMON XXII.

Luke xii. 20.

But God said unto him, Thou fool, this night thy soul shall be demanded of thee.

THERE are two ways of arguing with sinners, and of endeavouring to reclaim them from their evil courses. The first is, to set forth sin in all its horrors and deformity, and represent it as an object of fear and detestation. The second is, to shew the folly and stupidity of it, and its direct opposition even to common sense, by which it becomes the object of scorn and ridicule. Both these ways are good in their kind: some persons will be most affected by the first, and others by the second method of reasoning. No man likes to be an object of abomination; and no man likes to be an object of contempt. But if a man must have his choice of the two, there are some persons who had rather be scorned than abhorred; and there are others who had rather be thought profligates than pass for fools; they had rather be hated than despised; and amongst the wicked, the latter sort seem to be the more numerous.

For this reason Sinners are represented in the word of God as fools; particularly in the Psalms of David, and in the Proverbs of Solomon, where Fool and Sinner often stand for the same thing. Nor doth our Saviour decline this method of instructing. He treats the proud Pharisees as blind fools; he represents indolent persons,

persons, who made no preparation for their last hours, under the image of foolish Virgins, who, when the Bridegroom came suddenly in the night, had no oil in their lamps, and were not in a condition to go forth and meet him, and so were excluded from the feast; and in the parable from which the text is taken, he paints in lively colours the supine folly of a worldly-minded man whose first care is to amass treasure upon treasure, and who after all his laborious industry resolves with himself to sit down at ease, and enjoy his possessions for many and many years. But the time for this is elapsed, the last hour is at hand, and a voice from heaven says to him, Thou fool, this night shall thy soul be required of thee; and then whose shall all those things be which thou hast heaped together?

(a) I have not repeated these words to you with a design to explain them in the following discourse. They are so clear as not to admit of a comment. Nor will I confine myself to the example here set before us, to the single case of the worldly-minded man, who heaps up riches, and whose heart is in his storehouse. The doctrine of the text may very well be applied in general to all the disobedient and impenitent; and it is easy to prove that such persons well deserve the name of fools, and that the tranquillity and the carnal security which lulls them asleep, is a true infatuation.

And certainly the proof of it which the text suggests is obvious, and lies level to every capacity. It is this, that an impenitent Sinner is liable to be surprised by Death every day, every hour, nay every moment, and in a thousand different ways; and then what becomes of the unhappy man? If in a danger of this nature, in this most precarious and deplorable situation, he can be easy, careless, cheerful, in good humour, and given up to mirth and joy, what name can you bestow

(a) Warenfels, *Serm.* X.

bestow upon this indolent security? None will suit it, except folly, or frenzy.

And yet amongst those who make open profession of believing the Gospel, there are too many who are, if not in this state, in a state which borders too nearly upon it. The fact being certain, it may be proper to inquire a little into the causes.

They are these: Either an impenitent person plainly discerns all his danger, and despises it; or he turns away his eys from it, and will not take it into consideration; or lastly he deceives and flatters himself that he is in no peril.

As to the first state of mind, certain it is that a man must have lost his senses, to see his danger, and to despise it at the same time, to be contented to resign everlasting happiness and to plunge himself into incurable misery. If bad men enjoyed in this world an uninterrupted state of ease, and moved in a perpetual circle of pleasures, a state which none of them ever possessed, yet would it be a great folly to prefer these momentary delights to the durable and substantial joys of the kingdom of heaven. In like manner, if good men were inevitably doomed to affliction and distress, to a misery alleviated with no worldly comforts, and appointed to last as long as they lived, which yet is belied by Scripture and by Experience, yet would this be but a slight and inconsiderable evil, compared with the punishment denounced against Sinners. It is therefore mere madness to chuse wickedness knowingly and deliberately, and to defy all its fatal and foreseen consequences.

If, secondly, the indolence of a Sinner ariseth, as it more usually doth, not from a clear sight of the danger and a fool-hardy contempt of it, but from shutting his eyes, and turning his thoughts upon other things, and occupying and amusing himself in any way that can supress such troublesome reflections, he is not at all less extravagant in his behaviour. Suppose a man to
be

be warned by a skilful friend that his house is sinking and will fall upon his head; instead of hastening to escape, he remains quietly at home, and to drive the thoughts of danger out of his mind, he eats and drinks, and busies or diverts himself, till the house falls, and buries him in the ruins. If such a thing were related to us, and sufficiently attested, we should conclude without hesitation that the man had lost his senses before he lost his life. Yet this is a faithful representation of every impenitent person. On the one hand, Reason and Experience tell them that Death may come and surprise them every moment: on the other hand, the Gospel assures them, that if this happen to them, they are excluded from the kingdom of heaven, and delivered over to a state of misery. How do they behave themselves in these alarming circumstances? Exactly like the man beforementioned. Instead of escaping for their life, and flying from an evil which is at the door, they employ themselves upon something else, upon pleasure, or business, or schemes of temporal advantage; and all this partly to stupify themselves and to overlook the danger they are in; as if a man could annihilate that danger by forgetting it. Can there be a stronger proof of vicious folly?

Many of the impenitent are in this state of false security, because they fancy themselves to be out of all danger, and in a condition to which they may safely trust. Their hopes are grounded on the acknowledged weakness and imperfection of human nature, and on the clemency of divine nature. But how can they thus delude themselves? Whilst they are walking in the broad-way that leads to destruction, how can they mistake it for the narrow and less-beaten path that conducts to heaven? After all the declarations of the Scriptures concerning these things, and the terms of forgiveness and peace which are there propounded, a sinner must have renounced common sense to fall into such illusions. He must be like the Athenian mad-

man

man recorded in history, who imagined that every ship which came into the harbour was his own. Much in the same condition is he, when he dreams that the treasures of heaven are all his own right and property, and that he cannot fail one day to possess them.

And whereupon doth he found this imaginary right? He will tell you, perhaps, that he founds it upon his baptism, upon his being a member of the Church, and a partaker of its ordinances. Just as if a man, who should daily commit capital crimes against the laws of his country, should call himself a good subject and citizen, because he hath an house, and pays his taxes.

Baptism can signify nothing, if we do not endeavour to fulfil all the engagements into which we then entered; and hearing the word of God is as useless for those who are determined not to profit by it. To frequent the house of God is labour lost for him who returns from it as bad as he went to it; and to appear at the Lord's Table is intrusion and insult in him who hath no intention to observe his Lord's commands. To join in praising and thanking God for all his benefits is the mere service of the lips, or rather mere mockery, when the heart agrees not with the mouth. No one, who is not void of sense, can alledge, by way of excuse, those very things for which the Devil will accuse him one day, and for which his own Conscience will accuse him, and be to him another Devil.

But we have not yet touched upon the more general cause of impenitence and false security. Such persons are too fully sensible and too well convinced that they are not in the right path, and by no means prepared to give an account of themselves, if they should be suddenly called away. But they propose to rectify all in due time, and they conclude that favourable opportunities will not be wanting for that purpose. Thus they compose themselves, and with these flattering hopes and fair projects they think that they may for a season continue their accustomed irregularities.

Now upon how weak a foundation is this hope erected? Who can promise himself length of days, surrounded as he is with numberless persons who are snatched away by a sudden death, at a time when they thought themselves as secure from it as any of us here present?

The rich man in the text was in good health, and at an age and in a condition to enjoy all the comforts of life for a great many years, as he imagined, when the heavenly voice said unto him, Thou fool, this night thou must depart.

The various and endless schemes and projects of mortal creatures in this transient state, are some of those supreme vanities which Solomon beheld under the sun, and thought worthy of particular observation. Men go on, as if their bodies were formed strong and durable as the sun and moon, which have continued for many ages, and may continue for many more.

But perhaps a man shall not die suddenly. The chances are on his side; and for one person on whom this lot falls, many escape it. Be it so. But there is another kind of sudden death, which is frequent; and that is a death of the organs of the body, or of the faculties of the mind, a loss of memory, a decay of the understanding, which incapacitates a man from performing either business or duty. Distempers also, the forerunners of death, seldom leave a man that freedom of thought, and liberty of acting, which a true reformation seems to require.

But, to suppose every thing as favourable to repentance as may be, is a man sure that he shall seize upon those happy opportunities, and improve them to the welfare of his soul? If amendment appears irksome and insipid to-day, it will hardly appear in a more alluring and amiable form to-morrow, or when evil habits have hardened and stupified the heart.

Why

SERMON XXII.

Why therefore should any one promise himself better dispositions and fairer opportunities of doing well hereafter than at present? Age, it may be said, age will be a great assister. Age moderates the heat of youth, and tames and corrects irregular passions. But to renounce any act of sin when it becomes impracticable can hardly be called a change of temper. Besides, let us not deceive ourselves in this point. Each stage of human life hath its follies, its vices, and its temptations; and if the heart be once thoroughly spoiled, age will rather harden than soften it. It is a strange illusion to fancy that a man is growing better, when from youthful debaucheries he proceeds to envy, malice, and dishonesty; and thence to rapaciousness, covetousness, uncharitableness, and discontent. If the Devil can hold him fast by any one vicious chain, it matters little with him which chain it is.

Well; but there is still the grace of God, which can triumph over vicious nature. That grace is not yet come; and when it comes, all opposition from the world, the flesh, and the Devil will fall before it, and the sinner shall be rescued, though late, from his bondage. But how can such a person reckon upon the assistance of this grace? He hath received graces, of one sort or other, all the days of his life, and hath rejected them. He hath therefore the more reason to fear that God, whose goodness and patience have been so long despised, should withdraw himself totally, and leave the man to his own frantic passions and reprobate mind, which is the most deplorable state that can be conceived on this side of hell.

We trust to some serious hours, and serious thoughts, which bodily infirmities, the forerunners of a dissolution, shall bring along with them. But there is something very unpromising and deceitful in a change of temper extorted by mere necessity. A man would continue in his evil courses, but he hath neither time nor strength for it. He must take leave of the world. In this

this extremity he thinks of his offended Maker, and he is sorry for what is past and irretrievable. God is merciful, and to that mercy he hath recourse. This in reality is all that he can do; and what security hath he that God will accept of this?

Even this little is seldom performed whilst there is any hope of life; and when is that hope given up? In the most dangerous illnesses people flatter themselves as long as they can; their friends flatter them also, partly to keep up their spirits, and partly out of pity and affection. This is the usual case of those whose days have been wasted in folly and iniquity. Evil inclinations are not altered suddenly: it is against experience, it is against Nature.

Thus far we have proceeded upon the supposition that the religion which we profess is really a divine revelation, and that its doctrines concerning this life and the next are infallible oracles. And upon this system, every one must confess that obstinate impenitence is the greatest of evils, and the greatest of follies. But it may be said that these religious doctrines should never be taken for granted, when we are speaking against the false security of the wicked; for that these persons are often of the unbelieving tribe, and reject the very fundamental maxims upon which our arguments are established.

It is true indeed that there are such people. This we know, and we feel the bad effects of it; for such a dissolution of principles must always produce an equal dissolution and profligacy of manners.

I would not suppose that I have here to do with persons of that character. They are seldom to be found in Churches. But yet it is not amiss to expose them, and to shew that they are fools, as much as those who believe right and do wrong.

I would ask them; How do they know with such absolute certainty that all ends with this life? and that the promises and threatenings of the Scriptures are

idle

idle tales? Have they examined this point sincerely and impartially, and without any vicious passions and prejudices? And upon this fair and strict inquiry, have they found full proofs and tokens that religion is an imposture? If so, they shall have our consent to reject it, and lead a wicked life. We will grant that they act consistently, so far as a future state is concerned; and as for the present state, they must take their chance; and the chance is usually against them.

But where is the Unbeliever to be found, who can truly say that he hath been this sedate, careful, and impartial examiner? The far greater part of these persons never deigned to give the Gospel an hour's hearing. They reject it together with all its doctrines, only because they find them severe and inconvenient: and this is one clear proof of a disordered understanding; though not so disordered as to make a man innocent.

Is our future state then such a trifle, that it is not worth the while to bestow a thought upon it? What are those more pressing and important occupations, which shall hinder or excuse a man from doing it? Unbelievers would be glad without question to live free from the dread of a judgment and retribution. How can can they acquire this delightful calm and security, but by a full conviction that the Gospel is a fable? And how can they be convinced of this, till they have examined what may be said for and against it; especially since all is at stake on the one side, and very little on the other? To reject the Gospel, if it be true, is infinitely more dangerous, than to receive it, if it be false; because a man had much better lose some sensual pleasure, than incur an incurable and extreme evil.

They will say perhaps that the Gospel is evidently false; that a wise man can discern this at the first sight, and without any careful and laborious disquisition; and that believers are all of them weak and deluded, and infatuated people. This is strage indeed!

But

But when a man comes to affirm that all his neighbours are diftracted, it is a fure fign how it goes with himfelf.

An innumerable multitude of perfons, of all ages, places, times, and ftations have received and efteemed as facred truths the doctrines of Chriftianity, from the days of the Apoftles to the prefent hour; and amongft thefe there have been many fo eminent in learning, fagacity, judgment, extent of knowledge, and bright abilities of every kind, that were all the Infidels taken together, and all their capacities collected and centered in one perfon, he would be as much beneath one of thofe Chriftians, as Hell is beneath the Heavens. Amongft the Chriftians there have been many, who for the fake of God and of religion have renounced all that the world can give, and endured all that it can inflict, and with a courage and a conftancy never enough to be admired have run the race of piety and glory which was fet before them.

Many nations have received this religion, forfaking their altars, their Deities, their ceremonies, and their opinions, and conquering the almoft infuperable prejudices of cuftom and education.

And is a religion, which hath fuch a force and fuch an influence as this, to be rejected with difdain, and without an hearing?

Is it not worth the while to confider the long feries of prophecies contained in the Old Teftament, and accomplifhed in the Author of our faith and of our Salvation; and the various miracles by which he afcertained his divine miffion? We find thefe miracles attefted by men, in whom were united every mark of fincerity, honefty, and fober fenfe, and who were eye-witneffes of thefe wonders, and of their happy effects. Their teftimony is confiftent and unanimous; and they confirmed it by a life conformable to the precepts of their divine Mafter, by a generous difdain of worldly advantages,

SERMON XXII.

tages, and by a patient enduring of persecutions, distresses, and sufferings of every kind.

Is it not worth while to consider a little how Christianity at first introduced itself in the world? Its morality is pure indeed and amiable, and worthy of being joined to a divine revelation; but still it is contrary to the loose maxims, and disorderly appetites, of flesh and blood. And yet, in spite of all opposition from every thing that was crafty, every thing that was powerful, and every thing that was wicked in this world, it made its way, and it still keeps its ground with the generality of persons in Christian countries.

What can we think of those who, in a point of so much importance, are quite indifferent, and satisfy themselves with an oath, or with a jest, and with saying boldly and at random that it is all a cheat?

Lastly, let us suppose that amongst our Infidels there are persons who have bestowed some pains in examining revealed religion, and have found, as they think, that something is to be said for it, and as much against it, and are therefore left in a state of hesitation, and can form no certain conclusions. This I should take to be the utmost that an infidel can pretend to, if he hath any share of sense or candor. He is a doubter then; and I would ask him whether these doubts can secure him from apprehensions concerning a future state? By no means. Such a security is only to be obtained by a thorough conviction that religion is a fable. There is no peace with doubters, especially if they be evil-doers at the same time.

If a man were journeying, after the close of the day, and in a path unknown to him, and some neighbouring persons were to call to him and bid him have a care how he proceeds, for there is a precipice hard by, and he will be dashed to pieces. He might think with himself, These men may perhaps impose upon me; but perhaps they may say true, and give me a friendly warning. Therefore I will stop, or return back.

The unbeliever is this man. He walks in darkness, not knowing where he goes, and where his road will end; and as he proceeds, many voices call upon him, voices of Prophets, Apostles, Martyrs, Pastors, Parents, Friends, and Neighbours, who advise him to stop and take heed, and tell him that he is upon the brink of ruin, and hastening to his destruction. He knows not, it seems, whether these Prophets and Apostles, these teachers and neighbours deserve to be believed, whether they do not deceive themselves. He doubts of their judgment, and of their veracity. But then the dangers which they set before him are in their own nature so alarming, that if there be the least probability, or even possibility, in their charitable and disinterested admonitions, he cannot proceed in his course, without renouncing common sense.

You see what judgment is to be pronounced upon that vain security and that stupid indolence, which is the character of many sinners, of whom some act against conscience, and others have no conscience to act against. In whatever point of view you place their conduct, its folly is apparent. And therefore, whatsoever honourable titles they may boast of, whatsoever high rank and station they may hold in civil society, whatsoever airs of importance they may give themselves, whatsoever scorn they may affect for the sober, the serious, and the honest, whatsoever wit they may have at command, or whatsoever learning they may possess, (though usually they have not much of that) they are at the bottom persons void of understanding. Though they are not confined in dark rooms, like some other unhappy persons, but are permitted to walk up and down, and to shine in the politest circles, yet is their frenzy not at all the less real, and infinitely more mischievous to the world.

As for us, we appear to be worshippers of God, and servants of Jesus Christ, and in communion with the holy Spirit. But, are these professions sincere, and
accom-

accompanied with suitable effects? If so, we may trust with humble reverence in the mercy of God; and that trust is the most valuable of all treasures. But if this be not the case, we have no time to lose, and no room for delays. The heavenly voice hath not yet sounded in our ears, and told us that the fatal moment is come: but none of us is certain that he shall not be called away to-night, or to-morrow. It is wisdom to prepare for that change, and for that hour. That is the time when sinners are usually first to arraign and condemn themselves, when their hidden vices come to light, and their borrowed virtues disappear.

Why do not these thoughts make more impression upon us, and send us to seek the Lord whilst he may be found? He can and he will assist us in the pious undertaking, and teach us effectually that the figure of this world passeth away, and that his favour endureth for ever.

SERMON

SERMON XXIII.

PROV. xxx. 7.

Two things have I required of thee; deny me them not before I die. Remove far from me vanity and lies; give me neither poverty nor riches, feed me with food convenient for me: left I be full, and deny thee, and say, Who is the Lord? or left I be poor and steal, and take the name of my God in vain.

SUCH was the prayer of Agur, a man celebrated for his wisdom, and whose proverbs are joined to those of Solomon. We will first explain the words in which his petition is expressed, and then make some remarks upon it.

There are two things, says Agur, which I would willingly avoid, and which I humbly beg that thou, O God, wouldst remove from me; for by so doing thou wilt preserve me from temptations to the worst and most dangerous sort of lying. Remove from me poverty and riches; give me my bread by measure, for so the words mean, which are translated, *food convenient for me*. Agur seems to allude to the ancient custom of feeding slaves in great families. They had a certain measure of food daily allowed them; so that a servant, who had an honest and wealthy master, was secure from want, though he had nothing superfluous; he was kept in constant dependence, but he received

received a constant supply of the necessaries of life. Agur might also have in view the manner in which God fed the people of Israel in the wilderness with manna, of which they were commanded to gather daily a certain measure, but none for the morrow. That God would thus supply his wants from day to day, was his modest petition; that so he might be induced daily to ask for subsistence, and daily to return thanks for the granted favour.

Now (*a*) follow the reasons for his request to be placed in a middle state between affluence and indigence.

I would not be rich, says he, lest I be full, and lie, and say, Who is the Lord? that is, lest too much plenty should make me worldly-minded, profane, and irreligious. To say in a contemptuous manner, Who is the Lord? is to deny the being, or the providence of God. They may be denied by words, or by behaviour. To deny them by words, is to utter a lie; and to deny them by behaviour, may be called, to live a lie, and a lie of the most detestable kind.

I would not be in extreme want, says he, lest I steal, and take the name of my God in vain. Stealing is a crime, into which a poor man is in danger of falling, as not only Agur's fear, but daily experience may tell us.

The second sin that Agur mentions, is taking the name of God in vain, that is, perjury, which would follow upon stealing, as stealing upon poverty. The danger of perjury, upon the committing of theft, was greater amongst the Jews than amongst us, by reason of a custom or law amongst them, to render an oath to those who were suspected of theft, and who were thus to clear themselves. For because theft was not punished by death in the Law of Moses, but by restitution,

and

(*a*) See a Discourse of Joseph Mede on this text, from which some re.. '. are borrowed.

and a certain fine or penalty; it was usual, if sufficient evidence could not be produced for or against the accused person, to administer an oath to him; and it was supposed that the guilty party, especially where the legal punishment was gentle, would rather ingenuously confess his fault, than incur the heinous sin of perjury, and the heavy judgments which God had denounced against this crime, and which he often inflicted on the offenders. Not to add, that he could expect no mercy, if his sin should afterwards happen to be discovered.

In countries where theft or robbery is punished with death, a trial by oath would be highly improper; for it is very true, though it was spoken by the Father of lies, *All that a man hath, he will give for his life*, and usually he will say or do any thing to save it. But this manner of trial by oath was practised in some cases amongst the Jews. Hence it is that the prohibition of theft and perjury are joined together in Leviticus, because the one often drew on the other: Ye shall not steal, neither deal falsely, neither lie one to another; and ye shall not swear by my name falsely, neither shalt thou profane the name of thy God. I am the Lord. Thou shalt not defraud thy neighbour, nor rob him. For the same reason, theft and swearing are coupled together in the prophet Zechariah, and a curse is pronounced against them both: The Curse, saith the Lord of hosts, shall enter into the house of the thief, and into the house of him that sweareth falsely by my name; and it shall remain in the midst of his house, and shall consume it.

And indeed, not only the religious Jews abhorred the taking of God's holy name in vain, or in attestation to a lie; but the very Pagans also, from the remotest times, accounted perjury to be a most heinous provocation of the Deity; and though loose enough in other points of duty, and not abounding with moral principles, yet thought that this was a crime which would not go unpunished.

Thus

Thus you see what particular reason Agur had, in regard to the custom of his own nation, to add to the first evil of stealing, the second of taking the name of God in vain, because the one was likely to bring on the other; for though, as we observed before, the punishment of theft was not usually very rigid, when the thief was willing and able to restore what the Law required, yet when a needy and a profligate man had secretly purloined any thing, and eaten it up, and had nothing to make restitution with, besides his own body, he lay under violent temptations to perjury, that he might avoid bondage and hard labour.

I shall now proceed to some general remarks upon the text.

We should interpret the prayer of this wise man in a favourable and candid manner, as put up by one who was religious and humble, and disposed to submit his own will to the will of God. We need not suppose of him that he prayed absolutely against riches, or absolutely against poverty; for poverty and riches are of themselves things indifferent, and the blessing of God may go with them both. But it is a prayer of choice, or a comparative prayer; as if he had said, Rather than either poverty or riches, Give me, O God, if it be thy will, the middle between both, and feed me with food convenient for me. For though all the three estates be so far indifferent, that a man may be good, and ought to be contented or resigned in any of them, yet, if it were matter of choice, the middle is the easiest and most desireable.

Riches, poverty, and a competency, these are things which cannot be accurately fixed, without reference to the state and condition of men. What would be wealth to one, might be poverty to another; what would amply suffice for a single man, and in a private station, that a master of a large family, a magistrate, a noble person might have, and be exceeding poor. Therefore food convenient for a man is such a competency as will maintain him in that order, degree, or calling, in which God hath placed him.

Agur's prayer, as to the sense of it, is very like the petition in the Lord's prayer, Give us this day our daily bread. Nothing can redound more to his honour, than that his judgment should be confirmed by divine wisdom itself. And what we have observed concerning Agur's petition, is in some measure to be applied, by way of interpretation, to the petition in the Lord's prayer, Give us this day our daily bread; first, that it must be a conditional request, accompanied with a submission to the will of God; and secondly, that by it is meant a supply of the things which our situation in life requires.

The moderation of Agur's prayer is highly commendable, if we consider that he lived in a time, when temporal blessings were more expressly promised, and spiritual blessings less clearly propounded, than under the Gospel; so that a good man might have carried his desires of worldly conveniences somewhat farther than becomes a Christian, who is trained up under a sublimer dispensation, and hath nobler examples to copy after: and yet Agur not only makes no petition for riches, but declares that he would be glad to have them kept from him, and makes it his choice to go without them.

A competency, or a middle state between want and superfluity, deserves to be preferred as the best and happiest condition. Such was the judgment of Agur, which stands recorded in Scripture as an instance of his wisdom. The wiser Gentiles were not of a different opinion; many of them have said the same thing in other words. They have observed, that poverty is exposed to ridicule and ill usage, that it cramps and depresses the mind, with-holds the means of improving the natural abilities, confines a man to servile labour, that he may supply the wants of the body, and often puts him upon sordid and dishonest tricks: they have

observed,

observed, that the Great and the Rich have often the inclination as well as the opportunity to indulge every vile and vicious passion, that they are looked upon with an evil eye, are envied and hated, and most exposed to danger in troublesome times, and have many cares and fears in all times; and that a middle condition is advantageously situated below envy, and above contempt.

It is observable, that the reasons which the Pagans give for their choice, are reasons of convenience, and that the end which they have in view is their own ease and satisfaction: But Agur, who was instructed in the law of God, gives a reason for his choice, of which they seldom thought, a religious and pious reason; he would not be rich or poor, because he would not be wicked, and offend God. This may serve to remind us how far superior not only Christianity is, but Judaism was to natural religion, as it was usually understood and practised by the Pagans.

And indeed if we carefully examine the political laws of Moses, we shall find that the divine providence intended the Jewish people for that very situation between poverty and riches, which was the object of Agur's wish. The means of accumulating great wealth by an extensive commerce, by circulating large sums of money upon large interest, by extending their dominions, and by planting colonies abroad, were withholden from them; and their own lands industriously cultivated, would, by the blessing of God, furnish them with the necessaries, though not the superfluities of life.

Poverty, or extreme want, is represented by Agur as an undesireable condition; and if his opinion be right, to deprive ourselves of all our possessions, and to make vows of poverty, is not the way to perfection, nor an act of religion acceptable to God. Many Christians of old fell into this error, and many Christians still retain it, or pretend to retain it, in their Religious

gious Orders of Monks and Friers. As to the poverty of such Saints, the case is far from being clear. A man who, having no private property, belongs to a wealthy society, and lives at ease, and wants for nothing, can hardly be accounted poor, but rather enjoys himself with more quiet and less hazard than many a rich man. These Religious Societies, instead of being poor, but making many rich, have often been rich by making many people poor, by swallowing up the fortunes of ignorant and superstitious bigots.

They alledge the counsel of our Saviour to the young man in the Gospel; If thou wilt be perfect, go and sell that thou hast, and give it to the poor, and thou shalt have treasure in heaven: where Christ seems to prescribe poverty as the way to eternal life.

(b) But this was an extraordinary case, and is therefore not to be made a rule of ordinary practice. Besides, it is to be observed, that our Saviour spake this to the young man by way of experiment. He made the proposal to him, upon his forward request, to prove him, and to teach him how much he was deceived, and how far his heart was short of that perfection which he fancied in himself, when he thought that he could attempt or undergo any thing that would recommend him to the favour of God. This was a trial indeed, for the text says, He went away sorrowful. And it is natural for us, when we read it, to be sorrowful too, for his sake, and to think it pity, that with all his virtues he should have been lost. But, since it is said of him, that Jesus loved him, loved him for his good qualities, there seems room to suppose, and to hope, that though he then departed from Christ, he might afterwards join himself to the Apostles.

Secondly, the practice of the first Christians is alledged, who sold their lands and possessions.

But these were Jews, Jews dwelling in Judæa, who did so. The Gentiles did it not, when the Gospel came
to

(b) Jos. Mede.

SERMON XXIII.

to them. None of St. Paul's Epistles contain any such precept, or intimate any such practice. But as for the Jews, who believed then in Christ, there was something particular in their case. They knew that Christ had foretold the destruction of their nation, which should come upon it before that generation were passed away; and therefore they thought it proper, whilst there was yet time, to improve to the best use their estates, which they should not many years enjoy. An occasion of liberality at that time presented itself; the Gospel then began to be published, and large collections were necessary, to relieve those Christians, who were in want, and had lost every thing for the sake of the Gospel, and to enable the first teachers to pursue their travels from place to place. For this reason, the believers amongst the Jews set an illustrious example of disinterestedness and charity; and when the Gospel was also spread amongst the Gentiles, the Apostles seem to have been careful to make collections in all the Churches for the relief of the poor Saints of Jerusalem; since it was very just and expedient that provision should be made for those who at the first had quitted and given up all, and at whose charges it may be supposed, the Gospel was at the beginning preached amongst some of the Gentiles.

There is then nothing commendable in superstitious and affected poverty. If poverty comes to us, we must be patient and resigned under it; it is no part of our duty to seek it out. But, to say the truth, there are few amongst us who are disposed to transgress this way.

Agur represents poverty as a state which exposes to the temptations of dishonesty and perjury. As to the first of these temptations, it attends poverty in all times and places; as to the second, it is plain from experience, that thieves and defaulters will forswear themselves even when nothing compels them to swear at all. And then, as to lying, which is next of kin to perjury, we know that to be the ordinary and almost unavoidable consequence of cheating and pilfering. So that Agur's reasons for which he desires to be preserved from indigence, will fit us well enough.

Agur supposeth, that though he were poor, and had not food convenient for him, yet it would be a sin to steal, which makes him pray against it, Lest I be poor, and steal. Necessity is no small extenuation of the crime, and perhaps where it is extreme, it may take it quite away. But such cases rarely happen; and in general, poverty is not an excuse for stealing.

If it be a sin for a poor man to steal from the rich, it is beyond comparison a greater crime for a rich man to cheat and defraud the poor. Want is a strong temptation to fraudulent dealings: therefore Agur says, Lest I be poor, and steal; not, Lest I be rich, and steal: for why should a rich man steal? And yet this they will do in effect, nor is it very uncommon; not indeed in the way that poor people steal, but with an high hand, by oppression and overbearing, by injuring the public, by refusing to pay their debts, except they be debts of honour, and by endeavouring to ruin those whom they have wronged. We may suppose all such to be of the number of those whom Agur represents as saying, Who is the Lord? for it seems impossible for a man to act in this manner, who believes, I will not say revealed religion, but a Deity and a future state.

Agur, in the text, prays that he may not be exposed to poverty, and to the temptations which accompany it. It is to be taken for granted, that he, who was a wise man, added his endeavours to his petitions, and that he not only prayed against poverty, but provided against it; and indeed when he proceeds in the chapter to treat of other subjects, he makes mention of the industrious animals, who provide their yearly food in the summer, and proposes them as examples of wisdom. If we pray that we may never become poor

poor and wicked, we must take care not to become poor by our own fault: for he who falls into want by living above his income, and by a love of pleasure, is trained and prepared for all villainy. When he hath the appetites and desires of the rich, together with the needs and nakedness of the poor, when he is too lazy and unskilful to work, and too proud to beg, he is truly undone, and Safety itself cannot save him. In all faults, but more especially in these, the commission of one offence draws on another; and, as a sinner is said to be in bonds, so is each single sin linked to another, and makes part of the chain which binds him fast.

Agur's desire was, that he might not be rich. Jacob's request to God was, that he would give him food to eat, and raiment to put on. Our Lord hath permitted us to ask for no more than daily bread, or a bare competency. Having food and raiment, says the Apostle, let us be content. When God gives food and raiment, nothing is wanting on his part; it is our concern and our part to give ourselves a contented mind. In the whole Scripture, there is not one prayer for superfluity.

It is not unlawful to possess riches: they are of their own nature indifferent; they are called in Scripture the gift of God, and which is more, the blessing of God. They are blessings when God offers them, though not blessings to those who covetously seek them. Many good men mentioned in sacred history were rich; but none of them are said to have been desirous of riches.

To those who never know when they have a sufficiency, and who are restless and mad after earthly things, to such persons riches prove no blessing. He that maketh haste to be rich, says Solomon, shall not be innocent. They that will be rich, says St. Paul, that is, whose principal care and concern it is to be rich, fall into temptation, and a snare, and into many foolish and hurtful lusts, which drown men in destruction.

Agur was apprehensive lest wealth should make him irreligious: and many things are said in the Scriptures, which shew that his fear was not without a just cause. God is represented offering prosperity to his people as an ambiguous gift, with some doubt and distrust, and hesitation, with a hand half extended and half drawn back, as though he feared it might do more harm than good. Like an indulgent parent, he gives this caution along with it, When thou shalt have eaten and be full, then beware lest thy heart be lifted up, and thou forget the Lord thy God, in not keeping his commandments, and thou say in thy heart, My power and the might of my hand hath gotten me this wealth. Again in Deuteronomy, Moses thus prophesies of Israel: Thou art waxed fat——Then he forsook God who made him, and lightly esteemed the rock of his salvation. And in Hosea, God complains of the completion of this prophecy: According to their pasture, says he, so were they filled, and their hearts were lifted up; therefore have they forgotten me. Great wealth and power and honours bring with them a variety of business, draw after them a multitude of flatterers, nourish pride and conceit, and afford continual means and opportunities of pursuing all sorts of pleasures; so that what with the cares, and what with the diversions of life, no time is left for God and religion.

It is indeed a strange and a perverse wickedness to abuse the abundance of God's gifts to the dishonour of him who bestows them, and by such a scandalous behaviour to furnish wicked men with arguments against divine providence. Ingratitude is ever odious even towards men, and for the favours which they can bestow. Much more detestable is unthankfulness to the giver of all good things. Yet the repeated benefits of generous friends will sometimes force an acknowledgment even from a thankless difpofition, though a fmaller kindnefs will not do it. But, on the contrary, fo much the more to wrong our Maker, the more he heaps upon us, this is not eafily to be matched in the dealings between man and man. And yet thus are men ufed to behave towards God, not only to be unthankful, which were bad enough, but to make their unthankfulnefs increafe and keep pace with their increafing fortunes.

There is then a plain and good reafon why God for the moft part with-holds a great abundance of outward things from thofe whom he moft loves, namely, left by enriching the man, he fhould lofe the fervant.

It is very imprudent therefore in men earneftly to purfue that which fo much endangers their welfare. It is a folly for a man never to think himfelf well, till he is in a ftate of peril. We daily pray that God would not lead us into temptation, and yet we long to be tempted. We have fo good an opinion of ourfelves, that we would fain be rich, for the advantage of the public, and that we may fet a bright example of generofity and moderation. But as it is not true courage to feek out danger which we may avoid without lofs of honour, fo it is not true wifdom to covet a condition which hath fpoilt many a good underftanding and many an upright heart, and turned its prudence and innocence into folly and iniquity.

They to whom wealth hath prefented itfelf, either unfought, or honeftly obtained, ought to be very cautious and confiderate. Their ftate is expofed to danger; and yet it is poffible to be wife and happy and fafe in it, if proper means be ufed. What thofe means are, they may learn from St. Paul, who hath fet them forth in the artlefs fimplicity of plain words: Charge them that are rich in this world, that they be not highminded, nor truft in uncertain riches, but in the living God,

God, who giveth us richly all things to enjoy; that they do good, that they be rich in good works, ready to diſtribute, willing to communicate, laying up in ſtore for themſelves a good foundation againſt the time to come, that they may lay hold on eternal life,

SERMON XXIV.

1 Peter v. 5.

—*Be clothed with humility.*

IN my remarks upon the subject of Humility, I shall follow the usual method of discoursing upon moral virtues.

I. I will consider the nature and the effects of humility:

II. I will represent the motives and inducements to the practice of it.

I. I will consider its nature and effects, and represent it in these three views:

As it relates to our own private thoughts, and is confined to ourselves:

As it respects our duty to God:

As it influences our conduct towards our neighbour.

Humility, as it relates to our own private thoughts and judgment, requires that we should entertain no better an opinion of ourselves than we deserve. To judge too hardly and severely of ourselves, and to fancy that we are guilty of faults from which we are free, cannot be acts of humility, because there can be no virtue in mistake and ignorance. Only, as we have all a propensity to extenuate our defects, and to over-rate our good deeds, it is safest to err on the other side, to correct this bent by forcing the mind somewhat towards the contrary way, and frequently to review our failings and the many causes which we have of rejecting all arrogant and conceited thoughts.

Our Maker hath conferred upon us several gifts which we cannot possibly value too much, as long as we acknowledge them to come from him, and endeavour to make a right use of them. It shews ingratitude and ill-nature to lessen and undervalue the benefits which we receive from our friends; and to behave in this manner towards God, is still more blameable. In forming therefore a mean and despicable opinion of ourselves in particular, and of human nature in general, there may be not only no sound judgment, no modesty, no goodness of any sort, but error, ignorance, malevolence, and depravity of heart.

Some of the unbelieving and irreligious tribe have said, that a persuasion of the soul's immortality and of future rewards arose from the presumption and vanity of man, who, being proud and high-minded, fancies himself a more considerable and important animal than he really is; whilst they, throwing aside these prejudices, and aspiring to no such dignity, meekly acknowledge themselves to be brethren to the brutes, and expect after a few days to perish with them. This is humility; but it is so only in a bad sense, in the sense which the Romans used to fix upon that word, intending to express by it a sordid and mean spirit.

Others have affirmed that man never performs any good action, that all his seeming virtues are real vices, because self-love and a regard to his own interest is at the bottom of them, and conducts him in every step that he takes.

They who entertain such injurious notions of human nature, forfeit all claim to the approbation and
esteem

esteem of others. Charity itself, which thinketh no evil, cannot judge favourably of those who would transform every thing into vice, and banish all virtue from the earth.

Others, who are much better persons than the former, think that it is God who does all in and for the righteous in an arbitrary and irresistible manner, giving to some and refusing to others that assistance without which every one must perish. And this notion is, as they pretend, the very character of humility; whilst they really, though I will not say designedly, detract from the goodness and justice, and wisdom of God, and confound the notions of virtue and vice.

Lastly, there are some who have too mean an opinion of their own abilities, and by fancying themselves to be useless, become so, and dare not attempt many things in which they are capable of succeeding, and which they ought to perform. This behaviour arises more from indolence or melancholy than from humility.

Humility then, as it relates to the judgment which we form concerning ourselves, is a due sense of our imperfections; of those which are common to human nature, and of those which are more peculiarly our own.

The imperfections common to human nature are these:

Mortality, which came into the world by sin, and all the bad consequences attending it, a body weak and frail, and exposed to various disorders and diseases, which, as it is united to the soul, hath a great influence upon its operations, and often proves an impediment to its progress towards wisdom and goodness.

A stronger propensity to evil than to good, which all persons at certain times and on certain occasions have

have experienced, and guilt from some degrees of which none was ever free.

An understanding liable to be frequently deceived, and a knowledge which at the best is much confined.

The infirmities peculiar to ourselves are those defects, either in goodness, or in knowledge, or in wisdom, by which we are inferior to other persons.

To be sensible of these weaknesses and faults, is humility, as it relates to ourselves: to lessen or overlook them, is pride.

Let us now consider the effects which humility produces towards God.

Here it is also necessary to distinguish between true and false humility. That God is most just and holy, and that we are sinners, that the Gospel contains a perfect rule of righteousness, and that the best of us in many things transgress this rule; these are truths of which we ought to have a serious and a constant sense.

But there are here also extremes which should be avoided; for we may form too abject and too bad an opinion of ourselves, or we may represent God as a most strict and severe and inexorable master, or we may imagine that a perfection which we are not able to acquire is enjoined to us as necessary to salvation, or we may fear that repentance and amendment shall avail us nothing, or we may make religion to consist principally in a set of trifling and difficult rules, from which if we swerve, our mistaken conscience will condemn us. Such notions as these have in a greater or a lesser degree possessed many minds; and hence hath arisen a slavish dread and horrour of God, and a devotion overrun with superstition and uncommanded austerities. This is not humility; but ignorance, abject fear, and religious melancholy.

True

SERMON XXIV.

True and rational humility, as it influences our behaviour towards our Maker, produces a religious awe, and banishes presumption and carelessness and vain-glory. The humble person, considering the perfections of God, and comparing them with his own imperfections, approaches him with reverence, and acknowledges himself unworthy of his favour, and unable without his assistance to perform his duty, to obtain either temporal conveniences or eternal life. He trusts not to his own heart, or wisdom, or strength. He frequently recollects and confesses his omissions and transgressions, and uses them as motives to greater industry and watchfulness. He receives temporal good from the hands of God with gratitude; and temporal evil with resignation, as a correction which he deserves, as a trial of his obedience, and as intended for his benefit.

The effects which humility produces in our behaviour towards men are now to be considered; and here also the same distinction is to be repeated which was made before, namely, that there is a deceitful and false humility, which ought to be avoided. Thus some speak contemptibly of themselves, and pretend that they are ignorant of things in which they are well-skilled, and acknowledge themselves inferior to those whom they surpass; some pay a servile deference to the opinions and directions of others, and dare not use that reason and understanding which God has given them; some shun the conversation of their equals, and chuse companions of the lowest sort; and all those persons either fancy themselves to be humble, or would be accounted so by the world. Yet in such a conduct there may be no humility and modesty, but hypocrisy, or affectation, or bigotry, or a meanness of spirit mixed with pride and vanity.

Between an unmanly contempt and disregard of ourselves, with an abject fear and blind reverence of others,

others, which is one extreme, and a proud, conceited, overbearing infolence, which is the other extreme, true humility proceeds, always uniform and decent.

The humble perfon never affumes what belongs not to him; he defires to poffefs no more power, and to receive no more refpect and compliance from others, than is fuitable to his own character and condition, and appointed by the laws and cuftoms of fociety.

He is not a rigid exactor of the things to which he has an undoubted right; he can overlook and excufe many faults: he is not greatly difturbed and provoked at thofe flights and affronts which put vain and haughty perfons out of all patience.

He is eafy and quiet in his ftation, though he may deferve a better; not inclined to trouble the world with complaints and follicitations.

He can behold the fuccefs, much more the abilities and virtues of others with the fame even temper, and is not difpofed to hate, or flander, or envy them upon that account.

The good and ufeful qualities with which he is endued he employs in a prudent and unaffected manner, neither concealing them when they ought to appear, nor putting them forth for the fake of applaufe.

He is obedient to his fuperiors in things juft and lawful, rendering tribute to whom tribute is due, cuftom to whom cuftom, fear to whom fear, honour to whom honour.

He is dutiful to his parents, teachers, and mafters, courteous towards his equals, condefcending towards his inferiors, merciful and placable towards his enemies, gentle and patient towards thofe who are in error, or overtaken in a fault.

He

He is candid in his judgment, and more inclined, when there is any room for it, to think and speak favourably than hardly.

He exercises power, if it be committed to him, with justice and impartiality, tempered with as much forbearance and lenity as is consistent with the public good.

II. The nature of humility has been considered. Let us now, secondly, consider the motives to the practice of it.

1. Humility is a virtue so excellent, that the Scriptures have in some sort ascribed it even to God himself.

Humility is a right opinion and estimate of ourselves, producing a suitable behaviour towards others. But as in ourselves we find much imperfection, a dependence always upon God, and often upon men, and no good quality which we can call entirely our own, and for which we are not indebted to our Maker, hence it is that humility consists principally in a due sense of our defects, our transgressions, our wants, and the obligations which we have received. Therefore such humility cannot be in God, in him who possesses all perfections. But there is a part of humility, as it relates to our behaviour towards men, called condescension; and this is sometimes represented in Scripture as a disposition not unworthy of the divine Nature. " The Lord is high above all, his glory is above the heavens; yet he humbleth himself to behold the things that are in heaven and earth." Again; " Though the Lord be high, yet hath he respect unto the lowly." Again; " Lord, what is man, that thou art mindful of him; and the son of man, that thou visitest him?" that is, that thou condescendest to take notice and care of him. This condescension is ascribed to God, not as if it were an occupation below him, or unworthy of his power and wisdom; but because a like behaviour in men towards their inferiors

is

is called condefcenfion. And in us it is called condefcenfion, becaufe we defcend, not from our dignity, but from that falfe and foolifh fuperiority and ftate which vain and conceited perfons ufurp and maintain.

2. The example of our Saviour is an example of every virtue, particularly of humility. He himfelf calls upon us to obferve and imitate it, to come and learn of him to be meek, lowly in heart, patient, calm, and condefcending.

His humility appears in moft of the actions and circumftances of his life; in his birth, by which he became the child of a parent not lefs poor than virtuous; in the obfcurity which he chofe till he entered into his miniftry; in his care to conceal his dignity upon moft occafions; in his fubmiffion to the ceremonial law, to the civil government, to wicked magiftrates, to extreme want, and to extreme fufferings; in continually promoting, not his own glory, but the glory and honour of his father; in his behaviour towards thofe who fought him, and towards thofe whom he himfelf took the pains to feek and to fave, towards the ignorant and the miftaken, the forrowful and penitent, the fick and needy, towards his friends and followers, and towards his accufers, betrayers, flanderers, perfecutors, and murderers.

3. In the behaviour of the Angels, as it is revealed to us in the Scriptures, we find that part of humility called condefcenfion, or a willing and cheerful fubmiffion to any offices by which the good of others may be promoted. We are there taught that they have been, and that they always are ready, at God's appointment, to guide, to direct, to fuccour, to comfort, to inftruct, to affift, to relieve, to protect, and deliver good men. Thus are they miniftring fpirits; and in the intercourfe between us and them, the labour and the attendance is theirs, the profit is ours; we are miniftered unto, and they minifter. Hence we muft

must learn to think it no disgrace to be, as our Lord says he was, the servants of all, to be occupied in procuring the ease, the improvement, the welfare, and the happiness of our brethren, and to account no acts base and mean, which produce so noble and excellent effects. In truth we cannot be more creditably employed; nor can the holy Angels better shew the excellence of their nature than in thus stooping to our necessities; for it is more blessed, and more honourable too, to give than to receive. They bestow upon us substantial benefits, and we can return them nothing besides reverence and gratitude. Whosoever best imitates these holy Spirits in humility and condescension towards his inferiors, approaches nearest to them in dignity; and whilst he abases himself his actions exalt him.

4. It is affirmed in many places of Scripture that humility secures to us the favour of God, and will bring down his blessing upon ourselves and our undertakings.

" He that humbleth himself shall be exalted: with the lowly is wisdom: before honour is humility: honour shall uphold the humble in spirit: God shall save the humble: he giveth grace to the lowly, and exalteth the humble and meek: whosoever shall humble himself as a little child, the same is greatest in the kingdom of heaven: thus saith the high and lofty one that inhabiteth eternity; I dwell in the high and holy place; with him also that is of a contrite and humble spirit; to this man will I look, even to him that is poor, and of a contrite spirit; and trembleth at my word:. them that are meek, will God guide in judgment, and such as are gentle, them will he teach his way: he hath hidden the most valuable knowledge, that is, religious knowledge, from the wise and prudent, and hath revealed it unto babes."

From

From thefe paffages we may obferve that humility is highly acceptable to God; in general, becaufe it is a virtue; in particular, becaufe it difpofes men to receive with modeft fubmiffion the great truths of religion, to be willing to receive inftruction, to yield to reafon, and when there is fufficient evidence that a doctrine or precept is from God, to believe and obferve it.

5. Humility ufually gains the efteem and love of men, and confequently the conveniences, at leaft the neceffaries, of life. Every one who has even flightly obferved what paffes in the world muft fee and know this. Since all love themfelves, they will probably approve and favour thofe who never provoke, infult, deride, or injure them, who fhew them refpect and civility, and do them good offices. The humble perfon therefore takes the fureft way to recommend himfelf to thofe with whom he is joined in fociety, to increafe the number of his well-wifhers and friends, and to efcape or defeat the affaults of detraction, envy, and malice. This amiable quality will ftand by him, will be a protector and benefactor to him in all ftations, and through all his days, particularly when he firft enters into bufinefs and appears in public. Then the want of this one virtue is enough to ruin the perfon who ftands fo much in need of affiftance, inftruction, and recommendation. He who is young and unexperienced, proud and infolent, will fcarcely be able to improve either his mind or his fortunes, and if he falls, will fall unpitied.

6. Such are the prefent advantages which humility ufually fecures to us from God and from men; ufually, I fay, but not conftantly; becaufe it is poffible that an humble perfon may be neglected by the world, and that God may not interpofe in his behalf, and may defer his reward to the next life. Therefore the moft certain prefent recompence of humility

SERMON XXIV.

humility is that which arises from its own nature, and with which it repays the mind that entertains it; and a very valuably recompence it would be, though it were the only one allotted to this virtue.

An humble person neither hates nor envies any one; therefore he is free from those very turbulent and uneasy vices which are always a punishment to themselves.

He is not discomposed by the slights or censures of others. If he has undesignedly given some occasion for them, he amends the fault: if he deserves them not, he regards them as little.

He is contented with his condition, if it be tolerable; and therefore he finds satisfaction in all that is good, and overlooks, and in some measure escapes, all that is inconvenient in it.

He has a due sense of his unworthiness and defects, by which he is taught to bear calamities with patience and submission, and thereby to soften their harsh nature, and to allay their violence.

He is free from pride and ambition; therefore he never sacrifices his integrity, his honour, and his peace of mind, those substantial blessings, to the splendid trifles which are the objects of pride and ambition. He desires not to obtain them at all, much less to obtain them in the common way, by sordid flattery, by sinful compliances, by dissimulation, by lying and slandering, by deceiving and over-reaching, by violence and oppression, by loss of time, by useless occupations, by dangerous attempts, by profusion and extravagance, by methods which have been pernicious to the fortunes, to the body, and to the mind, of multitudes.

7. Lastly; From the account which we have given of humility, we may draw this conclusion; that it is not, as the insolent and haughty are inclined to imagine, an unmanly and sordid disposition. It is true

that the word (a) *humility* is used by Latin writers in a bad sense for meanness of spirit; but the Pagans were not ignorant of this virtue, and have recommended it; only they gave it another name. Christianity indeed hath taught us juster notions of humility than they commonly entertained; for they usually considered *humility*, which they called *modesty*, or *moderation*, as a social virtue, as it influenced our behaviour towards ourselves and towards men; but humility towards God few of them seem to have sufficiently apprehended. It is indeed a virtue so remote from meanness of spirit, that it is no bad sign of a great and exalted mind. An humble person is one who is neither puffed up with approbation and applause, nor greatly provoked or disturbed by censure and ill usage, who envies none placed above him, and despises none below him, who dares examine his own conduct, and condemn whatsoever is faulty in it, who is gentle to others and severe to himself, who desires to obtain no more than he deserves, who can quit even that also, if his duty requires it, who is contented to act the part which Providence allots to him, who is free from irregular self-love, that is, from one of the most insinuating and prevailing weaknesses of mankind, which may not improperly be called the inner garment of the soul, the first which it puts on, and the last which it puts off. If this be not, it will be hard to say what is greatness of mind.

On the contrary, if we would know what meanness of spirit is, and how it acts, let us look for it amongst the proud and insolent, and we shall not lose our labour. A proud man is one who is glad to receive homage and flattery, though it be offered to him by the most ignorant or worthless, and cannot bear contempt even from them; who therefore is the servant or slave of all, not in a good sense, but because his happiness

---

(a) See *Disc.* VII. on the Christian Religion.

happiness depends upon their opinion and behaviour; who has no heart to own his obligations to God and man, whose life and conduct is one continual lie, who assumes good qualities which he has not, and is blind to his own faults; who desires to possess what he should not, and what he often cannot obtain; and who is much dissatisfied when he is disappointed. These are the persons who despise humility, and by despising recommend it.

SERMON XXV.

MATTH. xxvi. 39.

O my Father, if it be possible, let this cup pass from me: nevertheless, not as I will, but as thou wilt.

THESE words of our Lord are generally and justly understood and acknowledged to contain a perfect act of resignation to the good pleasure of God; yet something of a difficulty there may seem to be in them. Not as I will, but as thou wilt. Our Lord then had a will quite different from the will of God. The will of God was, that he should suffer a painful and ignominious death: his own will was, not to suffer it. But how could this will be in Christ, when we know that he performed in all things the most exact obedience, and that to do the will of his Father, was his meat and drink, his constant employment, and his greatest delight?

We must observe then that our Lord was made like unto us in all things, sin excepted; and that upon this and other occasions he experienced in himself what we also frequently find within us, two contrary wills, or, to speak more accurately, a strife between inclination and reason; in which cases, though reason gets the better of inclination, we may be said to do a thing (*a*) willingly, yet with an unwilling mind.

(*a*) Ἑκὼν, ἀέκοντί γε θυμῷ.

mind. Thus a good man placed in such circumstances, that he must undergo great hardships, or act against his duty, is desirous, as he is a man, not to suffer pain, for human nature shuns and dislikes it; but he is more desirous of doing his duty; and when he is resolved to chuse what is right, and for the sake of it to submit to that which offends and crosses his natural inclinations, he may say, with our Lord, Not my will, but the will of God be done. Thus Christ, foretelling to Peter what death he should die, says; When thou wast young, thou girdedst thyself, and walkedst whither thou wouldest; but when thou shalt be old, thou shalt stretch forth thy hands, and another shall gird thee, and carry thee whither thou wouldst not; that is, to crucifixion, to a punishment which thou, as all other men, wouldst naturally desire to avoid. And yet that St. Peter suffered it with Christian fortitude is not to be doubted.

The great end of our Lord's sufferings, was to save and redeem us: but there are many other excellent ends for which they serve; as, for instance, to set before us an example of resignation to God's will in all calamities, and to be a comfort to us under them. In this view I shall at present consider them; proposing,

I. To shew, how the Son of God exercised this virtue here upon earth:

II. To recommend to ourselves the imitation of his example.

I. I shall shew how our Lord exercised this virtue here upon earth.

Christ pleased not himself, says St Paul, did not consult his own pleasure, ease, and quiet, and for the sake of them neglect any part of his office; he came, as himself tells us, not to do his own will, but the will of his Father; and by the wise appointment of God he was through the course of his ministry exercised with variety of heavy trials, subject to many inconveniencies and pains, from which men desire to be free, and deprived

prived of many good things which they desire to possess, that so he might practise in its full extent the duty of acquiescence to the divine will. A distinct view and consideration of all that he thus endured may be very useful to us.

We all desire to enjoy the conveniences of life, and to be above dependence. Even they who set not their hearts upon wealth and honours, yet start at the thoughts of the opposite state, and cannot look Want in the face, and are ready to say with Him in the Proverbs, Give me neither poverty nor riches. Yet to this extreme poverty our Lord humbly submitted. He was born and educated in a family, which was noble indeed, and of royal descent, but in very low circumstances; he had no house of his own where he could lay his head, nothing except what he received from some liberal and charitable persons, who ministered to him of their substance, and no money to pay the tribute, when it was demanded of him. Ye know, says St. Paul, the grace, that is, the loving kindness of our Lord Jesus Christ, that though he was rich, yet for your sakes he became poor, that ye, through his poverty, might be rich. For your sakes he became poor. The (*b*) word in the original is stronger, and means, for your sakes he was in the utmost indigence.

Yet, though in the New Testament we find proofs and instances of the extreme poverty of our Lord, we read of no complaint there upon that account, not a word expressing a dislike of such a state: on the contrary, he speaks favourably of poverty, recommends it to those whose lot it is, as a condition exposed to fewer temptations and dangers than worldly prosperity, and which patiently undergone shall turn to their advantage in the next life.

Hard labour, attended with weariness, is disagreeable. Even those active spirits who hate idleness, and

delight

(*b*) Ἐπτώχευσε.

delight in employment, would not have the toil long and uninterrupted, and love intervals of repose. Our Saviour's life, during his miniſtry, was a life of hardſhip and fatigue. He was conſtantly taking journeys on foot, diſcourſing whole days to the people, and often at night, when others were at reſt, retiring to bleak mountains and deſerts, to ſpend thoſe hours in meditation and prayer, and the next day renewing his accuſtomed toils.

Hunger and thirſt, when long endured, are enemies to our nature, and put us to violent uneaſineſs, till they are ſatisfied. Theſe alſo our Lord often ſuffered, oftener in all probability than the Evangeliſts have mentioned, as he was frequently buſy, and ſometimes in places where no refreſhment was to be had; nor do we read that he ever wrought a miracle to feed himſelf.

All this he underwent, not only without any impatience and repining, but willingly and readily, loſing no opportunity of doing good to mens minds and bodies, where he was intreated to come, and where he was not intreated, ſeeking and ſaving that which was loſt, converſing freely with ſinners, and eating with them, that he might win them over to the love of virtue, and rejoicing to ſee the multitudes gathered together to hear the word of God from him. Never did he then diſmiſs and diſappoint them, to conſult his own repoſe, and to avoid the inconvenience and trouble of ſo much company; but taught them heavenly truths, as they were able to receive them; and if his diſciples ſhewed any diſlike when the people preſſed into his preſence, he rebuked them for their forward and impatient behaviour.

When after his long faſt in the wilderneſs he was hungry, and the Devil tempting him, adviſed him to turn ſtones into bread, he anſwers; Man ſhall not live by bread alone, but by every word that proceedeth out of the mouth of God. When his diſciples bring him proviſions, knowing him to be ſpent, and in great
need

need of them, and intreat him, Master, eat; he puts it off: I have meat to eat that ye know not of. Therefore said the disciples one to another, Hath any man brought him ought to eat? Jesus saith unto them, My meat is to do the will of him that sent me, and to finish his work.

To those who have the instruction of others committed to their care, it is agreeable to meet with persons teachable, and of good capacities, and tiresome to inform slow understandings. Our Lord, knowing that the glory of God, and the good of mankind required it, chose for his disciples persons of mean rank and education, honest and well-disposed men, but ignorant, and dull, and apt to mistake him. Yet with these he spent most of his time, when he was not teaching the people; these he instructed with the greatest patience, and by repeated lessons, and never said any thing harder to them than, Are ye also without understanding? How is it that ye do not perceive?

Returns of baseness and treachery from our intimates whom we have loaded with benefits, are most grievous to be borne, and will wring from the mildest temper such complaints as these; It is not an open enemy that hath done me this dishonour; for then I could have borne it: but it was even thou, my companion, my guide, and mine own familiar friend. Christ amongst his disciples nourished a viper and a traitor, whom no warnings could call to repentance, no kindness could soften, and was forced, knowing that it was part of his office, to converse familiarly with this abandoned man, whose heart and inmost thoughts he perfectly saw: and even to him he shewed great lenity. He let him know that he was acquainted with his treachery, and charitably foretold him the consequence of it: The Son of man goeth, as it is written of him; but woe unto that man by whom the Son of man is betrayed. This would not reclaim him; and therefore Christ gave him up as one irrecoverably lost; but yet without reproaches:

SERMON XXV.

reproaches: What thou doſt, ſays he to Judas, do quickly: and when he was delivered up to the Jews, his reproof was; (c) Companion, wherefore art thou come? Betrayeſt thou the Son of man with a kiſs?

A good man, whoſe office it is to inſtruct others in religion, will be grieved when his charitable labours are loſt, and he hath to do with ſtubborn offenders, who are deaf to all reproofs and admonitions. Our Lord was unſucceſsful in his miniſtry. The harveſt indeed was great; but he ſaw it not whilſt he lived upon earth. He drew all men after him; but he was firſt lifted up, diſobeyed, ſet at nought and crucified by that faithleſs generation. How much this affected him we plainly ſee from the complaints which he often poured out, and the juſt anger which he expreſſed on ſome occaſions. Yet this pity and grief, mixed with indignation and reſentment at their obſtinacy, was for their ſake. He continued his kind endeavours to win them over to obedience and to ſave them from ruin.

To be injured in our reputation, and expoſed to malicious calumny, is a great trial of human patience; for it is our duty in theſe circumſtances both to forgive our enemies, and alſo not to be over-concerned at reproaches which our conſcience tells us that we deſerve not. But they who have not learned by repeated endeavours to govern their paſſions, find ſuch an evenneſs of temper, and ſuch a charitable diſpoſition, hard to be acquired. This trial our Saviour long endured: never was man more defamed and ſlandered than he. Yet ſtill he went about doing good, and ready to relieve, to inſtruct, and to pardon them. He told them that whatſoever they ſpake againſt the Son of man might be pardoned; and his dying words were prayers to God to forgive them, becauſe they knew not what they did.

To ſee multitudes involved in a great calamity is a grief to a charitable man, eſpecially when they are his country-men,

---

(c) So it ſhould be tranſlated; Ἑταῖρε, Sodalis, Companion. *Matt.* xxvi. 50.

country-men, when they are miserable through their own fault, and might have avoided those evils by amending their ways. Our Lord loved all mankind with an unparalleled love: greater love hath no man than this, that a man lay down his life for his friends. For a good, or a merciful man, peradventure some would even dare to die: but whilst we were yet sinners Christ died for us. But though he was thus affected towards all mankind, yet, like other men, he had a more particular love for those of his own nation; and amongst his disciples and acquaintance some seem to have had a greater share in his friendship than others, as Lazarus and St. John. His love for his ungrateful country caused in him the utmost sorrow, when he reflected upon the miseries that would shortly overtake it. The Jews had then nigh filled up the measure of their iniquities, the days of vengeance were at hand, and evils which eye had not seen, nor ear heard. When Christ was entering into Jerusalem, the sight of it brought to his thoughts those divine Judgments: the dreadful scene was as plainly before him as if he had seen it all acted; and it made him burst into tears, and passionately lament over that unhappy city.

Future evils, when we see them coming, and are sure that we cannot escape them, torment us near if not quite as much as when they are present. And though it may seem a folly to make ourselves uneasy at things which we do not yet endure, or which must unavoidably come to pass, yet so we are (*d*) made, and, cannot possibly help it. With great (*e*) kindness therefore

(*d*) ——— the expectation more
Of worse torments me than the feeling can.
I would be at the worst; worst is my port,
My harbour, and my ultimate repose,
The end I would attain, my final good.

Milton.

(*e*) Prudens futuri temporis exitum
Caliginosa nocte premit Deus.

fore God hath concealed from us future events, and keeps us in a happy ignorance, and reserves from us a knowledge which might make us miserable creatures all the days of our life. Our Lord, who was a man like to us, had this human infirmity. He was cast down at the foresight of the painful and ignominious death which he was to suffer. Long before it came, the thought of it was still uppermost in his mind, and he often told his disciples what he should endure: so that he might be truly said to die daily. As it drew near, he says; Now is my soul troubled; and what shall I say? Father, save me from this hour: but for this cause came I unto this hour. On the evening before his passion, he was troubled in spirit, and testified and said, Verily, verily, I say unto you, that one of you shall betray me. Afterwards he began to be sorrowful and very heavy, and said; My soul is exceeding sorrowful even unto death: tarry ye here, and watch with me. Yet in all this hard conflict which he endured within himself, this extreme dejection, this fear and anguish and horror and consternation, no impatient word fell from his mouth, nothing that did not express a perfect submission to the will of God.

Lastly; Men love life, and are unwilling to lose it. Death in any shape and at any time is usually unacceptable: a death attended with great pain and infamy is so grievous and terrible, that it requires an uncommon strength of mind to meet it with constancy. St. Peter, who was by nature courageous, and who drew his sword in defence of his master, and would have laid down his life undauntedly in the heat of the action, was quite overcome by the fears of suffering as a malefactor, and shamefully denied his Lord.

Most painful and ignominious was the death which Christ endured; and he bare it, as a good man might, with humble resignation to the will of God, yet not without that dislike, those fears, that concern and dejection,

jection, to which natural infirmity makes the best of persons often liable.

When we consider the unspotted innocence of our Saviour, and the great and good ends for which he laid down his life, and his certain knowledge that he should arise again, and ascend into heaven, and sit at God's right hand, it may seem strange that he should have shewed so much consternation at the approach of death. If all this will not support human nature under afflictions, what is there that possibly can? But it was the good pleasure of God, doubtless for many wise reasons of providence, that our Lord should be in an eminent manner a man of sorrows and acquainted with grief, according to the predictions of Isaiah.

Before he suffered, he fell into an agony at the thoughts of it, and when they came to seize him, the manner and the circumstances of it somewhat raised his resentment; and we see in his expressions, though they were tempered with great moderation, the offence which a man conscious of his own innocence takes, when he is treated as a villain. Are ye come out as against a thief, with swords and staves? When he was upon the cross, he cried out, My God, my God, why hast thou forsaken me? We must not imagine that God was then angry and displeased with him, who never loved him more than at that instant. But you should observe that these words of our Saviour are the very words of David in the beginning of the twenty second Psalm; and our Saviour repeated them on this occasion, to shew that he was the person foretold in that Psalm, and that in his person the words of David were accomplished, and that therefore he was the true Messias. It appeared that God did not forsake him entirely; for after this, he uttered no more complaints: he said, It is finished: his work was ended, and so were his sorrows. With serenity and composure of mind he recommended his soul into the hands of his Father, and gave up the ghost.

II. Such

SERMON XXV.

II. Such was the meek and refigned conduct of our Lord under trials as many and as great as can well be conceived. It remains, fecondly, to recommend his behaviour to be copied by Chriftians in trials of a like fort.

To fuffer in fome degree is as unavoidable as it is to breathe and to think. Through fuch trials we muft all expect to pafs: we cannot, and our Lord would not efcape them. That man is born to trouble, is a law which he came, not to deftroy, but to fulfil; and as he became a man, he became alfo a man of forrows. But though he would not free us from our calamities and inconveniences of life, yet, which is more than we could have expected, and as much as we can reafonably defire, he enables us to bear them by the religion that he hath taught us. Nature fays, Man is born to trouble: Revelation fays, A good man is born to happinefs. Nature fays, Man is born to die: Revelation fays, A good man dies to rife again unto life eternal. We muft fet the one againft the other, and be thankful that fince, as we are men, labour and forrow is our patrimony; as we are Chriftians, glory and immortality may be our inheritance.

The motives which we have to refignation under any inconveniences, any diftrefs or evil that may befall us, cannot be fully difcuffed in the remaining part of this difcourfe. I fhall in few words lay them before you.

One great motive to it, and which comprehends in it almoft all the reft, is the goodnefs of God. Upon this all our hope and comfort is founded. A belief of this will make us fubmit to any thing that God fhall impofe upon us; it will reconcile us to inconveniences, even for this reafon, becaufe it is his pleafure.

Another motive to refignation is, that calamities, if we make a right ufe of them, may be very profitable to us, and that they plainly conduce to excellent ends. They remind us to enter into ourfelves, and to examine the paft faults of our lives, they lead us to repentance,

they

they wean us from too great a fondness for a world which we must soon leave, and set our affections on proper objects, they keep us out of the reach of many temptations to which a state of affluence and prosperity lies continually exposed, and they soften our hearts and teach us humanity and compassion towards those who are in affliction.

Another inducement to resignation is that reward in heaven which we may secure.

If indeed it were evident that this state was our all, these few days our only portion, men, at least the unhappier part of men, could scarcely account themselves the offspring of a good and merciful Author, but children of Sorrow, forced into being they knew not how or why, and exposed to all the injuries that unrelenting Nature should lay upon them. A future state removes all pleas for discontent; and when eternal happiness is promised to sincere endeavours, we may well submit with decent patience to afflictions of a short continuance, and to imperfections which we shall soon cast off, and in all circumstances pay to divine Providence the reasonable duty of believing that it orders all for the best.

Lastly, Another motive to resignation is the behaviour of our Lord, which we, who assume the honourable name of Christians, should be ambitious to imitate. Would we learn to act as we ought under the evils that may probably some time or other overtake us? We need no other book besides the New Testament, and no other example than our Saviour's to instruct us. His sufferings and conduct under them is one of the most agreeable and most useful meditations that can occupy our minds, especially if we ourselves are in any of the same hard circumstances. To reflect then upon the majestic and resplendent parts of his life and character affords not the same relief to a dejected mind. To view him commanding all nature, saying to the sea and to the winds, Peace, be still; and to the dead, Come forth;

forth; to view him striking to the ground those who came to him, by only saying, I am he; and rising triumphant from the grave, and ascending in the clouds to heaven; to view him thus, will excite our reverence, and confirm our belief in him: but there is nothing in all this that we can imitate and apply to ourselves. It is more pleasing to view him, where he appears as one of us, as much distressed and as little regarded as any of us can be; to consider him possessing nothing, and attended with a few friends almost as poor as himself; enduring hunger, thirst, cold, and weariness, slandered and reviled, despised and betrayed, scourged and crucified; to consider him bearing afflictions, not with Stoical scorn and unconcern, as though he neither felt pain, nor was sensible of injuries, but deeply affected with fear and horror, with sorrow and despondency; bending to the earth under the heavy hand of God, offering up prayers and supplications with strong crying and tears, and almost asking what, as he well knew, was not to be obtained; to see him thus compassed about, as with afflictions, so also with human infirmities; to see him in all these trials persisting in an uniform obedience to God, exercising the utmost charity and long-suffering towards men, towards his enemies and persecutors; encountering evils most disagreeable to human nature with patience and silent meekness, without repining and without murmuring.

In these things he is to us an example not so vastly above us; an example which, by the assistance of God, we may hope, though not to equal, yet in some degree to resemble. The Apostles recommend it to us, supposing that we may come somewhat near to it. The Apostles recommend it to us, supposing that we may come somewhat near to it. They exhort us in general to live as he lived; in particular, to imitate the humility, patience, and resignation, which he shewed when he suffered for us, leaving us an example that we should follow his steps.

If

If we carefully meditate on the life of Christ, and study to conform our own to it, and apply for aid to Him who is always found of those who seek him, peace of mind, and that silent and sedate pleasure which ariseth from obedience will follow us through all states, making the best far more agreeable than it would else be, and administering a relief under the worst which will render it supportable.

I am sensible that to talk to gay and inconsiderate persons of any degree of pleasure joined to adversity, is in their opinion to talk in an enthusiastic strain; but there are pleasures of the serious and even of the melancholy kind. The joy of the first believers under ill usage and heavy trials is mentioned in the New Testament, and St. Paul thought it no contradiction to say of himself and of other servants of Christ, that they were sorrowful, yet always rejoicing. Our Saviour, without question, though in a most eminent manner a man of sorrows and acquainted with grief, yet often enjoyed a sober and exalted pleasure, which no man besides himself ever felt, as he was the most holy and beneficent of all men, and the only one in whom no sin was found. To rejoice in prosperity Nature will teach us: To rejoice in the hope of immortality our Lord will enable us if we consent to be guided by him; and of this joy adversity itself will not deprive us.

SERMON XXVI.

Rom. ii. 6.

Who will render to every man according to his deeds.

OF the doctrines contained in the Christian religion, there are some which only a divine revelation could have ascertained to us, and there are others which human reason was capable of discovering. Of the first kind is the resurrection of the dead, by which is to be understood that we who now are men, consisting of soul and body, shall again be what we now are, human creatures, knowing ourselves to be the same persons; and that this shall in all respects be a happy change for the righteous, whose souls shall be improved in every thing that is good and great, and whose bodies shall be exempted from the imperfections, diseases, and decays, which are inseparable attendants on frail mortality. Nearly of the same kind is the gracious promise made to sinners in general, that upon their repentance and amendment they shall be forgiven, and received hereafter into a state of peace and content, in some of the various mansions appointed for the servants of God, which is a greater favour than they could have collected with full certainty from the mere light of reason. Amongst the Christian doctrines which the human understanding might have discerned, are the being of one supreme God, most powerful, wise, and good,

good, the continuance of the soul after death, and a state of retribution.

A great part of the doctrine of the Scripture concerning another life and a future judgment was plain enough in itself, and might have been generally known, but through the ignorance and the wickedness of men was in a manner lost to the world, and for that reason may be truly said to be brought to light by our Saviour.

Not only in the text, but in other places of the New Testament, it is declared that all men shall give an account of themselves to God; that not only all Jews and Christians, but they who never heard of any revelation, shall be judged according to their works; whence it manifestly follows that all men might have expected a future state, and by a right use of their understanding might have supposed it very probable.

This doctrine, as it hath the greatest influence upon the actions of thinking beings, is so far of all doctrines the most important. That men are less wicked, or more virtuous than they would else be, is to be ascribed to the belief of this more than to any other motive; and they who can persuade themselves that it is false, are beyond the power of reason, and nothing besides immediate pain and punishment can awaken and convince them.

There are many considerations which concur to shew the certainty of this doctrine.

1. We may easily perceive, that we brought not ourselves into being, and that we owe what we possess to some Cause more powerful than ourselves; that the world, in which we are placed, bears in every part of it visible signs of great wisdom, power, and goodness. It is impossible that the world should be the work of beings many in number, and immensely remote from each other, and consequently much limited in knowledge, power, and wisdom. It is impossible that it should have been formed, either in time, or from all eternity,

by

by itself, or by chance, or by neceffity. It is therefore moſt reaſonable to ſuppoſe that there is one great Mind, which placed in proper order, and preſerves, and directs, and governs all that we behold, which is without beginning and without end, adorned with every perfection, moſt good, and the author of all good.

If we live according to the laws of reaſon and virtue, we find that we can free ourſelves from many wild and extravagant deſires of wealth, and worldly power, and vicious pleaſures, from deſires of revenge, cruelty, and oppreſſion; but one deſire ſticks faſt to us as human nature itſelf, the deſire of immortality. We would willingly continue for ever, for ever enjoy the power of reaſoning and reflecting, of viewing the various works of God, of inquiring after truth, and acquiring knowledge and experience. If we could poſſeſs an endleſs life, with an exemption from bodily pain, and from the ill offices of wicked beings, we ſhould think ourſelves moſt happy, and beyond expreſſion obliged to our Maker.

It is hard to ſuppoſe that he hath created us thus deſirous of immortality, and thus capable of eternal improvement, unleſs he intended us for ſomething more, and ſomething better than a few years of vanity and vexation.

2. The (*a*) evils and calamities of life, which though they have been frequently exaggerated, as grief is querulous, yet are certainly numerous and heavy, and the unequal diſpenſations of providence, are to us an earneſt of a future ſtate.

We are called and commanded into being, without our own conſent, by a ſuperior power; and if this earth were our only habitation, and theſe few days our all,

---

(*a*) Herodotus, vii. 46. Heſiod Ερy. 101. Homer *Odyſſ.* Σ. 129. Pliny ii. 7. Plautus *Amphitr.* ii. 12. Diphilus in Stobæus, Euripides, and many others, have treated of this ſubject; but the evils of life are no where better deſcribed than in Æſchines, *Dial.* iii. Περὶ θανάτȣ, p. 92.

all, the miserable part of mankind might with some reason (*b*) expostulate with their Creator, and question his goodness, who had forced upon them a being in which they could take no satisfaction. To reply that God is of supreme and irresistible power, and may do as he thinks fit to his creatures, is not a sufficient answer. As it removes none of the pain, and answers none of the desires, so it would satisfy none of the objections of the unhappy. They could never think a Creator to be merciful and wise, who should compel them into a miserable life upon such hard conditions, a life which they would have refused, if it could be conceived possible that they might have had their choice. Many of the Pagans used to say, by way of consolation, If life becomes insupportable, men should not complain, because they are not compelled to bear it, and have the remedy in their hands; the door always stands open, and they may go out when they will. But upon the supposition that there is no future state, the question would still remain, Why were they called in? A question which it is not easy to answer.

They who reject the doctrine of another life, do indeed usually reject along with it the moral attributes of God, and allow him neither goodness, nor equity, nor a regard to the virtues or vices of men; but only suppose him to be endued with supreme power, and consummate wisdom, that is to say, wisdom in the contrivance of the universe, and in the distribution of its parts. This is a favourite notion with some of our modern infidels; but it is surely a most absurd description

---

(*b*) It may be replied, that perhaps men suffer here for faults committed by them in a former state. But, first, the supposition of a former state includes in it the supposition also of a future state. Secondly, it seems not equitable, that there should be a state of punishment, which is not attended with a reminiscence of former transgressions; and this affords a strong argument against the doctrine of an antecedent state, and a transmigration of the soul.

tion of the Deity; for power without goodnefs is tyranny, and wifdom without goodnefs is little better than ignorance, and fails in its moſt eſſential part.

Again, as to the evils of life, it is not a fatisfactory folution to reply, that moſt of our calamities are to be afcribed to ourfelves, and that if we were virtuous, we might be happy, at leaſt contented with our condition.

It is true, that virtue is always amiable, and commonly convenient; that vice is always odious, and commonly hurtful. But this is not enough. It feems juſt and fit and regular, that as happinefs and goodnefs are neceffarily united in God, fo by his appointment they ſhould be united in all other beings. Virtue, which brings us nearer in refemblance to God, fhould for that very reafon be attended with a proportionable degree of happinefs; and vice, which deſtroys that refemblance, fhould be united to fhame and remorfe.

And yet, by an irregular tranfpofition, and an unnatural alliance, virtue is not only attended with mifery, but is, not feldom, the very caufe of it; whilſt fin fometimes flouriſhes, and many wicked perfons enjoy more worldly profperity, and fall into fewer calamities, than many good men. To reconcile which with the perfections of God, we muſt fuppofe that there will be a ſtate of retribution.

Man hath received from God reafon and liberty, and is accountable for them to him, as to his Creator. From him he muſt expect approbation, favour, and bleſſing, if he be obedient; and due correction, if he be ſtubborn and undutiful.

Man is obliged to perform good offices to his fellow-creatures, and hath a right to expect the fame returns. This is one of thofe evident truths which no rational creature can deny. It is therefore fit that they who defpife thefe obligations, and violate this great and plain duty, and by their cunning, by their high
ſtation

station in life, and their extensive power, or by the defect of human laws, escape the punishment which they deserve, should undergo it hereafter; and that they who love their neighbour as themselves, and are friends to mankind, should be rewarded, especially when their good deeds are overlooked, or misrepresented, or repaid with insults and injuries, in this unkind world.

Man, besides his public behaviour, acts a secret part in his own breast, and doth many things invisibly in imagination and design, which are buried in the mind that gave them birth, and receive for the present no punishment or recompence. Therefore there should be a state in which those good or bad dispositions shall be attended with suitable effects.

It may be urged, that future rewards are unnecessary, because there is none good. The best of men are guilty of so many failings, and are transgressors in so many respects, that they do not merit, and cannot claim of their Maker, as their due, a state of happiness after this; and God would not deal hardly with them, if he gave them no other life than this; and in this such a portion of good and evil mixed together, as time and chance should allot them.

Merit, and a right to demand rewards from God, are odious and insolent expressions. The necessity of future rewards appears not from the goodness of the best men considered in itself, and tried by the strict laws of justice, but from their comparative goodness in which they greatly surpass others. Thence the certainty of a future state may be collected; for it is not reasonable, that he who hath committed fewer faults, and performed some laudable actions, should fare worse than he who hath been very wicked, that all things should come alike to all, and that the greatest sinners, and they, who compared to them may be called righteous, shall perish together.

It

It may also be objected, that future punishments are the less necessary, because all vice is its own punishment even in this life.

Vice indeed usually draws after it many inconveniencies and disorders, many losses and calamities, and constantly deprives men of the superior pleasures which arise from virtue. But vice is not a proper and sufficient punishment to itself in this life, because many wicked men suffer far less here than many virtuous persons. Besides; happiness consists in opinion; he who can think himself happy is happy; and a sinner in this situation cannot be miserable, though he might have been happier with good dispositions, and though no wise man would change conditions with him.

3. If there were no judgment to come, or no evidence of it, men would want sufficient motives to well-doing, particularly when a steady adherence to righteousness would expose them to sufferings.

It hath been said, that since there is an unalterable difference between right and wrong, what is reasonable ought to be preferred by a reasonable creature, whatsoever the consequence may be; that there is a decency, dignity, and beauty in virtue, and that it is eligible for its own sake. All this may be granted; but it must be remembered, that man is not all mind, all intellect, all spirit. He is exposed to bodily pains so sharp and grievous, that whilst they last he must be miserable, though he should make them his choice, and approve his own conduct. He would therefore want a sufficient encouragement to endure such trials, if there were no life besides the present. The only motive upon that supposition would be this, that a rational creature ought not to act in a manner which his reason condemns, and for which he will be reproached, perhaps by others, but certainly by his own conscience (c). The

---

(c) The force of this motive is extremely well expressed by Juvenal:

—Phalaris

The fitness and rectitude of such a behaviour is a dusky and a refined kind of truth, which will escape the notice of the bulk of mankind. Some exalted minds might perceive it, and feel it, and act suitably to it; but men in general are no such creatures. They want hopes and fears, they want rewards and punishments, to make them chuse what is right, rather than what is agreeable to the senses, and convenient for the present; and Virtue which hath no recommendation besides her own decency, is an object which will hardly raise their affections. And therefore in the Scriptures, which are calculated for common use, you shall find few exhortations to goodness taken from the bare decency of it, but many from the advantages present and future of piety, and from the dreadful misery which follows vice by the just appointment of God.

4. The general consent of men concerning a future state ought not to be accounted a slight argument in favour of it.

In all ages and places the consciences of men usually bear witness to a future judgment. Their minds are full of disquiet, when they have acted against their known duty, though at the same time they may think themselves safe from punishment in this life.

On the contrary, good actions repay the virtuous with satisfaction; and something within tells them, that though their present condition be in many respects inconvenient, yet all shall be well at the last, and that there are undiscovered blessings reserved for them in a better world.

5. Lastly, upon the supposition of a future judgment, the present state and course of things, the unequal and promiscuous distribution of good and evil,

―――― Phalaris licet imperet ut sis
Falsus, et admoto dictet perjuria tauro,
Summum crede nefas animam præferre pudori,
Et propter vitam vivendi perdere causas.

evil, though it may seem at first sight irregular and unreasonable, is really a wise and a kind administration. Goodness is often not recompensed in this life, and sometimes exposes to many temporal evils. But hereby God hath given to mankind in all ages an intimation and a prospect of another world, hath added strength to those arguments which reason suggests for such expectations, and hath directed us to look forwards, and expect a more glorious scene, where the wisdom and goodness and equity and righteousness of the Creator and Governor of the world shall be fully justified, and cleared from every objection which the present confused and disorderly state can suggest. If goodness had been always immediately and amply rewarded; if length of days had been always in her right hand, and in her left hand riches and honour ; righteous men who lived before the coming of Christ, and the more express revelation of eternal life, might have been inclined to fear, that they had received their reward, especially when they considered their own imperfections and offences. To which we may add, that such an uninterrupted flow of prosperity might have made them too fond of this world, and too unwilling to leave it.

But indeed these large promises of temporal blessings contained in the Old Testament were found liable to so many limitations and exceptions, that wise and good men must have discerned that they were to be understood as frequently but not constantly made good, and must have drawn the obvious inference, that all present failures of this kind would be compensated hereafter.

The best persons often suffer in this world; but if by those transitory sufferings they improve their better part, and for the sake of them shall receive a greater reward, happy are the evil days which produce effects so desirable.

Vice sometimes escapes here with impunity, and is attended with conveniences, and with the pleasures of sense. But in this there is nothing unreasonable; for if sin were always instantly and duly chastised, if it infallibly produced sudden pain of body, and anguish of mind, and want, and scorn, and reproach, and infamy; if these were its sure and unavoidable companions, who would be wicked? or perhaps, rather, how few would be good? For to abstain from evil by mere (*d*) compulsion, and that we may escape instant misery, seems not to deserve the honourable name of virtue.

Though vice is sometimes united to temporal prosperity, and virtue attended with inconveniences, through the perverseness of men, yet these are not, and indeed they ought not to be, the natural and regular effects which they produce; for if every good man certainly knew that he must undergo perpetual disappointments, pains, calamities, and ill usage; and if every wicked man might as certainly conclude, that he should meet with constant success, and gratify all his desires; the temptations to wickedness would be too strong, and the discouragements from piety too violent. And therefore the course of things is so ordered, that righteousness is generally profitable to all things, and wickedness usually hurts both the body and the mind, and brings more uneasiness than pleasure.

These are the ordinary effects of moral good and evil; to which we must add, that there have been instances of wicked men, who seemed to have secured themselves from vengeance, and yet have been punished in so wonderful a manner; and of good men, who beyond all expectation have been so signally delivered and rewarded, that the world hath acknowledged something

---

(*d*) Εἰ τοῖς ἡμαρτηκόσιν εὐθὺς ἠκολούθων αἱ δίκαι, φόβῳ δικαιοπραγοῦντες ἀρετὴν οὐκ ἂν εἶχον. Sallustius philosophus.

something divine in it, and ascribed it to an over-ruling Providence.

These are the arguments by which the doctrine of a future state is confirmed; but these are not all, and to them are to be added two other proofs.

The first is taken from the nature of the soul itself, which, upon the most careful enquiry, and upon the best judgment that we can form, seems to be a substance active, simple, uncompounded, so that no external enemy, no impression of the surrounding elements, none but He who made it, can destroy it.

The second proof, which with Christians ought to weigh more than all the rest, is taken from the express testimony of the Gospel; so that every thing that confirms the truth of our religion assures us at the same time of a future state.

The numerous passages in the New Testament relating to the day of judgment, to the manner in which that judgment shall be executed, to the inquiry which shall be made into our behaviour, and to the subsequent state of happiness or misery, contain without question things which are to be literally understood, and things mixed with them, which are figurative, or spoken in condescension to our capacities. It is not easy to separate accurately the one from the other, nor doth it concern us to distinguish them exactly, since this clear and important truth is contained in them all, that every one shall finally receive according to his works.

The inference from which is as plain as it is important, that we should live as it becomes those who must give an account of their thoughts, words, and deeds.

Therefore; Let us not delude ourselves with foolish hopes, that God will receive us into happiness, though we perform not the conditions which he requires.

Let us not delay our reformation to an uncertain time. If our task remains unfinished, a long night succeeds, and after it comes a day of retribution.

Let

Let us reverence our conscience, and do no violence to it. God hath established it, as a judge within us, a judge in some respects like himself, a judge whom usually we cannot deceive, and from whose presence we cannot fly.

Let us not set our affections on unlawful objects, or too immoderately love any of the things which are earthly and transitory, and for the sake of the one or the other, neglect our duty and our eternal welfare. We must soon go hence, and leave all these follies and vanities; and when we arise again, it will be to behold a quite different scene. Sinners will then see no more that world which they have so much loved, or will see it only for a moment: it will consume away before the presence of the Lord, and nothing will be left that can give any pleasure, or comfort, or relief to a wicked mind.

Let us not value ourselves on account of any temporal advantages, nor despise nor insult those who are placed beneath us. These distinctions are of a very short continuance: a day is coming when they shall cease and be forgotten for ever. Death and judgment set all upon the level. All must lie down undistinguished in the dust, and all must arise and give account of their works to Him who is no respecter of persons, and who regards no other difference than that which ariseth from virtue and from vice.

Let us so live, that we may be able to reap the present benefit which every good person will certainly find from the belief of a future state. Peace and patience, and resignation and contentment must dwell in every mind that hopes and expects everlasting happiness.

'These are great and immediate rewards which faith would secure to us, if our behaviour were suitable to our profession; but because it is not, the thought of a future judgment carries with it more terror than consolation; the soul startles at it, and puts the important question

question to itself, What shall be thy portion in that day?

There is a religious fear, which is the beginning of wisdom, and the parent of virtue. If the thought of a future judgment awaken in us this fear, happy is it for us: diligence in well-doing will accompany it, and peace and hope will follow it in due time.

SERMON XXVII.

Eccles. v. 1.

Keep thy foot when thou goest into the house of God, and be more ready to hear than to give the sacrifice of fools; for they consider not that they do evil.

THIS first verse, and the four following ones, contain instructions concerning our duty and behaviour in the public worship of God, and concerning the religious vows which we make to him. I shall explain them, and then add some remarks upon them.

What Solomon calls, the House of God, is a place appointed for the worship and service of God. To erect and set apart such places for the exercise of religious rites is derived from the dictates of human nature, and approved of God from the remotest antiquity. It began not with the Tabernacle which Moses by divine appointment caused to be made, but was much more ancient. Noah built an altar when he came out of the ark. Abraham, Isaac, and Jacob, wheresoever they pitched their tents, had places for divine worship, that is, altars with their enclosures, though they had no express command from God, that we know of, concerning it. Moses, before the Ark was made, and that Tabernacle which God appointed, erected a tabernacle for the same purpose without the camp, where every one who sought the Lord was to go. And all this seems to have been done

SERMON XXVII.

done as a thing of cuſtom, and as men by tradition had learned to appropriate ſome particular place for the more ſolemn worſhip of God. Concerning places thus ſanctified and ſet apart, God thus ſpeaks to Moſes; In all places where I record my name, I will come and bleſs thee; that is, in every place where the remembrance or memorial of my name ſhall be, and which I have appointed for the performance of religious acts and duties, there will I come to thee and bleſs thee. And accordingly the tabernacle of the Lord is called, The tabernacle of meeting, not only becauſe men met there together to worſhip God, but becauſe God condeſcended to come and meet them. The Old Teſtament abounds with inſtances of God's manifeſting his preſence and his glory in the Tabernacle, and in the Temple; and it is needleſs to cite them.

This conſecration of particular places, and the performance of particular rites, which were not to be ſolemnized elſewhere, was of ſingular uſe in thoſe ruder ages, both as an help to excite reverence and devotion, and as well adapted to preſerve the poſterity of Abraham from Idolatry.

Our Saviour, who brought into the world a brighter light and a ſublimer religion, taught that it mattered not where God was worſhipped, if he were worſhipped in ſpirit and in truth; that of all temples a pure heart was that which he moſt approved, and that where two or three of his diſciples ſhould meet together to ſerve God, there would he ſpiritually be in the midſt of them; doctrines agreeable to reaſon, and ſuitable to the enſuing times, when Chriſtians ſhould be ſo far from enjoying ſplendid temples to repair to, that they often would hardly have a place where to hide their heads. As ſoon indeed as perſecution declined, and a calm ſucceeded, Chriſtians built themſelves Churches, and ever ſince have ſet

apart

apart such edifices for public worship; which is very right, so long as we remember that it is only for conveniency and decency.

(a) When thou goest to the house of God, says Solomon, keep thy foot.

In these words there is an allusion to a custom of taking off the shoes, which was practised by the Jews and by other nations of the East, when they entered their temples and sacred places. Concerning this ancient custom the Lord himself spake to Moses, and afterwards to Joshua: Put off thy shoes from thy feet; for the place where thou standest is holy ground. Therefore the meaning of Solomon's direction is this; Take heed to thyself, that thou act with decency and reverence in the house of God, bearing in mind into whose presence thou comest; and so it relates to the outward and bodily worship which is due to God. For God is the maker of our bodies as well as of our souls, and therefore we ought to serve him with both. As the outward worship without the inward is dead; so the inward without the other is not complete, is not the service of the whole man. Bodily worship indeed, being considered in itself, is one of the lesser things of the Law, and the honour done thereby to God is of no great value and esteem in his sight; and yet a voluntary and scornful and presumptuous neglect even of so small a duty may be no small sin, because such a neglect must proceed from a profane and hardened heart. For a sin is not always to be estimated according to the value of the duty omitted, but from the disposition of mind causing us to neglect it.

When thou art in the house of God, says Solomon, Be more ready to hear than to give the sacrifice of fools; for they consider not that they do evil.

Now,

(a) See a Discourse of Joseph Mede on the text.

Now, to hear, as every one knows, hath two senses, a natural and a figurative sense. To hear, in the natural or literal sense, is to attend to and to perceive what is said: to hear, in the figurative sense, or to hearken, is to obey. If we take the word in the first sense, it may be thus explained; Part of the service of the Temple, as it was instituted by David, Solomon's father, consisted in Psalms and Hymns which were sung by the Levites. When thou comest to the Temple, says Solomon, be attentive to the praises of God which are sung there, and to the prayers which are offered to him, and join in celebrating and invoking thy Creator, which is a better service than offering up sacrifices to him. The second sense, according to which to hear is to obey, amounts nearly to the same effect. The meaning then is; When thou comest to the Temple, bring with thee a religious mind, which is better than bringing sheep and oxen for a sacrifice. Return thanks to God for his mercies, implore his pardon for thy offences, acknowledge thy sins, pray to him for his assistance, and resolve to obey for the future. This is much better than any sacrifice, and infinitely better than the sacrifice of fools.

By the sacrifice offered by persons who persist in a wicked life, or who place too great a trust in sacrifice, as if it would be accepted of God instead of obedience, or who prefer the ceremonial to the moral Law.

Thus the direction given by Solomon agrees with that proverbial saying in Scripture; Obedience is better than sacrifice, and to hearken than the fat of rams.

Though sacrifices were appointed by the Law, yet the Prophets speak of them sometimes in a slighting and disparaging manner, as if God neither ordered nor approved them; which seeming contradiction may be thus removed.

First, according to the style of the Hebrew language, things are forbidden or rejected abfolutely, which are only meant comparatively with fomething elfe. So that when it is faid that God defires not and approves not facrifices, but goodnefs and righteoufnefs, the meaning is that he prefers thefe to facrifice.

Secondly, God feems not to have commanded facrifice as a thing of its own nature right and fit, but only as ufeful or needful by confequence. It was ufually a rite by which men renewed a covenant with God, and it fuppofed fome tranfgreffions. So that if men had never finned, it would perhaps have had no place.

When God accepted it, he approved it only as it was a teftimony of contrtion, an humble acknowledgment of unworthinefs, a defire to honour him with a prefent, and to be received again into favour and alliance with him.

Hence it is that God rejected and abhorred all oblations where there was no purpofe of amendment, no intention to keep his commandments; he would not allow them to be ordinances of his, when thus perverted and abufed.

The houfe of God at Jerufalem was an houfe of facrifice, which they, who came thither to worfhip, offered to God, to make way for their prayers, and to find favour in his fight. Solomon therefore gives them a caution not to place religion only or chiefly in the external rite, but principally in their readinefs to hear and keep the commandments of God, without which that rite alone would profit them nothing, but be no better than the facrifice of fools, who when they do evil, think they do well. For without this readinefs to obey, this purpofe of heart to live according to his will, God accepts of no facrifice from thofe who approach him, nor will pardon their tranfgreffions. He therefore

SERMON XXVII.

therefore who makes no confcience of offending God, and yet thinks to atone for it by gifts and offerings, is an ignorant and a wicked fool, how wife and how religious foever he may think himfelf. The reafon is, becaufe God requires obedience in the firft place, and abfolutely; but facrifice only confequently, and even then not chiefly, and for itfelf, but only as it is a real fign and a true teftimony of contrition.

After this introduction, Solomon proceeds to give fome directions concerning prayer, and fays;

Be not rafh with thy mouth, and let not thine heart be hafty to utter any thing before God; for God is in heaven, and thou upon earth; therefore let thy words be few.

That is; When thou art going to pray to God, recollect thyfelf; confider that thy Creator is great and good and wife above all, and that thou art a poor dependent mortal being, an inhabitant of this lower world; weigh thy expreffions; think before thou fpeakeft, and take heed to ufe few words, and to afk for nothing improper.

Thus faid the Wife man; and a greater than he, even Divine Wifdom itfelf, hath confirmed this advice; for our Lord hath given us the fame direction concerning prayer.

For a dream cometh, fays Solomon, through the multitude of bufinefs, and a fool's voice is known through a multitude of words.

The fenfe may perhaps be this; In our prayers to God, as in our converfation with men, a profufion of words often arifeth from want of judgment, refpect, difcretion, and decency. The prayer of fuch a perfon is like the dream of one who hath been oppreffed with a multitude of bufinefs, all confufion, jumble, and incoherence. Such fenfelefs and impertinent petitions cannot be acceptable to God.

Then Solomon proceeds to give fome prudent cautions concerning vows. When thou voweft a vow unto God, defer not to pay it; for he hath no pleasure in fools; pay that which thou haft vowed. Better is it that thou fhouldft not vow, than that thou fhouldft vow, and not pay. The words are fufficiently plain; and it is no lefs plain, that upon the whole they rather difcourage than recommend the practice of vowing.

The cuftom of making vows to God feems, as to antiquity, to have been almoft as old as mankind; and as to extent, to have been practifed by all nations, and entered into all religions.

Nor is this to be wondered at, fince it hath its foundation in the nature of man, in his defires and fears, which when they are ftrong will ufually get the better of right reafon. For of all practices which ftand not condemned in Revelation, and which by indulgence have been permitted to men, there are hardly any more injudicious than the making of vows, and in behalf of which lefs can be offered; fo that, at leaft under the Chriftian difpenfation and the light of the Gofpel, they ought to have been totally difcarded.

In the Old Teftament we find mention of vows made by Abraham, Jacob, and others, before the giving of the Law; and it feems to have been a thing which men fell into of their own accord, and which God, as he did not command, fo neither did he forbid and difallow.

It is obfervable, that from the beginning, when God revealed himfelf to men, he did it in a manner accommodated to the infirmities of men, and to the greater or leffer degrees of their knowledge. So that the holy Scriptures of the Old Teftament are a perpetual proof of this divine condefcenfion. When he converfed with men, he did it after the manner of men, and he fuffered them to behave themfelves in fome meafure towards him as they did towards each other; he fuffered them to reafon, to interrogate, to complain,

SERMON XXVII.

complain, to expostulate, and to make covenants with him.

As to vows, they seem to have been a kind of compact or bargain which men made with God. When they desired or feared something greatly, they declared that if God would do so or so for them, they in return would give him this or that thing, or perform this or that action in honour to him.

There were some conditions requisite to a vow, to make it in any sense a religious act; these for instance; What was asked of God, must have been what was harmless, innocent, and lawful, what might be fairly desired, and honestly enjoyed; and likewise what a man promised must have been something that he might lawfully give, and that he was not before obliged to perform by any law. Without these conditions, vows would have been childish and frivolous, and in some cases little better than affronts and abominations.

At the best, they seem to have been mixed with imperfect notions of the Deity, as if by promises and offerings he might be induced to grant what else he would with-hold, according to the Pagan notion, that a gift had power with Gods and men, and would prevail when prayers and intreaties were ineffectual.

And yet it is plain that God permitted good men to act thus in days of old, partly in condescension to their apprehensions, to their weaknesses, and to common practice; and partly for the sake of some good effects arising from this intercourse and covenant which men made and entertained with him. It kept up in their minds a firm belief of the presence, the power, and the clemency of God, and of his over-ruling providence, and was a fence against profaneness, irreligion, atheism, and idolatry; so that the benefit arising from it seemed to be a compensation for all that was imperfect and injudicious in such a behaviour.

In

In the Law of Moses, vows are never commanded, but they are often mentioned as actions to which the People had been accustomed of old, and some directions are laid down concerning them; and to prevent some inconveniences which might arise from an indiscreet use of them, a permission is granted to a father and to an husband, to annul vows made by a daughter or by a wife.

In the Book of Judges there is a particular account of Jephtha's rash vow, and of his unwilling performance of it, as it were on purpose to deter men from binding themselves under such imprudent obligations. It is not to be supposed that he offered up his daughter as a sacrifice, but rather that she was doomed to an unmarried state and to perpetual servitude in the Tabernacle of God, which was very disagreeable to her father and to herself, and a cause of great sorrow to both. The same practice was common amongst the (b) Gentiles, of devoting persons to the service of their Deities and Temples.

In the writings of the Prophets there are no exhortations to make vows, but only to fulfil them when they were made, and not to mock God by promising and not performing.

According to (c) Philo, an ancient and celebrated Jewish writer, if a father, a husband, or a king, vowed any thing that might be very grievous and detrimental, or even dangerous and destructive to his children, his wife, his servants, his subjects, they were indispensably obliged to perform it, and to submit to it. This was establishing a complete form of oppression and tyranny both public and domestic, and

treating

(b) See Euripides *Phæniss.* 210.

(c) Ἐὰν ἐπιφημίσῃ τροφὴν γυναικὸς ἀνὴρ ἱερὰν εἶναι, τροφῆς ἀνέχειν. Ἐὰν πατὴρ υἱῷ, ἐὰν ἄρχων τῷ ὑπηκόῳ, ταυτόν. Si vir uxoris suæ alimento Deo sacra esse voluerit, alimentis ei suis abstinendum. Si de filio pater, si princeps de subditis simile quiddam statuerit, fixum idem habendum ac ratum. Vide Eusebium, *Præp. Evang.* viii. p. 338.

treating rational creatures like brutes; as if a man's family stood in the same rank with his ox or his ass.

Even in the Old Testament it should be observed, that some of the (*d*) vows, whereof mention is made, were not strictly and properly vows, but only serious and solemn resolutions of gratitude and of general obedience, that is, of duties which men were obliged to observe, whether they vowed, or vowed not.

It is also a (*e*) saying of some Jewish Doctors, that vows for the most part proceeded from some evil principle; and therefore they advise those who would consult the quiet of their minds to be very cautious in making them.

Our Saviour, as far as it appears from the New Testament, never made a vow himself; nor did he ever give any precept concerning vows. The same is true of the Apostles; and if St. Paul bound himself once by a vow, as he is thought to have done, it was probably in condescension to the Jews, to whom as he says he became a Jew, and with whom he was willing to comply in any thing that was not unlawful, and immoral.

When Christianity was once well established, it might have been expected that these vows, together with all that was Jewish and Ceremonial, would have ceased. But the spirit of bigotry, fanaticism, and superstition soon began to operate, and at last was poured out like a torrent, till the Christian world was over-run with Monks and Monkish devotion. The Church of Rome hath a singular art of separating the chaff from the wheat; and then she gathers the chaff into the Ecclesiastical garner, and throws the wheat away. By a perverse choice she retains what was bad, or weak, and exceptionable, in the preceding ages of Christianity, and rejects very often what ought to have been preserved. She applauds and recommends and enforces
religious

(*d*) S. Clarke, Serm. CLXVI.
(*e*) Stillingfleet, *Miscell. Disc* p. 12.

religious vows and engagements, by which superstitious persons bind themselves to pay a blind obedience to the precepts of men, to practise uncommanded austerities, to live single and solitary lives, and to have no possessions.

Now let it be supposed that the things thus vowed are good and commendable, which is more than can be granted, yet it is wiser to stand fast in the liberty which God hath given us, and to do such actions freely and unconstrained; for then we can do them with a better grace and with a better will; whilst oaths and vows are a snare to us, and an occasion of sin and sorrow, if either we neglect them, or perform them with reluctance. The Religion of Christ, as it is laid down in the New Testament, is such, that we need not aspire to any thing beyond it; and happy is he who can in a tolerable degree conform his practice to it. Let him do that first, before he thinks of superadding will-worship, and excelling his rule.

Father Paul, who was himself of a Religious Order in the Church of Rome, and who was an honour to his Order, hath delivered his opinion fairly and freely upon this subject, without valuing the censures of the Zealots of his own communion. He declares his disapprobation of religious vows, and of a Monastic life. He says that such persons solemnly promise that they will observe a multitude of voluntary, unrequired, unnecessary things, without considering how a change of temper, and how human weakness may operate, and without well weighing what is practicable and possible. Thus uncalled and unforced they throw themselves into temptation, and often contract the guilt of perjury, and commit faults which in another state of life they might have avoided.

These are some of the corruptions which Protestants have observed and censured in the Romish Communion. It is to be wished that Protestant States were themselves altogether free from the same blemishes,

and

and from any defects of a like kind, and in particular, that public oaths and solemn declarations were more sparingly required. What good ariseth from multiplying such impositions, it is not easy to prove; what evil ariseth from them it is easy to discern.

Since religious vows are not common amongst us, the less need be said by way of caution against them; but it becomes us likewise to beware of every thing that bears any affinity to vows in our conduct towards God and towards men. Pious resolution, and prayer to God for his assistance, and a sense of human frailty, and a distrust of ourselves, these are dispositions which best suit a Christian: and to this nothing should be added by way of promise concerning a future behaviour. We know that St. Peter was too forward in making large protestations, and that his heart failed him when he came to the trial. Instead of making new vows, let us take heed to keep that which we formerly made, namely, the baptismal vow. In our transactions also with men, oaths, and covenants, and bonds, and suretyships and solemn engagements, and protestations, and promises, are things to be well weighed, and entered into with serious deliberation. In matters of consequence, a man should think an hour before he speaks, and a week before he promises. Sufficient to the day is the sorrow thereof. Causes of uneasiness will arise in human life as naturally as the sparks fly upward; and there is no occasion to add to them by indiscretion; by laying ourselves under obligations which we cannot accomplish, we shall make ourselves enemies, and lose our friends, our credit, and the peace of our mind. David, describing a righteous person, says of him among other things; He sweareth unto his neighbour, and disappointeth him not, though it were to his own hinderance. Promises are sacred, and religion, honour, reputation require that they be observed; and doubtless he who sweareth to his neighbour, and disappointeth him, is a contemptible and an infamous man.

man. But a perſon who is both righteous and wiſe is one who never ſwears to his neighbour when he can lawfully avoid it, and keeps himſelf free from temptations to perjury. He can ſcarcely break his promiſe, becauſe he ſeldom makes any promiſe, and never unleſs upon conditions which he knows he can fulfil; he chuſeth to be better than his word, and to perform more than was expected from him.

SERMON XXVIII.

ACTS ii. 6.

These were more noble than those in Thessalonica, in that they received the word with all readiness of mind, and searched the Scriptures daily, whether those things were so.

THE Jews of Beroea are here commended by St. Luke for examining and embracing the doctrines propounded to them. St. Paul, who preached the Gospel to them, was hated by the greater part of the Jews, his brethren and theirs, as an apostate, as one who taught false doctrines which he had once violently opposed. He had been persecuted by the Jews of Damascus, of Jerusalem, of Antioch, of Iconium, of Lystra, of Thessalonica. These transactions could hardly be unknown to the Jews of Beroea; and yet they shewed no prejudices against his doctrine upon that account, but were willing to give him a hearing, and received the word with all readiness of mind. On the other hand, though probably they were not ignorant of the success of the Gospel, and of the report concerning the wonderful works wrought by Christ and his Apostles in confirmation of it, yet as St. Paul undertook to reason with them out of the Scriptures, they on their part thought that they had a right to examine his proofs. They searched the Scriptures daily, whether those things were so. This their prudent conduct in receiving the Christian religion with docility and readiness, yet not without due enquiry and consideration, the Writer of the Acts of the Apostles hath recorded to their praise, that wheresoever the Gospel should be preached in the whole world, this also that they had done should be told for a memorial of them, and for an example to others.

St. Peter advises Christians to be ready to give an answer to every man who asketh them a reason of the hope which is in them; by which words seems to be meant, not only that Christians by their exemplary lives should justify themselves from the imputation of evil-doing, but that they should also be ready, and consequently able, to give some account why they were the servants of Christ, and to shew that they had just reason for their behaviour, and for their faith.

In many places of the New Testament, the word faith means the whole duty of a Christian, all that he is to believe, and all that he is to do. Thus it is said that they who believe in Christ shall receive remission of sins, shall be justified, shall not perish, but have everlasting life; where faith or belief in Christ is both a belief and an obedience.

But if we consider faith, in itself, it is a belief of the revelation which God hath made to us by his Son, entertained upon just grounds.

It is a belief that God sent his Son into the world to save and instruct us; it is a belief that the doctrines taught by our Lord are true; it is a belief that we ought to practise what he requires from us, the substance of which is that we must live soberly, righteously, and godly, because there is a time appointed when he will judge mankind, and reward his servants. As the motives to religion arise principally from things future and invisible, faith is therefore said to be the substance, or well-grounded expectation of things not seen.

Faith is not only, first, a belief of these things, but it is secondly, a belief of them entertained upon sufficient evidence.

For

For if we assent without a reason, this cannot properly be called faith. It is rather credulity, or prejudice, or positiveness; and if we believe what is true, it is by chance.

Such an imperfect faith, which, though it have a right object, hath no foundation, will probably be unstedfast, and unfruitful, or productive of nothing that is good.

Such a belief cannot be acceptable to God, who requires to be served, not only by the lips, but by the understanding. He gave us an understanding, and he expects that we should use it. When therefore any thing is proposed to our assent, as coming from him, we dishonour the abilities which he hath conferred upon us, if we believe without an enquiry whether he be the author of such a revelation.

Thus faith is a belief of the revelation which God hath made to us by his Son, entertained upon just grounds, when we know what that revelation requires from us, and when we have sufficient evidence that it is a divine revelation.

But it may be asked: If faith be little better than presumption and confidence and credulity, unless it be established upon the grounds above-mentioned, how shall the common people, the bulk of mankind, who have neither leisure, nor opportunities, nor abilities, inquire into all this?

This is a question of importance, and the proper answer seems to be this:

To whomsoever little is given, from them little is required. They can only examine to the best of their abilities; and serious consideration and upright intentions will certainly suffice. But besides this, be pleased to reflect upon the following observations, observations founded upon reason, truth, and plain matter of fact.

(*a*) Amongst those who stand lowest in rank, in knowledge

(*a*) Le Clerc, *De L'Incredulité*, P. II. ch. 1.

ledge and genius, and who could never apply themselves to close study and to deep reflection, there are many who are blessed with honest dispositions and an upright heart. The things relating to religion which concern such persons are so few, so clear, and so reasonable, that they enter into their mind as easily as light into the eye. They admire and embrace the truths of the Gospel at the first hearing, though they are not able perhaps to dress their thoughts in proper expressions, and to give a clear account of their sentiments. There is a simplicity, a majesty, and a beauty, in the precepts of the Gospel, in Christian morality, which wins their affection, and commands their respect; and as they see nothing in the doctrines which offends their notions, or crosses their innocent views, they receive them with submission, and a full acquiescence of mind. It is certain that the disposition and the conduct of these persons is praiseworthy, and that many great men and subtle reasoners are not near so wise as these are, in the true and religious sense of the word.

Every person, when he searches the Scriptures, that he may learn his duty, ought to separate what is plain and easy from that which is intricate and obscure, and to conclude that these plainer things are his principal concern. No parts of Scripture can, strictly speaking, be objects of our faith, so long as we cannot find out their meaning. Thus much we ought to believe concerning them, That they contain truths which we cannot discover. This is implicit faith, in a good sense of the word, and a very reasonable duty.

Concerning the assurance which every one may have of the truth of his religion, the case stands thus:

When the disciples of Christ preached the Gospel, multitudes of different nations, religions, ages, and professions, attending to this doctrine, and observing that it was pure and reasonable, and supported by many miracles, embraced the Christian religion. The faith of of these first converts was founded upon the excellence of Christianity, and upon the wonderful works by which it was confirmed, and which they had seen.

The evidence which we now have of the truth of the truth of our religion is somewhat altered. It consists partly upon the goodness of its precepts, and the importance of its doctrines; and partly, not indeed upon the evidence of sense, but upon the testimony of numerous and most unexceptionable witnesses who had such evidence.

The Apostles wrought kind and beneficial miracles, taught men to repent, to live good lives, to love and obey God, to love and assist one another, to expect a state of retribution; and they wrote treatises and epistles for the instruction of their brethren.

The first Christians, quitting the strong prejudices of education, and every worldly interest, received this religion so taught and so confirmed, wrought some miracles themselves, received extraordinary gifts of the holy Ghost, suffered cruel persecution for the sake of the Gospel, lived virtuously, delivered down these important truths to their children and successors, not by word of mouth only, but by leaving copies of the New Testament, which, soon translated into various languages, and read in all churches, and studied and reverenced by Christians from age to age, have been transmitted to us.

Thus our evidence for the Christian religion ariseth partly from the testimony of the most credible witnesses, and is founded upon the concurring authority of multitudes, whom we have no reasonable cause of suspecting.

The argument for the truth of the Christian religion, which is taken from its excellence and importance, is not only adapted to every capacity, but is wonderfully persuasive and full of conviction. The more it is examined, and the nearer it is viewed, the greater is its lustre, and the fairer its appearance. The doctrines of of the Gospel will ever be found amiable, useful, and necessary, tending to compose our passions, to improve our minds, to make us obedient to God, good magistrates, good subjects, good friends, good parents, good children, and serviceable to all in our several stations.

The Gospel discovers to us what human unassisted Reason could never have discerned; it promiseth more than we ever could have expected; and it alarms us with those just fears of God's displeasure, which together with pious hopes, are the main springs of action, and incentives to well-doing. A religion thus intrinsically excellent, and thus supported ought to be received with thankfulness, and held fast without wavering. To doubt of it, is folly: to reject it, is madness.

To these grounds of our Christian faith is to be added the completion of a great variety of prophecies contained both in the Old and in the New Testament, of which several are very clear and circumstantial; and the event, which is the great unfolder of predictions, hath sufficiently explained them to us; and when they are considered as a system or chain of prophecies, as all tending to one and the same end, they give strength and light to each other, and the argument built upon them acquires more weight and stability.

There is another proof of the truth of Christianity which hath been urged by several very good and well-meaning men, and it is this; that when pious persons meditate upon the holy Scriptures, an assurance ariseth in them that these Scriptures are the word of God: which assurance proceeds from the influence of the holy Spirit of God upon their minds.

If I treat this people as defective, it shall not be with any harsh censure or contempt thrown either upon it, or upon those who embrace it. But, all things duly considered, the case seems to stand thus:

The ordinary influences of the holy Spirit upon well-disposed persons are supposed and promised in the Scriptures. But whether a Christian can feel and discern

cern them from the workings of his own mind, he himself must determine. The best and wisest men have acknowledged that they felt no such impulses overbearing and over-ruling their natural faculties; and so have concluded, that the divine assistance concurs in such a silent and secret manner with the human abilities and with human reason, and with the operations of the human mind, as not to be distinguishable from them. So then, the proof above-mentioned, which may be called, the inward voice or testimony of the Spirit, unless it be accompanied with visible, external, and miraculous proofs, can convince no by-stander, none except the person who feels it. And how, I pray, shall we know whether that person is not under a delusion? If he who makes such pretensions to the Spirit, either acts dishonestly, or reasons childishly, all wise men will conclude, either that he intends to impose upon others, or that he is imposed upon himself by his own weak head, and warm imagination.

Thus far we have considered faith, as a belief founded upon good grounds. To this we must add, that it is a belief producing good works.

For if, upon an impartial inquiry, and sufficient evidence, we are convinced of the truth of our religion; if we receive the precepts of Christianity, not as a burden, but as a blessing and a favour, and account our duty to be a reasonable service; if we believe what is revealed to us concerning the invaluable rewards annexed to our obedience, and the dreadful misery which shall be the punishment of obstinate wickedness; if we think the approbation of God to be more desireable than all the unlawful or all the lawful pleasures of this world, and a perseverance in well-doing the only way to obtain it; if faith be the confident expectation of good things not seen; if it makes our future recompence appear certain, and as it were placed before our eyes; it seems to be a just inference, that faith and disobedience can never dwell together.

True it is that man is an inconsistent creature, whose heart and understanding are often at variance, who frequently suffers his inclinations to get the better of his reason, who approves one thing, and doth another, and who consequently may have faith, or something very like faith, and yet act contrary to it.

A distinction must therefore be made between faith, as it is a bare assent, and as it is a Christian virtue, acceptable to God. There is a faith, which is only an habitual and historical belief of religion, a faith which dwells in the memory or understanding, but hath no influence on the heart. They in whom this faith is found, disbelieve not the Gospel nor call it in question; they assent to it, as they assent to many other facts and truths upon which they never meditate and reflect. There is a faith which is an active faith, which embraces and receives God's revealed will, the affirmations, the promises, the threats, and the commands contained in it, assenting to the affirmations and doctrines, depending upon the promises, fearing the threatnings with a religious awe, and resolving sincerely to obey the commandments. Thus faith is not separable from good works; the former may have a place in the most vicious and corrupted minds.

I shall add some inferences and remarks.

1. Since faith is founded upon a knowledge of God's revealed will, every person hath a right to examine the Scriptures, and to determine for himself.

This indeed will make every man a judge of his religion, and of the doctrine of his teachers, which is said by many to be a pernicious liberty; producing errors and heresies: and the same may be said of all God's blessings, and of all our powers and abilities, namely, that they may be abused and misapplied; and therefore such objections are not just.

2. Since faith is founded upon a knowledge of God's revealed will, every Christian is obliged, according to his abilities and opportunities, to acquaint himself with

his duty, and to use all the helps which God vouchsafes to him, such as a knowledge of the Scriptures, prayers to God, a careful shunning of evil, and of acting against his own conscience, an attendance upon the public worship of God, a benevolent and charitable disposition, humility, and a due sense of his own offences and unworthiness, repentance, faith, and a sober serious temper. If a man will not act thus, how can he expect the blessing of God, and the divine assistance?

3. Since it is the duty and the privilege of every one thus to inquire and determine for himself, and since in so doing he may fall into great mistakes, the general causes of error should be well considered, and carefully avoided. These we shall find to be prejudice, or pride, or hastiness of determining, or a neglect and unconcern for religion, or all sin is general.

Prejudice is a judgment which the mind passeth upon a subject, before it has received due information, or whilst it is partially inclined to one side of the question. That in all our inquiries we should divest ourselves of prejudice, is commonly acknowledged. But who is intirely free from prejudice? Very few, to be sure. There are many differences of opinion amongst Christians; and in these differences there must be error on one side or other, as when in casting up a sum by different persons, different numbers are produced. But certainly favourable allowances are to be made for the prejudices of good persons, for such prejudices as arise from the prevailing force of education, from a modest distrust of their own understanding, from the example and authority of those of whose abilities and integrity they have a high opinion. Mistakes arising from such causes are often almost irresistible, and so far pardonable. But such prejudices as arise from vice are intirely different and inexcusable.

Pride is certainly another cause of error. It leads to singularity, and singularity seldom leads to truth in points of morality. Pride makes us love the praise of men more than the praise of God, and see things, not as they really are, but as our turbulent passions, our ambitious views, and our worldly interests, represent them. Pride makes men infallible in their own opinion, and therefore liable to more and worse mistakes than humble and diffident persons.

Hastiness of determinining is another cause for which we stray from truth, a cause arising from the small esteem which some entertain of religion. When they condescend to make any inquiries about it, they do it in a careless impatient manner, and are led away by every deceitful argument that lays hold of them in reading or in conversation. They find difficulties in revelation, which they cannot fully clear up, and thence they make a weak conclusion, that it is false. And this probably will terminate in atheism, because natural religion also hath its difficulties and obscurities. It had been well for several persons, if they had shunned the reading of irreligious books, and the conversation of profane companions. By impious doubts and scoffs, dressed up in a plausible manner, and seasoned with vivacity and impudence, many have received an incurable wound, and departed from the right way, and never found it more.

Vice is another cause of error. It would be uncharitable and cruel to suppose that every mistake in religion proceeds from the will, and is a proof of a wicked mind. And yet it is a sad and undoubted truth, that vice is constantly accompanied with error, and that there never was an habitual sinner who had not something wrong in his notions of religion. How in the nature of things should it be otherwise? Vice inflames the passions, and disturbs the understanding, and sinks and debases the mind, and fixes it upon low and mean objects, and takes from it the love of truth and right. It makes men wish that there were no differences between good and evil, no God, no providence, no future punishment of wickedness. And in what can this end, except

cept in false opinions concerning God and morality? That such must be the effects of an irregular life reason assures, and experience testifies, and the word of God plainly and frequently affirms.

From these causes of error we should free ourselves, and inquire into our duty with a love of truth, with a mind humble and desirous of receiving instruction, and cautious not to be deceived by itself or by others, with prayers to God to direct us, and with a sincere resolution to serve him, and to perform all that he requires from us.

If we proceed thus, we may be certain of success; for nothing is more evident, than that a person carefully endeavouring to inform himself of his duty, and using the means which God hath afforded him, and doing nothing that his conscience condemns, shall find out all that is necessary for him to know. To this also the Scriptures agree, containing great and clear promises to those who purify their minds from evil affections, and seriously apply themselves to the study of divine truths: whence this favourable conclusion may be drawn, that if any person be good, he shall be wise so far as it concerns his salvation, and secured from every thing that leads to perdition.

4. Since faith is a well-grounded belief, producing obedience, it follows, that it is a vain notion of faith to suppose it to consist entirely in a confident reliance upon the merits of Christ, and in a persuasion, that God hath fastened his love upon our very persons, without any consideration of our dispositions and qualifications; and that by such a faith as this we are justified.

If this were true, such a faith would most certainly be the greatest of all Christian accomplishments: but St. Paul will not let us say so; for he positively affirms, that charity is greater than faith; and therefore a Christian is more likely to be justified by charity than by faith, faith considered abstractedly from good works.

Justification,

Justification, in few words, and in plain words, means the same thing, as being acquitted and accepted of God, and being in his favour. And how are we justified? We are justified by faith, and not by works, saith St. Paul: we are justified by works, and not by faith, saith St. James. Yet these two Apostles require of us the same thing, namely, a religious belief and trust, accompanied with a sincere though imperfect obedience. St. Paul calls it faith, as it is a belief producing obedience: and St. James calls it works, as it is an obedience proceeding from belief. The works which St. Paul rejects are the works of the Jewish Law, or perhaps any works relied upon as perfect and meritorious in themselves. The faith which St. James rejects, is faith of the Devil, who believes a God, but fears him and hates him, and the faith of any man who holds that a bare assent to the Gospel is sufficient, without morality and common honesty.

5. Faith, in some sense, is a moral virtue, as it is an act of the will. If it were a bare act of the understanding, it would be the less commendable. It can scarcely be accounted a virtue to believe what seems so evident to us, that we cannot reject it. But he who possesseth that faith which the Gospel requires, hath first desired to know the will of God, and resolved to obey it, he hath inquired into it carefully, and as far as his abilities and circumstances would permit. His diligence therefore, and love of truth, and caution, and serious meditation, and good intention, cause his faith not improperly to be accounted a virtue. And this shews the unreasonableness of separating true Christian faith from Christian works, because even faith itself is a good work, and an act of obedience.

Besides, in the Scriptures, faith in God, or believing in God, often means, trusting in God; and indeed trusting in God is usually implied in the word, faith. Now to trust in God's promises is undoubtedly a moral act, or a good work.

Suppose

Suppose a man converted from Paganism to Christianity, and dying soon after. If any one can be said to be saved by faith, and not by works, it must be such a person. And yet in the faith of this man there are necessarily contained good dispositions, good resolutions, and a good behaviour, which is more than barely believing.

6. Lastly, Since without faith it is impossible to please God, and to be happy either here or hereafter, let us join in that honest and earnest prayer, which the Apostles once addressed to Jesus Christ; Lord, increase our faith. Let us beg of God that he would deliver us from cruel doubt and distrust, from evil inclinations and evil actions, and confirm in us a belief and a reliance in Him, the fountain of all good; and in his Son, our only mediator and Saviour; and in his holy and sanctifying Spirit. This faith and this reliance is the only sure refuge and comfort in every station and situation, in the day of prosperity, and in the day of adversity, in the passage through this life, and in the hour of departure from it.

SERMON XXIX.

II Tim. i. 10.

—Who hath brought life and immortality to light through the Gospel.

OF light and darkness there are various degrees, as every one knows; and as one night differeth from another night in darkness, so doth one day differ from another day in brightness. The light may shine upon a place that was quite dark before, and it may shine upon a place that was only gloomy and dusky, and make it conspicuous beyond what it was. The light also which dispels a total darkness may be stronger or fainter.

Light and darkness, in a figurative sense, is knowledge and ignorance; and nothing is more usual than this kind of expression. And of knowledge and ignorance there are as various degrees as of light and darkness.

The reason for which I have premised these remarks is this, that although our Lord is said to have brought life and immortality to light, it must not be inferred from such expressions, that nothing or very little was known, believed, and expected concerning a future state, before he discovered it. This interpretation, though adopted by some, is not to be reconciled with fact, and with the state of the world before the coming of Christ, both amongst the Gentiles, and amongst the Jews. They had a knowledge of it, though an imperfect

fect knowledge, compared with that which he superadded. The proofs of this shall be offered under these two heads.

I. Our Lord hath given us a clearer knowledge than without him we could ever have acquired of our state after death.

II. By his resurrection he hath fully assured us that he can and will raise up his servants to eternal life.

I. Our Lord hath given us a clearer knowledge than without him we could ever have acquired of our state after death.

It is true that reason furnishes us with very probable arguments for the soul's future existence, and that many in all ages have believed it, have hoped for it at least. Nevertheless it is true also that our Lord hath given us a clearer knowledge of our future condition.

For first, the best arguments which human reason suggests for the immortality of the soul, are founded upon right notions of God and of morality. But before the Gospel was revealed, the common people among the Gentiles had low and imperfect notions of those important truths, and consequently they were not persuaded upon good grounds of their future existence.

The proof of the soul's immortality, which are taken from its own nature, from its simplicity, spirituality, and inward activity, are by no means to be despised, they have much probability, and they never were or will be confuted. But they are calculated only for those who are used to deep reflection and abstract reasoning, and they produce not that full assent and acquiescence of mind which one could wish.

The moral arguments, as they are called, in behalf of the soul's immortality, as they are more familiar and intelligible, so are they more satisfactory. Here they are in few words.

There is one God and Father of all, endued with all perfections, with supreme wisdom, goodness, justice, and power. Man is a free, rational, moral agent, made

by

by this great Creator, and accountable to him for his actions.

Now it cannot be supposed that God, who is perfectly wise, would endue the soul of man with a capacity of well-doing, and of perpetual improvement, unless he intended it for other purposes than to live here for a very short space, and then perish for ever. He did not create the sun to shine for one day, and the moon to shine for one night, and then, to be turned out of being. The human soul is more excellent in its own nature than the sun and moon, or any material and visible object in the universe, and could never be made for no other purpose than to begin and to cease almost in an instant, like a flash of lightning in a dark night. As God is perfectly good, it cannot be supposed that he would make man desirous of living for ever, and yet incapable of obtaining his desire. As God is most just, it cannot be supposed that it is all one to him whether his creatures serve him or serve him not, that he will suffer the wicked to sin with impunity, and make no distinction between them and the righteous; for as things go in this world, no such proper distinction is made.

These sort of arguments, obvious and persuasive as they are, yet were usually overlooked in the Pagan world; polytheism, vice, and ignorance, hath made men insensible of their force: these arguments shone forth along with Christianity, and were in a great measure owing to the Gospel.

Secondly, though the belief of a state after this was much received amongst men, yet was it entertained by the vulgar rather as an ancient and long-established opinion, that as a truth founded upon just reasoning. Their ancestors had believed a life to come, and they retained the sentiments that had been delivered down to them by tradition; but they could not trace up this tradition to its rise, nor fix it upon an authority which might be trusted. Their opinions of the next state

were

were confused and unsettled, both as to rewards, and as to punishments. We may therefore suppose, that these fluctuating notions had no great effect upon them, to restrain them from vice, and to incite them to well-doing.

Thirdly, they who argued justly enough to conclude from the nature of God and of man, that it was reasonable to believe the immortality of the soul, and to hope that a future state of happiness should be the reward of a well-spent life, yet could not hence fairly draw any conclusions to their own full satisfaction. For they must have been sensible that they had not lived up to the laws of nature, and to the dictates of their own reason, and that they had offended the Author of their being in many instances. It is true, they might have recourse to repentance and amendment of life, and think it the most proper method which they could take to recommend themselves to God. But how far this would avail, they could not certainly know; and could only conclude, that it would be better for them if they repented, than if they repented not. They could not promise themselves an endless felicity. The best of them, who had committed the fewest faults, could scarcely hope for much more than to be removed after death into some other world, some other state perhaps not much better than this.

Fourthly; Many who believed the immortality of souls, believed also a continual and successive removal of souls from one body to another, and no fixed state of permanent happiness. After death they were to dwell in some other body, and still to continue thus changing their abodes, as they supposed that they had already done in ages past. And as in this life they had no memory of their former condition, so the memory of their present state was to be lost in the next. Thus their remembrance at least, which seems to be no small part of one's self, was to perish by death. Our Lord hath opened to us a better prospect than this, promising us an

incorruptible

incorruptible body, a life that shall not be taken from us, an unchangeable state, and an house eternal in the heavens.

Fifthly; Some who in words acknowledged the immortality of the soul, seem in reality to have taken it away, by imagining that the human soul was a part of the great Soul of the world, of the Deity, and that, upon its separation from the body, it was reunited to it.

Some endeavoured to prove the soul's immortality by arguments, which proved too much, which shewed, if they shewed any thing, that the soul was from all eternity; whence it followed, that the soul upon every change of condition forgot all that was past, and so lost what may be called the most valuable part of itself.

Some supposed indeed, that the soul should outlive the body, and receive a reward of well-doing; but they thought that the soul was material, and subject to dissolution, and that a time must come when it should perish.

Lastly; Many had so far debased their understanding, as to persuade themselves that death was a dissolution of the whole man, and that there was nothing to hope or to fear beyond this life.

These were the notions of several Pagans concerning the future condition of the soul, which seemed not improper to be here mentioned, because we may hence learn to value what the Gospel hath taught us about these things, and thankfully to receive the light which it hath let in upon our minds.

The Jews had not only, in common with the Gentiles, the light of reason to guide them to the discovery of a future state, but probably a tradition delivered from our first parents of a restoration to a lost Paradise; they had several examples, and several passages, in their sacred writings, whence it seems easy to have been collected, that God reserved better things for those who served him, than they received in this troublesome world,

SERMON XXIX.

world, and that the good, when they go hence, live to him. But notwithstanding the knowledge which the Jews had of these things, our Lord may justly be said to be our instructor in them, since he was a Light to lighten the Gentiles, as well as the Jews, and since the Gospel hath given us a more clear, more circumstantial, and more satisfactory account of it, than God had before revealed to his people.

1. The Gospel assures us, that we shall rise again.

I am the first, and the last, says our Lord. I am he that liveth and was dead; and behold I am alive for evermore, and have the keys of death. I am the resurrection and the life. He that believeth in me, hath everlasting life, and I will raise him up at the last day. The hour is coming in which all they that are in their graves shall hear the voice of the Son of God, and shall come forth. The Sea shall give up the dead that are in it; and Death and the Grave shall deliver up the dead that are in them.

St. Paul, in his Epistle to the Corinthians, gives an account of the resurrection full of encouragement and consolation, assuring us that the dead shall rise, and that we who are now clothed and encumbered with bodies, weak, frail, corruptible, subject to diseases and pain, shall in that day be raised with bodies bright, glorious, incorruptible and immortal. And in his Epistle to the Romans he says; He that raised up Jesus from the dead, shall also quicken, shall make alive, shall raise up your mortal bodies. And again: We, who have the first fruits of the spirit, groan within ourselves, expecting the redemption of our body; that is, as he says in other places, that our body may be delivered from the bondage of corruption, that mortality may be swallowed up in life, that this mortal may put on immortality, that Christ may change our vile body into the likeness of his glorious body.

This account of the resurrection is sufficient fully to satisfy us, and to teach us what it concerns us to know,

which

which is, that we, who now live in a frail and mortal body, shall rise, and live in a spiritualized body, liable to none of the inconveniences of this earthly tabernacle. Whether the dying body and the glorified body be or be not made up of the same particles of matter, is a question of no moral use, or importance, so long as the mind is the same, and the person the same, which is all that properly concerns us.

2. We are assured, that the happiness of the good shall be complete, unchangeable, and endless. This the Scripture declares in a copious variety of terms. The writers of the New Testament seem to labour for expressions, and to want words strong enough to represent it; and there being nothing within the compass of our knowledge that can answer to it, they are forced to have recourse to different images and similitudes, to set forth to us as much as they can of it. They call our reward an exceeding and eternal weight of glory, an unfading crown, an incorruptible inheritance. They tell us that the righteous shall shine forth as the sun in the kingdom of their Father, and shall for ever converse with the holy Angels, live with Jesus the mediator of the new covenant, and see God, and rejoice in his presence; and that fear, and ignorance, and doubt, and trouble, and sorrow, and tears, are eternally excluded from those blissful regions.

3. We have also reason, from some places of Scripture, to suppose that the souls of the good are not deprived of thought, but are in a place of peace and contentment, during their separation from the body.

In the Revelation, the souls of the Martyrs under the altar are said to call upon God to judge the earth; and a present recompence is given to them for their sufferings. These things indeed are spoken in a figurative manner, yet they seem to imply thus much, that the spirits of the Faithful after death are in a state of sensibility. St. Stephen, when dying, commends his spirit to Christ, praying him to receive it. Christ promiseth his fellow-sufferer on the cross, that he should on that day be with him in paradise, a place of happiness, no doubt, and understood to be so by all the Jews. St. Paul desires to depart hence, and to be with Christ, which is far better; judging that to die would be gain to him, and an advantageous exchange. The same Apostle says to the Corinthians: We are confident, and willing rather to be absent from the body, and to be present with the Lord; where he seems to speak of the state after death, and before the resurrection. The writer of the Epistle to the Hebrews speaks also of the spirits of just men made perfect: where by the spirits of just men are to be understood their souls separated from their bodies; and these, he says, are made perfect; by which he can hardly be supposed to mean less than this; that they are in a happier condition than they were in here on earth. Lastly, we have also the testimony of the holy Spirit, who declares; Blessed are the dead that die in the Lord: they rest from their labours, and their works follow them.

Blessed then are the dead that die in the Lord. But how are they blessed, if they lie in a silent state of senseless inactivity? if they are dead to themselves, and as it were blotted out of the creation? How can we reconcile such an annihilation with blessedness? To be free from trouble and pain is then only happiness, when we are sensible that we are free from them. The death of the good is indeed called rest and sleep, but that implies not a state of inactivity. It is called rest, because it is to them a rest from the cares and pains and toils of life: it is called sleep, because they cease for a while to converse with men and with this visible world, and because they shall wake again to both in the last day. But their souls are alive and awake, and our Lord hath told us that they live to God; they are in his custody, and secure from all evil, expecting the completion of their happiness at the resurrection of the just.

This

This seems to be a fair and probable inference from the passages of the Scriptures above mentioned; though little be revealed to us concerning the immediate state of the good, and scarcely any thing concerning the intermediate state of the bad. These are points, of which it may be said, to use the words of St. Paul, Now we see darkly, now we know in part.

II. The second thing which we proposed to prove is, that Christ, by his resurrection, hath fully assured us, that he can and will raise up his servants to eternal life.

The time which passed between the death and the resurrection of our Lord was a gloomy interval, a time of triumph to his enemies, of trouble, doubt, fear, and perplexity to his disciples.

Whilst he lay in the grave, his enemies concluded that he who had saved others could not save himself, that God in whom he trusted had forsaken him, and would not deliver him, that his pretensions of being his well-beloved Son were groundless, and that they had delivered themselves from a most troublesome adversary, whose good example had been a reproach to them, who had been always censuring their vices, and confuting their cavils, and exposing their hypocrisy.

He had told his disciples that he would give his life a ransom for many. But there was no proof that God had accepted this ransom. He had told them, Because I live, ye shall live also. But he who was to confer eternal life, lay dead himself, and with him were buried these fair promises.

But on the third day he proved himself to be the expected Messias, of whom it was prophesied that he should be afflicted and glorious, humbled and exalted, that he should give his life an offering for sin, and yet prolong his days and prosper. The resurrection of Christ declaring him to be the son of God with power, gives us just grounds to believe and receive as undoubted truths all the doctrines which he teaches, and all the assurances furances which he hath given us, particularly that he hath reconciled us to God, and that he lives to assist us, and to intercede for us.

If it be certain that Christ arose from the dead, the consequence is plain and unavoidable, that the religion taught by him is true. Thus much the adversaries of Christianity are not backward to grant; and chuse rather to deny the fact than the inference. If Christ be not risen, says St. Paul, our faith and our hopes are vain: if he be risen, it is to us a pledge and an earnest of a resurrection. If you ask the Apostle what proof he had to give of the fact? he says, Christ was seen of more than five hundred brethren, and of me also. If you ask him why their testimony should be admitted? he says, because by me and by other disciples of Christ the signs of an Apostle are wrought in wonders and mighty deeds. Thus the main evidences of Christianity lay in a small compass, and were as clear as the light of the sun: and therefore the Apostles, as well they might, speak severely of those who rejected the Gospel, and represent them as men who withstood the truth, not because it was embarrassed with difficulties, and wanted arguments and proofs, but because they had no heart and no will to do what was right, and to suffer temporal inconvenience, or forego sensual pleasure for the sake of it. Now though we in these ages have not the same kind of evidences, yet what was once plainly true, must always remain true.

I have only a few inferences to lay before you.

1. Our Lord hath taught us that our souls are immortal. As we are Christians, we have learned this from our earliest infancy, and we usually assent to it without hesitation: and yet, by a strange inconsistency, this important truth lies useless in our minds, and is seldom duly considered. Too many speak and act as if man consisted of nothing besides that earth from which what is visible of him was taken. Thus the soul, like a trifling and imprudent guest, neglecting its own con-

cerns, is very busy in caring for the body, for the decaying house in which it dwells for a few days. And yet the Father of every good gift hath liberally adorned the soul with a variety of accomplishments. It is an object worthy of its own serious contemplation, and in this world it can find nothing equal to itself. A being endued with so many excellent powers; a being capable of perpetual improvement; a being of unwearied activity, a fountain of thoughts that never ceases to flow; a being made to imitate its Author, and, if it perseveres in the love and practice of virtue, to enjoy his favour, and continue for ever safe under his protection. Such reflections upon the value of our souls should raise in us a rational esteem of ourselves, should fill us with an honest and laudable sort of pride, should make us ashamed to be wicked, should teach us to think every thing that is vicious to be mean and altogether beneath us, and to account nothing to be great, the contempt of which is great; should incite us to piety, and give us an indifference for the vanities of a world which we know that we must outlive.

2. Our Lord hath taught us that death is only the death or sleep of the body, that the souls of the good live to God, and that at the last day, when he shall appear, they shall be clothed with immortal and glorified bodies, and dwell for ever with him. And to confirm these truths, he arose himself in power and splendor, and became the first fruits of them that sleep.

Thus hath he delivered us from a state of doubts and fears, and hath in a great measure disarmed death of its terrors. The grave is not our last home, where we should sleep for all ages; but we commit our bodies to the earth, as to a fruitful field, faithful to the sower, which will return us back an hundred-fold, by restoring them to us incorruptible and immortal.

3. The resurrection of Christ contains in it the strongest motives to cast off our sins, and to prepare
ourselves

ourselves for the glories which shall be revealed, and to take off our affections from this world, and to set them on things above.

The resurrection of our Lord is a proof that God hath performed all that could be hoped on his part to bring us to him. But then it remains on our part that we rise instantly, as the Scripture expresses it, from the death of sin to the new life of holiness, that we work out our own salvation with diligence, and provide without delay for our future well-being. In vain did Christ die and rise again for us, if we lie buried in trespasses and sins, and put off our conversion to the hour of death, when it is forced and deceitful; to old age, when it is unable to bring forth fruits meet for repentance; to the morrow which we may never see.

Christ, the author of our better hopes, is risen from the dead, and lives to intercede for us, and is gone before us to prepare us a place in his kingdom. But if we would be the better for having such an advocate, and would secure to ourselves an inheritance above, our affections must be there, and we must live, not as children of this world, but as the candidates of heaven. If the things below possess our hearts, and have all our thoughts and wishes, if our time be all consumed in cultivating perishing friendships with earthly objects, we have no friend in heaven, and no mansions there prepared for us. If we do not think eternal life worth the seeking, it will not be obtruded upon us; and it is too valuable to be bought at so low a price as a few wishes for it at the close of our life, accompanied with a shame and a sorrow that we never thought of it before.

Let us turn from these motives of fear, to motives of hope, and love, and gratitude at this season, when the voice of joy and health is in the dwellings of the righteous, and we commemorate the mighty things which the right hand of the Lord hath brought to pass. Let us encourage ourselves to well-doing, by reflecting upon the victories of our Redeemer over the powers of darkness, and upon the promises which he is so able and so willing to perform.

SERMON XXX.

Acts i. 8.

But ye shall receive power, after that the holy Ghost is come upon you.

IF we consider the Apostles of Christ, to whom these words were spoken, in their public and in their private character, we find that they had a double office to perform, as they were Apostles, and as they were Christians. As Apostles, they were appointed to convert, and to instruct and guide those whom they had converted: as Christians, they were obliged to live suitably to the religion which they professed and taught. That they might perform these several duties, they had a promise of assistance from the holy Ghost, who is said in the New Testament to be the dispenser of all the gifts and helps necessary both for the promulgation of the Gospel, and for the sanctification of Believers; concerning which different gifts I shall now discourse; and first I shall consider the miraculous gifts which the holy Spirit conferred upon the Disciples.

I. Our Lord, intending to establish his religion in the world, made choice of means and instruments in appearance most disproportionate and unequal to the accomplishment of that end. He sent men to teach his will, who before he gave them his Spirit were not qualified

to

to execute the great things for which they were designed; that in the establishment of the Gospel the immediate assistance of God, and the power of the holy Ghost, might the more manifestly appear.

Christ at his ascension commanded the Apostles to go and teach all people. This they seemed not capable of performing upon many accounts, particularly because they understood not the language of foreign nations, and had neither leisure, nor opportunity, nor perhaps a genius, to learn them.

The holy Ghost therefore conferred upon them the knowledge of the languages. A great concourse of people from different and remote places was present at this miracle, and each heard the Apostles speaking in their tongues. Thus began the promise of divine assistance to be fulfilled, and a way was opened for the publication of Christianity, which immediately had its effect, and converted three thousand persons.

The gift of tongues was a miracle in which there could be no deceit and illusion. The Apostles were well known: they had always dwelt in Judæa; their manner of life, the circumstances of their education, the meanness of their condition, were notorious. Several things concurred to shew that they could not have acquired this knowledge in an ordinary way. If they had learned languages by the help of men, that would surely have been discovered; if we should say, by their own sagacity and industry, that is too improbable to be supposed; and whether without or with the assistance of others, the labour of some years would scarcely have been sufficient.

This was also a miracle new and singular in its kind, and therefore adapted to affect the Jews in a particular manner. They would probably be most moved by wonderful works of which the fewest instances had been known.

This was a power which neither Moses, nor the Prophets, nor John the Baptist had received, nor had
Christ

Christ himself during his ministry ever exercised it. The blind man who had been so from his birth, to whom Christ gave sight, immediately observed that since the world began, it had not been heard that any man opened the eyes of such an one. He concluded that his kind Benefactor had not only wrought a miracle, but a great miracle, because it was singular.

And moreover, it was not only the speaking new languages, but teaching sacred truths in a new and effectual manner. We hear them speak, say the multitude, the wonderful works of God. This doubled the miracle, and was all that a reasonable person could desire for his satisfaction and conviction.

The gift of tongues was of particular service to Christianity. It increased the number of believers at Jerusalem, and engaged the admiration and favour of the people so much, that the enemies of Christ could not accomplish their designs against the Disciples, and it served to convey the Gospel to distant regions.

For at the time of Pentecost there was a great resort of Jews and Proselytes from various and remote countries. The gift of tongues conferred upon the Disciples served to convince and convert many of these persons, and they were serviceable in carrying Christianity with them to their several abodes. Afterwards the Æthiopian Eunuch, Cornelius the Roman Centurion, Sergius Paulus the Proconsul, Dionysius the Areopagite, and others were converted. By these persons, and by the travels of the Apostles and of their disciples, Christianity was established in the Roman Empire, and in the East; and then the Greek tongue, which was so generally spread, together with human industry in learning other languages, might be sufficient to carry the Gospel as far and as soon as Providence intended; and accordingly the gift of tongues seems to have been of no long continuance in the Church.

The Apostles were to be witnesses of the things which they had heard and seen. It was therefore necessary that

that they should produce sufficient proof of their veracity, and of their divine mission; for it was not to be expected that men should give credit to obscure and unknown persons, and believe what they attested, only because they confidently asserted it. But the holy Ghost bare witness to them, by enabling them to perform various miracles publicly and frequently.

The Apostles were sent to instruct the world in divine truths, and to preach a doctrine amiable to unprejudiced hearers, but opposite in many things to the opinions in which the Jews and Gentiles had been educated. That they might perform this, they had a promise from Christ that they should be endued with a wisdom and with a strength of reason which none of their adversaries should be able to withstand. And indeed without divine assistance they were not qualified for so high an office. They had profited little from the instructions of their Master, they had been slow to understand, and ready to misunderstand what he taught. But the divine Spirit wrought a sudden change in their minds, enabled them to recollect all that Christ at various times had said to them, and taught them to persuade, to convince, and to triumph over all opposition.

The Apostles were to teach all necessary truths. This they were not able to perform; for some of those truths they knew not, or they were not disposed to believe. Christ says to them; I have many things to say to you, but ye cannot bear them now. Howbeit, when he, the Spirit of truth, is come, he will guide you into all truth. The truths which they were at that time unfit to receive, seem to have been these;

That the kingdom of Christ was spiritual, that he came not to conquer the nations, to make the Jews a flourishing people, and to reign here below; but would ascend into heaven, and thence send his Spirit to govern and instruct his Church:

That

SERMON XXX.

That the Meſſias came as much for the ſake of the Gentiles as of the Jews, and that all men ſhould be invited to partake of the bleſſing and benefit of the Goſpel:

That the Jewiſh diſpenſation ſhould not laſt long; that the Law, though divine, was only temporary, and muſt give place to a better covenant.

The employment to which the Apoſtles were called was honourable, but difficult and dangerous. Our Lord promiſed them ſucceſs in planting the Goſpel, but he concealed not from them the labours and the ſufferings to which they ſhould be expoſed. Whilſt their Maſter continued with them, they entertained flattering hopes of temporal happineſs; but he took care to undeceive them, he aſſured them that their labours would not be rewarded here below, that they muſt take up their croſs and follow him, and tread in his ſteps, and paſs through tribulation; and he commanded them not only to bear thoſe evils with patience and reſolution, but to meet them with chearfulneſs and joy.

This he required of perſons who ſhewed a want of courage and conſtancy upon every occaſion, who deſerted him, and fled ſhamefully from him, and were under great fear and conſternation at the firſt appearance of danger.

But the holy Spirit ſupplied theſe defects, and gave them a reſolution and courage which aſtoniſhed their perſecutors, a conſtancy and patience which no repeated ſufferings could ſhake; he taught them to glory in reproaches and afflictions, and to rejoice that they were found worthy to lay down their lives for the ſake of Chriſt.

The Church at firſt wanted ſpiritual guides and governors who ſhould inſtruct and confirm Chriſtians in the faith, who ſhould convert unbelievers, who ſhould have proper qualifications to preſide over a ſociety deſtitute of all ſecular authority, deprived of the

advantages

advantages which attend and secure human governments, discountenanced and oppressed by the civil powers. For these ends the holy Ghost imparted to the Apostles many excellent gifts. He conferred on them the knowledge of all necessary truths, and of some future events; he enabled them to heal the sick, to raise the dead, cast out devils, to work various miracles. It is commonly thought that they had also a power which our Lord himself never exercised, a power of inflicting diseases as corrections upon disobedient and dissolute Christians, to bring them to a better mind. They were also sometimes enlightened so as to discern the hearts of men, and to know who were secret enemies to religion, though they outwardly professed it. These extraordinary powers were variously imparted to the disciples; nor were they confined to them, but were communicated by the hands of the Apostles in different degrees to other Christians of that time.

II. I proceed, secondly, to speak of those gifts which the holy Ghost imparts to all sincere believers, to all good persons in all ages.

If any one should say that there can be no such thing as a divine assistance acting upon the human mind, because men are not sensible of it, or because such influences would destroy human liberty, he would affirm more than he would be able to prove. God, who made us, who is a Spirit, who is ever present to us, in whom we live and move, may doubtless act upon our minds by many ways unknown and undiscoverable. He may by his holy Spirit awaken us to a sense of our duty, may cherish our good dispositions, may comfort us in affliction, may strengthen us in difficulties, may animate us in dangers, without any act of compulsion. We cannot prove the impossibility of this, and therefore we ought not to conclude that there can be no such thing.

SERMON XXX.

It is frequently declared in the New Testament that God dwells in the Good, that Christ dwells in them; that the holy Ghost dwells in them; every Christian is said there to have the Spirit; to receive the holy Ghost, and to be a disciple of Christ, is represented there as one and the same thing; and in a word, frequent mention is made of the assistance of the Spirit.

God hath given us in the Gospel a rule for our actions; he hath promised us, upon our repentance and perseverance, forgiveness of sins and eternal life. These benefits Christ has acquired for us by his sufferings; and the truth of these things is confirmed by the holy Ghost, the author of the miracles and prophecies upon which our religion is founded.

By the assistance of the Spirit must be meant, either no more than these motives and encouragements to piety; or something more must be understood, which must be an influence upon our minds.

That something more is meant by the aids of the Spirit than the bare external motives to obedience, may be shewed, without an examination of particular texts of Scripture, by this argument:

Christians ought to request of God only those things which God hath promised to grant. If God has promised to his servants nothing besides remission of sins and eternal life, a Christian would indeed have cause to return daily thanks to God for the revelation made to him in the Gospel; but he would have no grounds to ask any thing of God relating to his spiritual concerns, except this, that God would accept his repentance and his religious endeavours, and make him happy in the next world.

On the contrary, it is plain from the doctrine of the New Testament, that a Christian hath leave and encouragement to ask that God would give him his holy Spirit, that he would give him religious wisdom, that he would assist him to overcome temptations, and to persevere in his obedience.

Why

Why in particular should a Christian ask of God, as he is directed to ask, that he would give him his holy Spirit, if by that Spirit is meant nothing besides the Gospel? That is given him already and once for all; so that he might with the same reason ask God to give him a body and a soul.

But that we may not fall into enthusiastic notions concerning this divine assistance, these things are to be observed; first, that the influence of the Spirit is only given at such times and on such occasions as require it; secondly, that it is not distinguishable from the operations of our own minds; thirdly, that it leaves us free agents, that it compels not, that it only inclines and aids, and that it may be resisted; lastly, that a life of obedience and righteousness is a proof, and the only proof, that the Spirit dwells in us. The fruit of the Spirit, say the Scriptures, is love, joy, peace, long-suffering, gentleness, goodness, meekness, temperance. The fruit of the Spirit is in all goodness, and righteousness, and truth. In this method of judging there is no difficulty, and there can be no deceit. These are clear proofs by which we may satisfy not only ourselves, but others also, that we enjoy the assistance which God hath promised to his children; whilst a light within, a call from heaven, a secret voice, an extraordinary impulse of the Spirit, and a conversation with him, are often the effects, not of divine favour, but of a weak understanding and a warm head; and sometimes something worse, even mere hypocrisy and unblushing assurance. Imagination, when it gets the better of Reason, is a dangerous guide: it is a good servant, but a bad master.

Good actions, as they are performed with a design of pleasing God, and according to the rules of the Gospel, are religious actions; as they are the result of choice and reason, they are moral virtues; and as the influences of the holy Ghost contribute to produce them, they are, in the language of the Scripture fruits of the Spirit; they are, to speak in the same figure, fruits of that seed

which

which God hath sowed and watered, but which would have withered and died, if it had not fallen into good ground, and been received by well-disposed minds.

The divine assistance, or the influence of the Spirit, or Grace, as it is commonly called, is to be distinguished and divided, as I observed before, into the extraordinary and the ordinary.

The true (*a*) difference between them seems to be this, that the extraordinary and miraculous operation of the Spirit is distinguishable by the person on whom it is conferred from the operation of his own mind, and that the ordinary influence of the Spirit is not thus distinguishable.

The former is communicated by a strong impulse, by visions, by an outward or an inward voice, revealing secret things past, present, or future, and conferring prophetic and miraculous powers.

The latter is an impulse of the moral kind, tending to the improvement of the servants of God. It is an act of the divine Spirit upon the human faculties, the chief and noblest of which is reason; and upon the human reason it must principally act, to strengthen and enlarge it.

It is possible indeed that the Spirit of God may also act upon the inferior faculties of man, that is, upon the imagination, and upon the passions, exciting hope, fear, sorrow, joy, desire, aversion. But then it must be in such a manner as to leave the passions obedient and subservient to the superior principle of reason; else God would counteract his own purpose, which is to preserve us moral and rational agents, to support that faith which was first founded on proper evidence, and a serious

---

(*a*) Dr. Middleton, in his Vindication of the Free Inquiry, (p. 327) derives the distinction between the ordinary and the extraordinary assistance of the Spirit, as Theological Jargon, and words without sense; and adds, that they who use them ought to define the precise meaning of them. In this latter point I agree with him, and follow his advice.

ous conviction of the truth of Religion. The overbearing impulses, emotions, and agitations, by which men are incited to foolish or unlawful actions, must needs proceed from other causes: they are the mere effects of a disordered body and mind; they are the effects of Enthusiasm, which I take to be a false persuasion of the Enthusiast that the Spirit acts upon him in a sensible manner, which he can certainly distinguish from the acts of his own spirit.

That the Spirit of God acts in a secret manner upon the minds of those who are fit to receive it, is a doctrine plainly taught in the (*b*) Scriptures.

But it may be said, Why should men imagine that they have this divine assistance, if they cannot discern it by any thing that passeth in their own minds? We answer that it is one of those doctrines which by the light of nature we could not have known. We might have thought it probable, but could not have proved the certainty of it to ourselves or to others. So it rests upon the authority of revealed Religion. And yet, I know not how it came to pass, but it seems to have been an opinion amongst the Pagans, that the Gods put men upon certain actions, suggested to them certain thoughts, and inclined their minds in a secret manner. We find this frequently in the (*c*) oldest Pagan writer that is extant. Afterwards, when Philosophy was cultivated, some of their wise men were of opinion that there was such a thing as a divine *afflatus,* or interposition, acting upon exalted and purified minds, and assisting them in well-doing.

I have only a few remarks to add relating to this subject.

1. The Apostles, in the exercise of miraculous powers, were not left to themselves, to use them at their own discretion, according to the dictates of mere human

---

(*b*) See Ezechiel xxxvi. 26.
(*c*) Homer.

man reason, or inclination and affection. They did not work miracles in every place through which they passed, or before every assembly to which they preached the Gospel. We may therefore suppose that they gave these proofs of the divine mission at such times only, and upon such occasions, as seemed proper to the holy Spirit by whom they were guided.

2. The holy Ghost imparted these gifts severally, and in various degrees, to the first Christians, according to his own good pleasure. They were designed, not so much for the benefit of those who received them, as for the benefit and conversion of others, and to be a testimony of the truth of the Gospel; and they were not constantly bestowed according to the moral qualifications of Christians. A person in those times by working miracles gave indeed a sufficient proof, that the holy Ghost dwelt in him. One person might do wonderful works in confirmation of the Gospel, and not live according to its rules: another might perform no miracles, and yet be a good man, and full of the holy Ghost; and therefore St. Paul prefers charity and the works of righteousness to all miraculous powers.

3. The gifts which the Apostles received were of two sorts; the first was of the miraculous kind; the second was courage and constancy, and a mind not to be deterred by dangers, or seduced by any worldly advantages from preaching the Gospel, and from observing its precepts.

These gifts differed in this respect, that the first were operations upon them as upon subjects merely passive; they contributed nothing on their part towards them, except sometimes Faith, or a trust and belief that they had such powers and such assistance. But it was not so in the second sort. Their piety, their courage, and their perseverance, were acts of their own choice, in the performance of which they were indeed supported and assisted in an uncommon manner, as they were called to great dangers, and to extraordi-

nary

nary trials; but still they were acts of choice, from which they had a natural power to refrain, and therefore they were virtues which God promised to reward with an exceeding and eternal weight of Glory.

4. Lastly; Since the ordinary assistances of the holy Ghost are promised to the faithful in all ages, we find in this doctrine proper motives to humility and to gratitude; to a sense of our own imperfections, which deprive us of all possibility of pleading any merits of our own; and to a sense of the divine goodness, which will add strength to our weakness, and support us in our Christian warfare. It is our duty therefore to pray to God, that he would give us his Spirit; it is our duty to purify our hearts from evil affections, and vicious habits, that we may be qualified to receive him; it is our duty to be thankful to this divine Guest, who condescends to be our guide, and our comforter; to be careful not to grieve and offend him by wicked actions, lest he should withdraw himself from us; to remember, that he, who is a pure and holy Spirit, cannot dwell in polluted hearts, in temples that are not his own.

SERMON XXXI.

LUKE xiv. 23.

And the Lord said unto the servant; Go into the highways and hedges, and compel them to come in, that my house may be filled.

IN this parable our Lord describes certain events relating to the Gospel, some things which then began to be accomplished, and some which were to be fulfilled after his resurrection; so that this, like many other of his parables, was also a prophecy.

He compares the kingdom of heaven to a king making a marriage feast for his son, and sending to call those who were bidden. By these are meant the Jews in general, to whom Christ came, and the Gospel was first preached. They who were bidden, refused to come, and returned rude answers, or frivolous excuses. Upon this, the Lord being angry, said to his servant; Go out into the streets and lanes of the city, and bring in hither the poor, and the maimed, and the halt, and the blind. By these are meant publicans, harlots, and the lower and meaner sort of the Jewish people; not that all the Jewish converts were such, but because the most considerable persons of that nation were usually the most averse from the Christian religion.

But there being yet room for more guests, the Lord said unto the servant; Go out into the highways and hedges, that is, go to the Gentiles, and compel them to come in; that is, invite them, intreat them, persuade them, press them, be importunate with them.

Upon a day which is set apart to commemorate a double deliverance from Popery and Tyranny, a discourse concerning the unlawfulness and great evil of persecution cannot be unsuitable. It is not a matter of mere curiosity and speculation; it is a practical point, a point of Christian morality. It may give us a due sense of the rational liberty which we enjoy, a resolution to preserve it, and right notions of the principles and practices of a Church, which requires a blind assent to numberless absurdities, and spares neither the body nor the soul of those who will not submit to her despotic government.

There have been Christians, who through much weakness of judgment, or wickedness of heart, have found the doctrine of persecution in the words of the text: Compel them to come in. Compel them, that is, according to their exposition, Compel persons who are in an error, to renounce it, and to join themselves to the true Church; compel them to it by severity and violence. This hath been, and is the doctrine and the constant practice of the church of Rome, the unreasonableness of which I propose to shew; observing first, that the arguments against it are so numerous, that the difficulty is, not to find out any, but to make a proper choice out of them, and that many Protestant writers have so effectually confuted the frivolous pretences of the Compellers, that they have in a manner exhausted the subject, and have left little for the diligence or sagacity of those who come after them.

Compel them to come in.

There are three ways of compelling men to come in, that is, of bringing persons over to our communion, and to our opinion, in matters of religion.

SERMON XXXI.

The firſt is, by ill uſage and perſecution, the unlawfulneſs of which I propoſe to ſhew.

The ſecond is, by perſuaſion, inſtruction, and conviction.

This is allowed on all hands to be a fair and honeſt procedure: this is a laudable and rational kind of compulſion and violence: this is the compulſion which is indirectly recommended in the text. Thus the Apoſtles preached the Goſpel, and thus they converted multitudes.

The third way is of an ambiguous kind, which it ſeems difficult to appraiſe; for it is neither ſo good, as to deſerve to be cried up for a virtue, nor yet ſo bad, as to be condemned for a vice. It is, overcoming men by kindneſs and courteſies, alluring and proſelyting them by favours, honours, profits, gifts and rewards.

Strictly ſpeaking, this is not the way to enlighten the mind, and to aſſiſt its inquiries after truth; but rather to ſeize a man on his weak ſide, and to give him a byas and a prejudice. And yet it cannot be altogether and abſolutely condemned. Something of this kind is unavoidable. Religious people will always be diſpoſed to favour thoſe who will come over to their principles; and if Chriſtian nations had never uſed worſe methods than theſe for converting unbelievers, hereticks, and ſchiſmaticks, they would have had both more ſucceſs in the undertaking, and leſs blame from all honeſt and equitable judges.

Now let us conſider the vile nature and the pernicious effects of perſecution.

1. Firſt; It is not a probable way to make men good.

If we would ſerve God in an acceptable manner, it is requiſite that we know the will of God, and that we pay him a cheerful obedience. When the firſt of theſe is wanting, there can be no religion; and when any act of religion is performed with reluctance and averſion, it is the ſervice of a beaſt, rather than of a man;

it

it is only a bodily action, in which the mind hath no share. This is acknowledged, I think, by all sects of Christians, and it evidently shews, that compulsion can have no good influence. For what is the pretended design and end of persecution? It is to instruct and to reform, to reclaim from error, and to give knowledge. But bonds and imprisonment, fines and stripes, racks and gibbets, will not inspire the art of reasoning justly, they will not cause a doctrine or system to seem more probable or more amiable to the suffering person than it appeared before he was punished. Ill usage may break his heart, but it will not open his heart, that he may understand the Scriptures.

2. Persecution will probably make men more wicked than they were, whilst they lived in error unmolested.

To prove this, I shall only take for granted, that men usually love the conveniences and fear the evils of life so much, that they will conform outwardly to a religion which in their hearts they detest, rather than endure infamy and contempt, hunger and rags, cold and nakedness; the consequence of which is, that such persons, when they are made external proselytes, have not freed themselves from any one false opinion to which they were slaves before, and have contracted the additional guilt of acting contrary to the dictates of their conscience. Conscience is a guide which every man is obliged to follow. Conscience is out of the reach of violence; oppression will not subdue it; the noise of whips and chains will not silence it. A man must be convinced before he can be converted; and till such conviction be wrought in his mind, it is better for him that he should act suitably to his own false notions, than that he should pay an unwilling and insincere obedience even to the precepts of God.

It follows not hence, that evil becomes good or innocent, because our conscience commands us to do it; for as we are obliged to act according to our judgment, so are we obliged to judge rightly, when we enjoy the means of getting information. When we use not those means, we offend God by our wilful carelessness and presumptuous ignorance, and are answerable to him for the errors and faults which we might have avoided.

3. Persecution is contrary to the spirit of Christianity. The religion of our Saviour is a religion like its author, full of humanity, lenity, and universal benevolence. Though he preached the Gospel in vain to many persons, whose unbelief proceded from a corrupted heart, as himself declared, who knew what was in man, yet he neither called down fire from heaven to consume them, nor sent Legions of Angels to dragoon them. To their obstinacy and malice he only opposed acts of kindness, and miracles, and arguments, and exhortations, and reproofs. He sent forth his Apostles into the world, not to persecute, but to be persecuted, and to establish the worship of God by such methods as himself had employed. It is not to be imagined, that, out of the mouth which said, Hereby shall all men know that ye are my disciples, if ye love one another, could proceed an order to exercise all sorts of cruelty upon men for their errors in religion.

4. The consequence of supposing persecution to be recommended by the Gospel, is that all sects of Christians would have the same call to plague and destroy those who differ from them. To say, that they alone who are the true church would have this privilege, is a childish evasion. All sects of Christians are the true Church, in their own opinion, and would apply such a commission to themselves, as their right, or their duty. And thus indeed they have acted. The Church of Rome hath signalized herself above all others in persecuting. It were to be wished, that the disgrace and guilt of such unchristian doctrine and practice had belonged to that Church alone; but it hath at certain times infected other Christian societies; and to the shame of the human understanding, there have been
persons,

persons, who though they had suffered persecution themselves, would yet needs persecute others, and were not taught better things by woeful experience, which usually softens the most inhuman, and instructs the most stupid.

It is easy to imagine what would be the consequence of a general persuasion amongst Christians, that men ought to be destroyed, if they refused to forsake their errors, what mutual hatred, cruelty, uncharitableness, malice and revenge would every where abound. Indeed such a deplorable and scandalous state of things could not last long, because the absolute necessity of mutual forbearance would appear with an irresistible evidence.

5. It is very strange that Christians in these latter ages can find the doctrine of persecution so plainly laid down in the New Testament, when the first Christians could see no such thing there. This argument ought to be of some weight with the Compellers, who commonly pretend to pay a great veneration to Christian Antiquity. To their sorrow and shame, they may observe, they may observe, that the earlier Christian writers are professed enemies to persecution, make very ingenious and severe remarks upon the inhuman behaviour of the Pagans, and reason most justly upon the liberty which every man ought to enjoy of following the dictates of his conscience in matters of religion, whilst in all things lawful he obeys the Civil Magistrate, and is a good and useful subject.

I deny not that the patrons of compulsion have in some sense antiquity on their side; they are able to prove that the doctrine of persecution is not very modern; and may object to us the examples of Christian Emperors of former ages; and they might as well add to them kings of France and Spain of the two last centuries; for it is not the idle parade of great names, either in Church or state, that can change oppression into virtue.

6. Lastly,

SERMON XXXI.

6. Lastly, since persecution is not a probable way to make men good, since it will probably make them worse than they would else have been, since it is so opposite to the spirit of the Gospel, and so terrible in its consequences, that if it were universally practised it must end in the subversion of Christianity; it evidently follows, that if it be commanded or permitted in the Scriptures, the order or permission should be contained in terms strong, plain, express, positive, very easy to be understood, like the precepts which require piety, charity, and justice. But that is not the case: the patrons of wholesome severity use the Scriptures, as they use those whom they undertake to convert; they give them the torture, and *compel* them, against the genius of language, and all rational exposition, to come into their sentiments. The words of the text are, Compel them to come in. Is it clear that these words mean, Use violence and punishments? All who have any sense or sincerity must confess that it is not, when they have seen the reasons which are given against it. It hath been fully proved that in many places of Scripture the expressions of compelling and of being compelled have a view to that compliance, which, to speak in the same Metaphor, is extorted by intreaties, by earnest importunity, by arguments, by promises, by other moral motives, and that in all languages men are said to be forced, necessitated, obliged, compelled, to do things, in a figurative sense. So, to give a single instance out of many, in this parable one of those who were invited, excuses himself, and says; I have bought a piece of ground, and I must needs go and see it. The word in the original is the same with that in the text; I am compelled to go and see it (*a*).

The scope therefore and turn of the parable lead us thus to explain the word, *compel*. It was an act of kindness,

---

(*a*) Βιαζεσθαι a stronger word than αναγκαζεσθαι is, thus twice used by Josephus, at the beginning of his Antiquities

kindness, not of rigour, in the Lord to send out his servants to those who could not expect so great a favour. He sends them to bid these strangers to the marriage-feast, as St. Matthew hath it; to compel them, as St. Luke more emphatically expresses it. We do not read that he sent them out armed, to use violence in case of refusal, nor is that the way of bringing people to an entertainment. Had such preposterous methods been used, they who were thus bidden might justly have said, Are ye come out, as against thieves, with swords and staves to take us?

This is not indeed the only passage in the New Testament, upon which Persecutors insist. They defend themselves by the examples of our Lord driving the buyers and sellers out of the temple, and throwing St. Paul to the earth, and of St. Peter putting to death, as they call it, Ananias and his wife. These are their proofs of the expedience of persecution, which in reality are proofs of nothing, except of the ignorance or disingenuity of those who use them.

But let us not altogether pass over their more plausible arguments.

1. They tell us, that it is good to punish men who are in error, to make them bethink themselves, to put them upon an examination of facts and reasons, which else they would not have considered.

To this it is answered, that on the contrary this is not a proper way to make men examine; for he who examines any point, particularly any point of religion, ought to be free from passion and prejudice. That punishment tends to byass the judgment, is too clear to admit a dispute.

We may also observe that in every religious sect, erring or not erring in points of faith, these three sorts of men are to be found; first, persons who look upon all religion with much indifference, and are outwardly of that to which chance or custom hath joined them; secondly, persons who are sincere in their profession,

fession, but have too great an affection for the things of this life; and thirdly, persons who are resolved to serve God according to the dictates of their conscience, and to suffer all things rather than act contrary to it. Surely it will be allowed by the most prejudiced, that these last are the best, the worthiest of the three sorts. Now these will be the chief sufferers, and the punishments inflicted upon them will not have the intended effect.

The first sort will probably comply without hesitation, and be joined in external communion with the persecuting Church; for all Churches are alike to them. The second sort, intimidated by punishments, will pretend to be converted, and still retain their errors. The last will perish, rather than basely dissemble, and will be Confessors and Martyrs, in their own opinion at least. Thus the Persecutors will furnish their Church with atheists and hypocrites, and destroy well-meaning although mistaken men. This is the honour, and these the advantages, which are to be gained by such proceedings.

But let us suppose that persecution may at last produce some good effect, that a sect may by that method be destroyed, and the division cease for the future; yet persecution is not the more lawful. We are not to do evil that good may come of it. Public calamities, pestilence, famine, and war, have sometimes made nations more religious than they were: it is not therefore fit that a prince should invade and ruin a wicked nation, that the inhabitants may learn righteousness.

2. Persecutors frequently object, that by permitting liberty of conscience, encouragement is given to scurrility and profaneness.

In this objection are industriously confounded liberty, and licentiousness; erroneous opinions, and wicked practices; mistakes which affect not civil society, and doctrines which tend to its ruin. No discreet defender fenders of liberty ever defired that encouragement or impunity fhould be allowed to impudence and vice.

3. Perfecutors object alfo, that by fuch indulgence herefies are propagated to the eternal deftruction of thofe who are deluded, and that therefore the utmoft rigour is true Chriftian charity, and, by the punifhment of a few, faves many from everlafting mifery.

One of the moft odious and pernicious doctrines of the Chuch of Rome is, that all who feparate themfelves from her are in a ftate of damnation. A man may believe a great quantity of nonfenfe, or may fancy that he believes it; he may worfhip a piece of wood, or a piece of bread; he may think that the fame body can be prefent in ten thoufand places at once; and yet he may have humanity and pity for his fellow-creatures, and love his neighbour as himfelf: but this uncharitable notion hath a plain tendency to corrupt the temper, and to make a man more favage than a brute to all who diffent from him. Hence arifeth hatred of thofe, who are fuppofed to be hated of God; hence thofe tribunals of iniquity called Inquifitions; hence plots and affaffinations; hence violating all faith, and making a jeft of all oaths, and treaties, and folemn promifes; hence equivocations and mental refervations; hence the forcing away children from parents, and wives from hufbands, and any oppreffion which tends to the bleffed end of extirpating herefy. This end fanctifies all villainies; all is done out of mere compaffion for the Souls of men, and piety towards God; a diabolical compaffion, and a piety worfe than profanenefs.

The Papifts who dwell amongft us, will, if I am not miftaken, ufually difown the doctrine of perfecution, when it is objected againft them: but in all places where the Church of Rome is the Church eftablifhed, it is openly avowed; and if any perfons be amongft them, who think otherways, as probably there

there are such, and especially of the Laity, it is not safe for them to say so, in a land of Inquisition.

The doctrine that all who are not of the Church of Rome are damned, must needs have horrible effects, when it is entertained by morose and insolent men, since it can spoil even a courteous and affable temper; as it appeared from the barbarous usage which the Protestants in France received from their own countrymen.

It hath been (*b*) observed of us, that seriousness and zeal for religion is almost the natural temper of the English, to which may be added a bent towards melancholy and fanaticism. This seriousness is easily turned into oppressive severity, when it is joined to bigotry and superstition; so that, if Popery were the prevailing religion amongst us, we may conclude that there would be no toleration for any thing else.

But liberty of conscience produceth many evils. True it is that liberty ever is and ever will be abused, and that where men are free to think for themselves, and to declare their opinions, seducers will be busy in making converts, and weak and unstable men will be led away. But this is an evil for which there is no remedy, except the utmost degree of severity; and this is a remedy worse than the evil. It is acknowledged to be so by several persons, who approve lower and less cruel severities. They should consider that moderate punishments have been found by long experience ineffectual towards reformation of errors, and that divisions cannot be intirely cured or prevented for the future, unless by destroying all the weaker party.

They should also consider, that there is nothing good and desireable which is not often the innocent cause and occasion of evil, and that many inconveniences must be borne, because the redressing of them is a greater evil.

There are for example in all nations many gluttons, drunkards, liars, slanderers, adulterers, dissolute and debauched

(*b*) Tillotson.

bauched persons, who are at least as bad members of society as those who err in matters of faith. Persecutors seldom desire that such should be destroyed; nor are they to be blamed for not desiring it. But then they should not have two weights and two measures: they should bear as much with mistaken men, as they bear with men vicious and usually self-condemned.

4. Another argument, of which persecutors make great use, is taken from the Laws which God gave to the Jews, by which idolaters and false prophets were to be put to death; and from the practice of those kings of Israel and Judah who put these laws in execution.

Of several answers which might be made to this, I shall only mention one at present, namely, that the laws of the Jews, as such, are no laws to us. To shew that any of the Jewish laws are to be observed by us, one of these two things must be proved; either, first, that it is a law of nature, as, Thou shalt not steal, Thou shalt not bear false witness; or secondly, that our Lord hath enjoined the observation of it. Before we can plead a command or a permission from God for persecution, we must find this doctrine either contained in the New Testament, or taught by reason. But when we consult the one or the other, we meet with nothing in favour of it.

God indeed may order that the breach of any of his laws be punished with death. He who gave life, may take it away himself, or appoint another to do it. He may command any nation to punish with death uncircumcision, or the profanation of the sabbath, or the worship of false Gods. He may command one nation to destroy another; but none of these things can be done without his appointment. Divine Wisdom alone can authorize them, and not *Public Wisdom*, as some mightily love to call it, which is too often *Public Folly*.

Great

SERMON XXXI.

Great reason have we to be thankful that we are not educated in such stupid and inhuman principles, nor under the dominion of a Church, which hath turned religion into absurdity and contradiction, and forces it upon every one over whom she can exercise her tyranny, which instead of administering wholesome food and spiritual correction, feeds with stones, and chastises with scorpions.

We enjoy as much liberty of judgment as any people in the world, and much more than many amongst us have deserved; for so it is, that he who takes care to avoid those grosser crimes which are punished by the laws of this and of all other civilized nations, may openly deride all religion, may expose his opinions and himself to the public, and be as profane and as rude as he can desire. Instead therefore of adding any thing more concerning the evil of persecution, I chuse to conclude this discourse with a few observations upon the contrary extremes, and the care with which we ought to shun them.

The spirit of persecution, when it is not owing to political maxims and self-interested views, to cruelty, oppressive pride, and the love of arbitrary power; when there is any thing of conscience and sincerity mixed with it, ariseth from a blind and impetuous zeal, but yet a zeal for religion: the contrary fault to this is a coldness, indifference, and carelessness for truth and virtue.

The spirit of persecution supposes that all errors arise from stubbornness and depravity of heart, and shall be punished with damnation: the contrary excess esteems faith to be of no importance, and morality the whole duty of man.

The spirit of persecution is a spirit of malice, hatred, and detraction, let loose upon all who differ in opinion; the contrary extreme consists in conversing much and cultivating friendships with persons of debauched principles and practices, for the sake of profit or pleasure.

The

The spirit of persecution is an inveterate enemy to examining matters of faith, and to reformation of the grossest abuses: opposite to this is the spirit of contradiction, and the love of novelty and singularity, with which whosoever is smitten, is ever framing new systems of religion and morality, and not able to conceal any of his awkward inventions.

Happy and wise is he who can keep at a proper distance from both extremes. He esteems the Gospel to be the greatest blessing which God hath conferred upon us; he carefully endeavours to understand and to practise it, and to recommend it to others. Acts of civility and humanity he exerciseth towards all; but avoids the society of those, who in their conversation and behaviour shew a disregard to God, to truth, to probity, and to religion. His faith depends not upon human authority, fashion, and custom; he reasons and judges and determines for himself, but never forgets the respect due to civil society, or hates those who differ from him.

This seems to be the middle way between superstition and licentiousness, the way to live in peace and reputation, to do no harm and to do good to mankind.

Of all moral qualities the most valuable is piety; the next to it is prudence; and they must be joined together; for piety without prudence becomes enthusiasm and bigotry, and prudence without piety sinks into knavish craft.

SERMON XXXII.

MATTH. xii. 39.

An evil and adulterous generation seeketh after a Sign, and there shall no Sign be given to it, but the Sign of the prophet Jonas.

UPON the perverse and unreasonable request of the Pharisees to Christ, that he would shew them a sign from heaven, our Lord replied that they should indeed have one remarkable sign given to them, a sign sufficient to convince them of his divine mission, though not one of their own chusing, even the sign of the prophet Jonas. The meaning of which is, that as the prophetic office of Jonas was confirmed to the Ninivites by his miraculous deliverance on the third day from the belly of the fish; so the divine authority of Christ should be confirmed to the Jews by his resurrection on the third day.

To this it may be objected, that Christ was not such a sign to the Jews, as Jonas was to the Ninivites, because Jonas appeared publicly, and prophesied in their streets; but Christ shewed himself only to a few, to his own disciples.

This objection I propose to consider, and to remove, by shewing that Christ gave as much, and indeed far more evidence to the Jews of his resurrection, than Jonas could possibly give to the Ninivites of his wonderful deliverance.

After

After this I shall consider some of the reasons for which Christ shewed not himself openly to all the people.

But first it will be proper to give some account of the history of Jonas, to which our Lord alludes, and which will add light and strength to our following arguments.

The prophet Jonas was commanded by the Spirit of the Lord to go to Niniveh, and to prophesy against it for its great wickedness, and to threaten it with utter destruction.

Niniveh was the capital of Assyria, a great city, remote from the sea, lying on the east of Judæa, and about six hundred miles from it, which was a land-journey.

The country of Israel and Judah lay extended not far from the coast of the Mediterranean Sea.

Jonas rose up, to flee from the presense of the Lord. Why he was unwilling to go, is not clearly mentioned in the very short book which bears his name. But many probable reasons for it appear.

Jonas knew indeed for a certainty that the Spirit of God was upon him, and that he had a prophetic errand; but God had not promised him any extraordinary and miraculous power by which he might prove his mission to others, nor given him any express assurance of his protection. Therefore he was unwilling to go, stranger as he was, to a city great, powerful, rich, insolent, and wicked. He (*a*) feared that the inhabitants would treat him as a disturber of the public peace; at the best, as an enthusiast and a man disordered in his senses; and would perhaps throw him into prison. He had before him the examples of prophets, who had been persecuted, imprisoned, slain by wicked Princes of Israel; and he had no reason to hope for better usage at Niniveh.

He

(*a*) Δείσας ἐκ ἀπῆλθεν, says Josephus.

SERMON XXXII.

He was apprehensive also that possibly, after all, his prophecy would not be accomplished, that God would perhaps spare the city, and that he then should be punished as a false prophet, or at least, that he should be exposed to scorn, infamy, and disgrace. Jonas intimates that he had been moved by some fears of this kind when he afterwards expostulates with God, and says, I pray thee, O Lord, was not this my saying, when I was yet in my country? Therefore I fled before unto Tarshish: for I knew that thou art a gracious God, and merciful, slow to anger, and of great kindness, and repentest thee of the evil.

God was pleased to put his faith thus to the trial; and his faith was weak. Swayed by these, or some motives like these, he fled from the face of the Lord. It may seem strange to us that a Prophet should imagine that he could conceal himself from omniscience, or go beyond the reach of omnipotence. But probably he supposed and hoped that the prophetic impulse would not exert itself out of the land of Israel, and that if he could but fly from thence, he should be at rest.

The Prophets had their weaknesses and faults, like other men; and wanted sometimes to be excused from performing the dangerous and painful office to which they were appointed. Jeremiah was in that condition, and (*b*) complained heavily; O Lord, thou art stronger than I.—I am in derision daily. Then said I, I will not make mention of God, nor speak any more in his name. But his word was in my heart as a burning fire, shut up in my bones, and I was weary with forbearing, and I could not stay.

Jonas therefore, to be released from his prophetic commission, went down to Joppa, a celebrated sea-port in the neighbourhood of Judæa, and entered into a ship which was going to trade at (*c*) Tarshish, or Spain.

(*b*) Chap. xx. 9.
(*c*) Probably, *Hispania Bætica*.

His orders were to take a long journey by land to the east; and he on the contrary took a long voyage by sea to the west.

A violent tempest arose; and Jonas, who knew that it was a divine judgment upon him, was flung into the sea at his own request, and swallowed up by a great fish, which cast him on the third day upon the shore alive and unhurt. What shore it was the Scripture says not: perhaps it was at Joppa, where he took ship.

To inquire what kind of fish it was, and in what manner Jonas could be preserved, seems to be a vain attempt. Who can account in a natural way for an event contrary to the ordinary course of nature? A miracle it was in all respects, but not beyond the power of God, who by himself, or by the ministry of an Angel, could both make the sea-monster fit to contain the man, and preserve the man, also in a situation, wherein without the divine interposition he must soon have perished.

Now Jonas had received a just correction for his disobedience, and a signal instance of God's mercy, and deferred no longer to perform his office. He had likewise, what he before wanted, proper credentials of his mission; for doubtless the fame of his punishment and of his deliverance flew before him, and reached Nineveh, ere he could arrive at it.

This is not a (*d*) loose conjecture, but the most probable reason that can be assigned for the dutiful and humble behaviour of the people of that city; for as soon as he delivered his dreadful message, that in a certain number (*e*) of days Nineveh should be destroyed, all the inhabitants

---

(*d*) Irenæus iii. 22. says that Jonas converted the Ninivites, *conterritos ab eo signo, quod factum erat circa Jonam.*

(*e*) The Hebrew, Aquila, Symmachus, and Theodotion have: *Yet forty days, and Nineveh shall be overthrown;* the Septuagint, τρεις ημεραι, *three days;* Josephus, μετ' ολιγον πανυ χρονον, *after a very short time;* Justin Martyr, *forty-three days,* Dial p. 366, 367. where see Thirlby.

Whether

inhabitants covered themselves with sackcloth, and fasted and prayed, and cried to God, hoping that he would forgive them, as he had forgiven his prophet Jonas; and God had pity on them, and destroyed them not.

At this Jonas was highly displeased. His grief and his anger on this occasion were most unreasonable; for his reputation was sufficiently secured by the things which had befallen him; every one accounted him a man sent from God, and he was safe from insult and ill-usage. So that he ought to have rejoiced at the repentance and deliverance of so many thousands. If the Ninivites had thought that the sentence of God was irreversible, they would have given themselves up to despair; and if they hoped that amendment and supplications might prevail, they could not hate the prophet, or slight him, or use him ill, because the event had shewed his threats to be conditional. Therefore God gave him a rebuke for his froward behaviour, but a rebuke far more gentle than his peevish and passionate humour deserved.

From the history of Jonas it appears that the threatning denounced against Niniveh was conditional, that there was a tacit exception in case of repentance, that the Ninivites did repent and humble themselves, and that therefore the sentence was reversed, or rather suspended: for the Ninivites, as we may justly suppose, when the alarm was over, and the danger past in all appearance, did in process of time relapse into their old iniquities, and then followed the divine judgments; for we learn from sacred and profane history that the Medes and Babylonians

---

Whether Niniveh was destroyed after as many *years* as *days* denounced by Jonas, we cannot say. We have not chronological evidence sufficient to direct us: but that a day often stands for a year in prophetic language, is certain. See Ezech. iv. 4. Vitringa in Isai. ii. p. 216. Jos. Mede p. 598. 720. More, p. 119.

Grotius on *Revel.* ii. 10. says that a day is never put for a year in the Prophets. He is much mistaken.

Babylonians utterly deftroyed that great and ancient city, and fo verified the prophecies of Jonas, Nahum, and Zephaniah againft it.

I now proceed to fhew that Chrift gave as much, and indeed more evidence to the Jews of his refurrection, than Jonas could poffibly give to the Ninivites of his wonderful deliverance.

Jonas indeed fhewed himfelf openly to the Ninivites, and prophefied in their city, but he wrought no miracles there; and if we confider what hath been faid concerning the fituation of Niniveh, and its diftance from the fea, we fhall find no reafon to fuppofe that any of the Ninivites were eye-witneffes of that which had befallen him; they heard the report of it perhaps from fome who had feen part of it, perhaps from fome who had converfed with thofe who faw it, and upon this evidence they believed.

Let us now compare with this the proofs which Chrift gave to the Jews of his refurrection.

Nothing can be conceived more public and undeniably evident than his crucifixion, death, and burial. On the third day, in which he had declared that he would rife again, his Sepulchre was found empty, and the body was gone. Not long after, his difciples came forth in public, and declared that Chrift was rifen from the dead, that he had converfed with them forty days, and that in their fight he afcended into heaven. This St. Peter teftified to the Jews, in his firft difcourfe to them, and the truth of this he confirmed to them by the beft of arguments. To convince you, fays he, that Chrift is afcended into heaven, he hath fhed forth this which ye now fee and hear; he hath enabled us to fpeak languages which we never had an opportunity of learning, and to difcourfe upon religious fubjects in a manner furpaffing our education and our abilities. This was proof enough; but to this he adds another equally ftrong and perfuafive: If you, fays he, will acknowledge
along

SERMON XXXII.

along with us this Jesus for your Lord and Master, you also shall immediately receive some of these gifts and powers which you see conferred upon us. Greater certainty than this God himself cannot give; and surely man ought not to require.

Well therefore might our Lord say; The men of Niniveh shall rise in judgment with this generation, and condemn it; because they repented at the preaching of Jonas, and behold, (*f*) *more* than Jonas is here. More is done, and shall be done by me, to call this stubborn people to repentance, and to convince them of my authority, than was done by Jonas to the Ninivites.

But still it may be said, (*g*) Why did not Christ shew himself openly to all the people, particularly to his enemies, to his accusers, and murderers, to confound or to convince them? I answer:

1. Christ did not shew himself to all the Jews, because it was not necessary for their conversion, because the descent of the Holy Ghost upon the Apostles, and the miracles wrought by them at Jerusalem were sufficient proofs of his resurrection. And as there was no reason why Christ should shew himself to the Jews for their satisfaction; so neither was it necessary for our satisfaction who live in these later ages. The evidence which we have of it would not have been the greater; for there were so many thousands of Jews and Gentiles converted within forty years after Christ's ascension, that if the unbelieving Jews had been converted and added to the number, the increase of the evidence arising from thence would have been next to nothing.

2. Christ did not shew himself to the unbelieving Jews, because they were upon all accounts unworthy

of

(*f*) πλεῖον.
(*g*) It is the objection of Celsus, to which Origin gives answers different from those which I have used. See p. 98. *Contr. Celf.*

of such favour; they could not reasonably expect it from him, towards whom they had shewed so much ingratitude, spite, malice, and cruelty; and deserved not to have their curiosity and their stubbornness so far gratified.

Add to this, that in proofs of religious truths, when persons are not contented with that which is sufficient in the opinion of fair inquirers, but desire still something more, this something more is never to be fixed, but varies and increases according to the extravagant fancies of perverse men. If our Lord ought to have shewed himself to all the Jews of his own times, he should for the same reason have shewed himself to the Gentiles; and so to all men, to the end of the world, to convert some, to satisfy and confirm others, and to recall others from a wicked life; and thus faith would be no longer what it is, and what it ought to be.

3. If Christ had appeared openly in the presence of his enemies, and ascended into heaven before their eyes, it is not certain that this would have reduced them to silence, and have put a stop to their objections. They who had said that he was possessed of the Devil, and wrought his beneficent miracles by the assistance of the Devil, might have said, on this occasion, that an evil spirit had taken his body out of the grave, and (*h*) entered into it, and carried it about Jerusalem for some days, to make the people believe his resurrection, and then had conveyed it through the air to some unknown place.

4. If Christ had appeared to the unbelieving Jews, there is no just reason to conclude that they would have heartily and sincerely embraced the Gospel. If Christ had given them the same proofs which he gave to his Apostles, possibly they would have believed his resurrection:

(*h*) The Devil performed such a thing at the command of Cornel. Agrippa. So the Jesuit Delrio assures us, *Disq. Magic.* L. II. Qu. 29. Sect. I. and, for aught I know, he might be fool enough to believe it.

rection: but to believe that Christ was risen, and to become his servants, and obey his precepts, were two different things; the first did not imply the second, nor is there sufficient cause to think that such conviction would have made them honester men.

We find that in the days of Christ and of his Apostles, there were persons who saw the miracles which were wrought in confirmation of the Gospel, and who acknowledged in their hearts that they were divine works, and yet either did not openly profess it, or apostatized from it, and opposed it, after they had professed it; that some forsook the Gospel, to escape persecution, and others from worse and baser motives. They who fell away through fear were less guilty; for fear is an imperious passion, and drives men to do things which they detest, and for which they are afterwards very sorry; but they who were seduced by their vices, were sinners of whose amendment there was little or no hope. St. Peter denied his Master, but it was through fear, and by surprise, and therefore he obtained pardon, and returned to his obedience: If he had denied him for thirty pieces of silver, he would have been quite lost to God and to goodness.

Let us suppose the unbelieving Jews to have been of this wicked temper; let us suppose that by conversing with Christ after his resurrection, they had been fully convinced of it, and that they had either concealed their faith, or had joined themselves to the Christian Church only for a time, and then had rejected the Gospel; if they had thus behaved themselves, it must be acknowledged that such proselytes would have been of no service to our religion, and that Christ would have shewed himself to them to no purpose.

There is room to suspect that the chief persons amongst the Jews, who opposed the Apostles at their first preaching, did believe that Christ was risen, or thought that it might be true, or at least were not fully persuaded that it was false; there is room, I say, to

suspect

suspect this, from their compact with the soldiers, from the foolish and inconsistent story which they raised, that the Disciples had stolen his body, and from their lenity towards some of those disciples, whom they punished with less rigour than might have been expected.

Perhaps it will be said; If they believed the resurrection of Christ they could not have been so wicked and perverse; they would have been afraid of offending him, lest he should destroy them.

But history, Sacred and Pagan, ancient and modern, will afford us examples of men, who have done many wicked things against conviction and conscience, and who have from time to time been plagued with apprehensions that they should suffer for their iniquities in this world or the next, or in both. Besides, as the miracles of Christ had all been of the gentle and merciful kind, the Jews were the less alarmed with a fear of his indignation.

It is easy to imagine how the Jews might have been brought to embrace the Gospel by a few miracles of severity. For example; If the Apostles after Christ's resurrection had threatened the Jews that if they did not immediately acknowledge him, God would deal with them as he had dealt with the Ægyptians of old, and their first-born should all die in one night, and if this had come to pass, they who survived would have made no delay to profess themselves Christians. But the divine Providence did not think fit thus to compel men to come in, and to frighten them into Christianity. To a sufficient evidence is joined those gentle means of persuasion which permitted faith to be an act of choice, and the result of a sound judgment, a tractable temper, and a virtuous disposition.

5. If Christ had shewed himself to all the nation, and to all the strangers in Judea, and thereby had converted both Jews and Romans, and if the Christian religion had been thus established suddenly and without opposition,

opposition, it is certain that we in these ages should not have had so good proofs of the truth of our religion as we now have. Many objections might have been made to a religion embraced by the powers of this world, propagated under their protection and authority, established by those whom it was not safe to disoblige, and attended with honour and profit. But the speedy and extensive progress of the Gospel, though it was opposed by the great and learned, and the hardships which its first professors endured with so much meekness and courage, and their perseverance in a faith which at that time was not consistent with their temporal interests, these are perpetual testimonies of the truth of our religion.

6. But lastly, if Christ had appeared publicly, and conversed for forty days with the Jewish nation, there is reason to suppose that it would have been a hindrance to the propagation of the Gospel.

The Jews were then in subjection to the Romans, they did about that time expect the Messias, they imagined and hoped that the Messias would be a temporal prince, who should deliver them from the oppressive dominion of the Gentiles, and make them a powerful and a glorious nation. Accordingly, many impostors arose amongst them, from the time of that Herod in whose reign Christ was born, to the destruction of Jerusalem, who stirred up the people to insurrections, and who with their deluded followers suffered what they well deserved. We read in the New Testament, that when the multitudes saw the wonders which Christ wrought, particularly his feeding of thousands miraculously, they presently thought to set him up for their king, supposing that they should easily subdue their oppressors and enemies under such a leader. Upon this, Christ withdrew himself from them, and during the whole course of his ministry took a particular care to give no offence to the magistrate. His meek and blameless behaviour seems to have been acknowledged

by

by the Romans; for when the Jews accused him to Pilate of making himself a king in opposition to Cæsar, and of stirring up the people to a revolt, Pilate was sensible that it was a calumny, and openly declared him innocent.

Hence it may be supposed that if Christ had shewed himself to all the nation, after his resurrection, the multitude would have received him as the Messias, as their king, and would have risen against the Romans; and the ensuing wars would have been laid to the charge of the Christian religion, which upon that account must have become odious to the Romans, and have been opposed by them in all their dominions.

These are ill effects, which could not have been prevented, unless many miracles had been wrought for that very purpose, and consequently such astonishing and overbearing evidence of the truth of the Gospel had been given to the world as none besides madmen could resist; which, as we before observed, destroys the nature of faith.

In a much better manner did our religion make its first public appearance. Christ, after his resurrection, shewed himself to a sufficient number of witnesses; after he had conversed with them forty days, he sent them to preach the Gospel, and ascended into heaven. Concerning Christ, they taught that he was the Lawgiver, the Teacher, and the Saviour, and would be the Judge of mankind; that he was a king also, but that his kingdom was of a spiritual nature, not of this world, and that obedience to his laws was perfectly consistent with obedience to the higher Powers here on earth; so that no Prince had any thing to fear from the Christian religion, which diminished none of his rights. Nor did it lessen the rights of subjects, as is weakly or dishonestly affirmed by some vile flatterers, who have endeavoured to establish systems of passive obedience and non-resistance, of tyranny and slavery, from St. Paul's Epistle to the Romans. The Jews behaved themselves

themselves towards the Apostles, as they had behaved towards Christ, ever accusing them to the Gentiles as pestilent fellows, movers of sedition, and enemies to Cæsar; but the Roman magistrates saw that it was a false and malicious accusation, and looked upon the Apostles and their followers as upon a new sect amongst the Jews, differing from their countrymen in matters purely speculative and religious, who being quiet subjects deserved to enjoy the same liberty which at that time was granted to the Jews. This appears from the behaviour of Lysias, and Felix, and Festus, and Gallio, to St. Paul, related in the Acts of the Apostles; where we also find that the Apostle, when he had appealed to Cæsar, and was sent to Rome, continued there two years, preaching the Gospel to all who would hear it, no man forbidding him. Thus the Christian religion in its beginnings met with no great opposition from the Romans; the persecutions which its professors then underwent, arose chiefly from the Jews.

SERMON

SERMON XXXIII.

II COR. xii. 7.

Lest I should be exalted above measure through the abundance of the revelations, there was given to me a thorn in the flesh, the messenger of Satan to buffet me.

ST. Paul met with great and constant opposition in his ministry from Pagans and from unconverted Jews; but he experienced a more vexatious contradiction from half brethren and false brethren, from Jews converted indeed to Christianity, but yet stubbornly attached to their old prejudices, and absurdly tenacious of their expiring rites and ceremonies. These men made it their business to lessen and defame him, and to render his preaching unsuccessful, and to draw away his disciples from him, representing him as an enemy to the Jews, a despiser of the Law of Moses, a companion, a friend, and a patron of the Gentiles, an upstart and an intruder into the number of the Apostles. St. Paul therefore found himself often under the unavoidable and the hard necessity of acting what he calls the part of a fool; that is, of commending and extolling himself, and of proving that he was beyond all comparison superior to these injudicious or envious men, and as a teacher, not inferior to any Apostle how eminent soever, not to Peter, the first in dignity, not to John, the beloved disciple of Jesus Christ.

His arguments in support of his own sacred office and authority are set forth with that strength and vivacity which

which were natural to him, with that juſt indignation which ſo baſe an oppoſition would excite in a man conſcious that he deſerved no ſuch treatment, with that ſecurity and ſuperiority which attend a diſputant who knows his proofs to be clear and unanſwerable, and with the vehemence and zeal of a teacher of truth, who is afraid left his diſciples ſhould be ſeduced, and his pious endeavours defeated.

He obſerves that he was miraculouſly converted, and called by Jeſus Chriſt appearing to him; that he was inſtructed in the Chriſtian religion, and appointed to teach it, not by men, but by the Lord Jeſus Chriſt himſelf; that he had as many ſpiritual gifts conferred upon him, that he had wrought as many miracles as any Apoſtle; that in his miniſtry he had been as diligent as others, and indeed more diligent, had converted more perſons, had founded more Churches, had endured more labours, and had undergone more afflictions and greater ſufferings than any of Chriſt's diſciples; that he had likewiſe ſet a remarkable and uncommon example of ſelf-denial and diſintereſtedneſs, in not receiving even a maintenance from ſeveral of thoſe whom he taught, and that at different times he had laboured with his own hands to get his bread. To this he adds that he had been favoured with viſions and revelations, that he had been taken up, once into Paradiſe, and another time into the third heaven.

Theſe extraordinary deſerts on his ſide, and theſe extraordinary favours and privileges ſo largely conferred upon him, were in one reſpect dangerous temptations, and ſuch as might inſenſibly lead the wiſeſt and the humbleſt man upon earth into the confines at leaſt of pride and vanity, and now and then ſuggeſt a conceited reflection upon his own eminence and ſuperiority, eſpecially when he was provoked to it by ill uſage, by ſlights and cenſures, and compelled to compare himſelf with his oppoſers.

Therefore

Therefore to all these favours bestowed upon our great Apostle, God was pleased to add another, namely, affliction and discipline; for he chasteneth him whom he loveth, and scourgeth every son whom he receiveth. This chastisement is called by St. Paul, A thorn in the flesh, and it was intended to remind him of his weakness, and to preserve him from arrogance; and the moral sense of it was, Be not high-minded, but fear.

Lest I should be exalted above measure; that is, lest I should think too well of myself, and fancy that I had a right to God's favours, and imagine that I surpassed as much in moral accomplishments and in goodness, as I do in spiritual gifts, in visions and revelations; in the success which hath attended my ministry, and in the numbers which I have brought into the Church of Christ; lest I should be thus puffed up, there was given to me a thorn in the flesh.

(*a*) This thorn in the flesh must have been, in general, something that had its seat in the body, something that was uneasy and painful.

But it could not be the ill offices and the opposition of wicked men, and the afflictions and the persecutions which he endured, like other Christians. This, he knew, was then the lot and the portion of all the servants of Jesus Christ, and from this he would not have expected or prayed so earnestly to be released. It must have been some grievance more personal and particular.

What was it then? I answer, It could not have been any vicious desire; a thing which should not even have been mentioned, if some injudicious persons had not adopted this (*b*) absurd notion. When St. Paul recommends

---

(*a*) Some of these remarks are taken from a Discourse of Bishop Bull on the same text.

(*b*) And yet, as absurd as it is, some may perhaps chuse to retain it, as affording a sort of excuse for themselves when they yield to the same inclinations which they impute to the

SERMON XXXIII.

commends continence and chastity to the Corinthians, he says, I wish that all Christians were like myself, in that respect. It is not to be supposed that God should send such temptations upon him, or that this aged, sober, chaste, distressed, and laborious Apostle should have been exposed to them, or that he should call it an infirmity, a name much too civil for it, as he afterwards calls it, or that he should even glory and boast of it, as he declares that he would. Nor indeed could it be a proper remedy to cure him, of pride; for one sin doth not usually expel another, any more than Satan casts out Satan, or if it doth, it leaves the sinner as it found him, in the condition of an insolvent debtor, who borrows from one creditor to pay another.

Some understand it to be Original Sin; and it is matter of astonishment that any man should ever have so understood it. The thorn, in some sense, was given of God, as it seems; but God is the author of no bad gift. The thorn was given to St. Paul in particular; but original sin, if it belongs to any of us, belongs to all of us. If by original sin be meant, the sin of Adam imputed to all his posterity, and making them guilty in the sight of God, it belongs to no one, it is a dream and a false interpretation of Scripture: if by original sin be meant the imperfections and the defects of human nature, and the mortality which Adam brought upon himself and upon his posterity, this indeed is true, but it hath no more to do with St. Paul's thorn in the flesh, than with his journey from Jerusalem to Damascus.

As it plainly could be nothing of the lewd and immoral kind, it must have been somewhat of a (*c*) bodily defect

---

Apostle. I mean those persons who extol faith and depreciate morality, and whose religion often dwells in the brain, and descends not *infra zonam*.

(*c*) Erasmus is against us, and delivers his sentiments in a very positive manner:

"*Nec enim audiendos arbitror, qui non minus indocte quam impudenter solent illud objicere ; Virtus in infirmitate perficitur ;*

defect and disease, which he laboured under, and which made him appear mean and despicable in the eyes of those who judge of another merely from his outside, from his manner, his address, and his appearance.

The ancient Christian writers, who lived nearest to the time of the Apostle, constantly understood it so, and might probably have learned it from a tradition preserved in those places where St. Paul had preached the Gospel. But what chiefly confirms it is that the Apostle himself seems to explain it so in other passages of his Epistles. He says to his disciples the Galatians, Ye know that through infirmity in the flesh I preached the Gospel unto you at the first. And my temptation which was in my flesh you despised not, nor rejected, but received me as an Angel of God, even as Jesus Christ. The thorn in the flesh, and the temptation in the flesh, mean the same thing. Again he says to the Corinthians, that one of the objections which his adversaries used to make to him was this, His bodily presence is weak, and his speech is contemptible. Again he says, We are weak and ye are strong, and I was with you in weakness.

Laying these things together, we may collect that this Apostle had an infirm constitution, a bodily disorder, an ill state of health, which might at certain times affect his speech and his delivery, so that there was something in his whole appearance that tended to depress him, and to make him less venerable.

This thorn in the flesh is called, A messenger of Satan; the meaning of which seems to be, that God, who

---

tur; SOMNIANTES Paulum gravi capitis dolori fuisse obnoxium, cum ille *infirmitatem*, vel animi tentatiónem, vel quod vero propius est, improborum hominum molestam infectationem appellet. Atque idem ille Paulus, inter Apostolicas dotes donum curationis recensuit." *De Laude Medicinæ.*

It is not we who *nod* and *dream;* but *bonus dormitat Erasmus.*

SERMON XXXIII.

who hath Spirits good and evil at his command, and fulfils his purposes by both, when he thinks fit, gave liberty to Satan to afflict St. Paul. We find that in those days the Apostles had, amongst other extraordinary gifts, a power of delivering wicked Christians to Satan, or of inflicting bodily pains and disorders upon them, to cure them of their spiritual diseases, when milder methods were ineffectual; and it is St. Paul who hath occasionally made mention of this correction, and who himself, as an Apostle, inflicted it sometimes upon the disobedient. The same method God thought proper to follow in chastizing this great Apostle, not by way of punishment, for he had not incurred it by his behaviour, but by way of prevention, and because he was in danger of being tempted to spiritual pride.

For this, says the Apostle, I besought the Lord thrice. He must have been very uneasy upon this account, and have laboured under some grievance that lay heavy upon him, since he prayed so earnestly for relief.

In all probability it was not the pain that he felt, or any contempt or censure which his condition might draw upon him from wicked or rash and injudicious men, that thus affected him. He was too wise and prudent, too good and too patient to have been so much moved by such trials. The true reason of his sorrow and anxiety seems to have been a fear lest the cause of religion, which he had so much at heart, should suffer by it, lest his infirmities should obstruct his preaching of the Gospel, and render him less able to do good, and less prevalent in his endeavours to convert and save others. He knew that there is a great deal in the outward appearance, the person, the countenance, the voice, the manner, and the address, to bespeak the favour, the attention, and the respect of the populace and of the public.

For this, says he, I besought the Lord thrice.

If it be asked, who is meant by the Lord? it seems

most probable from the context, that it was not God the Father, but (*d*) Jesus Christ.

For the Lord answered St. Paul, and spake to him; but God the Father never thus appeared and manifested himself in this manner. All the visible or audible manifestations of God, of which mention is made in the Scriptures of the Old Testament, seem to have been appearances of the *Word* or the *Son* of God, acting and speaking in his Father's name; as after the incarnation he acted and spake in his own person; as when he appeared to St. Stephen, to St. Paul, and to other Saints and Disciples. In this the ancient Christians and most of the (*e*) moderns are agreed.

Secondly, according to the common style of the New Testament, the word *God* means the Father, and the word *Lord* means Jesus Christ.

Thirdly, the Lord said to St. Paul, My grace is sufficient for thee. This word *grace* is also commonly used of Christ; the grace of Christ, and the love of God, and the communion of the Spirit.

Fourthly, The Lord here promiseth to St. Paul his grace and his strength; and therefore the Apostle immediately adds, I will glory in my infirmities, that the power of Christ may rest upon me.

Christ shewed himself to St. Paul, when he converted him, and appeared to him afterwards at other times, and upon other occasions; and we may suppose that he did so now.

St. Paul being under much uneasiness on account of this thorn in the flesh, and remembering that Christ himself before his sufferings prayed earnestly to his Father three times that the cup might pass from him, followed

---

(*d*) Schlictingius, and other Socinians, allow that this is a prayer directed to Jesus Christ.

(*e*) Except those who admit not the pre-existence of Christ, as the *Word* or the *Son* of God. But they who are not influenced by this hypothesis will find no cause to reject this very old and probable opinion.

lowed the example, and befought Jefus Chrift with great earneftnefs three times that he might be relieved from this diforder.

Our Saviour then fpake to his Apoftle, and gave him this kind anfwer, My grace is fufficient for thee; for my ftrength is made perfect in weaknefs. Be patient and contented; it is enough that I love thee, that I am always with thee, to affift thee in the performance of thy office and miniftry. Thy weaknefs and infirmities fhall not hinder thee from being a fuccefsful preacher of the Gofpel; and then thefe very imperfections will fhew forth my power, and prove to the world that by the moft incompetent and unpromifing means and inftruments I am able to bring about the good of my Church and the eftablifhment of my Kingdom.

St. Paul, upon receiving this anfwer, not only humbly acquiefced in his Lord's determination, but declares that it was matter of joy to him, and that he would thenceforward glory in his infirmities, fince they were not only not detrimental, but ferviceable to Chriftianity, and tended to the good of the Church, and to the edification of his brethren.

It feems probable that this bodily infirmity of St. Paul was upon fome extraordinary occafions fufpended and removed for a time; as when he pleaded his caufe before Princes and Roman Governors, by whom he was favourably heard; and when with Barnabas he difcourfed to the Pagans of Lyftra, who took them to be Gods in an human form, and him to be Mercury, the God of eloquence (*f*).

Indeed, when we confider the infirmities of St. Paul, together with his innumerable toils and fufferings, we cannot account it lefs than a miracle that he was able for fo long a time to do what he did, and to bear

---

(*f*) Longinus, in a Fragment, amongft the Orators reckons Paul of Tarfus.

bear what he underwent; so that his bodily weakness, instead of being an objection to his character, afforded a proof to all who knew him that he must have been supported by a divine power in an extraordinary manner.

The moral reflections and practical uses arising from this subject are various; and I can only just review them, and touch upon them.

1. We see the very dangerous nature of pride, to which the best of persons are obnoxious, since such a man as St. Paul stood in need of some corrective to humble him, to check and to damp any conceited thought that might arise in his mind from reflecting upon his great labours and services, his high station in the Church, and the extraordinary gifts which he had received. This chastening and this bodily weakness had its due effect upon him; and one cannot but admire that sober and wise moderation, and that singular discretion, when he talks of himself. He represents his own exemplary conduct, his unblameable and disinterested behaviour amongst his converts, when he would animate them to follow his example; but then he ascribes it to the grace of God and the Spirit of God working with him, and helping his infirmities. He magnifies his Apostolical powers, when he was under a necessity of exerting his authority to repress the insolence of his adversaries, and to drive false teachers out of his flock; but at the same time he humbles himself by frequent acknowledgments of the crime which he had committed before his conversion, in persecuting the Church of Christ. On this account he places himself amongst the greatest sinners, only pleading his ignorance at that time, not as a sufficient excuse, but as an extenuation of his fault, for the sake of which he obtained mercy; and then he proposeth himself as an encouragement to penitent sinners. Thus he makes use of his past transgressions, of his spiritual gifts, of his religious behaviour, of his

bodily

bodily infirmities, of his afflictions and persecutions, his labours and his industry, to comfort, to instruct, to reprove, to warn, and to reform others.

If we have not so many gifts and graces as St. Paul had, and so by reason of our imperfections are not in so much danger of conceit and vanity as he might be, yet from imaginary accomplishments real pride will often spring up, and we have not the Apostle's goodness and discretion, to enable us to repel such temptations. We should therefore beware of every kind of pride, and like him keep it in subjection by a serious and frequent consideration of our many defects. Motives and inducements to humility we can never want, if we deal fairly and honestly with ourselves, and compare our practice with our duty.

2. We see from this, and from many other places in the New Testament, that the Apostles had not the power of working miracles at their own discretion, but had some particular impulse of the holy Spirit directing them when and how this gift should be exercised. For St. Paul could not cure himself of this bodily disease, nor could he give his beloved disciple Timothy a better state of health, nor relieve some of his friends when they were sick. If then even in the Apostolical days miracles were not daily lavished, but performed moderately, and sparingly, and with a kind of sober frugality, we have great reason to suspect that wanton and endless profusion of miracles pretended to have been wrought in following ages, often in a most fantastical manner, and to no good end that we can discern, and often for bad ends and base purposes.

3. We all desire temporal peace and happiness, and would willingly shun every thing that gives us uneasiness and pain; and these desires are natural and not sinful. St. Paul also earnestly wished to be delivered from his infirmities, and to have more health and strength and vigour of body. But from his example

ple we may learn to regulate these desires, and not to expect that things would fall out just as we could wish. We may pray to God, as he did, either to obtain a present good, or to be delivered from a present evil; but such prayers must always be conditional, and the condition must be either expressed or understood, if it shall seem good to God. Perhaps it will not seem good to him, and then we must not think ourselves hardly and unkindly used, nor imagine that our requests are unsuccesful, merely because they are not granted. If God should not deliver us from temporal evil, yet if he intends it for our benefit, if he gives us strength to support it, if he bestows upon us other blessings to counterbalance it, and if he will in due time reward our faith and resignation, our submissive temper and humble acquiescence, we are infinite gainers upon the whole.

Consider the case of St. Paul. He underwent something that was very grievous, no doubt, since he begged three times with repeated importunity to be relieved. For when he was scourged, and cast into prison, and fettered, and beaten, and stoned, and shipwrecked, and driven from place to place, and deprived even of the necessaries of life, he endured it with all intrepidity and resolution, and never once desired to be exempted from such severe trials. When it was revealed to him, or when he plainly foresaw, that he should soon suffer martyrdom, he speaks to his disciples, not only with calm composure, but with pleasure and exultation, that he should leave this world, and go to his Lord and Master. But this thorn in the flesh, this bodily disorder grieved him much, and yet he was not relieved from it, and in all probability he carried it with him to the grave, afflicted, and yet acquiescing, as well he might, in the will of his Lord. Suppose we were exactly in his case, and were to receive the same answer from Jesus Christ, and he should say to one of us, Be satisfied with this, that I am thy friend

friend and protector, that I love thee, and will always take care of thee; certainly such an answer would be worth all the health, all the strength, all the respect, and all the worldly prosperity, that any man ever enjoyed.

4. This leads me, lastly, to observe that in the present state of things, a mixture of temporal good and evil is best for us upon the whole. An uninterrupted flow of prosperity, as it is hardly possible in the nature of things, so it is not expedient for strangers and sojourners here below, who want some motives to remind them of the end for which they are designed, and of the home to which they are repairing, and to keep them from trifling and dallying with their great concerns, and from making every frivolous and fading object the object of their affections.

A Pagan Moralist hath represented the folly of an attachment to this world almost as strongly as a Christian could express it. Thou art a passenger, says he, and thy ship hath put into an harbour for a few hours. The tide and the wind serves, and the pilot calls thee to depart; and thou art amusing thyself, and gathering shells and pebbles upon the shore, till they set sail without thee.

So is every Christian, who, being upon his voyage to an happy eternity, delays and loiters, and thinks and acts as if he were to dwell here for ever.

An infirm habit of body, and a frequent return of sickness, is reckoned, amongst temporal calamities; and yet it is not without some alleviations and advantages, which may teach us to be resigned under it, if it prove our lot and portion.

It often keeps persons out of the way and the reach of many temptations; as on the contrary, health and strength, and a flow of spirits, lead them to gaiety and dissipation, to everlasting amusements and diversions, and sometimes to worse things, to mischievous undertakings and vicious actions.

It

It teaches compaſſion and charity towards the unhappy and miſerables; and on the contrary, they who are ſtrangers to pain and ſorrow are ſeldom diſpoſed to pity it much in others.

It is uſually joined to ſeriouſneſs and contemplation, to thinking and reaſoning; and thus the capacity is enlarged and the underſtanding improved, and though the body be weak, the mind is active; and it is obvious to obſerve that the moſt ſickly are not the leaſt ingenious.

It makes the world leſs engaging and leſs dear, and thereby teaches and enables to live more prudently, and to depart more willingly.

Chriſtians are directed to pray to God for all things, and to return thanks to him for all things, becauſe if they endeavour to ſerve God conſtantly and faithfully, nothing very diſaſtrous ſhall befall them, but whether in proſperity or in adverſity, or, which is more common, in a mixture and viciſſitude of both, all things ſhall, by the divine bleſſing and appointment, work together for their advantage.

SERMON XXXIV.

TITUS iii. 2.

To speak evil of no man.

THERE are several reasons for which Christians ought to be exhorted to refrain from evil speaking.

First, it is not only a mean and shameful, but a pernicious fault; it produces much harm in society, and is a cause why many live hateful and hating one another, and die in the same unfriendly disposition.

Secondly, it is a common and wide-spread fault, and few, very few are entirely free from it. It is not confined to wicked and profane persons; it is to be found in some measure even in those who have their virtues, their good and useful and amiable qualities and accomplishments, who live soberly and honestly, who are just and true in their dealings, who love their friends and are active to serve and oblige them, who are not uncharitable to the poor, who have a sense of religion, and worship God both in public and in private.

Thirdly, they who are addicted to it, either seldom reflect upon its odious nature, or are not sensible when and how often they thus offend, or have several plausible though vain excuses to justify themselves.

Upon

Upon all these accounts therefore it is necessary that it should be set in a true light, and have its share of rebuke amongst other sins from which we are commanded in Scripture to abstain ourselves, and to dissuade others.

Evil-speaking consists in spreading reports to the disadvantage of our neighbour; and of this fault there are three distinct kinds or degrees.

The worst kind of it is to spread lies of our own invention concerning them.

The next is to report things to their disadvantage, of the truth of which we are not sufficiently assured.

The lowest degree is to say of them that evil which we know to be true.

There is no occasion to prove and expose the folly and dishonesty of the two former kinds. It would be losing time and words. I shall therefore chiefly discourse of the latter, and shew how blameable even this is for the most part. I say, how blameable it is for the most part, because we should not condemn it in the gross, and without distinction. To speak what we know concerning the faults of others is one of those acts which by a change of circumstances becomes lawful or unlawful, and therefore we should first examine and consider in what cases it may be allowable.

They who are forwardly and impertinently busy in detecting smaller offences for the sake of lucre, undertake a disreputable office, and receive part of their just reward in the contempt and abomination which is usually bestowed upon them. But where the common good and the wise laws of society absolutely require it, it is allowable, indeed it is a duty, to make known the crimes of others which we can prove. Pity, and gratitude, and friendship, and every affection, should give place to the love which we owe to virtue and to our country. It must be confessed that to one who has any generosity and good nature, few things can be more disagreeable than to be an informer or accuser; but there

there may be cases in which it may be undergone. The Law of God expressly commanded the Jews to discover any person, even a brother, a friend, or a wife, who should attempt to seduce others to idolatry, which in that government was high treason; the laws of our country, and of all countries, upon some very great occasions require a like behaviour; and indeed charity itself forbids us to conceal what cannot be kept secret without grievous injury to the public. But this is a duty which we are seldom called upon and compelled to practise.

The Roman Law (a) says; Let no one be forced against his will to accuse or prosecute; which for the most part is reasonable, though liable to exceptions.

Under the general rule, that we may speak of the faults of others when the common interest demands it, are contained these particular cases:

If we are injured in our reputation, it is lawful for us to clear our character, though we do it by casting infamy upon him who has defamed us. We are no where commanded to love our neighbour more than ourselves; and it is much better in all respects that a slanderer should by our detection of him be exposed, than that we by his calumnies should be misrepresented.

So, if we be wronged, not only in our reputation by slander, but in any other manner affecting our fortunes and our welfare, to discover those injuries and complain of them, that we may obtain our right, and be secured from such ill usage for the future, or that the offending person may be brought to a sense of his sin, and to a better mind, can be no fault, if it be done with due temper and with moderation.

And if in the defence of our own good name, of our own property, we may proceed thus far in proclaiming the faults of others, we may do as much for our neigh-

---

(a) *Invitus agere vel accusare nemo cogatur*, says Dioclesian, *Cod.* L. III. *Tit.* VII.

neighbour, when he suffers in like manner, because it is our duty to love him as ourselves.

This regard which we owe to mankind will also justify us in speaking of the obvious faults of others, when by it we may preserve any person from great evil and mischief. If one be in danger of falling into bad company, and by their instigation and example into wickedness and ruin, to mention to him the vices of those whom he ought to shun, can be no fault or breach of charity.

We may also observe that there are offences committed daily in the world so notorious and scandalous, that they can neither be concealed nor excused. To be afraid to mention such offences in common discourse, would be to lay too rigid and scrupulous a restraint upon our tongue.

And again as young persons are more (*b*) affected by examples than by precepts, if a parent or master, dissuading a youth from this or that vice, should point out to him some person impudently barefaced in the practice of it, and shew him the bad consequences of such a behaviour, this would not properly be called evil-speaking.

These are particular cases in which to say what we certainly know concerning the faults of others is either a duty, or no crime. And to these, more, perhaps might be added. It is in this as in some other actions; a change of circumstances alters the nature of it, and makes it good, or evil, or indifferent; and these cirumstances are sometimes such, that it is no easy matter to fix the exact bounds between right

---

(*b*) ———— Insuevit pater optimus hoc me

Ut fugerem exemplis vitiorum quæque notando.

Cum me hortaretur, parce, &c. *Horat.* Serm. I. iv. 105.

See *Locke* on Education, § 82. 94.

SERMON XXXIV.

right and wrong. But to this general rule we ought to keep, namely, to be very cautious and reserved in speaking even the ill of others which we know to be true, and to abstain from it, unless we can shew a just cause; and that for several reasons, which I shall now set before you.

1. We should not be too forward to publish the faults of others, because it is no sufficient excuse for us, that what we say is true, and that they against whom we speak deserve such usage. This excuse seems to be the strong-hold of the better and more moderate sort of evil-speakers, who think that they do nothing amiss, when they can prove what they affirm, and when the person whom they censure is really worthy of correction. They consider not that they assume an undue power, and that they have not a general and unlimited right to speak against evil-doers, and to deliver them up to shame and infamy. If every one should take this liberty, the ill effects would soon be visible, and the offender would often suffer more than is fit, his character being thus exposed to the rabble, to be worried at their discretion. Resentments, retaliations, grudges, and quarrels would unavoidably ensue, and human society would be what some have imagined of a state of nature, a state of war, and a trial of skill who should be best able to plague and expose his neighbour.

By publishing the faults of others, they not only judge but punish. Now let us suppose that the person punished deserves all this, yet how have they deserved so ill of themselves, that they must needs administer the correction? Let offenders punish offenders, since it will always be so. Let it be left to tale-bearers, to busy bodies, to the spiteful, the envious, and the malicious: they will do it sufficiently.

And here one cannot well omit the mention of a fault, nearly related to evil-speaking, but more pernicious, and that is evil-writing, or Satire, in which the defects, weaknesses, indiscretions, follies and vices, not of cor-

rupted

rupted human nature, but of particular perſons are expoſed to public view. If theſe writers can ſay for themſelves they keep exactly to truth, yet they exerciſe an authority to which they have no legal and juſt claim. But they ſeldom have even that excuſe to plead; they often beſtow their cenſures as intereſt, partiality, ignorance, ſpleen, and prejudice direct, and are uſually the moſt malicious revilers of ſome, and the moſt ſordid flatterers of others. Thus a perſon ſhall preſume to paſs ſentence upon his neighbour's reputation, who is not fit to open the cauſe, and ſhall ſet himſelf up for a Judge, who has not the qualifications requiſite even for an ordinary Evidence.

And of this tribe of men the moſt odious are thoſe, who ſhoot their arrows from the dark, who wear a maſk, not out of modeſty, but of fear and ſelf-preſervation, who themſelves write without a name, and abuſe innocent perſons by name; a crime which deſerves other correction than words.

I will not ſay that every thing which may be called Satire is unlawful, or lay ſo hard a reſtraint upon poets, and indeed upon Divines too; for Sermons againſt Vice, Error, Folly, and Fanaticiſm, may perhaps be thought to fall under that denomination. Fables and Parables are a ſpecies of Satire, and an uſeful way of correcting mankind, and conveying good inſtruction. Characters of pride, conceit, folly, avarice, impudence, &c. may be preſented to public view, and perhaps they may be drawn from the life; but when the Original is not pointed out, no one is obliged to take it upon himſelf, or ſhould pretend to be offended.

2. Another argument againſt cenſoriouſneſs is contained in this plain precept of the Goſpel; Whatſoever ye would that men ſhould do unto you, do ye ſo unto them.

Every perſon has his defects, and yet loves himſelf notwithſtanding his imperfections. He takes it ill of thoſe who deride or expoſe his faults, and he thinks himſelf

himself obliged to those who excuse or defend him. He calls the former his enemies, and the latter his friends. Thus nature acts within us; and reason adds, that we we ought to be such towards others as we wish them to be towards us.

Charity in men, like mercy in God, is a perfection which we admire and esteem, especially when we stand much in need of it; then he to whom much hath been forgiven, will usually love much. One part of Charity consists in passing over and covering transgressions, when it may be done without injury to others, and the divine mercy displays itself in the promise which God hath made that he will blot out transgressions, and remember them no more, if we amend, and in particular if we deal with men as we desire that he should deal with us. As we hope therefore at the great day of account to have the follies and failings of our life pardoned, and not exposed to our shame and confusion before that solemn assembly of men and Angels, we must take care not to be extreme ourselves to mark and to expose what is done amiss by others.

3. We should not accustom ourselves to discourse about the faults of our neighbour, because it may betray us by degrees into a worse kind of evil speaking. From saying every thing to his disadvantage that we can prove to be true, from omitting no opportunity to indulge his humour, when we can plead some excuse for it, we shall perhaps proceed to tell what we learn by uncertain hearsays, and thence to make large additions of our own invention, which is the height of slander and calumny. By much speaking upon useful subjects we learn the art of discoursing with fluency and justness; and by much talking in the censorious way, we learn the art, such as it is, of evil speaking; with this difference, that the latter is by far the easier to be acquired, our irregular passions greatly assisting us, and small pains and abilities being requisite to get any bad habit.

4. We

4. We should not be forward to expose the faults of others, because by so doing we may bring upon them a punishment too heavy for the offence. Our words we account to be mere sounds, which can do little or no hurt, and yet be they very swords; they are often most pernicious instruments of mischief, and inflict wounds never to be healed. By spreading about one single fault of another, we may perhaps raise him up irreconcileable enemies, we may lessen very much the peace of his mind, his reputation, his fortunes, and the welfare of an innocent family, who depend upon him; and thus may we contribute to bring him into inconveniences and troubles, which bear no proportion to his folly, and which he may no more deserve to suffer than we ourselves.

5. We should be cautious how we censure others, because we may misrepresent them, and yet say nothing of them that is not true. Men have their bad and their good qualities, and in forming a judgment of them as much regard at least should be had to the good as to the bad ones. By exposing all that is faulty in a man, and suppressing all that is commendable, we may make him appear far worse than he is, and transform an imperfect mortal into a detestable creature.

A person hath committed a fault, and we publish it. Perhaps he has been sensible of it, has repented, and is amended. God hath forgiven it; and shall not men cease to throw it in his face? They ought; but very often they do not. God pardons a transgression, when a new course of life follows it, and there is joy in heaven at the happy change; but here below, one folly shall live upon the tongues and in the memories of men an unreasonable length of time, and not be expiated by the most exemplary behaviour, and an honourable series of virtuous actions; so that in this, to our unspeakable happiness, the thoughts of God are not our thoughts, nor his ways our ways.

6. Again;

SERMON XXXIV.

6. Again; To disclose the faults and indiscretions of others, is often very pernicious to society, raises infinite variances amongst men, and tends to destroy the slender remains of love and charity which subsist in the Christian world. By this ill-natured loquaciousness the peace of families, of neighbourhoods, and of cities, is disturbed, and strife and hatred take place, where concord and civility might have flourished; for since through pride and passion and inadvertence we often throw out rash censures and reflections, many receive and return good offices, who, if they knew what the one has blabbed concerning the other, would become desperate enemies.

No employment then can be more base and uncharitable than to gather up every unguarded and idle word, and carry it to those who will infallibly resent it, and to force men out of an ignorance, a quiet and happy ignorance of the things which have been said against them.

7. It is farther to be observed upon this subject, that, since for the most part we cannot discern the exact nature and degree of other men's faults, we may easily think too hardly, and judge too severely of them. Their faults, when we know not the circumstances attending them, are like objects seen by us at a great distance, or at twilight; we see them neither in shape, nor in size or colour, such as they really are.

It must be owned, that there is much open, and much secret wickedness in the world, that even the apparent virtues of men are sometimes the offspring of mean or bad motives, and may rather stand in need of excuse or forgiveness, than deserve commendation.

But as the seeming virtues of men are not always what they seem; so their faults are sometimes less odious than they appear to us, and are attended with favourable circumstances which diminish the guilt.

Thus we are in a great measure incompetent judges of the actions of others, and therefore should decline the office of judging them, when nothing obliges us to it. If we want to be exercising this faculty, we may do it at home, upon ourselves; for we best know the motives of our own actions, and cannot easily impose upon our own conscience.

It is not to be inferred from this, that we should be afraid to call vice, vice; and error, error; and to condemn bad actions. We ought not to justify evil either in ourselves, or in others. But we should remember, that in all faults there may be many circumstances either aggravating, or lessening the offence, which are not known to us; and in that case Charity teaches us to hope the best, and to speak and think and judge as candidly as we possibly can, in which if we err, and cause others to err with us, there is no great harm done, and it is much better to be mistaken on that side than on the other. (c) Thus the Heathen Moralists direct us to behave towards those whom we ought to love and esteem, to make all fair allowances for their imperfections, and to represent their defects in the most favourable manner than the thing will admit. What an honest Pagan would have done in this case to a friend, a Christian should do to any and to every man.

And of all the persons whom we are inclined to censure, and to condemn, there are none who usually deserve it less than they who differ from us in their opinions which tend not directly to debauch the mind, and have no necessary connection with profaneness and immorality. Nothing is more reasonable than to allow them sincerity, and to suppose that they design well, though they judge wrong.

Vice indeed is the parent of error; but there are errors which are of a better family, and come from parents less scandalous, and arise from causes which rather

deserve

(c) Vellem in amicitia sic erraremus et isti
Errori nomen Virtus posuisset honestum.
Horat. Serm. l. iii. 4ᵗ.

deserve to be ranked amongst weaknesses than amongst crimes. Such are the prejudices of education, a reverence for parents, friends, and teachers, a superstitious turn of mind, a small capacity, and an infirm judgment. Of all false doctrines we may freely express our dislike, since whosoever loves reason and religion, must hate falshood. But the erring persons, who may possess many good qualities, have not forfeited their right to our favourable opinion. It is no wonder to see ignorance and implicit Faith attended with uncharitable insolence; it can hardly be otherways; but a man of sense and knowledge, who has been used to think, and reason, and examine, and correct his own mistakes, cannot hate those who are in error, without hating himself.

8. That we may restrain ourselves from talking of the faults of others, we should also consider, that such discourse is produced by bad causes, and proceeds from a corrupted heart; and that all good and wise persons who hear us, will judge of us accordingly. Speech is the child of thought; and a child it is which greatly resembles its Parent. When the discourse is censorious and malicious, the mind which conceives it is no better. Pride, anger, self-conceit, self-interest, ill-nature, spitefulness, envy, are often the causes of this talkativeness concerning the defects of our neighbour; at the very best, it must be ascribed to heedlessness and impertinence, qualities which every one would willingly disown.

9. Besides; This is an offence which seldom escapes correction. If human laws cannot chastise it, except in some few cases, the persons who are ridiculed or censured will fully supply that defect. Though we be cautious, inoffensive, and courteous, adversaries will spring up we know not how; they are weeds which will grow, though neither planted nor watered; not only our vices, but our virtues, will produce them. Yet of all men the backbiter hath the most, and those very troublesome and implacable, who want neither inclination,

clination, nor power, nor abilities, to plague him; for unkind ufage will make a man ingenious even in fpight of nature; it will fharpen the dulleft capacity, and render it quick in fpying out the defects of an enemy, and fkilful in expofing them.

10. Laftly, we fhould be cautious not to give way to an inclination of talking againft others, becaufe if we be once accuftomed to it, there is no probability that we fhall ever leave it off. They who are cenforious, not now and then only, by chance, by fudden paffion, by refentment, by a thoughtlefs indifcretion, but by trade and profeffion, by long cuftom and habit, who, like their Father, go to and fro in the earth, and walk up and down in it, to do mifchief; fuch perfons will change for the better, when the Æthiopian changes his fkin, and the leopard his fpots.

Of all bad habits, thofe of the tongue are perhaps the hardeft to be cured. The reafon is this: We deceive ourfelves in thinking that words can do little or no hurt, and that the guilt of them is inconfiderably fmall, and confequently we fpeak at random, what comes uppermoft. The wicked actions which we commit are bulky things compared to our difcourfe, take up more time, force themfelves more upon our obfervation, and fink deeper into our memories; but words which have wings, and fly away, flip from us unregarded, and the remembrance of them, as to us, often perifhes with them, efpecially of thofe words which we have a habit of uttering. Thus the perpetual talker, the common fwearer, the vain boafter, and the old liar, often perceive not their feveral defects. So alfo the habitual backbiter knows not his own temper and character; and when that is the cafe, his amendment is almoft impoffible, and as long as he hath the ufe of fpeech, the abufe of it will probably continue.

Thefe are reafons why we fhould not be inclined to fay of others that ill which we know, and can prove to be true.

SERMON

SERMON XXXV.

II TIM. iii. 2.

Men shall be lovers of their own selves.

SINCE it is certain, that there is an innocent love of ourselves, and yet self-love is here condemned, and has the foremost place in a long catalogue of crimes, it will be proper to state the difference between innocent and vicious self-love.

That there is a love of ourselves, which is natural and necessary, and consequently innocent is a plain truth, and yet a truth which has been opposed and denied. There have been pious and well-meaning persons, who, in their refinements on morality and religion, have taught that a man must not only consider the will and the honour of God in all his actions, but that he must forget himself entirely, and have no kind of regard to his own good. Now this is not only to require impossibilities of men, but to talk to them in a language which most of them cannot comprehend, that is, in a language quite contrary to the style of the holy Scriptures, which, in teaching us our duty, condescend always to our capacities, though never to our perverse inclinations.

God has given us a being which is necessarily attended with a love of it, with a desire to preserve and enjoy our life, with an endeavour to shun the things which hurt us, and to provide the things which conduce

duce to our ease and support. This Nature implants in us, and to this it leadeth us.

Our Reason, which judges of good and evil, teaches us to use our skill and industry in getting and securing whatsoever is agreeable and useful to us, under these limitations, that we do no wrong to others, that we transgress no law of God, and that we seek not what upon the whole will do us more harm than good.

This love of ourselves, which is natural to us, and which reason confirms in us, is plainly allowed in the Scriptures; for there we learn that by divine appointment our duty and our interest are inseparably connected, and that whilst we serve our Maker, we serve ourselves: we have there set before us as motives to obedience a variety of rewards both temporal and eternal; we have there dissuasives from vice enforced by denunciations of punishments here and hereafter. Such a method of treating us supposes that we love, and that we must love ourselves, else it would be unaccountable. Praise and blame, exhortations and discouragements, promises and threatnings, rewards and corrections, are designed for those who love their own happiness, that is, who love themselves.

God has placed us in a world abounding with all good things suited to our natural appetites and inclinations; he has made an ample provision for our real wants and just desires, so that we might generally pass our days here with tolerable ease and satisfaction, if it were not for our own fault, and for the ill usage which we give and receive. Now God would not have set these things before us in our reach, unless he had intended that we should enjoy them, unless we might seek and possess them. Self-love therefore, as it directs us to provide discreetly at all times for our welfare, is lawful.

God has required of us a disposition to do good to all, he has recommended the social virtues in the strongest terms; yet even in this he makes the love which we

have

SERMON XXXV.

have for ourselves the measure and the rule of our love to others. Thou shalt love thy neighbour as thyself: and, whatsoever ye would that men should do unto you, do ye so unto them.

Hence we learn, that there is a self-love which is natural, innocent, and unavoidable.

But there is an affection for ourselves which is irregular and pernicious, and which we call self-love; for this word is usually taken in a bad sense. By it is meant an esteem and fondness for ourselves, arising from evil causes, exceeding its true bounds, hurtful to others. The particular kinds of it are many, and shall now be considered distinctly.

1. Self-love is vicious, when it leads us to judge too favourably of our faults.

Sometimes it finds out other (*a*) names for them, and by miscalling them, endeavours to take away their bad qualities. Thus, according to self-love, covetousness is frugality, selfishness is œconomy, profusion is liberality, ambition is a generous desire of excelling, censoriousness is impartiality, severity is justice, and the spirit of persecution is religious zeal.

Sometimes it represents our sins as weaknesses, infirmities, the effect of natural constitution, and deserving more pity than blame.

Sometimes it excuses them upon account of the intent, pretending that some good or other is promoted by them, and that the motive and the end sanctify the means, or greatly lessen the faultiness of them.

It leads us to set our good in opposition to our bad qualities, and to persuade ourselves, that what is laudable in us far outweighs what is evil.

It

(*a*) Nemo se avarum esse intelligit, nemo cupidum.—Dicimus; Non ego ambitiosus sum, sed nemo aliter Romæ potest vivere. Non ego sumtuosus sum, &c. *Seneca* Epist. l. 50.

Timidus vocat se cautum, parcum sordidus. *Publius Syrus.*

It teaches us to compare ourselves with others, and thence to draw favourable and flattering conclusions, because we are not so bad as several whom we could name; it shews us the general corruption that is in the world, represents it worse than it is, and then tells us, that we must not hope, and need not endeavour, to be remarkably and singularly good.

2, Our self-love is irregular, when we think too well of our righteousness, and overvalue our good actions, and are pure in our own eyes.

This religious conceit and spiritual pride destroys that humility which God requires even of the most virtuous; it prevents that improvement in goodness which has its foundation in humility. They who trust in themselves that they are righteous, will also usually despise others, and become rash and censorious. They consider not that God prefers the sorrowful acknowledgment even of a great offender, followed by amendment, to the insolence of a vain boaster, who magnifies his incomplete obedience, and thinks himself arrived at perfection.

At the best, we are, as our Lord tells us, unprofitable servants: we have received much from God, and we have made him a small return.

We should state the account fairly, and see what assistance we have had from others; first from God, who hath made us what we are, and caused the light of the Gospel to shine upon us; then from our parents, friends, and teachers, for education, advice, reproof, instruction, and encouragement; from good examples, both those which are recorded in history, and those which have offered themselves to our view amongst the persons with whom we converse.

We should examine our past and present conduct, not by comparing ourselves with profligate persons, whom it is no credit to surpass, but by judging our actions according to the laws of God; in which inquiry if we proceed impartially, we shall find enough to mortify our pride. He who surveys himself thus, will see many things which stand in need of pardon, and few which deserve approbation. The thoughts of man are often running upon follies and trifles, his affections too much fixed upon transitory objects, his desires extravagant and irregular, his passions disorderly, his hopes and fears, his joy and sorrow, raised by small causes, and carried beyond decency and discretion, his heart frequently cold to spiritual things, his resolutions of amendment weak and inconstant, his behaviour to others not uniform, his obedience at the best incomplete, his most commendable actions imperfect, mixed and sullied with little views to something that did not deserve his regard. There is none who can pronounce himself clear of such faults and defects. To think ourselves free from them would be a great fault. A sincere endeavour to amend and improve is not more our duty, than a due sense and meek acknowledgment of our imperfections.

3. Our self-love is blameable, when we overvalue our abilities, and entertain too good an opinion of our knowledge and capacity: and this kind of self-love is called self-conceit.

One evil which men reap from it, is to be disliked and despised. There are some faults which the world is disposed to forgive, or not to censure very severely, such for example as intemperance, extravagance, and rash courage; and there are faults which every one blames, such as ingratitude, covetousness, malicioufness, and self-conceit.

The reason why self-conceit is so much disliked, is plainly this, that it is always attended with a mean opinion of others. There never was a person vain of things which he possessed or thought that he possessed in common with multitudes: it is a superiority, real or imaginary, on which this self-love is founded. As

therefore

therefore the conceited person sets himself above others and looks down upon them with scorn; they in revenge will endeavour to abase him who would thus be exalted. On this account worldly wisdom bids us avoid the appearances of vanity, and not commend in ourselves what really deserves commendation: and herein religion also joins with worldly wisdom, teaching us to use the same caution, and to let another praise us, and not our own lips.

From self-conceit arise rash undertakings, indiscreet attempts, hasty determinations, stubbornness, insolence, envy, censoriousness, confidence, vanity, the love of flattery, and sometimes irreligion, and a kind of idolatry, by which a man worships his own abilities, and places his whole trust in them.

The unreasonableness of this conceit appears from the imperfections of the human understanding, and the obstacles which lie between us and wisdom. All knowledge is attained with much pains and difficulty: the utmost that we can acquire of it bears no proportion to our ignorance; it is kept up, as it was at first attained, by labour; it is gradually lost and forgotten, unless it be frequently reviewed and recollected; it is suddenly snatched away, and quite blotted out by many bodily distempers; the mind is soon wearied in the search of it, is misguided by prejudices, is deceived by false appearances, is disturbed by the various alterations which the body undergoes, and has several diseases of its own, which are so many impediments in the way to wisdom.

Hence it is that knowledge is in a great measure hidden from the eyes of men, that the most inquisitive and learned differ in their opinions, that the most careful and considerate vary and change their sentiments, and that the most judicious are the most sensible of their own weakness.

To remember this, to love truth with all our heart, to seek it with all our strength, and to perceive that
we

we can discover only a little of it, is to be as wise as we can be here below. Whosoever entertains higher thoughts than these in favour of himself, has employed his time and pains to no purpose, has not only much to learn, but much to unlearn, and is farther from wisdom than he was in his childhood.

To be conceited through an opinion of superiority of judgment, sagacity, and experience, is foolish, because in all probability it is groundless. For why should we fancy ourselves so much above others? There are in every age a few of uncommon abilities and great knowledge; and there are some as remarkably deficient. These two sorts excepted, the rest of the world are more upon the level than some vain heads are willing to think. The powers of the mind are not extremely different in different persons; sense and understanding and the means of improving them are common blessings; sincerity and industry are not qualities peculiar to any of us. Others therefore may seek the truth as successfully, and reason as judiciously, and act as discreetly as we.

Besides; they who are wise and prudent, are not always so, but with their good sense and acute discernment have a mixture of frailty, and imperfection sufficient to keep them modest and humble. Every one has his dark intervals: there is nothing so silly that some wise man hath not said, and nothing so weak that some prudent man has not done.

3. Our self-love is irregular when we are proud and vain of things inferior in nature to those before-mentioned, when we value ourselves upon the station and circumstances in which not our own deserts, but chance or favour or birth hath placed us, upon mere shew and outside, upon these and the like advantages in which we surpass others.

This conceit is unreasonable and foolish; for these are either things which the possessors can hardly call their own, as having done little or nothing to acquire them, or they are of small value, or they are liable to

be

be irrecoverably loſt by many unforeſeen accidents. They often bring more hurt than good with them, expoſe men to dangers and temptations, hinder them from improving their underſtanding, have a bad effect upon their minds, and make them fools if they do not find them ſuch; and whoſoever uſes them rightly, yet poſſeſſes them in common with ſome of the weakeſt, the moſt contemptible, the moſt profligate and vileſt perſons.

5. Laſtly, our ſelf love is vicious when we make our worldly intereſt, convenience, humour, eaſe, or pleaſure, the great end of our actions. This is ſelfiſhneſs, a very diſingenuous and ſordid kind of ſelf-love. It is a paſſion that leads a man to any baſeneſs which is joined to lucre, and to any method of growing rich which may be practiſed with impunity. It occupies the mind with low and mean views, and weakens or deſtroys the deſire of reputation, the fear of contempt, and the compaſſionate and friendly and charitable and generous diſpoſitions. If it meets with good abilities, it diſgraces and ſpoils them, and turns a man's wiſdom into craft, and his ſagacity into tricks.

A ſelfiſh perſon thinks and acts as if the world and every thing that is in it were made for him, for his ſole uſe and pleaſure, as if his concerns muſt be preferred to the intereſt of all others. But it is unreaſonable that one man ſhould expect to be conſidered as if he were more than one man, that he ſhould want to be ſet above his equals or his betters. A more abſurd and ridiculous creature can hardly be conceived, than a perſon who deſires every thing, and deſerves nothing.

Selfiſhneſs is unreaſonable, as it is contrary even to our preſent advantage.

The end which it purſues, is worldly happineſs; but in reality it tends more to leſſen than to promote it; for it knows not the pleaſure of doing good offices, it enjoys not the eſteem of the virtuous part of mankind, it is accompanied with envy and with inſatiable deſires, and it is often the cauſe of diſappointments; for men

take

take a delight in oppoſing, croſſing, and over-reaching ſuch perſons, and when they are ill-uſed, they are ſeldom pitied; for he who is in love with himſelf alone, is ſure to love himſelf without a rival.

Laſtly, ſelfiſhneſs is unreaſonable, becauſe the objects which it purſues are not worthy to be ſought ſo earneſtly and loved ſo immoderately.

Man's life conſiſteth not in that much-envied and unprofitable thing called abundance. Our Saviour hath ſaid ſo; and moſt men have ſaid or thought ſo, who have had the trial of it. Abundance cannot give underſtanding to the ſimple, nor health to the infirm: it cannot prolong life; it is very well if it doth not ſhorten it; it cannot ſecure from ſlander and detraction, or calm the diſquiet of a guilty conſcience, or become a certain or a laſting poſſeſſion.

Hence it is manifeſt that a man, who is endued with reaſon and liberty, and can employ them to ſo good purpoſes, for whom Chriſt died, to whom heaven is propoſed as a reward of well-doing, who in this world finds nothing equal to his deſires, acts in a fooliſh perverſe manner, when he ſacrifices better things to ſecure his temporal intereſts, to thruſt himſelf into ſome ſtation for which he is unfit, to obtain more wealth than he wants or knows how to employ, more power than he can diſcreetly uſe, or more outward reſpect from perſons who perhaps in their hearts hate or deſpiſe him.

Hence we may alſo ſee the folly of that repining uneaſineſs which ſelfiſhneſs raiſes in us when we are neglected by the world, and behold others, though our inferiors, thrive and ſucceed better than we. If this life were our only portion, this earth our firſt and laſt habitation, we might have ſome pretence to grieve that bread ſhould not be to the wiſe, nor riches to men of underſtanding, nor favour to men of ſkill. But if there be a better world to come, in which we may ſecure to ourſelves an everlaſting habitation, theſe ſmall and transitory inconveniences should not much offend and disturb us; especially since by possessing little in this place of sojourning, we shall find a safer and easier passage to our home; and our treasure not being here, neither will our heart be here in all probability.

Thus much distinctly concerning the several kinds of irregular self-love; to which I shall now add a few geral remarks concerning this fault.

St. Paul says in the chapter whence the text is taken, In the last days men shall be lovers of their own selves, covetous, boasters, proud, blasphemers, and guilty of many other crimes which he there mentions.

St. Paul seems not to have placed self-love first in this catalogue of vices undesignedly and by chance, but because it is the root of much evil, and the parent of many sins.

Sins against God frequently proceed from an undue love of ourselves. We prefer our pleasure and our interest, as we call it, to his favour. Thence arises disobedience to his laws when they cross our inclinations, when they require any thing disagreeable, when the observance of them exposes us to any inconvenience. We prefer our will to his; and therefore when things happen not to us just as we desire, thence arise impatience and discontent, and dishonourable thoughts of divine providence. We have too high an opinion of ourselves; thence we ascribe all the good which we enjoy to our own labours and merit.

Sins against our neighbour proceed as often from the same cause. From an irregular self-love we grow covetous, rapacious, proud, insolent, envious, malicious, ungrateful, and uncharitable.

Such are the bad effects which self-love produces. It is true, indeed, that it ought to be particularly observed, that all who are lovers of themselves have not always every bad quality which we have reckoned up. Self-love works differently and causes greater or lesser, more or fewer disorders in the mind, as it is counter-
balanced

balanced by more or fewer good dispositions; but some or other of the faults before mentioned always arise from it.

Thus it appears that self-love is a dangerous corruption, which may be also proved by this observation, that Christ absolutely required of all who would join themselves to him a virtue directly contrary to it, namely, self-denial. Whosoever will come after me, says he, let him deny himself, and take up his cross, and follow me. This is a commandment which he who loves himself in an undue manner cannot possibly obey. No such person could follow him, at a time when all, even life itself, was to be laid down for his sake. No such person ever died a martyr, except to his own follies and vices, and even in times when no persecution or disgrace attends the profession of Christianity, yet to such an one the Gospel is disagreeable; he is as little disposed to obey some of its precepts, as he would be to undergo stripes and imprisonment, and loss of life.

Lastly; self-love is dangerous, because it is of a deceitful nature, it finds an easy admittance into our hearts, and is usually attended with much blindness and ignorance.

But the ignorance is voluntary, and the means to remove it are in our hands. Our Saviour hath given us this precept concerning our behaviour towards others: Thou shalt love thy neighbour as thyself. In this rule we may also find how we ought to love ourselves as our neighbour; that is, we ought to have such a love for ourselves as we know that we ought to have for others, and what we reckon an honest and upright conduct towards one whom we esteem, and whose prosperity we heartily desire, will inform us how we must deal with ourselves.

Now it is easy to know what sort of behaviour that is. If our affection be virtuous and prudent, we value our friend according to his deserts, and pay him a due
regard

regard, honouring whatsoever is commendable and amiable in him, but neither ascribing to him accomplishments which he has not, nor placing him above his superiors or his equals, nor giving him praises which may insensibly lead him into pride and insolence. We are not blind to his faults, we set them before him, and tell him disagreeable truths when it is necessary that he should hear them. We never encourage or help him to pursue things hurtful to himself or to others; we industriously promote his welfare by all innocent methods, more especially we have in view the welfare of his mind, and his improvement in those good qualities upon which depend the favour of God, and eternal life.

Thus a good man would act towards his friend; and thus every one should deal with himself, and approve nothing there which he would not approve of in another person.

END OF THE SECOND VOLUME.

www.ingramcontent.com/pod-product-compliance
Lightning Source LLC
Chambersburg PA
CBHW031954300426
44117CB00008B/762